The Cambridge Handbook of the
Ethics of Ageing

We're all getting older from the moment we're born. Ageing is a fundamental and ubiquitous aspect of life. Yet in ethics, not much work is done on the questions surrounding ageing: how do diachronic features of ageing and the lifespan contribute to the overall value of life? How do time, change, and mortality impact on questions of morality and the good life? And how ought societies to respond to issues of social justice and the good, balancing the interests of generations and age cohorts? In this Cambridge Handbook, the first book-length attempt to stake this terrain, leading moral philosophers from a range of sub-fields and regions set out their approaches to the conceptual and ethical understanding of ageing. The volume makes an important contribution to significant debates about the implications of ageing for individual well-being, social policy and social justice.

C. S. Wareham is a researcher at the Ethics Institute, Utrecht University, and Honorary Associate Professor at the Steve Biko Centre for Bioethics, the University of the Witwatersrand. He has published a number of journal articles on ethics and ageing.

Cambridge Handbooks in Philosophy

Cambridge Handbooks in Philosophy are explorations of philosophical topics for both students and specialists. They offer accessible new essays by a range of contributors, as well as a substantial introduction and bibliography.

Titles published in this series

The Cambridge Handbook of the
Ethics of Ageing

EDITED BY

C. S. Wareham

Utrecht University & University of the Witwatersrand,
Johannesburg

CAMBRIDGE
UNIVERSITY PRESS

University Printing House, Cambridge CB2 8BS, United Kingdom

One Liberty Plaza, 20th Floor, New York, NY 10006, USA

477 Williamstown Road, Port Melbourne, VIC 3207, Australia

314–321, 3rd Floor, Plot 3, Splendor Forum, Jasola District Centre, New Delhi – 110025, India

103 Penang Road, #05–06/07, Visioncrest Commercial, Singapore 238467

Cambridge University Press is part of the University of Cambridge.

It furthers the University's mission by disseminating knowledge in the pursuit of education, learning, and research at the highest international levels of excellence.

www.cambridge.org
Information on this title: www.cambridge.org/9781108495134
DOI: 10.1017/9781108861168

First published 2022

A catalogue record for this publication is available from the British Library.

ISBN 978-1-108-49513-4 Hardback
ISBN 978-1-108-81704-2 Paperback

Contents

Contributors

Samantha Brennan is Dean of the College of Arts and Professor of Philosophy at the University of Guelph. She is co-editor (with Sarah Hannan and Richard Vernon) of *Permissible Progeny? Moral Considerations and Procreative Choice* (2015).

John K. Davis is Professor of Philosophy at California State University, Fullerton. He is the author of *New Methuselahs: The Ethics of Life Extension* (2018).

David DeGrazia is Elton Professor of Philosophy at George Washington University. His most recent book, co-authored with Joseph Millum, is *A Theory of Bioethics* (2021).

Axel Gosseries is Senior Research Fellow of the FNRS (Belgium) and Hoover Professor of Economic and Social Ethics at UC Louvain. He is the author and editor of several books, including *Institutions for Future Generations* (2016), and has published in journals including the *Journal of Political Philosophy*, *Politics, Philosophy & Economics* and *Economics and Philosophy*.

Daniel Halliday is Associate Professor in Philosophy at the University of Melbourne. He is the author of *Inheritance of Wealth: Justice, Equality, and the Right to Bequeath* (2018).

Christopher Hamilton is Reader in Philosophy at King's College London. His most recent book is *A Philosophy of Tragedy* (2016).

Søren Holm is Professor of Bioethics at the University of Manchester and Professor of Medical Ethics at the University of Oslo, Norway. His publications include *The Future of Human Reproduction: Ethics, Choice, and Regulation* (2000) and he is editor of the Routledge Ethics, Law and Society series.

Nancy S. Jecker is a professor at the University of Washington School of Medicine, visiting professor at the University of Johannesburg Department of Philosophy, and visiting professor at the Chinese University of Hong Kong. Her most recent book is *Ending Midlife Bias: New Values for Old Age* (2020).

Diane Jeske is Professor of Philosophy at the University of Iowa. Her most recent book is *Friendship and Social Media: A Philosophical Exploration* (2019).

Simon Keller is Professor of Philosophy at Victoria University of Wellington. He is the author of *The Limits of Loyalty* (Cambridge 2007) and *Partiality* (2013).

Jeff McMahan is White's Professor of Moral Philosophy at the University of Oxford and a Fellow of Corpus Christi College, Oxford. He is the author of *The Ethics of Killing: Problems at the Margins of Life* (2002) and *Killing in War* (2009).

Thaddeus Metz is Professor of Philosophy at the University of Pretoria. He is the author of *A Relational Moral Theory: African Ethics in and beyond the Continent* (2022).

Christine Overall is Professor Emerita of Philosophy and holds a University Research Chair at Queen's University, Kingston, Ontario. She is the author of *Ageing, Death, and Human Longevity* (2003) and *Why Have Children? The Ethical Debate* (2012), and the editor of *Pets and People: The Ethics of Our Relationships with Companion Animals* (2017).

Tom Parr is Associate Professor in Political Theory at the University of Warwick and a Marie Skłodowska-Curie Individual Fellow in the Department of Law at Universitat Pompeu Fabra. He is the author of *Introducing Political Philosophy: A Policy-Driven Approach* (2021).

Geoffrey Scarre is Professor of Philosophy at Durham University. His publications include *After Evil: Responding to Wrongdoing* (2004) and *Death* (2007), and he is the editor of *The Palgrave Handbook to the Philosophy of Aging* (2016).

Mark Schweda is Professor for Ethics in Medicine at the Department of Health Services Research of the School of Medicine and Health Sciences at the University of Oldenburg. He is the co-editor of *Planning Later Life: Bioethics and Public Health in Ageing Societies* (2017, with Larissa Pfaller, Kai Brauer, Frank Adloff, and Silke Schicktanz), and *Aging and Human Nature* (2020, with Michael Coors and Claudia Bozzaro).

Anthony Skelton is Associate Professor of Philosophy at the University of Western Ontario. He has published articles in journals including the *Journal of the History of Philosophy* and *Ethics*.

L. W. Sumner is University Professor of Philosophy Emeritus at the University of Toronto. He is the author of six books, including *Assisted Death: A Study in Ethics and Law* (2011) and *Physician-Assisted Death: What Everyone Needs to Know* (2017).

C. S. Wareham is Assistant Professor at the Ethics Institute, Utrecht University, and Honorary Associate Professor at the Steve Biko Centre for Bioethics, University of the Witwatersrand. He is the editor of this volume and has published articles in journals including *Ethical Theory and Moral Practice* and *History and Philosophy of the Life Sciences*.

Acknowledgements

Thanks to Veli Mitova, who helped get the ball rolling on this volume and gave it a level of ambition it might not otherwise have had. She has been a great person to turn to throughout.

Hilary Gaskin from Cambridge University Press has been an essential guide through this process and has been helpful, responsive, and forgiving in the face of delays.

Felicity Knight's painstaking editing under pressure added polish to the book.

I am grateful to my mentors, Thaddeus Metz and Kevin Behrens. Thad provided invaluable comments on my chapter drafts and has long been a go-to source of guidance, even before I conceived of this book. Kevin has supported me with time, advice, and other resources for this process, and was a great sounding board.

Anthony Skelton provided valuable feedback on parts of the manuscript late in the process.

Colleagues at the Steve BIko Centre, especially Tebogo Dithung, provided helpful contributions. Nezerith Cengiz did excellent work organising and collating the references. Rita Sephton did a wonderful job on the index. Thanks for saving me from this!

Of course, I am tremendously grateful to the contributors who have worked through the worst pandemic in living memory. Some have had to work whilst looking after small children in lockdown conditions, others have lost loved ones. I am indebted to those who pulled through and more than sympathetic to those who did not.

My extended family and in-laws, including Mario, Marisa, and nonna Giuliana, have helped me throughout in various ways. I am grateful to my siblings, Paul, Nicola, Mary, James, and Anna for their interest and for helping me to develop as I have. It is partly your fault.

Many of the fascinating ethical things about ageing concern the shifts that occur between generations from young to old. So it is important to thank my children, Giacomo and Alba, who (I would argue) have aged beautifully across the time spent developing this volume. I am indebted to my parents, who have taught me (or from whom I ought to have learned) a great deal about ageing, morality, and wisdom, and the relations between them. By the time they read this, my parents will both have seen more than eighty springs. While the pandemic meant that I could not spend my mum's eightieth birthday with her, I nonetheless look forward to celebrating her twenty-first birthday over and over again. She is not just a presence in my life, she is ever-present, for which I am very grateful.

More than anyone, I am grateful to Beatrice, who shares the times of my life and has put up with me for most of them.

Introduction

Ethics is home to numerous subfields such as procreative ethics, environmental ethics, and 'genethics'. By contrast, there is far less work on ageing and ethics, and there is at present no subfield explicitly devoted to ethical issues related to ageing. This is surprising given that ageing is a fundamental aspect of life; perhaps even more fundamental and ubiquitous than procreation. Moreover, significant ethical questions confront us as ageing persons: How do features of ageing and the lifespan contribute to the overall value of life? How do time, change, and mortality impact on questions of morality? And how ought societies to respond to issues of social justice and the good, balancing the interests of generations and age cohorts? The practical and theoretical importance of these questions, and their inextricable relation to the ageing process, makes it curious that there are few other volumes specifically dedicated to what might be called ageing ethics, or the ethics of ageing.

Whatever the explanation for this relative lack of attention, the full range and content of ageing ethics is yet to be explored. This volume is the first book-length attempt to engage this content and stake the conceptual terrain. As is evident from the chapters that follow this introduction, the area to be covered is philosophically rich in and full of potential new directions. Ageing as an ethical topic should not be conceived of as a drab, dreary, lonely, and perhaps painful period at the end of life. Instead, we are all ageing, and the significance of this process for morality and the good life are areas ripe for sustained ethical reflection.

I do not mean to imply here that there is a dearth of relevant ethical literature about ageing. Ruminations on the topic have been common since ancient times, with Seneca's *On the Shortness of Life* a particularly influential example. Indeed, most great philosophers have had something to say about ageing, particularly when its effects become apparent. For instance Hume, upon becoming mortally ill, explained his 'detached' attitude to his inevitable death: 'I consider ... that a man of sixty-five, by dying, cuts off only a few years of infirmities' (Hume 1985, xl). This substantive ethical and empirical claim unfortunately did not receive the same degree of scrutiny as those made in his other work. If it had, he may have given greater weight to the lines surrounding this quote, in which he points to his later years as those he might 'most choose to pass over again', and in which he acknowledges that his reputation is 'breaking out at last with additional lustre'. If the latter years can be so good (a claim revisited in many of the chapters in this book), should Hume not have been more loath to lose them? Certainly, the world might have been better off had Hume more time to dedicate to this and other issues.

So I am not suggesting that there is a lack of work on ageing by great philosophers. For the most part, though, as in Hume's case, philosophical reflections on ageing ethics tend to be addenda in the works of the greats. There are few concentrated efforts to consider the implications of ageing for morality and the good life, or the implications of morality and the good life in understanding and interpreting the (dis)value of ageing. The gap I am pointing to, then, is not in the lack of existing high quality literature and contributors, but in the lack of *focussed* treatments of the topic of ageing in the field of philosophical ethics.

By contrast, there is a tremendous amount of literature on ageing and the elderly in health policy, public health, clinical disciplines, and behavioural sciences. While this work is often valuable, it tends to view ageing as a problem that needs to be solved, and elderly people as problematic objects for treatment or care. Philosophical understandings of age and ageing, by contrast, appreciate ageing as a ubiquitous process that can shed light on questions about how we should structure our societies and live our lives meaningfully or virtuously as ageing subjects.

This volume aims to bring together some of the world's finest moral philosophers and bioethicists to contribute to developing this area. In selecting authors and topics, it was important that there should be breadth of perspective, including more and less senior academics, and a range of traditions, spanning Western analytic and (European) continental traditions, as well as African and Eastern approaches to ethics. There was no intention to prescribe a comprehensive list of topics. Instead, part of the book's aim is to showcase the many existing subjects worthy of further exploration, to generate debates relevant to people at various stages of ageing, to inspire new and fruitful lines of research, and to invigorate ageing as a topic for ethical reflection.

The volume comprises three parts. Contributions in the first part, 'Ageing and the Good Life', consider what makes lives go better or worse at different stages of the lifespan. Chapters in the second part, 'Ageing and Morality', address rights and duties that may change, becoming weaker or stronger as we, and those close to us, age. The final part, 'Ageing and Society', comprises contributions that engage problems of social justice and fair distributions, and how a good society should look, particularly in light of social ageing.

The contributions are outlined below.

Ageing and the Good Life

There are few philosophers who have contributed so valuably to work about the persistence of prudential value across time as Jeff McMahan, so it is fitting that the volume begins with his contribution. McMahan considers limitations of the preference towards the future (which Parfit referred to as a 'bias'), according to which we prefer goods to be in the future and harms to be in the past. The preference applies far less forcefully to non-experiential goods, particularly the good of achievement, with significant implications for well-being at different life stages and the overall goodness of life. Amongst other contributions to a good life, connection to a life's achievements can contribute to the psychological unity of a person across time. If so, this should influence how we live earlier in life, in order to create a store of value in old age.

The entwinement of ethics, ageing, and *time* is the focus of Mark Schweda's chapter. He considers this interaction across three levels of temporality: our coordinates in time as finite entities; our passage through different, increasingly indeterminate phases of life; and the trajectory of our life as a narrative whole. Significantly, Schweda's analysis points to the need for an ethics of ageing, not just as an ethics for older people. Instead, understanding the philosophically neglected temporal dimensions of the structure of human life can illuminate understandings of meaning and the good life more generally.

This idea of ageing as a process occurring *across* a life, and not merely the last part when we are older, is reflected in the chapters that succeed it. Anthony Skelton's chapter concerns the prudential goodness of lives for children. Surprisingly, the intuition that children's *lives* have value for children themselves (as ageing subjects) is not well accounted for by dominant strands of thinking about prudential value. Skelton addresses this shortcoming, whilst also dissecting significant questions about the relation between well-being in childhood and its relation to the value of a life as a whole.

Mid-life, too, tends not to be at the forefront of one's mind when considers ageing. However, Christopher Hamilton's discussion of *The Swimmer*, a haunting film based on Cheever's equally haunting short story of the same name, clarifies that middle age is a pivotal phase in ethical development. The surreal and dream-like nature of the protagonist's journey through time conveys significant realities about the experience of ageing and time and our ethical relation to them.

Christine Overall poses and interrogates the 'odd' question of whether ageing, as a life stage, is good. While ageing is typically associated with some negative aspects, there are great goods to be found in ageing, such as renewable pleasures and enriching relationships with younger generations. Although extracting the potential of later life is mediated by material and social conditions, there are strong moral and political justifications for holding that ageing can be good, not least to overturn dominant and damaging ageist stereotypes.

Simon Keller argues that common accounts of mental health fail to capture the diachronic character of ageing. In particular, he critiques functionalist and welfarist definitions of mental health and finds that they fail to cope with human differences at various stages of the lifespan. Assessments of the mental health of the elderly should not rest on empirical findings about the 'natural function' of elderly minds. Moreover, identifying mental health with fulfilment of apparently objective criteria for welfare, such as productive work, appears to exclude both the elderly and children, thereby judging mental health by a mid-life standard that neither children nor the old are likely to fulfil. Instead, Keller defends a resourcist view that mental health is a matter of having the right resources to live a good human life. In considering the good life, it is important to take into account the life narrative: that which constitutes a good life changes as one ages and thus so do the resources required for mental health.

David DeGrazia considers whether ageing and death are to be feared. Death is generally thought to be a harm, and ageing inevitably brings us nearer to this end. In this case, what is the correct attitude towards ageing? DeGrazia claims that ageing is not to be feared if a person's life is likely to be achieve a 'normative baseline' of decent quality and length. Such a baseline represents a reasonable standard against which to compare the goodness of our lives (and the disvalue of our deaths). This baseline is important so that we can overcome what DeGrazia refers to as 'cosmic narcissism' – the tendency to view our lives as more important than they actually are and compare the value of life against unachievable standards.

Ageing and Morality

Søren Holm's chapter provides a wonderfully clear exposition of the concept of personhood in bioethics, before applying it specifically to questions about personhood across the lifespan. 'Personhood theory' ties full moral status to the possession of certain cognitive capacities. The loss of these capacities in old age presents problems for ethical theory and moral duties towards the very old, similar to those posed by infants and foetuses. These problems point to poten-tial limitations in personhood theory and perhaps direct us to consider more relational understandings of what it is to be a person.

In this vein, Thaddeus Metz draws attention to relational perspectives on personhood and ageing that tend to be neglected. In a deft handling of two enormous ethical traditions from the global East and global South, he points to significant similarities in the ethical understanding of ageing, and significant differences from Western thought. Confucian and African traditions propose a stronger role for ageing in achieving harmony and virtue than do Western traditions. The increased value of, and esteem for, the elderly has important practical implications for questions regarding filial duties and the allocation of life-saving resources. Such implications may complement or compete with Western approaches in valuable ways.

Diane Jeske discusses the obligations generated by friendship across time. Typically, we become more reliant on others as we near and reach old age, raising questions regarding duties in the care of the elderly. Jeske makes the case that long-term, intimate friendships, whilst adding joy to the ageing process, also create especially strong reciprocal obligations. She argues against the idea that having one's friend act from motivations of *obligation* or *duty* is undesirable because this implies burdensome responsibility. Instead, acting from a motivation of duty coincides with reasonable understandings of what it is to care for a friend.

When ought we to forgive offences that occurred long ago, and what is the role of forgiveness in improving our own lives and those of others? Geoffrey Scarre explores the moral duties and needs of victims and offenders with regard to forgiveness. He argues that forgiveness can play a crucial role in bringing about successful closure to narratives of aged victims and offenders.

A controversial issue in applied ethics concerns when it is justified to withhold and withdraw, and to offer and accept, life-extending treatments. In her chapter, Nancy Jecker focusses on the conditions for a life worth extending, making use of 'experience machine' thought experiments. The conditions she generates shed light on questions about when life-extending resources can justifiably be allocated to people with dementia.

L. W. Sumner engages four questions about suicide and medically assisted dying for the elderly: When, if ever, is suicide rational for the elderly? When is it ethical to assist in a rational suicide? Can medical practitioners be reasonably expected to provide assistance? Should being 'tired of life' be accepted as a criterion for providing assistance in dying? Sumner provides detailed and informed answers to these questions, employing real cases to argue that their being 'tired of life' can indeed be justified grounds for providing medical assistance in dying to the elderly.

Ageing and Society

Samantha Brennan provides a thought-provoking overview of ways in which age, gender, justice, and ethics intersect. For instance, she interrogates the idea that women's longer lifespans are unjust, examines the differential role of beauty stereotypes played in the lives of older women, and poses the question of whether the 'front-loading' of responsibility in women's lives may some-times contribute to a richer and freer experience of being older.

As societies age, questions about the social and economic role of the elderly, and what is owed to them by younger age groups, are thrown into sharp focus. In a piece of great conceptual clarity, Axel Gosseries considers the circum-stances under which contributions of 'active' population in ageing societies may be unjust. How can societies avoid the unjust overburdening of younger age groups, whilst securing at least a minimal standard of well-being for all, but particularly the elderly poor? Gosseries makes the case that injustice in ageing societies is not necessarily more pronounced than in non-ageing societies, and that, surprisingly, increases in longevity may, to an extent, alleviate this tension.

Questions about when and whether it is justified to require older people to retire, perhaps depriving them of work from which their lives derive meaning, are important issues of intergenerational justice. Daniel Halliday and Tom Parr provide a valuable contribution to these debates, proposing that even the most promising justifications of mandatory retirement support a more modest proposal: that employers might justifiably reduce the number of work hours of older workers.

In my contribution, I discuss a curious phenomenon in studies of population well-being: the upward curve of happiness in advanced years, known as the 'happiness curve'. I point to some interesting ethical implications of the curve for individual well-being, applied ethical questions, and for society as a whole. As an example of the role that this empirical finding can play in ethical arguments, I consider Peter Singer's critique of life extension, and Walker's response to it based on the happiness curve. An empirically justified outlook on later life encourages a sunnier view of the prospect life extension.

Unsurprisingly in a book about ageing, many of the chapters in the volume touch on issues related to the value of longer lives (particularly those of Jecker, Overall, and my own chapter). However, John K. Davis's contribution provides the only sustained discussion of the science and ethics of this. If, as many expect, lifespans continue to rise as interventions aimed at increasing the lifespan become available, what ought the response to be, from the perspectives of societies and the individual? Davis succinctly discusses a myriad of objections to life extension, such as the prospect of overpopulation and the likelihood of unjust distributions of lifespan. He argues that, like other scientific advances, life-extending interventions are unlikely to be all good, or all bad, and that their ethical use will require considerable efforts to ensure fair distribution and prevent overpopulation.

Part I

Ageing and the Good Life

1 Old Age and the Preference for the Future

Jeff McMahan

> It is a sad scene, the last – the last act of life – to see beauty and eloquence, sense, mouldering away in pain and agony under terrible diseases, and hastening to the grave with sundry kinds of death – to witness the barren silence of him who charmed us with his exuberant fancy and gaiety never to be exhausted – to gaze upon wrinkles and yellowness and incurvations where we remember beautiful forms and smiles and smoothness and the blush of health and the bloom of desire, to see – but here I recollect I am not in the pulpit, so I stop.
>
> Rev. Sydney Smith, letter to Lady Holland[1]

The Preference for the Future

As one enters and progresses through old age, one experiences various unwelcome changes. One suffers declines in most physical abilities as well as in certain cognitive capacities; one becomes physically less attractive – or, perhaps, more unattractive; one's friends and loved ones succumb with increasing frequency to illness and death, leaving one submerged in grief and loneliness; and the familiar world one has known continues to recede into a past that few remember. Perhaps worst of all, the goods of life that remain in prospect are few, and rapidly become ever fewer.

This is particularly distressing because we are strongly disposed to want the goods of life to be in the future and the ills to be consigned to the past. Derek Parfit calls this feature of our psychology 'the bias towards the future'. I will refer to it as the 'preference for the future', as Parfit's pejorative label begs the question against the rationality of these asymmetrical attitudes to the future and the past (Parfit 1987, 160).[2]

Just as it is a cause of grief to us when, in old age, life's goods are disproportionately in the past, so it should be a cause of relief that life's ills are also largely in the past. Yet, even though we are in general more concerned with avoiding grave ills, such as suffering, than with enjoying correspondingly

---

[1] Quoted in Pearson (1977, 291).

[2] On p. 177, Parfit (1987) says that his claim in section 67 that the bias towards the future is bad for us 'does not beg the question about the rationality of this bias'. That is true; it could be bad for us to act on an attitude that is rational. What does beg the question is the description of the attitude as a 'bias'.

significant goods, the thought in old age that most of our ills are behind us provides little solace. This is because, even though in old age the ratio of good to ill tends to diminish, we still expect the goods to outweigh the ills and thus prefer, given that they are inseparable, to have both in the future rather than in the past.

Parfit illustrates the preference for the future by noting how our reflecting on certain goods and ills makes us feel. 'Looking forward to a pleasure is', he writes, 'in general, more pleasant than looking back upon it. And in the case of pains the difference is even greater' (Parfit 1987, 160). Our attitudes to the timing of goods and ills are, however, deeper than this, as Parfit himself reveals in an ingenious thought experiment.

Amnesia

You are in hospital for a procedure that requires no surgical incision but is nevertheless excruciatingly painful because it cannot be performed with anesthesia. To avoid aftereffects such as Post Traumatic Stress Disorder, patients scheduled to have this operation are, on entering the hospital, given a drug that induces amnesia, so that at no point during their time in hospital are they able to remember anything that has happened to them while they have been there. You therefore have to ask the nurse whether you have had your procedure. She replies that you are either the patient who had a ten-hour procedure yesterday or the one who will have a one-hour procedure later today. While she goes to check, you consider what you hope she will discover. (Parfit 1987, 165)[3]

As Parfit observes, you will naturally hope that you had much greater suffering yesterday rather than having to undergo lesser suffering today. What this shows is that it is not just that anticipating pain is itself more painful than recollecting pain; it is also that we *prefer* to have had ten times more pain, and fervently *hope* that we had that much more pain, because of the pain's temporal location: in the past.

Parfit argues that the preference for the future is bad for us. For this reason, he contends, 'we ought not to be biased towards the future' but ought instead to be 'temporally neutral'. If we were temporally neutral, 'looking backward . . . could be equally cheering' as looking forward (Parfit 1987, 177), 'or in the case of pains equally distressing' (Parfit 1987, 174). If we were this way, Parfit comments, 'we should then greatly gain in our attitude to ageing and death.

---

[3] My statement of the case differs from Parfit's in that it eliminates ways in which you might infer that you are the patient who had the procedure yesterday. In Parfit's statement, for example, the drug that induces amnesia is administered when one has the procedure, so that the patient in his example, who has no memory of ten hours yesterday, should be able to infer that he is the patient who had the longer procedure during that period.

As our life passes, we should have less and less to look forward to, but more and more to look backward to' (Parfit 1987, 175).

As I noted, however, our attitudes to time are not just matters of how pleasant or painful it is for us to contemplate past or likely future goods and ills. They can also, as the Amnesia case shows, be intense preferences, hopes, or fears about whether goods or ills have been in our past or will be in our future. One might wonder, therefore, whether it could be rational, or psychologically possible, to be indifferent in old age to the fact that the great majority of the goods in one's life are in the past rather than in the future. Could one hope to have great suffering later today rather than having had greater suffering yesterday? I will not address these issues. It may be that, even if it would be better for us to be temporally neutral, the preference for the future is ineradicable. It may even be that this attitude to time – which, for obvious reasons, is favoured by natural selection – is neither rational not irrational but is rather a brute or primitive feature of our psychology. Asking whether the preference for the future is rational may be like asking whether it is rational to have desires.

Rather than considering whether the preference for the future is rational or irrational, good or bad for us, or eliminable or ineliminable, I will enquire about its *scope*. As Parfit rightly observes, what he calls the bias towards the future 'applies most clearly to events that are in themselves pleasant or painful' (Parfit 1987, 160). There are, however, many experiences that can be good for us without necessarily being pleasant and many that can be bad for us without being painful, and the preference for the future seems to apply quite broadly to all such experiential goods and ills.[4] But, assuming that there are dimensions of well-being, or ways in which our lives can go well or badly for us, that are not essentially experiential, it is possible that there are goods and ills to which the preference for the future does not apply, or does not apply to the extent to which it applies to experiential goods and ills. This is, indeed, acknowledged by Parfit, who writes that 'this attitude does not apply to events that give us either pride or shame: events that either gild or stain our picture of our lives' (1987, 160).

This is an important insight, though overstated. Most of us, I think, would in general prefer that sources of shame in our lives be in the past, if only for instrumental reasons – for example, so that we could express appropriate remorse and demonstrate that we have reformed. We prefer a pattern of reform to one of degeneration. Similarly, as I will try to show, the preference for the future also applies to objects of pride, though to a lesser degree. But what is important for the evaluation of old age is that the preference for the future is indeed weaker in its application to certain non-experiential goods, perhaps

---

[4] For a defence of an experientialist account of well-being in which pleasure is understood as a comparatively minor element of well-being, see Kraut (2018).

particularly those in which we can justifiably experience pride, than it is in its application to purely experiential goods.

The Good of Achievement

One good that has a non-experiential dimension is achievement. I will assume here that achievement is objectively good – that is, that it is good for people if their lives contain significant achievement and that their lives go better for them, if other things are equal, the more they achieve. This is true, I believe, even if the process leading to achievement fails to enhance the experiential dimension of their well-being and even if they never know of their successful achievement. Achievement is, in other words, an object-ive, intrinsic, and non-experiential good. There are other goods of this type. They are often forms of action that are virtuous and admirable, such as caring devotedly for a loved one, but that we are reluctant to describe as achievements, in part because they are not normally objects of ambition. In the remainder of this chapter I will concentrate the discussion on achieve-ment, but taking it as a representative of this broader class of non-experiential goods.

Usually, achievement and the efforts leading to it are good for people both experientially and instrumentally as well as non-experientially. Significant achievement is seldom, if ever, accidental. It is preceded by purposeful activity intended to achieve a goal. And purposeful action is an important element of experiential well-being. One psychologist who has devoted his career to the study of happiness writes that 'happiness is *experiences of pleasure and purpose over time*' (Dolan 2014, 3).[5] This, I believe, is too simple, for there are non-experiential dimensions of well-being, one of which is successful achievement (McMahan 2020). But the psychological literature and our own experience both confirm that absorption in an activity directed towards a goal one believes to be worth pursuing is a source of profound satisfaction.[6] (This is echoed in the familiar 'paradox of hedonism', which is that happiness cannot be successfully pursued directly, but is instead a side effect of immersion in some other activity pursued for its own sake.) The achievement of the goal can, moreover, be not only gratifying in itself but also instrumental in securing other goods. These claims are well summarized by Bertrand Russell:

The satisfaction to be derived from success in a great constructive enterprise is one of the most massive that life has to offer . . . [Those who successfully pursue worthy goals] do work which is itself delightful; while they are doing it, it secures them the respect of those whose respect is worth having . . . They have also the most solid reasons for thinking well of themselves (Russell 1930, 214–15).

---

[5] Italics in the original.   [6] See, for example, Mihaly Csikszentmihalyi (1990).

Achievement as an objective, non-experiential good – that is, considered apart from the experiential goods involved in its pursuit and realization – is less subject to the preference for the future than experiential goods are. It may therefore have special significance for us in old age. In his *Autobiography*, John Stuart Mill wrote of his father, James Mill, that 'his principal satisfaction, after he knew his end was near, seemed to be the thought of what he had done to make the world better than he had found it; and his chief regret in not living longer, that he had not had time to do more' (Robson and Stillinger 1981, 211). This contrasts with the ability to look back on a life of unproductive, even if intense, pleasures. As Thackeray observes, 'recollections of the best-ordained banquets will scarcely cheer sick epicures' (Thackeray 1937, 257). But, as I noted earlier, what matters most here is not how looking back on an important achievement may make us *feel*. A more significant issue is whether one might look back on one's achievements in a way that parallels the way one looks forward to pleasure, or other experiential goods.

The Significance of Past Achievement

Those who in old age have significant achievements in their past are often admired and envied by young people who aspire to realize great achievements in their own lives. These old people are secure in the possession of something that the ambitious young people want, but that only a relatively small proportion of them will ever have. Some of these young people might prefer to have a life that contains significant achievement rather than a life that would be longer and would contain more experiential goods but would lack significant achievement.

Suppose, for example, that a young scientist, having just completed her doctoral work, reasonably believes that there is a high probability of her being able to do important work in science, yielding significant achievements, if she devotes much of her life to her research. The necessary work would, however, unavoidably involve exposure to toxic chemicals and radiation, so that there is an equally high probability that her achievements will cost her several years of good life. To sharpen the example, suppose that it is reasonable for her to believe that, if she consistently devotes herself to her research, there is a high probability that she will achieve important results in science, though only shortly before the end of her life, which will come roughly three years sooner than it would if she were to pursue less promising but safer and equally enjoyable research instead. She understands, therefore, that the achievement would likely cost her several years of pleasant life and that she would be unlikely to have long to savour her achievement or the fame that it would be likely to bring. Even so, she might well judge that the achievement would compensate her for the loss of a longer life with more good experiences but without achievement.

This judgement would, however, be compatible with the preference for the future. Both the achievement and the additional years of enjoyable life would be in the distant future. Her judgement might therefore indicate only that she now values great achievement in the future more than she values several further years of good experiences in the equally distant future. It might indicate nothing about her attitudes to time.

To test for these, we might inquire whether it is plausible to suppose that, having chosen to pursue great achievement, this scientist would, near the end of her life, be glad that she chose as she did even though, had she chosen differently, she would be able to continue to live for several more years. But this test may be unreliable if her achievement is one that has important, beneficial consequences for others and would not have been brought about by anyone else had she not pursued it. For in that case it might be difficult, even for her, to separate her gladness for the beneficiaries of her achievement from her gladness or regret for her own sake.

The best test for our intuitions is a variant of Parfit's Amnesia case.[7]

The Amnesiac Scientist

The scientist, having finally realized her great achievement but nearing the end of her life, is in hospital for palliative treatment of the illness caused by her earlier exposure to chemicals and radiation in the course of her research. One of the effects of her condition is temporary but total amnesia. Although the beliefs and values that have guided her life are intact, she can, at the moment, remember nothing of her previous life. She asks the nurse who she is, but the nurse is uncertain which of two amnesiac patients she is. One of them, the nurse explains, is a prominent scientist who has recently achieved a great advance in scientific understanding but is terminally ill and will certainly die within a month. The other is a wholly undistinguished scientist in the same field who gave priority to frivolous pleasures over the serious pursuit of science and who is also terminally ill, but is confidently expected to live comfortably and pleasantly for another few years.

It seems reasonable to suppose that, given the values that informed the scientist's earlier decision to pursue achievement at the cost of a shorter life, she would now hope that the nurse brings her the news that she is the scientist with a great achievement in her recent past. We can appreciate, in other words, how she might prefer to have a great achievement in her past than to have more experiential good in her future.

If that seems reasonable, then we have an example in which the preference for the future is not overriding. That preference may, of course, still apply to some degree. Suppose that earlier, at the beginning of her career, she would

---

[7] An earlier version of this example, along with some similar discussion, is in my essay, 'The Lucretian Argument' (McDaniel et al. 2006, 213–26, Section 5).

have been willing to accept the loss of *five* years of additional life if that had been a necessary cost of her great achievement. But now, in the hospital, if she were told by the nurse that the prominent scientist had only a month to live while the undistinguished scientist could expect to live for five more years, she might well prefer to have five years of experientially rewarding life rather than to have a great achievement in her past. If so, that would reveal a preference for the future. But if she would prefer to learn from the nurse that she is the prominent scientist with only a month to live rather than an undistinguished scientist with *two* years to live, this would show that, in her case, the preference for the future is not absolute but is instead a matter of degree. She can reasonably prefer a greater good of a non-experiential kind in the past to a lesser total of experiential goods in the future.

That these speculations about the scientist's preferences are not unrealistic is shown by there being some expressions by actual people of a preference for past achievement over years of future life. The writer Harold Brodkey, for example, wrote shortly before his death from AIDS at the age of sixty-five that 'I like what I've written, the stories and two novels. If I had to give up what I've written in order to be clear of this disease, I wouldn't do it' (Brodkey 1996, 176).

There are, of course, reasons for preferring to have one's achievements in the future rather than in the past. One of these emerges when we consider the types of achievement with peaks that tend to occur early in people's lives. The most obvious of these is athletic achievement, but there are also some types of intellectual achievement – for example, in mathematics – that require forms of intelligence that reach their zenith in early adulthood and then gradually decline (Posner 1995, chapter 7).

Suppose, for example, that an athlete, beginning in childhood, trains intensively for many years and finally, in his early thirties, breaks a world record in his particular sport. He has, at that point, almost certainly reached his peak. He will not break the record he has set and, if his sport is a competitive one, it will not be many years before he has to retire from competitive play. When that time comes, he will still be a young man, but his athletic achievements will be behind him and, because he has devoted all his time to his sport, he will be unlikely to be fitted for significant achievement in any other domain of activity. It may be dispiriting for him to know that, at this comparatively early age, the remainder of his life is likely to follow a descending trajectory.[8]

If a person knows that his most important achievements are in the past, this may diminish his motivation to pursue new goals that, even if achieved, will matter much less than what he has already accomplished. But if he is uninspired to pursue lesser goals, he may come to lack any strong sense of purpose

---

[8] Compare Jeff McMahan (2002), p. 140.

in life, which is likely to result in a substantial diminishment of his experiential well-being.

But even apart from such instrumental considerations, we tend to believe that an ascending pattern of good in a life is better than a descending pattern – hence my earlier comment that we prefer a pattern of reform to one of degeneration. This applies to the good of achievement. We can imagine two lives with overall equally great achievements. In one, the greatest achievements occur early and the person then accomplishes less and less over the remainder of her life. In the other, the achievements are modest at the beginning but become progressively more impressive and significant, with the greatest achievement coming near the end. To many of us, the second seems the better life, if other things are equal, for it has the better *pattern* of achievement.[9]

It may seem that the preference for an ascending pattern of good in a life is just a manifestation of the preference for the future, since at any time during one's life, even at a point of early achievement, one wants the sequence of goods, including achievements, to be ascending simply because one cares more about the future than about the past. But even though the preference for an ascending pattern tends to coincide with and thus reinforces the preference for the future, it is nevertheless distinct. This is shown by the fact that, if one were surveying one's life from a point near its end, so that all of one's achievements were in the past, one would still prefer an ascending to a descending pattern even with a fixed total level of achievement. We could devise a variant of the Amnesia case to elicit this preference.

It is perhaps worth mentioning that even Parfit, despite his defence of temporal neutrality, may have been subject to the preference for the future in his attitudes to his own achievements. As he gradually progressed into old age, he was working on the three volumes of *On What Matters*. During that time, he would be disappointed, and hurt, if anyone whose judgement he respected expressed the view that his later work was in any way less good than his earlier book, *Reasons and Persons*. There are, however, alternative possible explanations of his attitudes. One is that he wanted his life as a whole to follow a continuously ascending trajectory. Another is that he wanted his later work to be better than the earlier because only if that were the case would he be able, while he was doing that later work, to attain the greatest level of achievement possible over the course of his life.

Even though there are the foregoing reasons for wanting our achievements to be in the future rather than in the past, there are also reasons for preferring them to be in the past. One such reason is compatible with the preference for the future. Many people care greatly about fame and even posthumous fame – or

---

[9] For a defence of the view that, in general, a pattern of improvement in life is better than a pattern of decline, see Velleman (1991).

would if they thought fame were possible for them. They would like to be widely known and admired, and favourably remembered after they die. Suppose for the sake of argument that these common desires are rational, and that fame and even posthumous fame are good for a person. In that case, one could explain the preference for having achievement in the past in prospective terms. Only if one has achievement in the past could one have the benefits of fame now and in the immediate future.

This consideration thus weakens the intuitive challenge that cases such as that of the amnesiac scientist pose to the application of the preference for the future to the good of achievement. But it does not undermine that challenge. The amnesiac scientist knows that if she is the patient with great scientific achievements in her past, she will have little time to enjoy the benefits of her fame. It seems unlikely, moreover, that in her present condition she would be motivated by thoughts of posthumous fame. If she prefers to learn that she is the patient with great achievement in her past, that can be sufficiently explained by her wanting to be the scientist who has succeeded in what she chose to devote her life to, even at the cost of having less to look forward to. To some extent, moreover, posthumous fame may be desired because it provides confirmation of the importance of one's achievements.

Even though the desire for fame provides a prospective reason for wanting to have achievements in the past, there are other reasons for wanting achievements to be in the past that seem to conflict with the preference for the future. These reasons are largely instrumental, and thus contingent, but are important nonetheless. One is epistemic – and obvious: if an achievement is in the past, one can normally be certain that one's life contains a significant good; whereas if an achievement is only a prospect, one cannot be confident that one's life will ever contain this significant good. (This is true of fame as well. Having significant achievement in the past offers a higher probability of fame in the future than an uncertain prospect of achievement in the future does.) Sometimes, of course, there is uncertainty about whether what one has done in fact constitutes a significant achievement at all. It may turn out to have been mistaken, trivial, or pernicious. On rare occasions, one has to wait a considerable period for verification. For example, predictions implied by the theory of relativity when Einstein presented it in 1905 were not confirmed until the Hafele–Keating experiment was performed in 1971, thereby conclusively verifying the theory.

But when, as with most significant achievements, one can be certain that one has accomplished a substantial and worthy goal, one then has the great good of knowing that, at least in one important respect, one's life has been well lived. One is then entitled to some measure of satisfaction and pride, and one can experience some relief from the pressure one may feel to ensure that one's life is not wasted. This may in turn give one licence to indulge oneself in other activities that were previously excluded by the imperative to pursue one's goal, thus enabling oneself to enjoy other dimensions of well-being, perhaps including the experiential benefits of fame, however modest.

As Mill wrote of his father, the knowledge that one has achieved something significant, perhaps making the world better than it would have been in one's absence, can help one to reconcile oneself to the approach of death – a view expressed more poetically by Friedrich Hölderlin, who wrote that 'if what is holy to me, the poem that rests in my heart, succeeds – then welcome, silent world of shadows!'[10] If, moreover, significant achievement can provide consolation in the face of death, it can also provide solace in old age. Solace is, of course, an experiential good, but it derives in this case from the assurance that one's life contains a fundamental, objective, non-experiential good.

Atemporal Goods, Lives as Wholes, and the Hierarchy of Achievement

But when this good is in the past, why should it be even partially exempt from the preference for the future? To most of us, as Parfit observed, it simply does not matter that we have experienced some physical pleasure in the past, except insofar as that may have some bearing on our present or future life. Why should the good of achievement be any different? Part of the explanation may be that experiential goods, such as pleasure, are ephemeral and good for us only while they occur, but not at other times. Although they contribute to our overall lifetime well-being, they do so in an additive way.

Achievement and many other non-experiential goods seem, by contrast, to be good for us in a way that might be described as atemporal. An achievement is not good only at the time it is completed, or even only during the period when it is being pursued and completed. It too affects the value of a life as a whole but not simply additively. The non-experiential good of achievement does not contribute to lifetime well-being by enhancing the goodness of some temporal part of a life; rather, to extend Parfit's metaphor, it gilds the life as a whole, imparting a lustre to all its phases, including old age. (This is an extension of Parfit's metaphor because the gilding is not of our pictures of our lives, or not *just* of our pictures of our lives, but of our lives themselves.)

Achievement, when it occurs, can affect the meaning and therefore the value of the past, particularly when it is the result of enduring effort. When one invests substantial effort, energy, time, and other personal resources in the pursuit of a goal, whether those investments succeed or fail affects their meaning and significance in one's life. If they result in failure, that can mean that part of one's life was wasted – though it need not mean that, for it could be that one's efforts were noble or heroic and therefore not to be regretted even though they ended in failure. Still, even noble and heroic efforts gild a life more

---

[10] 'To the Fates' by Friedrich Hölderlin. Available at: https://allpoetry.com/To-The-Fates

brightly when they succeed, resulting in noble achievement rather than noble failure.

Just as successful achievement enhances the meaning and significance of the efforts by which it was brought about, so those efforts can reciprocally enhance the value or significance of the achievement within the life of the one who, through those efforts, has brought it about. The more time and effort one willingly invests in the determined pursuit of a worthy goal, perhaps including years of arduous training in the relevant field of endeavour, the more the achievement of that goal does to enhance the goodness of one's life as a whole. (When, in the course of a disgraceful lawsuit he brought against John Ruskin in retaliation for a harsh review, James McNeill Whistler was asked sneeringly by the Attorney-General whether he asked 200 guineas for only two days' labour on a painting, he responded with a related and, in this one instance, plausible point: 'No; I ask it for the knowledge of a lifetime' (Hilton 2000, 398). The quality and therefore the value of the painting had been enhanced by the years of effort he had devoted to enabling himself to paint it.)

There are, of course, many types of achievement, some of which do more to enhance the goodness of a life than others. Some achievements benefit no one other than the achiever. Although there may be impersonal value in breaking an athletic record or climbing to the summit of a mountain, the motivation for such achievements is normally self-interested: to be the one who surpasses all others in some way, to do something exceedingly difficult that few others can do, and so on. Other achievements are wholly altruistically motivated – for example, Mamoudou Gassama's rapidly scaling four storeys of a building to save a child dangling from a balcony.[11] (This was a single, spontaneous act, but there are also people who devote their lives to a moral cause without any thought of personal glory – for example, the recently deceased civil rights activist and congressman John Lewis).[12] Many other achievements – particularly in the sciences, humanities, and arts – are motivated by a blend of personal ambition and a desire to do something that matters for humanity, such as increasing our understanding of the world or of ourselves and our place in the world.

There is a hierarchy among these different types of achievement and there are various general criteria for determining where different achievements fit along the scale that measures their worth.[13] First, achievements with effects that are important for others are higher, other things being equal, than those

---

[11] Many sources. For example, *The Guardian*, 29 May 2018, https://bit.ly/3DuvDZ9.

[12] When, in 1973, I was in my second year at a little liberal arts college in the American South, I invited Lewis to speak there and was his host for a couple of days. Even now I am prone to become tearful when I recall the humility, selflessness, and magnanimity of that exceptionally great man.

[13] For a more extensive discussion of the comparative goodness for people of different forms of achievement, see Gwen Bradford (2015, chapter 5).

that are not. Second, an achievement does more to enhance the goodness of a person's life the more it was motivated by a concern for matters outside the achiever's own life. Morally motivated achievements are thus higher in the hierarchy than ones that were self-interestedly motivated, if other things are equal. And even an achievement that provides significant benefits for others, such as the manufacture of a product that many people enjoy, contributes less to the goodness of the achiever's life if was motivated by self-interest, for example, by the desire to make money. (Moral goodness, I believe, is a highly important element of a good life for a person, even if it is not a component of well-being, which may be only one dimension, though perhaps the dominant one, of a good life.) Third, achievements that require great effort, persistence, discipline, sacrifice – in short, a high degree of investment – are more valuable than those that require less. Fourth, and relatedly, achievements that require unusual skills and talents and are therefore rare or even unique are higher or more valuable than those that are common, again if other things are equal. Thus, an achievement worthy of recognition by the awarding of a Nobel Prize in Physics contributes more to the goodness of a person's life than, for example, receiving a bonus at work for exemplary performance on the job, even if, improbably, the latter required more effort and personal sacrifice.

What this means, as should be obvious in any case, is that the forms of achievement that do most to enhance the goodness of a life as a whole are quite rare. Thus, in thought experiments such as the Amnesiac Scientist, the preference for achievement in the past over further experientially good but unproductive life in the future may be limited to achievements that are comparatively rare. And this, of course, limits the significance of my claims about the importance of previous achievement to well-being in old age. The less significant one's achievements are, the less likely one is to prefer having them in the past to having more experiential good in the future. All the same, having achievements in the past, even ones that are neither great nor rare, is good for us in the present. Even lesser achievements imbue our lives as wholes with some degree of value of a non-experiential sort, and in old age are also sources of pride, satisfaction, and consolation.

There is another way in which the significance of my arguments about achievement is limited. Achievement as an objective, non-experiential good is, I have suggested, an atemporal good in that it enhances the goodness of a life as a whole. And the goodness of a person's life as a whole is not equivalent to the aggregate or sum of the goods in the life from moment to moment.[14] If there were a sentient being without any psychological connections between itself at one time and itself at any other time – no memories, no desires for the future, no persisting beliefs – the goodness of its life as a whole might be just the net sum of its pleasures over time. Indeed, such a creature would have no life at all

---

[14] For a further defence of this claim, see Velleman (1991).

except in the biological sense. It would simply be the location in which a sequence of disconnected experiences would occur.[15] But the lives of persons and animals are unified psychologically over time to varying degrees, and the value of a life as a whole varies with the degree of unification.

Let us, following David Velleman, refer to a person's level of well-being at a particular time, measured by reference to the nature of her state at that time, as her 'momentary well-being' (McMahan 2002, 2021). Next, imagine two lives with equivalent aggregate totals of momentary well-being over time. If one of these lives is tightly unified over time by memory and by continuities of character, belief, desire, ambition, value, and so on, while the other is only loosely bound together by these forms of psychological continuity, the first matters more as a whole, and is a better life to have, than the second. My claims about the significance of prior achievement in old age are thus stronger and more compelling in their application to lives as wholes that are more rather than less psychologically unified over time.

Furthermore, the strength of one's reason, at any particular time, to care specially about one's life *as a whole* depends, I believe, on the extent to which one is, at that time, psychologically related to oneself in the past and will be (or will likely be) psychologically related to oneself in the future. Similarly, the extent to which a significant achievement at one time in one's life contributes to one's good at another time depends on the strength of the psychological relations between oneself at the one time and oneself at the other.

These claims, if correct, have special significance for those who suffer cognitive decline in old age. In particular, those who develop severe forms of dementia, especially forms involving substantial loss of memory, may become so weakly psychologically related to themselves as they were earlier when they pursued and achieved important goals that their earlier achievements may have little effect on the extent to which their lives are good during the period of dementia. Imagine, for example, an elderly demented individual who did legendary work in mathematics when she was in her twenties but cannot now remember her work or even do simple addition or subtraction. Her past achievements may have suffused her subsequent life with a special value as long as she remained strongly psychologically related to herself as she was when she did her great work. But as the psychological connections with her earlier self weakened with the progression of her cognitive decline, this special value gradually drained out of her life in the present, leaving it not so much gilded as only faintly illuminated by her earlier achievements. It is, to echo one of Parfit's claims about what matters in a life, almost as if her earlier achievements were the work of a different person.

Dementia is, of course, an abnormality, an illness. In the absence of such pathology, the adoption, pursuit over a lengthy period, and eventual

---

[15] For further discussion, see McMahan (2002, 75–7 and 475–6) and McMahan (2021).

achievement of some purpose or goal is one of the most important ways in which a life can become unusually highly unified psychologically over time by means of a person's own action. In normal circumstances, therefore, achievement contributes to the goodness of a life in several distinct ways: it constitutes a non-experiential good that enhances the value of the life as a whole; it helps to unify the life as a whole psychologically, thereby making the life as a whole more significant as a locus of value; and it requires forms of action that are normally among the higher forms of experiential good.

Conclusion

Insofar as it is rational for us to care about our future well-being, it should matter to us, in advance of old age, to do what we can to ensure that we will have as high a level of well-being as possible when we become old, assuming that we will be sufficiently fortunate to reach that stage of life. If my claims in this chapter are correct, we would be well advised to spend less time pursuing passive pleasures, such as watching television, and more in active pursuit of worthy purposes that may yield achievements that impart meaning and value to our lives, and of which we can be proud.

2 Ageing and the Temporality of the Good Life

Mark Schweda

Introduction: Finding Time in Ageing

'We find time in *ageing*' the Austrian writer Jean Améry explains in his essay *On Ageing: Revolt and Resignation* (Améry 2011, 11). The amount of lived time behind us incessantly grows and adopts the shape of a past life that may come to appear alien and even meaningless to us. '[T]he old have life behind them, but this life that is no longer actually lived is nothing but time gathered up, lived, passed away' (Améry 1994, 14). At the same time, the reserve of future time left to live before us progressively shrinks and finally trickles away like sand running through an hourglass. With each passing moment, we have 'already partly left the space in which [we] can remain a bit longer' (Améry 1994, 26). Thus, in growing old, the fundamental temporality of human existence, its transience and finitude, become manifest and ultimately inescapable. 'While their time passes away in the twinkling of an eye', the old 'are still only creatures of time. Each of them says "I" and means "my time"' (Améry 1994, 26).

With these considerations, Améry closes a remarkable lacuna in classical existential philosophy. Undoubtedly, in his *Being and Time*, Martin Heidegger had already established temporality and finitude as the fundamental features of human existence as such. 'Dasein' is the one 'entity which in its Being has this very Being as an issue' (Heidegger 2008, 68). Looming behind the manifold practical concerns and endeavours in which this central existential structure of 'Care' becomes manifest is the crucial question of the ultimate direction and destination of our own finite and ever-elapsing existence in time. In this sense, 'temporality makes up the primordial meaning of Dasein's Being' (Heidegger 2008, 235). However, ageing as a process or old age as a phase are seldom mentioned in the context of Heidegger's 'existential ontology'. In this respect, his profound analysis of human existence in time remains peculiarly abstract and formalistic. The infamous notion of the individual's 'running ahead towards death' (Heidegger 2008, section 53) does not seem to pay much systematic attention to the route of this course, with all its various stages and trajectories, twists and turns.

This contribution proposes that an in-depth analysis of ageing can assist us in developing a deeper understanding of human temporality and its relevance for the good life. The experience of growing old makes clear that life is essentially a process in time with a particular temporal extension and structure that has important eudaemonic implications. While the last few decades have witnessed a renaissance of ethical discussions about happiness, human flourishing, and meaning in life, little attention has yet been paid to these temporal aspects and dimensions. Taking ageing as the starting point and frame of reference for exploring the temporality of human life and its ethical significance, I begin by distinguishing three ethically relevant levels of human temporality that become manifest in the process of ageing. Firstly, I take a closer look at the level of fundamental co-ordinates and parameters of human existence in time such as finitude, processuality, directedness, irreversibility, and finality, and discuss their implications for the good life. Secondly, I examine the ethical significance of culturally variable models of the life course and life stages such as childhood, adolescence, middle adulthood, and old age, each linked to particular statuses and passages as well as to specific roles, expectations, and life prospects. Finally, I consider the unique individual trajectory through life, highlighting the ethical relevance of different sequences of biographical events and processes, as well as their narrative interpretation. Taken together, these considerations underline the need for a more appropriate appreciation of the temporal dimension and structure of human existence in ethical discussions about the good life.

Ageing and the Levels of Human Temporality

If we follow Améry, ageing is more than some arbitrary fact of life among others. It points right to the core of our existence in time and reveals fundamental aspects and dimensions of human temporality. Ageing is 'living in a temporal perspective' (Baars 2020). In particular, three levels of time and temporal structuredness of life come to the fore as we grow older: the basic co-ordinates and parameters of human existence in time; the life course, with its different stages and passages; and the unique individual trajectory through life (Schweda 2020).

The most fundamental temporal condition of human life is usually deemed its finitude. In contrast to the timeless existence of the gods, the eternal cosmic order of things, or the ever-revolving cycles of nature, human beings are traditionally characterized as 'mortals'. Their life has a definite end and is ultimately short and fleeting, like a breath of wind or a flare of sunlight. Psalm 90 declaims: 'Our days may come to seventy years, or eighty, if our strength endures; yet the best of them are but trouble and sorrow, for they quickly pass, and we fly away'.[1] The Greek poet Pindar even calls humans 'ephemeroi', a term that originally refers to short-lived insects and flowers and literally means 'creatures of a day' (Hubbard 1985). In modern existential

---

[1] https://biblehub.com/psalms/90-10.htm.

philosophy, this fact of our mortality has become the focus of systematic scrutiny. For Heidegger, death marks the central point of reference of our existence, 'Dasein' means 'Being-towards-death' (Heidegger 2008, sections 46–53). This also accounts for the fundamental processuality of human life. Life is not a permanent state but unfolds and proceeds over a limited temporal stretch and thus involves change. 'Everything flows', as Heraclitus famously observed (Narecki 2012). All things constantly evolve and perish, come and go, and are in continuous transformation. This means that life must be understood in diachronic categories of past, present, and future, now and then, before and after. The different events occurring and steps taken do not take place all at once, but follow each other, and therefore stand in a certain consecutive relationship and order. This temporal succession of life events and phases eventually also entails the directionality, irreversibility, and finality of human existence in time. The 'arrow of time' only points in one direction. There is simply no way back. What happened in the past is irrevocable and cannot be reversed. It forms the starting point from which everything inevitably proceeds towards the end (Paul 2014).

The experience of ageing reveals these fundamental co-ordinates and parameters of human existence in time. It first involves a realization of the temporal finitude of life. Influenced by Heidegger, Améry describes growing old in terms of an increasingly inescapable confrontation with mortality in which we are eventually forced to face death as the ultimate and definite temporal limit of our own existence. The ageing person is 'like a man condemned to death: he still has five hours till his execution, then two more; finally, when the steps outside can already be heard, it's just a few minutes, seconds, and the poor sinner would like to make this most horrible moment tarry a while because it is so lovely' (Améry 1994, 9). However, according to Améry, ageing not only points to death as an impending terminus of human existence in time, but also means that death slowly infiltrates individual life from day to day and therefore represents an incremental, piecemeal 'death in the midst of life', a process of decline and expiration of life perspectives and possibilities. Ageing makes us realize that '[d]eath is already in us, making room for equivocation and contradiction. We become I and not-I. [...] We become more alienated from ourselves and more familiar with ourselves. [...] Alienation from oneself becomes alienation from being, no matter how faithfully we still attend to the day' (Améry 1994, 52). Eventually, this intensifying experience of passing time, of fleetingness and the transience of life, sheds light on the directionality, irreversibility, and finality of human existence in time. Améry describes this as a dramatic escalation in which the inevitable expiration of our limited lifetime becomes more and more acute and pressing: while the young still seem to have an immeasurable abundance of time before them, 'the ageing, who all at once know how to count the autumns and the winters with horrifying exactness, since they still measure the seasons against those that have passed [. . .], understand the passage of time as an irreversibility – too horrible to complain about, since so much has slipped by and already run past' (Améry 1994, 17).

Beyond these fundamental co-ordinates and parameters of human existence in time, ageing also involves the experience of a specific *internal* temporal shape and structure of life, a segmentation of the continuous life process into an ordered sequence of phases, stages, and passages. In literature and the arts, this 'life course' is frequently modelled after larger natural cycles like the change of the seasons, which suggests the embeddedness of human life in the comprehensive order of nature (Burrow 1986; Sears 1986). Behind these different schemes is a notion of human life as a structured and foreseeable process in time evolving through a fixed sequence of phases and passages that each have a specific meaning and involve particular activities, challenges, and expectations. In the eighteenth and nineteenth centuries, this notion became graphic in the popular depictions of staircases marking the different 'steps of life'. They arranged the human life course according to the contemporary bourgeois career ladder as a climbing and then descending curve, and devised a whole parkour of stages with their respective statuses, tasks, and opportunities (Joerißen and Will 1983). With the progress of modernization, the roles and responsibilities of these life stages became increasingly defined through the functional requirements of modern industrialized society. In the context of its working life and welfare state administration, the 'institutionalization of the life course' took place (Kohli and Meyer 1986). Legal regulations came to standardize socially relevant biographical phases and thresholds according to clear-cut chronological age limits (for example, school enrolment, access to professional positions and public offices, or entitlements under pension schemes). As a result, our still familiar 'three boxes of life' emerged: a childhood and adolescence dedicated to education and professional training, an adult life focussed on work and biological reproduction, and an old age defined through retirement, social disengagement, and physical decline (Kohli and Meyer 1986).

In the process of ageing, this internal temporal structuredness of the life course and the variety of its phases and trajectories inevitably become manifest. After all, growing older ultimately means successively passing through the different stages and passages of human life and consequently experiencing the pertinent changes regarding one's own body and physical functioning, one's personal viewpoint and perspective in life, and one's social status, roles, possibilities, and responsibilities. A famous early modern example is the monologue 'All the world's a stage' in William Shakespeare's *As You Like It* (1623), which compares a person living their life to the actor in a play with 'his acts being seven ages' (Shakespeare 1623, 2.7): going through life, the protagonist assumes different roles, starting with 'the infant, / Mewling and puking in the nurse's arms', and 'the whining schoolboy, with his satchel / And shining morning face', subsequently turning into the sentimental 'lover', the 'soldier' with his heroism and thirst for glory, the wise and righteous 'justice', and 'the lean and slippered pantaloon'. Thus, while young children and adolescents can only know of the full range of life stages from a third-person perspective, for example as embodied in their own parents or grandparents, people who have reached later life have indeed lived through and directly experienced the complete life cycle first-hand. Consequently, they personally know that the different stages of life do not represent strictly discrete states or classes of individuals, but rather phases of an encompassing, more or less continuous temporal whole. Of course, this does not necessarily mean that older people are generally privileged or superior to the young. In fact, Shakespeare himself draws a rather bleak picture of 'deep' old age. For him, the 'last scene of all, / That ends this strange eventful history / Is second childishness and mere oblivion / Sans teeth, sans eyes, sans taste, sans everything' (Shakespeare 1623, 2.7).

Of course, the process of ageing does not simply consist in the accurate execution of a clear-cut generic time schedule. On a third level, it is always entangled with the concrete temporal shape and trajectory of our individual lives. This unique personal 'journey of life' is the result of an interplay of innumerable factors, comprising our own decisions, plans, and actions on the one hand, as well as the multitude of accidental events and processes interfering with them on the other. In ancient philosophy, this fundamental contingency of human existence in time, the ultimate unavailability and incalculability of our life's concrete course and outcome, was usually discussed in terms of fate (Eidinow 2011). This perspective did not necessarily imply the fatalistic view that our life is completely determined by higher powers or by external factors and circumstances. Yet, it meant that, as humans, we inevitably must acknowledge and deal with these existential imponderabilities. From a temporal perspective, this aspect of the human condition was often captured in the notion of *kairos*. Originally, the concept alluded to a god in Greek mythology. He had a lock of hair hanging over his face, but the back of his head was bald. Thus, one could only grab hold of Kairos when he was approaching. Once he had passed by, he had irretrievably escaped (Smith 1969). The allegory captures the experience of the irresolvable entanglement of pursuit, achievement, and luck during the course of a human life, as we are exposed to forces that are beyond our own control and must react to them. One important implication of this contingency of human existence in time is that the course of our lives can never be fully explained as a consequential series of rational decisions and intentional actions. Life's actual trajectory cannot be deduced from a set of general principles or preconditions, just as its future direction cannot be outlined in advance. Instead, the interplay of our personal conduct and the manifold external factors interfering with it calls for an ex post reconstruction in narrative terms. Only in the narrative form of a biographical storyline are we able to grasp the inextricable entanglement of purposeful courses of action, and contingent conditions and accidental events that simply happen to us (Horsdal 2011).

Again, ageing and old age play an important role for understanding this contingent temporal structure of the individual path through life. As an individual's fate cannot be derived from the generic structure of the human life cycle or from individual projects and plans, it essentially needs time to unfold and to take shape before we can understand it. Only time can tell how an individual person's life will turn out, and the more time has passed, the more we know about his or her fate. In ancient and medieval thought, this connection between the contingency of the individual trajectory of life and the passing of time was a prominent topic. Thus, according to Herodotus, the ancient Greek statesman and poet Solon once met the legendarily wealthy King Croesus and discussed with him whether we can appraise a person's fate, that is, assess an individual life, before it has come to a definite end. *Respice finem* – consider the end – was Solon's somewhat foreboding admonition to Croesus (Shapiro 1996). In a similar sense, medieval thought captured the vagaries of human life, the persistent twists and turns of individual fate, in the allegory of the 'wheel of fortune'. Invoking the ancient notion of celestial spheres, the image of the wheel symbolizes the persistent ups and downs of human existence in time and summarizes its erratic movements in an overarching circular motion that alludes to the fully completed life cycle (Radding 1992). The general connection appears clear: the older a person becomes, the more their fate, the overall 'arc' of their life, takes shape and becomes palpable. This corresponds to the specific temporal perspective framing the narrative representation of individual biographies. The point of view of the narrator is essentially a retrospective one. Looking back upon our lives, we recount important events and developments, draw connections, and thus compose a more or less coherent life story. This may also explain the common association of old age with ideas of reminiscence and narrative life review (Kenyon et al. 2010).

Ageing, Human Temporality, and the Good Life

It seems astonishing that current ethical theories of the good life have given comparatively little consideration to the temporal aspects and dimensions of this life. After all, many of these theories were originally formulated to counter the abstract normative viewpoint of contemporary moral philosophy by renewing certain ancient approaches of ethical reasoning. Their theoretical perspective can be described as eudaemonistic in the sense that they deliberate on the value of the goals, projects, and activities we pursue in our personal lives. This kind of ethical reasoning thus asks about what must be regarded as prudent and desirable in the context of an individual life, comprising aspects of happiness, well-being, self-fulfilment, and flourishing, but also of meaning and purpose in life (Martin 2012). It may appear understandable why the dominant utilitarian or deontological branches of moral philosophy that are primarily concerned with the ultimate foundation of universal norms that govern social interactions do not pay much attention to changes over time and differences between life stages (Rentsch 2016). However, an ethical perspective that explicitly focusses on the question of the success or failure of individual life cannot afford to ignore the fact that this life is a process in time that has a particular temporal extension and structure. Taking ageing as a starting point and frame of reference, the following sections set out to explore the ethical significance of the different levels of human temporality for the discussion of the good life.

The Value of Mortality: Ageing, Finitude, and Meaning

From the beginning, the confrontation with finitude has given rise to questions about the meaning of human life. In ancient myths as well as in biblical tales, the insight into our mortality frequently sparked the concern that our existence might be nothing more than a blink of an eye, a brief and completely irrelevant episode in the immeasurable cosmic aeons. Thus, the book of *Ecclesiastes* contemplates human mortality and the ceaseless passing of individuals and generations as well as the rise and downfall of great empires in powerful images of breath, dust, and wind that depict all human aspirations and endeavours as vain and ultimately futile (Christianson 2006). The Mesopotamian epic of Gilgamesh or the Greek myth of Tithonus deal with the individual's struggle with transience and finitude and the longing for immortality and eternal youth (Burton 1997). Philosophical reflections such as Seneca's *De Brevitate Vitae* or the *Meditations* of Roman Emperor Marcus Aurelius investigate the possibility of true, lasting value, considering the brevity of human life and the perishableness of power and glory (Holowchak 2008).

At the same time, there is a long tradition that assumes a dialectical connection between finitude and meaning. According to this line of thought, it is precisely the experience of limited and fleeting time that gives human life its existential weight and value in the first place (Hauskeller 2020). In fact, mythical and literary tales of immortality often suggest that an eternal life would necessarily be characterized by boredom, weariness, and pointlessness. If we were immortal, there would be no need to set priorities in life or even make any existential decisions between conflicting options at all. We could simply wait and postpone any decision ad infinitum, or just as well sample every single possibility one after the other. By contrast, only the existential experience of a limited amount of lifetime running out makes our time valuable and gives our lives meaning. Thus, the insight into one's own transience and finitude appears as the necessary condition for appreciating life as a unique and precious good, for seizing opportunities that present themselves, and for making meaningful use of the limited lifetime available (Williams 1973). In this sense, the famous epigram 'carpe diem' of the Roman poet Horace calls for a determined exploitation of life and its possibilities in face of the inevitability of death (Krznaric 2017). The idea that finitude is a necessary precondition for fulfilment and meaning in life is taken up and varied throughout intellectual history, from medieval sources and Baroque poetry right up to existential philosophy (White 2017). Thus, according to Heidegger, only the acute awareness of our own mortality calls us back from the conventional existence of the 'They' and the busy distraction by the variety of things and matters to self-contemplation and the pursuit of an authentic life (Heidegger 2008, section 62).

Indeed, the confrontation with death can take place at any point in life. Yet, as Améry underlined, the fundamental processuality of life that we experience as we grow older establishes a specific sense of urgency and gravity of human existence in time. At a young age, the future normally appears to be wide open, and an unlimited number of possibilities seem to be available to the individual. However, with each decision and each turn, a course is set that increasingly narrows the range of future choices, determines points of no return, and thus effectuates an ever-increasing degree of determinacy. This may explain the common experience that, in old age, the shape of one's life becomes more and more solid and definite: 'At this point the whole of a long life is set and fixed behind us, and it holds us captive' (Beauvoir 1996, 373). This incremental increase of determinateness of human life over time has far-reaching ethical implications. Thus, it makes clear that we can never escape the life we have already lived. We cannot shake off our past in order to start all over again or make up for missed opportunities. We must proceed from where we stand. Even radical reorientations or dramatic conversions cannot turn back time or wipe our biographical slate clean. Life – as Kierkegaard says – must be lived forwards (Stokes 2010). This temporal directionality and irreversibility of human existence not only accounts for the ideas of responsibility and guilt, promise and trust, regret, apology, and forgiveness that are constitutive of our moral thinking and practice (Dyke 2003). It also has important consequences for our prospects of a good life. If living basically means accumulating more and more lived time behind us and finding less and less time to live ahead, the question of the success or failure of life becomes increasingly acute, urgent, and pressing as we grow older. Ultimately, the experience of ageing thus makes clear that human existence in time is serious. It does not provide for any hypothetical or tentative state. There is no grace period or dress rehearsal. We must lead our lives 'in real time' within an ever-closing time horizon. With each lived moment, lifetime has already irretrievably passed and thus definitely 'counts'.

Thus, if advancing in years gradually intensifies our awareness of human finitude and makes it harder to avoid our own transitoriness and mortality, one might assume that it also produces an intensifying concern with meaning in life, a specific yearning and struggle to make sense of our finite existence in time. Indeed, intellectual history shows that the confrontation with human mortality can provoke very different responses, from the hedonistic maxim of 'living in the moment' savouring the limited amount of lifetime and exploiting the opportunities for pleasure and enjoyment that it offers, to more circumspect approaches in the tradition of the Stoic philosopher Seneca that emphasize the importance of methodical plans and provisions ensuring the efficient individual utilization of our lifetime (Hauskeller 2020). Yet, under the title of 'generativity', contemporary developmental psychology and social gerontology have indeed pointed out a specific kind of concern with mortality and meaning in life that may appear as characteristic for the experience of ageing and of later phases of life (Erikson and Erikson 1998). The concept of generativity generally describes the idea of 'outliving the self' (Kotre 1996), that is, overcoming the confines of one's own limited individual existence in time through self-transcendence and embedding one's life in the more comprehensive temporal horizon of generational succession. According to this perspective, the effort to leave something permanent or pass on the quintessence of one's own existence to posterity in the form of a legacy can convey a sense of continuity or even of symbolic immortality in the chain of generations (Kotre 1996). Indeed, gerontological studies suggest that such generative motives can be found in a whole variety of social and cultural practices in old age, from care and support for one's own children and grandchildren or passing on life experience and knowledge to younger and future generations, to volunteering for the community or ecological engagement for nature and sustainable development (Weiss and Bass 2002).

The Autumn of My Years: Ageing and Life-Stage Ideals

While the fundamental co-ordinates and parameters of human existence in time have found at least some consideration, the renewed philosophical discussion of questions of the good life has paid remarkably little systematic attention to the internal temporal structure of this life, and the different stages and passages of the life cycle that we pass through as we grow older. It could almost seem as though the subject of the good life were a completely ageless, disembodied individual, a Cartesian ego that stays exactly the same over an indefinite period of time. However, upon closer inspection, this seemingly abstract ethical subject usually bears a striking resemblance to an independent and fully functional (male) person in the middle of their adult years. In light of this implicit 'standard individual', other phases of life like childhood and old age are easily perceived as deviant or even inferior and deficient modes of human existence.

This ethical 'midlife bias' (Jecker 2020a) appears particularly problematic in view of questions of the good life. In fact, in everyday life contexts, we usually speak not so much of *the* good life as such and in general. Instead, we consider different conditions and criteria of happiness, self-fulfilment, flourishing, and meaning for the different phases or stages of human life. For example, a good childhood is traditionally associated with notions of a carefree and joyful existence and autotelic activities like playing. Although this vision may convey a romanticized image of the child as the embodiment of an original and unadulterated existence, it has proven to be extremely influential throughout modern cultural history (Kennedy 2006). By contrast, a good adult life is frequently characterized by completely different attributes, most notably the performance of and excellence in instrumental activities and tasks that correspond to the various responsibilities and objectives in the context of a grown-up individual's professional career, family life, and public functions (Hudson 1999). For old age, perspectives of social disengagement and separation are traditionally considered relevant, often going hand-in-hand with the image of a life dedicated to reminiscence, theoretical contemplation, or spiritual opening (Weiss and Bass 2002). However, a good life is usually not just perceived as the sum of these separate ideals. The passages between them and their temporal order and sequence also matter, for example when we exhort someone to 'grow up already'. Thus, the stages of life are seen as connected, successively forming a structured and meaningful course. In this sense, life constitutes a temporally organized whole, comparable to a literary narrative or a musical composition. Its individual components cannot be moved, rearranged, shortened, extended, or exchanged without changing the identity and meaning of the whole, just like, for example, the beginning of a novel or the final chord of a symphony.

Obviously, the traditional ideals of the life course have long since started to erode. The course and segmentation of life, as well as the meaning given to its different stages, are changing due to increasing life expectancies and additional processes of de-standardization and individualization of the life course. In other words, we are growing out of the constraints of traditional biographical patterns. This is particularly evident with regard to later life, which has become subject to renegotiation and redefinition. A 'fresh map of life' (Laslett 1991) is emerging in which the phase of old age is not only temporally extended, but also differentiated. Today, gerontologists envisage a 'third age' that seems to continue the life of late maturity with its emphasis on enduring activity and high expectations for quality of life and social participation, and a 'fourth age' characterized by failing health, progressive frailty, and increasing need for help. At the same time, our traditional ideals and orientations concerning later life carry less and less force. The classical industrial society's model of ageing, retirement, deserved repose, and impending demise loses ground. The 'greying of the baby boomers', with their pronounced orientation towards youthfulness, personal fulfilment, and social engagement, is overturning long-standing cultural paradigms of ageing and old age. In gerontology, this corresponds to new models of 'successful ageing' that seek to replace traditional deficit-oriented notions of ageing in terms of decline and degeneration with more positive perspectives that emphasize the resources and potentials of later life (Pruchno 2012). Yet, in the respective debates, the actual goal or decisive standard against which the 'success' or 'failure' of ageing is measured is often taken for granted, mostly involving medical, psychological, or sociological notions of physical functioning, psychological well-being, or social adaptation. Like analogical conceptions of childhood in pedagogy, gerontological concepts of successful ageing hence often mirror the society and the value systems of their time (Bearon 1996).

By contrast, a philosophical discussion of good life in old age needs to dig deeper: It must address the goals and standards of ageing well as such and in general, as well as discuss why and to what extent they can *actually* be considered justified and desirable. For example, a fundamental ethical question regarding ideas of 'successful ageing' concerns the central value ascribed to activity (Pfaller and Schweda 2019). It is not self-evident why activity as such should be constitutive of a good life. After all, major strands of classical and medieval philosophy, as well as spiritual thought, traditionally considered a life dedicated to intellectual insight, perception, or contemplation as superior to any form of active life. In modern ageing research, similar ideas were incorporated in the disengagement theory of ageing and related gerontological approaches suggesting that it is natural and appropriate for the ageing person to withdraw from relationships and professional obligations, look back onto his or her past life, and contemplate finiteness and approaching death. The accompanying lessening of social interaction was frequently associated with a welcome release from social norms and thus with a vision of 'late freedom' (Rosenmayr 1987). In a similar vein, conceptions of generativity or gerotranscendence rehabilitate ideals emphasizing the increasing relevance of self-decentralization and self-transcendence in old age, drawing attention to holistic dimensions of communal and historical as well as cosmological and spiritual awareness (Tornstam 2005). Therefore, it is not sufficient to simply counter negative stereotypes of ageing and old age with more positive ones, such as ageist images of decrepit dodderers with today's active and attractive 'young old' seniors. Rather than replacing one biased stereotype with another and thus merely reversing the underlying value system, we need to achieve a more profound and balanced understanding of what it actually means from a eudaemonistic perspective to age and to be old (Baars 2012).

The Temporal Shape of Life: Ageing and Individual Fate

Just like the generic patterns of the human life course with its different stages and passages, the unique route of an individual person's path through life has found little systematic consideration in the renewed ethical discussions of the good life. This appears particularly perplexing because this individual fate seems to be exactly what the ethics of the good life is ultimately concerned with: the question of whether a person's life turns out well or not on the whole. However, the dominant temporal perspective in contemporary ethical deliberations on the good life seems to be a purely additive one in which an individual life appears good if – and to the extent that – it consists of a considerable number of valuable units or portions of time, or at least on balance comprises a greater amount of valuable than worthless lifetime. In this calculation, the specific temporal shape of this life, that is, the concrete order and sequence of the 'eudaemonic time quanta', does not seem to have any special ethical significance.

In contrast to this 'aggregationist' perspective of modern discussions about the good life, the specific temporal structure of the personal trajectory played an important role in ancient philosophy. Thus, Aristotle contemplates the ethical relevance of this individual 'arc' of life in a number of intriguing passages of his *Nicomachean Ethics*. For example, he explains that true happiness (eudaemonia cannot be just a matter of a few happy days or periods in life but essentially involves the aspect of the duration of eudaemonia and therefore must be considered on principle as the signature of a whole lifetime. According to him, it takes more than one swallow to make a spring (Aristotle 2005, 1098a18–20; Farwell 1995)). In close connection with this aspect of the temporal duration of eudaemonia, Aristotle then takes up and discusses the aforementioned problem posed by Solon of whether we can really call a person happy, that is, evaluate the success or failure of an individual's life, before it has been fully completed (Aristotle 2005, 1098a18–20; Irwin 1985). The lesson of Solon's encounter with King Croesus had been to consider the end of the respective life. In a similar vein, Aristotle reminds the reader of other famous examples of honourable and well-to-do individuals who suffered devastating blows of fate in later life and ended their days in deep misery and despair (Aristotle 2005, 1100a5). He even ponders the possibility that a man's nefarious descendants could posthumously compromise the overall balance of his life by disgracing him, but eventually discards the thought as implausible (Aristotle 2005, 1100a10–31; Scott 2000).

Some strands of contemporary ethical theorizing have tried to recover aspects of this awareness of fate and the contingency of human life in terms of 'moral luck' (Williams 1981). Taking up this problem from a decidedly eudaemonistic perspective, Martha Nussbaum revisited ancient philosophy and literature to remind us of the 'fragility of goodness'; that is, the fact that human happiness and flourishing as well as the success or failure of individual life also depend on external goods that are not necessarily at our autonomous disposal, so that considerable up- and downturns of individual fortune can occur over time (Nussbaum 2001). More recent contributions follow this line of thought further and also reflect on the eudaemonic significance of a life's concrete temporal shape (Velleman 1991; Campbell 2015; Dorsey 2015). For example, there are good reasons to assume that it makes a difference whether a person experiences existential misfortune and crises at the beginning or towards the end of his or her life. Prima facie, many would probably prefer the 'ascending arc' of a life that starts in the midst of hardship and adversities but moves on towards success and happiness to the reverse 'declining arc': a life that begins carefree but is later afflicted by blows of fate and ends in misery and despair (Velleman 1991). However, the reason for this preference may not only be that a 'happy ending' somehow feels more satisfactory and comforting. In fact, facing tragic failure in a lifelong fight for a worthy cause may even appear preferable to a completely unforeseeable streak of good luck after a trivial life of irrelevance and tediousness. Thus, what matters from the perspective of the good life is neither just the overall balance of happy and unhappy moments in life, nor their sheer temporal order and sequence, but rather the way we are able to connect the different moments and life events in a coherent and significant biographical storyline in order to give our life meaning (Kauppinen 2012; Dorsey 2015).

This reconfirms the close connection between the ethical question of the erratic shape of the individual trajectory through life and the problem of time, ageing, and narrativity. As already indicated, the fundamental contingency of human existence in time entails an element of irreducible facticity that requires an ex post reconstruction in narrative terms. We can only do justice to the entanglement of purposeful courses of action and accidental events and developments that make up our life in the narrative form of a biographical storyline. However, the relevance of narrativity is not just a matter of representation of an independent biographical reality. It rather gives our lives meaning and significance in the first place. Some philosophers even argue that it accounts for our individual character, our unique personal identity (Schechtman 2010). This idea of narrative identity, that it is our individual life 'history' that ultimately makes us the persons we are, corresponds to traditional ideas of ageing as 'becoming oneself' (Rentsch 2016), a process of self-development, individual maturation, and personal growth. In any case, biographical meaning is not simply a given fact. It is produced in the face of variable biographical discontinuities, transitions, changes, and disruptions that question the unity of the person and the coherence of his or her life. Of course, the symbolic orders of our culture, mythology, literature, and the arts provide us with an abundance of generic narrative schemes of the life course that we can take up and adapt in order to construct and reconstruct the individual arc of our own life story. This includes, for example, the idea of a 'prime of life' common to classical and medieval ethics, a zenith or peak where all of a person's capabilities and possibilities are developed to the fullest extent (Dove 1986), or the consoling thought that the 'journey of life' moves towards a final meaningful closure in the end, thus becoming a complete, well-rounded whole (Cole 1992).

Conclusions: Ageing and the Temporality of the Good Life

Ageing is living in a temporal perspective. Therefore, a closer examination of the various aspects of ageing and old age can help us to understand the relevance of human temporality for the ethical discussion of the good life. In particular, three levels of temporality come to the fore: the basic co-ordinates and parameters of human existence in time, the life course with its different stages and passages, and the individual fate and trajectory through life.

At each of these three levels, ageing and human temporality have important implications for the discussion of the good life. The confrontation with finitude and mortality that we experience as we grow older is often considered a necessary precondition for valuing our limited lifetime and setting priorities in life. In this sense, it could arguably even be regarded as constitutive of the ethical point of view itself, the very perspective in which it actually matters what we do and how we live. Furthermore, as we age, we pass through the life course, with its different phases and passages, and come to realize that the internal temporal extension and structure of human life is also relevant with regard to happiness and meaning in life. Different things become important at different points in life. Finally, the unique trajectory through life that unfolds as we grow older reveals the contingency of individual fate and raises questions of the ethical relevance of the temporal shape and narrative structure of the good life.

We must acknowledge the heuristic nature of the analytical distinction between these three levels of temporality. They do not refer to separate strands of life that run parallel without ever touching each other. In fact, they are closely intertwined in the process of ageing. Thus, as we have seen, our viewpoint on and awareness of our own finitude as human beings changes throughout the life course, and the challenge of mortality for meaning in life arguably becomes more acute and pressing as we approach old age. At the same time, the manifold social patterns and cultural representations of the life course provide different interpretative frames of reference for making sense of the erratic individual trajectory of life from a narrative perspective. It makes an important difference whether we understand our pathway through life in terms of the change of seasons in the annual cycle, or as a long, protracted voyage that leads into new, uncharted territories.

This entanglement of the different levels of temporality also has important consequences for the ethical discussion of the good life. Thus, tensions and conflicts between the different temporal levels can impede and complicate a person's prospects of leading a good life. For example, protracted difficulties with acknowledging the fundamental condition of human finitude and coming to terms with one's own mortality may endanger the possibility of appreciating and actually using one's limited individual lifetime in a sensible way. In this regard, certain forms of the denial of human finitude may have rather problematic individual consequences, such as the transhumanist quest for 'radical life extension' or 'biological immortality' (Kass 2004). Another example pertains to the gap between our increasing average life expectancy and the traditional lack of appropriate social positions and meaningful cultural narratives for later life. In fact, in the wake of demographic ageing, a 'structural lag' has been diagnosed, a discrepancy between the scanty roles and prospects traditionally assigned to the later phase of life and the ever-increasing amount of lifetime available (Riley et al. 1994).

It seems surprising that the renewed ethical discussion of the good life has not engaged in a more substantial manner with ageing and the temporal aspects and dimensions of human life. While there may be famous philosophical works on old age as a specific topic of ethical considerations, there is hardly any systematic reflection on the fundamental implications of ageing and human temporality for ethical theorizing as such and in general (Small 2007). What does it mean for ethical thought that human lives are essentially determined by certain inevitable and irreversible changes over time? What is the role of specific images, conceptions, expectations, and ideals regarding childhood, adolescence, adulthood, and old age? How can we appropriately reflect the ethical relevance of the unmistakable temporal shape of an individual life? An ethical discussion of the good life must address these questions and engage with the attendant temporal aspects and dimensions in order to foster an open debate on their significance and justification. If ageing means living in a temporal perspective, what we need is not so much a specific ethics of ageing, an ethics for older people, but an appropriate ethical appreciation of the temporal dimension and structure of human existence as such and in general.

3 Children's Prudential Value

Anthony Skelton

Introduction

Until recently, the nature of children's well-being or prudential value remained all but unexplored in the literature on well-being. There now exists a small but growing body of work on the topic.[1] In this chapter, I focus on a cluster of under-explored issues relating to children's well-being. I investigate, in specific, three distinct (and to my mind puzzling) positions about it, namely, that children's *lives* cannot on the whole go well or poorly for them, prudentially speaking; that the prudential goods of childhood *count for less* than the same goods of adulthood towards the prudential value of an individual's life as a whole; and that children's prudential goods (or goods more generally) are (at least in some cases) in some way *special*.

This chapter is divided into four main sections. In the first section, I briefly describe some accounts of the nature of children's well-being. In the next three sections, I address the three somewhat puzzling positions mentioned above.

Children's Well-Being

What is non-instrumentally or basically prudentially good for a child? Recent literature on well-being has produced a range of answers. The most well-developed seem to fall into two categories.

The first category comprises so-called objective list views of well-being. The distinguishing feature of such views is they hold something (friendship or play) is non-instrumentally good for a child (or other individual) independently of whether the child possesses a pro attitude towards the item in question. In line with this, Guy Fletcher describes objective list theories as including 'all and only those that specify particular things as non-instrumentally prudentially good (or bad) for people whether or not they have any pro (or con) attitude towards them' (Fletcher 2016, 151; Lin 2020). For example, spending time engaged in sport may be good for a child even if it is not, for her, enjoyable or what she wants. True, it might be better were she enjoying or satisfying

---

[1] For treatments of what is non-instrumentally prudentially good for children, see Alexandrova (2017), Brennan (2014), Brighouse and Swift (2014), Gheaus (2015a; 2015b), Kraut (1994; 2007), Lin (2017), Skelton (2015; 2016; 2018), and Skelton, Forsberg, and Black (2021).

a desire for sport, but enjoyment or desire satisfaction is not necessary for sport to be good for her. To take another example, it might be non-instrumentally bad for a child to be in some way ignorant or in the possession of false beliefs even if she enjoys it. Ignorance need not be painful or frustrate a desire to be non-instrumentally bad for her.

Samantha Brennan adopts an objective list view of what is good for children. The items she thinks basically prudentially good for children include:

Unstructured, imaginative play. Relationships with other children and with adults. Opportunities to meaningfully contribute to household and community. Time spent outdoors and in the natural world. Physical affection. Physical activity and sport. Bodily pleasure. Music and art. Emotional well-being. Physical well-being and health. (Brennan 2014, 42)

Anna Alexandrova also appears to adopt an objective list view of what is basically prudentially good for children, on which the following two items are good for children:

Develop those stage-appropriate capacities that would, for all we know, equip them for successful future, given their environment ... And engage with the world in child-appropriate ways, for instance, with curiosity and exploration, spontaneity, and emotional security. (Alexandrova 2017, 69 [emphasis removed])

Included in the so-called stage-appropriate capacities are the ability to reason, to make decisions, and to use one's body (Alexandrova 2017, 69). These are basically good for children in part because they develop skills for use that (it is reasonable to expect) will be useful when one is an adult. Included in child-appropriate ways of engaging with the world are both psychological states (pleasure, happiness, awe) and behaviours (spontaneous action) and many of the goods on Brennan's list (Alexandrova 2017, 74).

Into the second category fall so-called hybrid views of well-being.[2] Hybrid theories of well-being (putatively) combine aspects of objective list views with aspects of so-called subjective views of well-being, the distinguishing feature of which is that some item is non-instrumentally or basically good for an individual only if that individual has a pro attitude toward the item in question, for example she wants it or values it in some way (Sumner 1996, 34ff).

The idea behind hybrid views is that one fares well only when one possesses or engages with something, for example a friendship, *and* one has a pro attitude towards that something, for example one wants it or finds it satisfying. In one hybrid view of well-being for children, well-being consists in happiness or satisfaction in play, intellectual development or activity, and valuable relationships (including friendships with peers) (Skelton 2015; 2016). According to this view, neither happiness alone nor play, intellectual development, and

---

[2] For detailed general discussion of hybrid views, see Woodard (2016).

valuable relationships alone have non-instrumental, basic prudential value. If a child experiences happiness in the absence of the other items, her happiness will at best be instrumentally good for her. Similarly, if a child develops intellectually in the absence of happiness, such development will at best be instrumentally good for her.

The views discussed so far are articulated explicitly for children. Alexandrova is most clearly committed to advocating for a distinct view of well-being for adults. She bears the burden, therefore, of showing that children's well-being is distinct from adult well-being. Proponents of the other views may at least in principle leave open whether children's well-being is distinct from adults' well-being.[3]

Not all views of adults' well-being are silent on the nature of children's well-being.[4] Richard Kraut defends a hybrid view of well-being applying to all (human) welfare subjects, which he calls developmentalism (Kraut 2007). According to this view, 'a flourishing human being is one who possesses, develops, and enjoys the exercise of cognitive, affective, sensory, and social powers (no less than physical powers)' (Kraut 2007, 137). Kraut thinks his view contains the flexibility to explain why different things are good for different human beings at different stages in their life and development. According to Kraut's view, then, a child is faring well when she is flourishing, and she is flourishing when she is enjoying or taking pleasure in the actual development or exercise of her physical, social, sensory, cognitive, and affective capacities or powers. As with the other hybrid view, Kraut maintains that pleasure in the absence of the development or the exercise of one's capacities or powers is not basically or non-instrumentally good for a child (Kraut 2007, 124–5, 129, 137, 166, 176) and (similarly) that the development or exercise of a capacity in the absence of pleasure is not basically or non-instrumentally good for a child (Kraut 2007, 128, 165).

These prominent theories of children's well-being face challenges. Take the hybrid view. It might be implausible to claim that happiness by itself or intellectual development by itself is at best merely instrumentally good, as the hybrid view implies. Happiness alone may seem basically good for a child; the same may be true, for example, of intellectual development and valuable relationships. If this is right, the objective list view may be the better account of children's well-being, provided the list includes happiness and goods like intellectual development.

In reply, the proponent of the hybrid view may urge that if the happiness in question really is not taken in one of the objective items the particular hybrid view favours, and the possession of objective items really does leave one cold, it

---

[3] For arguments in favour of the view that children's well-being is distinct from adults' well-being, see Skelton (2015); for doubts, see Cormier and Rossi (2019).

[4] Of course, hedonism and desire-fulfilment views of well-being may provide accounts of children's well-being; for discussion and criticism, see Kraut (1994; 2007) and Skelton (2015; 2016).

may not be all that implausible to deny them non-instrumental, basic prudential value. Most views of well-being will have to declare that at least some items
appearing non-instrumentally good will turn out in fact to be merely instrumentally good (e.g., hedonism). The hybrid view of well-being is not unique in
this respect.

We shall want to know which of these views to accept, if any. I will not
adjudicate the dispute here. Instead, I focus on what seem to be matters of
agreement between the views. These views agree that their favoured basic
prudential goods contribute to making a child's life go well, or at least that
a sum or other combination of the goods determine how well a child's life is
going. Children's lives as a whole can go well on these views. In addition, these
views do not (on the face of it) claim that children's prudential goods contribute
less in themselves to the non-instrumental prudential value of one's life as
a whole. They do not, that is, discount children's prudential goods when thinking
about how well one's life is going or has gone. Some of these views of children's
well-being suggest, as noted, that children's well-being is distinct (or possesses
features that are distinct) from adult well-being, but they seem not to hold that
there are special prudential goods in childhood because, for example, certain
goods are accessible only (or more readily available) to children.

In the remainder of this chapter, I explore the following positions rivalling
those agreed to by the views of well-being discussed so far: that children's lives
cannot go well or poorly for them on the whole, prudentially speaking; that the
prudential goods of childhood count for less than the prudential goods of
adulthood towards the prudential value of an individual's life as a whole;
and that children's prudential goods (or at least some of them) are special.

Do Children's Lives Go Well?

David Velleman defends a conception of prudential value implying that children (at least when young) may fare well or poorly at a time but not over time
(Velleman 2000). Children may be able to fare well in a moment; their lives as
a whole cannot go well or poorly for them.

This conclusion follows from the premises of an argument Velleman relies on
to show that the lives of certain non-human animals (e.g., cows) cannot go well
or poorly for them. He argues non-human animals can 'fare well or ill only at
particular moments' (Velleman 2000, 83). This is because a cow is able to care
only about what happens to it at a time or in a moment. A cow cannot care
about what happens to it over time or in a period of time or in its life as a whole,
because a cow is unable to conceive of itself 'as persisting through a sequence
of benefits' or ills (Velleman 2000, 81). And since a cow is unable to care about
how well or poorly its life is going over time or across time or as a whole, what
happens to it across time or in a period of time or in its life as a whole is not
'intrinsically good for' it (Velleman 2000, 81).

By contrast, because 'a person can care about what his life story is like' or her life as a whole, what happens to her across time or in a period of time or in her life as a whole is intrinsically good for her (Velleman 2000, 84). In addition, like non-human animals, persons can care about what is good for them in a moment or at a time. Persons therefore, according to Velleman, can fare well at a time and across time; that is, they have both synchronic or momentary welfare interests and diachronic welfare interests (Velleman 2000, 71).

Velleman contends further that, in the case of persons, the value of a life as a whole is a not a matter exclusively of the sum of the momentary goods comprising it. The value of a life has to do in addition with the meaning of various events in the life. The meaning of an event is determined by how it figures into the narrative structure or story of the life. There is value to be found in the sequence of harms and benefits (Velleman 2000, 81 and 83). The value of the life or meaning is not reducible to the sum of the values of the moments comprising it.

To illustrate, imagine two different lives. One involves a troubled marriage of ten years ending in divorce, which is quickly followed by a very happy second marriage to someone else. A second life involves a troubled marriage ending not in divorce, but in 'eventual happiness as the relationship matures' (Velleman 2000, 65). Velleman says even if the sum of momentary well-being in the two lives is equal in value, the second life is basically prudentially better for one as it includes a better sequence of events. In the first marriage the struggle is a 'dead loss' whereas in the second the struggle is 'redeemed' (Velleman 2000, 65). The (better) story of redemption adds value to the life beyond what (the sum of) momentary values contribute.

What does Velleman's view imply for children? It is unclear whether Velleman means to include children in the category of 'persons'. Like much work in well-being, his focus seems to be on adults in full possession of their faculties (Skelton 2016). But it appears to follow on his view that, like cows, children, especially when young, can fare well or ill only at particular moments. This follows presumably in part because children, at least when young, can care only about what happens to them at a time or in a moment. Such children cannot, it seems, care about what their life story is like or about extended periods in time or about their life as a whole.

Of greatest significance for Velleman is the 'value of a particular sequence' of harms and benefits, for example struggle in a marriage followed by reconciliation and redemption. Children cannot care about such sequences because they cannot take up the diachronic perspective from which they may be valued. They cannot conceive of themselves persisting through a sequence of benefits or ills and so cannot care about the relations between them. Since they cannot care about their lives as a whole, their lives cannot go better or worse for them. They appear, then, like non-human animals, to have no diachronic prudential interests; they have only synchronic prudential interests.

Key to Velleman's position on non-human animals and on children is a form of internalism: 'unless a subject has the bare capacity, the equipment, to care about something under some conditions or other, it cannot be intrinsically good for him' (Velleman 2000, 81). The variety of internalism is weak, requiring only that subjects have a 'bare capacity' to care about something rather than that they actually care about something or have the disposition to care about something under some (possibly counterfactual) condition(s). But, still, it has bite. If children lack the capacity to care about their life as a whole or the relationship between sequences of events in their life, children cannot be said to have good or bad lives, prudentially speaking.

The implications of Velleman's view seem highly counterintuitive. We speak of children's lives going well or of individuals having had a good childhood. Velleman himself at points suggests one can have a good or 'happy' childhood (Velleman 2000, 73, also 72, 60, 68). It is part of common sense that a child's life can go well or poorly for her. News items frequently report, for instance, some children's lives have gone less well (or badly) for them during the pandemic because lockdowns and school closures have had a negative impact on their mental health. A child soldier might be said to have had a bad childhood or lived a bad life while she was a soldier.

Such claims are not, it seems, the same as the claim that children have suffered or things have gone poorly for them only in various moments or at discrete times in their life. The claim seems to be that their lives have on the whole, taking into account all the relevant bits, gone less well for them or did not go well for them during the worst parts of the pandemic or during their time as a child soldier. We, of course, speak in similar ways about non-human animals. We might say, for example, that Melanie's cat Taz has a good life on the whole, taking into account all she does, frolicking, napping, and eating. Or that abused dogs or cows in factory farms have lives that go poorly for them on the whole.

In what sense do we make those claims? There is a natural sense in which we may be talking about a cat having a good life. The cat's life, it seems natural to suppose, contains on balance more positive experiences than negative experiences (Bradley 2015). A life is going well when the benefits outweigh the harms. We might think something like the same is true for children. It is not implausible that in the case of at least some (young) children, their lives are going well in the sense that on balance they have more of what is non-instrumentally, basically good for them than they have what is non-instrumentally, basically bad for them.

Velleman denies this kind of summing or aggregating in the case of non-human animals, because

any method of combining the values of a cow's good and bad moments will be purely arbitrary and consequently defective, insofar as it fails to represent what values things have specifically for the cow rather than for some other perspective. (Velleman 2000, 83)

It seems to follow that, for children, this way of determining what makes their lives good on the whole is not acceptable because it is arbitrary 'insofar as it fails to represent what values things have specifically for' the child.

This is too strong. It does not follow automatically that a judgement about how well a child's life is going on the whole or as a whole would be arbitrary given Velleman's supposition. It is not clearly arbitrary that the value of a life as a whole or over some period in a life is equivalent to the sum of the values of the moments in that life or period. It might be wrong. It might be true that the sum of the values of the parts is not the whole story. Perhaps the distribution or arrangement of goods matters, too. In this case the value of a life as a whole would in part be a function of how equitably prudential goods (e.g., happiness, friendship) are distributed in this life (Sen 1979, 470–1). This view does not seem arbitrary, either. In any case, it is not as if we lack intuitions about what makes lives good or bad on the whole for children, for example, that other things being equal, a life containing surplus prudential value on balance is better than one containing surplus ill-being on balance. Insofar as we rely on such intuitions, we seem well suited to avoiding the charge of arbitrariness.

Velleman's worry must be that it is dubious to make judgements about the prudential goodness or badness of a child's or non-human animal's life as a whole without reference to their perspective, for without reference to that we can no longer be certain we are talking about prudential value anymore.

But it is not clear this follows. We seem to have intuitions about what makes a life good or bad for a child. A child would certainly live a bad life on the whole were they forced into sexual or slave labour. This life would be worse on balance than a life lived as member of a loving, protective family. Our judgements about what is basically prudentially good or bad for children will have to rely on intuitions like this rather than about what they can care about from their perspective. It is not clear that we think one's perspective is of the utmost importance in the case of (especially young) children and animals in any case.

We have a clash, then, between internalism and the idea that children and non-human animals can have lives that are good or bad on the whole. Since it seems clear that (young) children can live good or bad lives, we should reject internalism (or Velleman's version of it) for them.

The point might be reached in another way. Velleman thinks that it is only in cases in which a non-human animal or a child has the bare capacity to care about something that we can say something is non-instrumentally good for or bad for them. But this assumes without argument that the only relation determining whether something is prudentially good or bad for one is that of being something one has the bare capacity to care about. It is possible there may be other relations in which an individual may stand to something for it to count as prudentially good or bad for them. It is possible that having the capacity to care or caring about something makes a difference to how prudentially good or bad for you it turns out to be. However, there may be other relations. It is possible in the case of children that something contributing to flourishing or development is the right relation a thing must bear to a child to make her prudentially better or worse off.

In any case, requiring that one could care is too strong in the case of children and of non-human animals. Suppose a very young child does not care about taking happiness in valuable relationships with family members. It is just not clear such relationships fail to contribute directly to making a child prudentially better off. So we must search for some other relation to make sense of the relation something must bear to a child to make her prudentially better or worse off. It is more plausible that such a relation exists than that young children cannot have momentary or lifetime well-being. It seems plausible to reject internalism for the purpose of thinking about children's well-being, or at least for the purpose of thinking about the value of their lives as a whole.

Now, of course, at some point children will, as they mature, develop the capacity to care about their lives as a whole and in particular to care about the narrative structure of the life. In this case, Velleman's form of internalism will apply to children. Should we think in this case (let's focus here on adolescents) that narrative structure or meaning in Velleman's sense matters in the way he suggests? It might matter to a degree. It might be good for a young person, say, to struggle at a sport or at school and then after a period emerge as a success or a leader in the sport or at school. It might be better to succeed at one's current sport or in one's current study than to fail and move on to another sport or vocation even if the momentary well-being of the life with success is the same as the life with failure.

But I am not convinced that narrative structure has the importance Velleman suggests it does for adolescents, for two reasons. First, once an individual can care about something, what she cares about (at least under certain circumstances) will have an important role to play in determining what is basically prudentially valuable or not for her. The idea is that once she can care, her schedule of concerns determines to a significant degree what is basically prudentially good (bad) for her. If an individual (whether an adolescent or not) does not care about narrative structure or the way in which sequences of events in her life fit together, it is plausible that it matters or seems to matter much less to how well her life is going. The extent to which it does is largely (though perhaps not solely) up to her.

Second, to the extent that what matters to an adolescent's lifetime well-being is not a matter purely of her schedule of concerns, it is plausible that things other than narrative structure matter directly to her well-being. What seems to be good for adolescents more than narrative structure is quite the reverse. It is a near platitude that among the important basic prudential goods of relevance to adolescent well-being are not pleasing stories or narratives but rather plentiful experimentation with different identities involving, almost as a matter of course, trying on new identities, jettisoning some, failing at others, and having only partial success at yet others. In short, a good bit of organized chaos. Adolescence involves dropping some things one has worked hard on and taking up others, and so on. It is far from clear whether it is better for an adolescent to stick to a sport she has worked hard at than to drop the sport and move on to a musical instrument. In light of the importance of experimentation in adolescence (Schaprio 1999; Franklin-Hall 2013; Gheaus 2015a) and – yes – failure, it seems narrative structure, as Velleman understands, is of (limited) non-instrumental prudential value for children.

Do Children's Prudential Goods Count for Less towards Lifetime Well-Being?

Michael Slote agrees children's lives can go well or poorly for them, prudentially speaking (Slote 1983). Momentary goods in childhood play a role in determining the value of a life as a whole, but they play a lesser role compared to the goods of adulthood. Slote makes this remark about discounting the goods of childhood in the context of his quarrel with Henry Sidgwick's claim that the temporal location of an individual's perfection or happiness is not directly or intrinsically relevant to its value (Sidgwick 1981 [1907], 381). Sidgwick is a proponent of temporal neutrality. For Slote, location in time (pace Sidgwick) can make such a direct, intrinsic difference to something's prudential value. More specifically, the stage in life in which a prudential good occurs is directly relevant to the value it contributes to the life as a whole. A good (success) or ill (misfortune) counts for less when it falls in childhood.

Slote's argument runs as follows. Individual lives can be carved up into periods by reliance on 'natural and socially influenced facts about the typical human life cycle' (Slote 1983, 13, also 14). Roughly, there are three periods: childhood, including adolescence; the prime of life; and senescence or old age. Slote defines the prime of life as the period 'containing precisely those goals, strivings, miseries, and satisfactions, that are to be taken most seriously in human life' (Slote 1983, 21).

Slote goes on to argue that we tend to treat with 'lesser seriousness ... the successes and misfortunes of childhood' (Slote 1983, 14). There are, he says, pursuits 'typical' or 'characteristic' of childhood (Slote 1983, 16, 17, 20, 23), including 'membership of the school team, scout merit badges', 'honour-roll marks', and 'captaincy of the basketball team' (Slote 1983, 16, 17, also 18). Successes or failures in these 'don't enter with any great weight into our estimation of the (relative) goodness of total lives' (Slote 1983, 14, also 20). In other words, he says, the 'successes and misfortunes' of childhood are less weighty when we are considering 'how fortunate someone has been in life'

(Slote 1983, 14). These count for less in determining the overall value of a life simply because such successes and misfortunes took place in childhood.

In support of the discounting of childhood goods, he offers as evidence that we do not think glories in childhood make up for, or in some way compensate for, adult misfortunes, and nor do we think that the misfortunes of a schoolboy or a schoolgirl by themselves make a life worse or much worse (Slote 1983, 14). For example, Slote says

A statesman known to have led a very happy and successful life may be discovered to have had a miserable childhood, but unless we imagine that that embittered his adulthood in ways not immediately obvious from other biographical facts, I don't think the discovery will make us wonder whether we haven't been over hasty in supposing the man (or his life) to have been fortunate, enviable. Within a very wide range, the facts of childhood simply don't enter with any great weight into our estimation of the (relative) goodness of total lives. (Slote 1983, 14)

The best explanation of this normative claim is, Slote says, that the successes and misfortunes of childhood are period relative goods: these are things that are valuable for children in childhood but not valuable 'from the perspective of human life as a whole' (Slote 1983, 17). This serves as a better explanation of their status than does an explanation according to which the typical pursuits of childhood lack value as irrational desires or addictions might (Slote 1983, 16, 21). Slote concludes from this that the value of the successes and misfortunes typical of childhood count for less towards determining the value of a life as a whole because they occur in childhood. Therefore, contra Sidgwick, the contribution a success or misfortune makes to the value of a life as a whole depends in part on when in time it occurs in a life.

It is not obvious the goods of childhood are to be discounted in the way Slote suggests. Slote's way of carving up life into discrete stages is problematic. He groups infancy, toddlerhood, pre-adolescence, and adolescence together into one category, thereby ignoring the vast intellectual, emotional, and physical differences between very young children and teenagers. It is not a stretch to suggest differences between children might affect the value their successes or failures contribute to lifetime well-being. An adolescent's failures or misfortunes may be much worse than a younger child's failures. Even if we concede that in general children's misfortunes are less significant in determining life's value, it does not follow that they are equally insignificant. The misfortune an adolescent experiences in being treated in an excessively paternalistic way may detract more from lifetime well-being than the misfortune a very young child experiences in being treated paternalistically.

Slote might grant this objection. He might simply suggest all he has to do is carve out another period of life – adolescence – and make claims that are distinct from but similar to those he makes about childhood. He could, for example, argue there are four periods in life, and that the goods of childhood are less important than the goods of adolescence, which are less important than the goods of the prime of life.

It is unclear if this reply on Slote's behalf does complete justice to the kinds of successes of which adolescents are capable, however. Some triumphs of adolescence and especially later adolescence seem not to be that remote from those indicative of the 'prime of life'. They seem to be precisely those things that are 'to be taken most seriously in human life' (Slote 1983, 21).

Consider an example to illustrate. In the 2012 Olympic games, a fifteen-year-old American, Katie Ledecky, won a gold medal in the 800-metre free-style swimming event. The fact that Ledecky was fifteen, and therefore by Slote's standards a child, does not by itself lead me to regard her success with 'lesser significance' when comparing it with the same success had later on in life. It appears to make as big a contribution to the overall value of her life as would the same success had in the 'prime of life'.

Indeed, this success seems (to me) to be 'determinative of what one's life has, for better or worse, been like' (Slote 1983, 21). In Slote's view, this is an important feature of the goods of the prime of life. This sort of triumph may well make up for future failures in coaching or in other pursuits relating to winning a gold medal.

Slote might reply to this by reiterating he does not think his claim about discounting applies to all the misfortunes or successes in childhood. His view is not that 'all, or even most, of the satisfactions … of childhood, are merely (period-)relative goods' (Slote 1983, 20). Rather, only some of the successes and misfortunes are discounted. Slote is concerned only with the successes and misfortunes that are 'characteristic' or 'typical' of childhood, for example captaincy of sport teams in school, honour-roll marks, scout merit badges, and the like. It is only to these successes and their corresponding misfortunes that his claim about the lesser significance with which we treat the successes and misfortunes of childhood applies. His claim is, if a success or misfortune is 'characteristic' or 'typical' of childhood, it is treated with less significance when we are thinking about how fortunate a person has been in life.

This reply weakens Slote's position. First, Slote relies on a distinction between goods (ills) that are characteristic or typical of childhood and goods (ills) that are not. He does not cut the distinction in a principled way. He offers only examples of what he has in mind. His examples of what seem to be typical or characteristic successes or misfortunes of childhood are very narrow and risk trivializing his main claim about the successes and misfortunes of childhood. We might grant that what he regards as typical or characteristic do not count for much and then argue that we ought to focus on other, more important goods in childhood instead (e.g., unstructured leisure and play and the opportunity to pursue them).

Second, what he characterizes as 'typical' or 'characteristic' seems not to exhaust all of what we think of as typical goods of childhood. Consider, for example, one very typical or characteristic pursuit of childhood, namely, the rich, intimate, and very enjoyable relationships children often or typically have with children (roughly) their own age or with their siblings or older adults (e.g., grandparents). Such friendships often involve knowing, loving, and interacting with others in very focussed, very intimate ways. It is very difficult to imagine this kind of typical or characteristic good as being one to be discounted in any way simply because it occurs in childhood.

Slote's point about typical or characteristic goods is more easily accepted if we focus exclusively on his examples. But in line with the point just made, it seems harder to concede his point if we look behind the various successes on which he focusses to the more basic goods they might serve to promote, including happiness, intellectual development, friendship, companionship, and so on. These seem not to be obvious candidates for discounting in them-selves. It is less than obvious that we have reason to discount happiness taken in a close, intimate relationships simply because it takes place in childhood. Such friendships might count for a lot in thinking about how well or not one's life has gone. They may even compensate for the lack of successful relation-ships in adulthood.

Third, we might grant in some cases that what Slote deems typical or characteristic goods of childhood are in some way of less significance, but on grounds other than their location in time or the fact that they occur in childhood. We might agree with Slote that, for example, captaincy or aca-demic success is better when had in the prime of life, but for reasons other than having to do with where they fall in the typical human lifespan. The reason the goods located in the prime of life may be better and contribute more to the value of a life may have to do with certain of their nature, not their location in time.

Let's suppose the successes constitute the achievement of a worthwhile aim. For adults this may well be a matter of one's 'choices and reactions . . . of how well the ends are selected and how successfully they are pursued' (Scanlon 1998, 125). Because features like choices are less prevalent in childhood successes or worthwhile aims, we may be inclined to discount the value of the successes as a result. Let's suppose, slightly differently, that the successes of childhood count as achievements, where, roughly, an achievement involves one competently causing something through a difficult activity. One sets out a plan for getting high marks, effortfully executes and works diligently on the plan, and succeeds in getting high marks. According to one influential view, the value of an achievement is a matter of how much effort and will one exerts to achieve it and how competently or knowingly one caused it using one's theoretical and practical rationality (Bradford 2015). Such features may be present to a lesser degree in the typical or characteristic successes and achieve-ments of childhood, making them (seemingly in themselves) less valuable than similar achievements in adulthood. Factors such as the ones highlighted above seem better at explaining the difference in value of the successes and misfortunes in childhood than does mere temporal location in the lifespan.

Are Children's Prudential Goods Special?

Slote sometimes puts his position more bluntly:

what happens in childhood principally affects our view of total lives through the effects that childhood success or failure are supposed to have on mature individuals. (Slote 1983, 15)

Based on what has been argued so far, this seems implausible. Certain things are non-instrumentally good for children whether or not they have a positive or negative impact on mature individuals. And they do not seem to be the sorts of things it would make sense to discount merely because they happen in childhood.

Recently, a more extreme version of Slote's view has attracted the attention of (mainly) political philosophers. It is the view 'that having a good childhood is ... valuable merely because it contributes to a good adulthood' (Gheaus 2015a, 6) or that 'childhood is a period of life in which the person is waiting and preparing for adulthood' (Brighouse and Swift 2014, 65). Some attribute this view to Slote (e.g., Gheaus 2015a). But it is not obvious, as we have seen, that this is his view, hence the 'principally' in the above-quoted passage. Indeed, it is rare to see the more extreme view explicitly defended in the literature, though it is certainly implied in at least some views in political philosophy.[5]

The main thrust of the response to the position that children's goods are merely instrumental is to argue there are certain things that are basically, non-instrumentally (or intrinsically) good for children. Not all the goods of childhood or the things good for children are good merely because they are conducive to a good adulthood or produce states that are basically, non-instrumentally good for the adults the children will become (Macleod, 2010; Brennan 2014; Gheaus, 2015a; Gheaus 2015b; Macleod 2015).

It is undeniable there are certain things that are basically, non-instrumentally good or bad for children, prudentially speaking. That said, it seems to be a matter of debate, at least amongst some political philosophers, whether there are such goods. That this requires debate is, perhaps, indicative of the undue influence Aristotelianism and Kantianism have over (especially) contemporary political philosophy.[6]

Those who reject the extreme view fashion themselves as defenders of intrinsic goods (or bads) of childhood. Typically, a defence of this takes the

---

[5] For discussion of this view's sources, see Macleod (2010) and Gheaus (2015a).

[6] For discussion of what Aristotle and Kant think about children's well-being, see Skelton (2018).

form of developing a list of non-instrumental goods, the value of which 'doesn't follow from their contribution to the goods of adult life' (Brennan 2014, 35). Brennan defends a list of intrinsic goods of childhood, which we noted above. Colin Macleod offers a slightly different list:

a valuable childhood will have its share of frustration, difficulties, and even emotional and physical pain ... we should think of the [intrinsic] goods [of childhood] as emerging from various forms of creative stimulation of distinctive human faculties. To realize the goods, we engage and activate the physical, emotional, aesthetic, cognitive, and moral faculties of children by exposing them to circumstances in which they can experience and give expression to their faculties and face challenges involved in using these faculties. (Macleod 2010, 187)

The specific goods realized include, Macleod says, 'adventure, and aesthetic exploration and experience', and a secure and loving family (Macleod 2010, 180, 181, 182).[7] Neither Brennan nor Macleod (at least in this paper) suggest these goods are in any way special. Their point is that certain things are good for children not only when and because such things enhance one's future good in adulthood. These may be good for children even when they are, to use Macleod's phrase, 'developmentally inert' (Macleod 2010, 182).

Some want to go further and argue in response to the extreme view not only that certain things are basically, non-instrumentally good for children, but are in addition 'special' to children (Brighouse and Swift 2014, 65; Gheaus 2015a, 2015b). Brennan and Macleod are correct that at least some items are basically, non-instrumentally good for children. We do not have to agree with their particular lists of non-instrumental goods to agree with their general position that there are things basically, non-instrumentally good for children.

Is there compelling reason to think at least some of the intrinsic goods of childhood are special? Brighouse and Swift think so:

some goods may have value only, or much more readily, in childhood. We do not have a full list, but we think that innocence about sexuality, for example, is good in childhood ... [a] certain steady sense of being carefree is also valuable in childhood but a flaw in most adults ... [o]ther goods are just more readily available in childhood than in adulthood: the capacities to feel spontaneous joy, to be surprised, and to be thrilled seem to diminish a good deal with age. (Brighouse and Swift 2014, 65)

Gheaus expresses a similar view in at least some places. She suggests a list of goods to which, she thinks, children have 'privileged access' (Gheaus 2015a, 8, 13), and which are easily available to children but 'largely' unavailable to adults (Gheaus 2015a, 8).[8] She lists goods such as 'intellectual curiosity', 'experimentation', and 'variety' (Gheaus 2015a, 11, 8, 12).

---

[7] Macleod also mentions 'fun', 'amusement', and 'pleasure' (2010, 187).
[8] Gheaus is not consistent in this view; for her doubts, see Gheaus (2015b).

In more recent work, Macleod says certain things non-instrumentally good for children are such that 'children as juvenile agents have privileged and perhaps unique access' to them (Macleod 2015, 59). His two examples are innocence and imagination (Macleod 2015, 59–62).

The articulation of these so-called special goods is key, in the mind of many of these thinkers, to defeating the claim that the goods of childhood are merely instrumentally good, good merely because of their role in promoting non-instrumental goods for adults (e.g., Macleod 2015, 59; Gheaus 2015a). It is not clear, however, why one would need to defend special goods for children in order to defeat this extreme view of children's goods (or bads). To defeat this position, it is sufficient to defend the claim that there are things that are basically, non-instrumentally good for children, for example happiness or satisfaction taken in valuable relationships or intellectual development, that may or may not be good for adults. It is enough to say it would be intrinsically bad for a young child to be deprived of playing sport even if it meant she would be a bit more rational in adulthood.

There is good reason to be chary of the idea that there are special goods of childhood. First, the claim there are such goods of childhood is controversial. Sarah Hannan has argued that in some cases sexual innocence and carefreeness can lead to bad outcomes and be bad for a child (Hannan 2018). For example, she argues that in some situations sexual innocence may have very bad outcomes for children; it may leave them vulnerable to exploitation. I am not entirely convinced by Hannan's arguments, but I am convinced that if we can get away without appeal to special goods in combating some of the positions discussed above it would be better. It seems better to abandon talk of special goods of childhood and focus on the idea there are certain things that are basically, non-instrumentally good for children.[9]

Second, we can make many of the points that special goods advocates want to make without the language of special goods. We can accommodate such goods in two ways (and in so doing perhaps deflect some of the worries Hannan raises).

First, most of the candidates for special goods are better understood as at best mere instruments (in some cases) for producing other basic, non-instrumental goods. For example, carefreeness or lack of anxiety seem merely instrumentally good, good for promoting other things that are uncontroversially good (e.g., happiness taken in play or in valuable relationships). And sexual innocence may facilitate certain kinds of relationships or be a source of happiness.

Second, the 'special' goods, insofar as they seem more than instrumental, seem more like elements or parts of wholes that are good for children. For example, carefreeness might add to the value of a whole consisting in happiness taken in intellectual development even though it is not clearly good on its

[9] For critical discussion of Hannan's position, see Skelton (2018).

own. The lack of anxiety or worry or concern may add to the value of a whole of which it is part, even if it is alone not good or of only very minor value when taken by itself.

Finally, we do not need talk of special goods to defeat the extreme view or the views of Slote or Velleman. Argument about special goods is a distraction and may involve merely parochial assumptions about what makes for a good or valuable childhood. We want a broad-based view for the purpose of articulating our ethical and political obligations to children. It is more beneficial to the cause of greater acknowledgement of children's goods in moral and political philosophy to focus our attention on matters other than special goods. What is important for ethical thinking and social justice with respect to children is clarifying the general basic, non-instrumental children's goods and the instruments most effective in producing or enhancing them.

Conclusion

In this chapter, my focus has been a cluster of under-explored issues relating to children's well-being or prudential good. I examined, in particular, three distinct (and to my mind puzzling) positions, namely, that children's lives on the whole cannot go well or poorly for them, prudentially speaking; that the prudential goods of childhood count for less than the same goods of adulthood towards the prudential value of an individual's life as a whole; and that children's prudential goods (or goods more generally) are (at least in some cases) in some way special.

In reply to these views, I argued that children's lives can go well for them, prudentially speaking; that there is no good reason to discount children's prudential goods in themselves; and that defending the claim there are non-instrumental goods for children does not require defending special intrinsic goods of childhood.

4 The Ethics of Ageing in Frank Perry's *The Swimmer*

Christopher Hamilton

> In middle age there is a mystery, there is mystification. The most I can make out of
> this hour is a kind of loneliness. Even the beauty of the visible world seems to
> crumble, yes even love. I feel that there is some miscarriage, some wrong turning, but
> I do not know when it took place and I have no hope of finding it.
>
> (Cheever 2010, 1)

The film *The Swimmer*, released in 1968, directed by Frank Perry and starring
Burt Lancaster, is based on a short story of the same name by John Cheever
(1990a), originally published in 1964 in *The New Yorker*. Cheever's work often
aims at exposing the banality, misery and hypocrisy that lies under the surface
of privilege and wealth. This is certainly true of both the story and film in
question, but I think the focus here is less on social critique than on personal
crisis. It might be tempting to think of this as the midlife crisis, and that would
not be wholly wrong, but the emphasis is not quite right. What is at stake here is
a kind of compressed and intense increase in ethical insight – shattering
insight, and insight connected with ageing, with middle age, but also with
the idea of a journey, the return home, which is important here, as Roger Ebert
has pointed out (Ebert 1968). That, at any rate, is what I wish to try to show
here. I shall be mainly concentrating on the film as, whatever its debt to the
story, it has more to teach us on the theme of the ethics of middle age than does
the book, though I shall advert to the story as and when seems appropriate and
helpful.

The basic plot of the film, as of the story, has a somewhat surreal aspect – and
surrealism is something of significance more generally here: a man, Ned
Merrill, decides to swim his way home from the house of some friends. His
aim is to visit the houses of a number of friends, houses which all have
swimming pools and lie on a route from where he starts out to his own home,
on each occasion swimming a length and then continuing on foot to the next
house with a pool. One of the pools will be the public swimming baths. He will
thus swim home across the county – the scene is Connecticut and the filming
was carried out largely in Westport.

The opening shots of the film provide us with images of woodland and we
infer that the camera's view is that of an as yet unknown person walking

through the woods. The mood is one of menace and we could be at the beginning of a horror film, as if we might have here an unknown stalker homing in on some hapless victim. That is certainly not at all the genre of the film, at least in any traditional or usual sense, but the film is clearly inviting us into such a sense and is doing so deliberately: there is going to be horror here, but it has nothing to do with the typical tropes of the genre – shadows falling across the window, unexplained whisperings, brutal murders, maimings and the rest of the stock-in-trade of the genre. The horror here is infinitely more subtle: it is the horror of a man's soul, and its writhing in agony takes place in glorious daylight, in the dappled light of the sun streaming through the branches of trees, and in cool, translucent water – it takes place, that is, just where everything invites us to imagine that a man's soul must be at peace. This is important for thinking about the ethical insights this film is dealing with; they are insights that are, after all, ordinary, insights that anyone can have who chooses to look, for they are there, clear in the sunlight, as clear as sunlight, but Ned misses them, and we miss them in our own lives, because they terrify us: they are insights, at a general level, into our 'boredom, failure, being ridiculous, being on the wrong side, dying', as W. H. Auden put it (Auden 2019 [2002], 241). The bright sunlight and blue skies of the film emphasise this: ethical learning is difficult because nothing is hidden; this only seems paradoxical because we are such self-deceived creatures, as the film goes on to explore.

Crucial to the film is this: we think we are witnessing one man's obsession with swimming home over the course of a day, but the sense of time is dislocated here, and what we are really seeing, from one point of view, is a man growing from middle age to early old age. The lessons he learns as he meets his friends – if that is what they are; it is what he takes them to be, hopes them to be – are the lessons learnt across midlife as his past catches up with him. In this sense, the day is, in reality, a number of years, and this is part of the surrealism of the film. We are being invited to occupy two time-scales simultaneously: one day and several years. It is only very gradually that we realise this as we watch the film, and the effect is disturbing and confusing: one keeps having the sense, as does Ned, that one has missed something, and this is the feeling with which we are left at the end of the film. What we *think* we have missed is something to explain various oddities; what we in fact have missed is the passage of several years. And that is itself a way of inviting us into Ned's experience: as he misses so much of his life, we miss that he is missing it, lulled into supposing that we have a grip on what is going on by the surface form of the film, with its dialogue so typical of middle-class life, just as Ned has been lulled into supposing he has a grip on his life when, in reality, he has been living an illusion, in flight from understanding his own condition.

Ned speaks at several moments in the film of his two daughters who are, he says, at home with their mother, his wife, Lucinda. He starts off at the home of the Westerhazys – I shall return to this beginning – and then visits the home of the Grahams. Betty Graham's first words concern her intent to go on a diet and lose weight, a classic middle-class, midlife ambition, at once utterly banal and replete with a sense of failure and loss; the issue had already surfaced when Ned, whilst he was with the Westerhazys, had commented on the increasing belly of another of his friends there, that of Stu Forsburgh. Howard Graham then turns up on a motorised lawnmower, whose motor Ned, in a gesture of vanity and conceit, says is not idling correctly, and proceeds to fix. But the key moment is the Grahams' look of perplexity when Ned says, speaking of his own house, that he would like his daughters to get married there. A quizzical look passes between them, and it seems that Howard is going to say something, but he is restrained by Betty. We can have no idea what the problem is and, indeed, never with certainty do come to know in any detail, but clearly there is something amiss.

Later, Ned comes to the home of some further friends and finds there Julie Ann, who had formerly been the babysitter for Ned's daughters – she is enjoying a day swimming in the pool and we first see her in the water. Ned tells Julie Ann that she should come over again to his place to look after the girls, but her reaction is one of complete bafflement. She is clearly thinking that his girls are now far too old to need a babysitter. Indeed, Ned had earlier told Stu that his girls were 'All grown up'. Later, Ned tells Julie Ann that he was only kidding with his comments about her baby-sitting, but this comes across very much as a retrospective correction or gesture of self-defence: his original comments seemed to carry no implication of joking and, indeed, such a form of joking hardly seems consonant with this man's character: beneath his immense revelling in the physical, there is something deadly serious in this man. Still later, when speaking to the young son of the Kilmartins, he says that his daughters are about his age – eight or nine, and then, when Julie Ann then introduces her brother, Vernon, to Ned, he is deeply surprised: he can only remember him as a little boy, as if he had no recollection of the years that have passed since he last saw him. The point is made subtly, as if this was nothing more than the usual surprise one has on seeing someone as a young adult whom one had last seen as a child. Yet the current experience on the part of Ned is different: his reaction shows that he thinks no time has passed so Vernon *cannot* now be a young man.

There are other dislocations in the experience of time, such as when Ned stops the Hallorans' driver, thinking him to be Steve, the driver he knew, but who was replaced by the current driver some two years before. And when Mr Halloran apologises to Ned for not having been able to help him out with money when he asked him last time they met, Ned says he has no recollection of having asked for any help. When visiting his ex-lover Shirley, he speaks of having seen her last winter in Toronto, but she says she has not been to Toronto for three years.

All of this is done subtly, and it gives a delicate but powerful sense of Ned as lost in the time of his own life. He is swimming in real water, but this is in part a metaphor for his swimming in time: he thinks that a day is passing, but actually time is passing, or has passed, much faster than he supposes, and leaves him intermittently as if stunned or numb, his mind suddenly blank. Burt Lancaster's glorious smile, which he uses to shake off the stunned mind, is a wonderful piece of acting that gives the sense: don't think about it and it'll be all right.

The insight into the phenomenology of time here is wonderful: who in middle age does not have on occasions the sense that *so much time has passed* but *cannot* have passed? In middle age, and as middle age passes and one gets closer to death, this passage of time seems impossible, as if all one has to do is to shake oneself and time will somehow adjust itself and one would discover that it had not passed in this way at all. The experience really is as if, let us say, a day, or some days, had passed, but in fact many years have gone past. My mother once said to me that she had the sense that one day she was a little girl, and the next day she was an old woman. That is exactly right, and is just what this film expresses, getting us to share in Ned's subtle confusion, whose confusions we too shake off as we go on following the story of this man's day, bizarre as it is with this attempt to swim home, but not bizarre in the sense of being lived on two planes of time – for we do not yet quite grasp that, cannot see it clearly, any more than we can in our own lives when we blink, as my mother blinked.

Let us, however, go back to the start of the film. As I indicated above, it opens with a sense of menace as the camera's view seems to be that of some kind of malevolent presence about to wreak havoc. As this presence moves through the wood and undergrowth, bushes and shrubs are shaken and animals are disturbed. There are even two odd moments in which we see an owl, which makes little sense from the point of view of realism, as the establishing shots have already made it clear to us that this is daytime – though it must be granted that these opening shots in general have a strangely autumnal feel about them, which may be a result of the persistence of shadow in the undergrowth or of the foliage.

In retrospect, we may wonder if these are intimations of the autumn of this man's life and, indeed, it seems that this is one of the last days of summer or even, perhaps, a day during an Indian summer, a final burst of the glory of summer out of season, ripe and bursting, but on the cusp of decay – as a person in middle age may feel him- or herself to be. There is a sense here that goes back at least to Dante of middle age as like being lost in a dark wood. Then we see the figure, which turns out to be an athletic man in swimming trunks and, as the camera draws up and away, we see him from behind entering into glorious sunlight and, clambering over some rocks, approaching a swimming pool into which he launches himself with a magnificent dive, a gesture of confidence and nonchalance. In Cheever's story, the explanation for Ned's presence by the Westerhazys' pool is that he has stayed overnight with his wife at a party with his friends. But in the film there is no explanation for his presence: the Westerhazys have had a party, but Ned was not there and, when asked about his sudden arrival at the Westerhazys', he simply says: 'I was around'. The Westerhazys ask him questions that make it clear that they have not seen him for a long time, at least for the whole summer, though he behaves as though he may have seen them just a few days before. In the film we have the sense that this man *comes from nowhere*, and I think that this is important for our sense of this man's life, his being in middle age, for that is what the experience of middle age is like: one suddenly *finds oneself* here, in this life, leading this life, as if from nowhere (cf. Dante, who says: '*mi ritrovai per una selva oscura*' [Alighieri 1321, canto 1, line 2]). One can tell the story of how one got here, the choices one made, the pressures to which one responded, the desires one sought to satisfy and the rest, but the problem is that, in middle age, somehow this no longer seems to add up, as if all of it were disjointed or arbitrarily put together, a matter more of chance and contingency than of anything one might think of as an organised or coherent life. One thought one was coming from there – the plans one had, the hopes and wishes one harboured and so on – and then one finds that all of that seems so vague and evanescent that it is as if one had come from nowhere. How did I get to be leading *this* life? 'So here I am, in the middle way', as T. S. Eliot has it in 'East Coker,' (Eliot 1986 [1963], 202) in a deliberate echo of Dante. The appearance of the swimmer from nowhere gives us then, I think, a powerful sense of middle age, *reminds* us of this aspect of middle age.

For all that, Ned is in some ways the envy of his friends. He is – at the outset of the film – physically in great shape, a magnificent specimen of manliness, powerful, muscular, lean, handsome. ('I don't know how you do it! You haven't changed a bit!' exclaims Stu.) Who would not want to be like that? He reminisces with Stu about days in the past when they swam together, but the latter remarks that they had 'nice, new pink lungs in those days'. This was before, he says, they had touched a drink or a cigarette. 'Or a girl!' interjects Donald Westerhazy. But his wife, Helen, comments that girls do not sap a man's strength. 'Or I'd be in a wheelchair today', says Ned. 'Still bragging', comments Peggy Forsburgh, but full of tenderness for him – she in no way means to criticise him; she is, rather, entering the game with delight.

Yet here, as elsewhere, there is a suffocating nostalgia in Ned: his immense physical impressiveness seems less a joyful acceptance of what *is* than a desire to hold on to what *was*. His bravado seems to come, not from an inner plenitude, but from a certain inner poverty. This is partly a matter of his seeming to protest too loudly, or to be somewhat evasive, when it comes to his affirmations of his life in response to his friends' questions, and partly an issue of a kind of arrogance. For instance, at one point he gatecrashes a party around the pool at the home of the Biswangers, people he has snubbed in the past, and is challenged by the hostess, who is clearly not at all pleased to see him. But he insists that he is one of her 'more distinguished gatecrashers'. He then gets into a conversation with a woman at the party who is curious about him – clearly attracted to him. And then, he tells her that he is an explorer and: 'I'm a very special human being. Noble and splendid'. She looks at him aghast and then another man appears – presumably her husband or lover – and leads her away. Ned then turns and the camera focusses on his face, on which there is an expression of absolute desolation and despair. The acting on Lancaster's part is superb, and there we see a moment of total loss, as if he grasped his true state just for a moment: a man in flight from himself, no doubt noble in some ways, but also weak and vulnerable, frightened and alone. Indeed, that sense of his being alone is very strong throughout the film and increases as he makes his way from one swimming pool to the next. This man passes through the lives of others but remains resolutely alone – and one way or another, now more, now less forcefully, this is something that is true of us and that we discover more acutely in middle age than before, though there are some parallels here with the experience of adolescence, which middle age seems in some ways to recapitulate in its confusions and unclarities.

The pool party at the Biswangers' is a key moment for Ned: after his bizarre exchange with the woman he dives into the pool and swims a length, but as he gets out he recognises his hot dog wagon. He is astonished and cannot understand what it is doing there. He tells the person manning it that he wheels his children around in it – not that he *wheeled* his children around in it. Again we see the dislocation of time, made all the worse by the fact that Mrs Biswanger tells him that she and her husband bought it in a white elephant sale. He cannot understand how it got to be in such a sale and Mrs Biswanger suggests that his wife must have donated it – even though, says Ned, he is crazy for the thing, and she knows it. We have long begun to suspect that all is not well in the Merrill household, but now we sense that something extremely dramatic may have taken place: has she left him and has he obliterated the memory of the event? When he offers to buy back the wagon, Mr Biswanger scoffs and, since at a previous stop of Ned's, with the Hallorans, they assumed he had stopped by to ask for some money again (the first time, as I noted above, they did not help him, and they have no intention of helping him this time round either), we begin to wonder whether the marriage has ended and he is financially in difficulty as well as emotionally bereft.

Indeed, we had intimations of this separation right at the outset when Ned was with the Westerhazys. Stu and Peggy Forsburgh had been intending to take an aeroplane that afternoon to go home, but Ned insisted that he take them over to see Lucinda. Helen looks baffled, a look we can only understand later, but it is a look that tells us, we realise in retrospect, that Lucinda is not there for him to bring the Forsburghs to her. And then there is Cynthia's catty remark to Ned, as they talk at the Biswangers' party, when she invites him round to dinner that evening, evidently with something more than eating in mind, and he replies that he will come along and bring Lucinda, as long as she has no other plans for them. Cynthia's violent reaction – 'Lucinda! Well, congratulations', she says, in a spiteful tone – suggests that she thinks Ned must have got back together with his wife, whereas he talks in utter ignorance of any possible separation with her in the first place.

But how *could* he not know what his situation really is?

That may be partly the point. Everyone else knows, and he does not. This is not so much a refusal, or incapacity, to acknowledge the facts, as he does not grasp what the facts mean: that the meaning of his life has suffered a massive shift or fracture, and that he needs to reassess his life. His life has become something he does not recognise, and this is a typical feeling of middle age – middle age is, one might say, a moment for many in which we do not recognise ourselves in our own life, and this can be so even when the facts of that life do not change at all. Indeed, it might be just when the facts do not change that we might least recognise ourselves, which is one reason why it is hardly to the point to object that Ned must somehow know his wife has left him and thus that the plot stretches credibility. Arguably, this may be thought of as part of the surrealism of the film, but if so it is a surrealism that returns us to a realism (there is nothing so real as the surreal, one might say).

By the end of the film, we have the final confirmation that Ned's wife and daughters are not at the family home. In fact, the house is abandoned, and clearly has been for some considerable time. We cannot, of course, ask what Ned has been doing all that time, or how he has been dealing with the practical matters of his life – where has he been living, what has he been doing for money, and the like.

In Ford Madox Ford's masterpiece *The Good Soldier* – which could profitably be read alongside Perry's film and Cheever's story – John Dowell says: 'But upon my word, I don't know how we put in our time. How does one put in one's time?' (Ford 2008 [1915], 44). Quite. How *does* one put in one's time? That is a question of middle age. No one who gets to middle age can escape the sense that most of (one's) life has consisted of what Virginia Woolf calls 'cotton wool' or 'non-being': empty moments devoted to nothing more than *carrying on* (shopping, cooking, cleaning and the like). In this sense, most of life seems simply to have evaporated. If I look back on my life, now in my middle age, I feel I could compress into a few years the things I have done that stand out for me: writing some books, going on memorable holidays, etc. What *was* I doing the rest of the time?

A parallel thought comes out in another marvellous film that is a study of middle age, Sofia Coppola's *Lost in Translation* (2003). At one point the middle-aged Bob Harris, played by Bill Murray, chatting with the young Charlotte (Scarlett Johansson), says that the difficulties of a long marriage are attenuated by the fact that one sleeps a third of one's life. So, the problems of about eight years of his married life have been resolved by his having slept a total of eight years since he got married. The wonderful deadpan humour of this carries a deep truth: most of life passes with nothing happening – and not just when one is asleep – and thus, in middle age, one has a sense of so much 'time/Torn off unused', as Philip Larkin (1990, l. 11.) puts it. So to ask what Ned has been doing all this time is to miss the key idea: he has not been doing anything because most of life is not doing anything; that is the deeper point behind his having been nowhere, doing nothing, during the time we can now see to have passed from the moment when his troubles began to where we catch up with him, and he catches up with himself, in the final scene of the film.

It may be that the collapse of Ned's marriage has something to do with the event – whatever it was exactly – to which Ned's friend Brian refers when he passes through the Bunkers' place – they too are having a party by a pool. Brian tells Ned that he is very sorry about 'what they pulled on you over at your place'. He thinks it was 'a stinking thing to do'. He then refers to a 'new guy'. It is unclear just what has happened, but it probably has something to do with his work, not least because, some moments later, a further friend, Denny, suggests that he may be able to put him on to a connection for a job if only he will take a pay cut at first. Ned rejects this out of hand and clearly Denny thinks that he is no position to be so dismissive: he is angered by Ned's response.

At a later point, when Ned swims in the local public swimming pool, he comes across four acquaintances who are angered by him: he owes them money and has failed to pay them back. They go on to mock him, claiming that they have heard his daughters ridicule him and, it seems, had been involved in some kind of vandalism, running around drunk and wrecking cars. This is a man, then, who has separated from his wife, has no job and is alienated from his daughters. Yet he is living as in a dream; he knows these things only in his flight from them. And is this not how we all are in middle age – knowing what we know in our fleeing from it?

I have often studied with my students, most of whom are in their early twenties, Conrad's *Lord Jim*. At one point, Marlow, the narrator for most of the novel, visits a certain Stein to get his advice about Jim's case: his Romanticism, his foolishness, his idealism, the strange, distorted wisdom buried somewhere in it all. Stein says:

Very funny this terrible thing is. A man that is born falls into a dream like a man who falls into the sea. If he tries to climb out into the air as inexperienced people endeavour to do, he drowns – nicht wahr? ... No! I tell you! The way is to the destructive element submit yourself, and with the exertions of your hands and feet in the water make the deep, deep sea keep you up. (Conrad 2007 [1900], 163–4)

I have remarked often that my students do not, generally speaking, really see Stein's point: the idea that life is a dream makes little sense to them. This is not because they are insensitive or unintelligent or unwilling to reflect. It is simply that they are young – too young to understand the point. Of course, they can understand the claim in the sense that they grasp that some people experience life (at times) in this way, but that remains a mere piece of knowledge, an externality to their personality, to their person. The sense of one's life as a dream is something that comes with age; with a sense of the recurrent experience of non-being (to use Woolf's terminology); with the sense that all those things that one took so seriously turned out not to be so important at all and that those things or moments one thought to be of little consequence have shown themselves to be, after all, of the first importance; that human beings keep making the same mistakes over and over again, however hard they try not to do so; that rarely are human beings able to solve problems – they are much better at shifting problems about in a kind of merry-go-round of error that looks at times as if it might be resolving something; that even though one thought one could not forgive oneself for all those stupid, foolish things one did, one did forgive oneself after all; that life goes on; that perhaps it does not matter much that one was able to forgive oneself and that perhaps, therefore, those failures did not matter, do not matter, so much after all; that one's foolishness is limitless; that one knows all this and refuses to know it. And so on. These are the kinds of things that make one feel one's life is a dream, and they are the fruit of middle-aged maturity. They can be taken as a source of despair; it is better to take them as a reason to be sceptical and wary, circumspect and ironic – as does Conrad's Stein.

Ned, we might say, has simply taken the dream to an extreme. For that is the danger in scepticism, wariness, circumspection and irony: they can be a hair's-breadth away from exhaustion of the spirit, cynicism and bitterness. The inevitability of self-deception – allowing the sea to hold one up without seeking to climb out – can be held on to ironically or, alternatively, with a kind of bitter will of desperation. Then comes Hamlet's 'for there is nothing either good or bad, but thinking makes it so'. Ned may look like the opposite of a cynic, but cynicism can be expressed in a kind of mask of riotous affirmation, as Nietzsche knew so well, and Ned's living in a dream is a kind of cynicism whose aim is to deflect from himself what he knows to be the truth about his life.

His cynicism is exposed on a number of occasions. It is there when he swims in Mrs Hammar's pool after his visit to the Grahams. Mrs Hammar challenges him, asking him who gave him permission to use the pool. He replies: 'I'm Ned Merrill'. This could be taken as a mere affirmation of his identity, but there is a note of defiance in it, as if his being Ned Merrill gave him the right to swim here. Mrs Hammar is far from pacified: Ned thinks that his being her son's friend should calm her, but it makes things worse. It becomes clear that her son was in hospital and died there – and Ned never visited him. Grasping his situation, he *runs away*, and then we see him reflecting for a moment. But he soon shakes this off and loses himself in pitting himself against a horse by running alongside it in a field to which he comes.

But Ned knows what he is about even if he also fights shy of such knowledge. At one point he comes to the house of the Kilmartins, but discovers that they are away. Only the son is at home, Kevin Kilmartin Jr., a boy of about eight or nine years of age. Ned asks if he may use the family pool and Kevin says he may. However, there is no water in it; his parents have had it drained since Kevin is not a good swimmer. Ned suggests that they make-believe swim a length, which they do. Kevin is disturbed: is this not cheating? 'If you make believe hard enough that something is true then it is true for you', says Ned. Ned would like this to be a cheerful acceptance of what one needs to get through life, but he knows the pose is threadbare.

When Ned meets Julie Ann, he tells her of his plan to swim home. Her friends find the plan rather absurd but she agrees to go with him. At one point during their journey, Julie Ann confesses at length to Ned that, when she was younger and baby-sat for his daughters, she had an almost overwhelming crush on him. Ned remains for much of the time impressively cool with this beautiful young woman, but when she tells him of some unwanted male attention she has been receiving at work, he suddenly expresses the wish to be a kind of protector to her, and this gets mixed up with his desire for her, which has been simmering beneath the surface, and he tries to kiss her – at which point she runs off. At this moment the film is clearly trading on what is by now a rather tired stereotypical image of the middle-aged man seeking to recapture his lost youth and assure himself that his virility has not faded, but the tiredness of the image should not blind us to the genuine pathos that there is in Lancaster's portrayal of such a man here, who expresses first foolish optimism and then personal devasta-tion: Lancaster is capable in this film of an impressive range of emotional response, one aspect of which is a persistent sense of loneliness as a kind of ground bass throughout.

One aspect of this pathos is that Ned is a Romantic at heart – his swimming home tells us that, if nothing else does – but is also driven by a raw sexual urgency. He has not given up trying to mediate these, give them their due and live with them – but, it appears, without much success. Twice he addresses women with words from *The Song of Songs*: when he first arrives at the house of the Westerhazys and sees Helen lying on a sun lounger, wearing sandals, he greets her with, 'How beautiful are your feet in sandals, O prince's daughter!' and, kneeling down, he takes one of her feet gently into his hands, lifts it reverentially, and softly kisses it; and later, when talking with Julie Ann, she is lying on her back and he places his hand on her belly – which she holds there – and says: 'Thy belly is like a heap of wheat, fenced about with lilies'. Yet these gestures of tenderness collapse when he comes to the swimming pool of his former mistress, Shirley Abbott. Cheever's story makes clear what the film expresses otherwise. 'If he had suffered any injuries at the Biswangers' they would be cured here. Love – sexual roughhouse in fact – was the supreme elixir, the pain killer, the brightly colored pill that would put the spring back into his step, the joy of life in his heart' (Cheever 1990a, 786).

When he arrives at Shirley's home, Ned sees that she is lying on a sun lounger as Helen Westerhazy was; she is trying to extract a wood splinter from her right foot. Ned replicates the gesture he made with Helen and, kneeling before Shirley, takes out the splinter for her. The inflection of tenderness would be there even without the echo of the previous greeting, but it is certainly deepened by it. And the echo is there even more sharply when he then kisses her foot. She responds by kicking him; his fantasy of being with her is shattered from that moment, and he gradually descends into a state of despair.

NED: I'm cold. What's the matter with that sun? There's no heat in it. Shirley, what happened?
SHIRLEY: What happened to what?
NED: Nothing's turned out ... Nothing's turned out the way I thought it would. When I was a kid, I used to believe in things. People seemed happier when I was a kid. People used to love each other. What happened?
SHIRLEY: You got tossed out of your golden playpen, that's what happened.
NED: My mother gave me 25 cents for mowing the lawn around our house. Seems only a minute ago. I could smell the grass ... It's so fast ... People grow up, and then they ... We're all gonna die, Shirley. That doesn't make much sense, does it?
SHIRLEY: Sometimes it does ... Sometimes at three o'clock in the morning.

Across the course of the film Ned has been feeling colder and colder, getting physically weaker and weaker, shivering and needing more and more drink to keep him warm – and keep his spirits up. This is one aspect of the passage of the years, but his bodily coldness is also a physical expression or reflection of his spiritual coldness, of his arrival at the insights that he offers to Shirley in the dialogue just quoted. Although the film has not quite ended, this is Ned's spiritual end, the moment when he knows that life can never be what he wants it to be, the moment of ethical insight when he grasps what life is. Like my mother, he has blinked and only yesterday he was the boy who mowed the lawn. And Shirley shares his view, which is why she can say that death sometimes makes sense.

But Ned continues to fight this knowledge and the key way he does it is to try and seduce Shirley. Gradually, his tender sexual advances cede to the violence of a desire to have her in any way he might, for she resists him, well aware that what he wants, still, is to go back in time – back to when they were lovers and wanted each other wholeheartedly. She is more open-eyed than he is: 'Do you really think it's that easy?' she asks when he proposes a trip away together. She can accept, however painful it is to her, that life is loss, and this is what Ned knows now but resolutely seeks to avoid acknowledging. He starts to shiver even more, and Shirley says she will drive him home. But he refuses, saying he has just *got* to swim home. In Cheever's story we read, referring to a moment when he has to cross a dangerous highway to get to the public swimming pool: 'Why, believing as he did, that all human obduracy was susceptible to common sense, was he unable to turn back? Why was he determined to complete his journey even if it meant putting his life in danger? At what point had this prank, this joke, this piece of horseplay become serious?' (Cheever 1990a, 782). The answer is that he is desperate to prove to himself that he is not middle-aged, that he can do anything he might have done twenty years before. 'Good Christ, Ned, will you ever grow up?' Shirley had said when he first arrived at her house and told him of his escapade.

No, he cannot grow up. Can any of us in middle age?

The final point I wish to discuss is the three significant ways in which liquid enters into this film. At the end, there is the rain: Ned arrives at his home under a storm that drenches him. Here the rain carries a sense of homelessness, of being abandoned to the elements as Ned is abandoned by life – by his friends, by his family, by himself. Then there is alcohol: just about everyone here is drinking; this is the way they get through the day. And then there is the water in the swimming pools. Water is purifying; this is what Ned wants it to do for him. Yet he becomes weaker and weaker as he goes from one pool to the next and the water, rather than purifying him, works to flush out and display all his weaknesses, his fears. One of Cheever's greatest short stories, 'The World of Apples' (Cheever 1990b, 789–802), concerns an ageing American poet living in Italy who becomes transfixed by images of sexual licence, freedom and crudity. He finally finds relief in a purifying drenching in a waterfall in the Italian countryside. There is no such relief for Ned. His is a hopeless case; his return home is no return home at all. I do not think we are all like this in our middle years; yet, 'There but for the grace of God go I' should, I think, stand as the epigram at the door to middle age.

5 Is Ageing Good?

Christine Overall

Is ageing good?

I will argue that the very question is an odd one, in several ways, and that, for three reasons, we do not usually ask it of other life stages. Nonetheless, to raise the possibility that ageing *is* good is to push back against ageist assumptions that old age is nothing more than an unhappy period of loss and decline. I consider several candidate reasons for saying that ageing is good. I also acknowledge the various factors that may readily detract from the goodness of ageing.

For the purposes of this chapter, I will interpret 'ageing' to mean 'getting or being old', and by 'old' I will mean 'over seventy-five'. I won't devote time here to discussing why I think it's appropriate to define 'old' as 'over seventy-five', but if the reader prefers another landmark – such as seventy or eighty – that's fine too. What a person takes to be old depends in part on the age of the person; the younger the person, the sooner they think oldness arrives, while the older the person, the later in life they regard as old (Arnquist 2009). While the landmark of oldness may vary[1] (it seems dependent on the conditions in particular societies, but it may also be dependent on individual situations and health statuses, including features such as life expectancy, cognitive function, and disability rates), the nature of the philosophical question itself, about the value of getting old, remains the same.

Why the Question Is Odd

When considered carefully, 'Is ageing good?' is an odd question. There are three facts that make it odd.

The first fact that makes the question 'Is ageing good?' a prima facie odd one is simply that literally all of us are ageing. A baby ages from six months to one year; an eleven-year-old ages to twelve; a twenty-nine-year-old ages into

This Chapter is dedicated to Kim Renders, gifted artist and generous friend. 1955–2018.

I'm grateful to Gisela Braune, Evan Alcock, Nancy Chapple, Carol Kavanaugh, Ted Worth, and Peter Sims for their contributions to this paper.

[1] Warren Sanderson and Sergei Scherbov suggest that old age be defined prospectively, by reference to individuals' life expectancy. Old age, they say, arrives when individuals have fifteen or fewer years left to live (Sanderson and Scherbov 2008, 7). Since life expectancy is increasing, old age is arriving at a later time than it did in the past.

her next decade; and so on. Some might say it makes little sense to ask whether a process that is normal and natural is also good. But if it does make sense, then the question could be asked in regard to every phase of human life. Hence, to ask whether ageing is good is, from this perspective, to ask a deeply existential question as to whether living is good, or whether being human is good.[2] But I will, for now, set aside this interpretation of the question.

The second fact that makes this question odd is that comparable questions are not asked about other demographic identities. People don't usually ask, Is being a woman good? Is being a person of colour good? But perhaps identifying with or belonging to a certain sex/gender or race is not the best comparison to ageing. Perhaps a better comparison of category to category would arise if we ask, Is being gendered good? Is being racialized good?

Now I do think it is worth asking whether being gendered, for example, is good, and I also think the answer is that in some ways being gendered is good and in some ways it is not good (Overall 2000). Gender may look like more of a social category than ageing is; that is, gender may appear to be entirely or largely socially constructed, whereas getting old appears to be a (biological) fact of life. Nonetheless, ageing is, to at least some extent, a social category; one is not simply a raw number – sixteen or thirty-nine or fifty-five or seventy-four or ninety-two. What one is, at those various numbers, is also a product of social forces, including material conditions that shape one's health care, housing, education, employment, etc., and also cultural influences that define what it means to be one of these ages, and how much one is able to thrive at those ages (Overall 2016, 20–1). In effect, as Margaret Morganroth Gullette (2004) argues, people are 'aged by culture', just as they are gendered and racialized by culture.

There is a third fact that makes the question odd. The question is most plausibly interpreted as being about a particular stage of life, namely, old age. But then it is noteworthy that most people – academic or non-academic – are unlikely to ask it about any other stage of life. Would we ask, Is childhood good? Is adolescence good? Is young adulthood good? Is middle age good?[3] Presumably we wouldn't.

The question looks even odder if it is applied to specific ages. Is being seventy good? Is it better than thirty? Or worse? Is it as good as being eighty? As good as being sixty? How exactly could we ever make these comparisons?

Why We Don't Ask the Question of Other Life Stages

I suggest that there are two reasons why we are unlikely to ask whether earlier life stages are good. These reasons do not necessarily *justify* the failure to ask

---

[2] It may also be to ask a question about the justification of suicide.

[3] However, there is good evidence for the existence of ageism even about people who are merely middle-aged. Gullette writes of middle ageism that its 'victims are not old – just "too old"' (Gullette 2019). So perhaps people should be asking whether or not middle age is good.

the question; they say more about the nature of life in the twenty-first century developed world than they say about the legitimacy of asking whether other life stages are good. Indeed, I suspect that it would be philosophically productive to ask the question in regard to earlier life stages, although I shall not try to defend that claim here, and obviously investigating the goodness, or otherwise, of earlier life stages is not the task of this chapter.

First, the fact that we are unlikely to ask whether earlier life stages are good may be partly because there is not the same widespread fear, dread, and loathing for those earlier stages of life as there is for old age. We live in an ageist society, and there are plentiful cultural messages that encourage and reinforce dislike of and impatience with people who are ageing (Gullette 2018). Old age is treated as a time of diminishment; it is a stage when one is, supposedly, losing more than one is gaining: losing physical and mental capacities, losing friends and family members, losing independence and autonomy, losing 'identity conferring jobs and roles', losing activities that make life worthwhile (Cowley 2016, 188).[4] Julian Barnes writes that in anticipating old age, he fears 'the nervous laugh I shall give when I don't quite get an allusion or have forgotten a shared memory, or a familiar face, and then begin to mistrust much of what I think I know, and finally mistrust all of it. I fear the catheter and the stairlift, the oozing body and the wasting brain' (Barnes 2008, 139–40).

Consequently, becoming old is regarded as a condition that must be fended off. There is a battle to be waged against the ravages of time. One can strive to stay 'forever young', or to be somehow ageless. In other words, ageing people are encouraged to attempt to 'pass' as not old. To the extent that an individual can resist old age, her ageing is conceptualized as 'successful', and if she does not or cannot resist, then it is unsuccessful (Ehrenreich 2018, 164–5). Similarly, ageing is seen as a process that can happen gracefully or not. One may strive, or fail to strive, to age 'well': 'Any faltering on this goal can seem a sign of laziness and lack of grit' (Paris 2018).

By contrast, we do not usually interpret other life stages in these ways. The assumption is that people at earlier life stages are growing and progressing in their capacities, independence, and understanding. Hence, no one is urged to 'resist' childhood, adolescence, or young adulthood (although they might be urged to resist middle age, because the negativity with which old age is regarded spills over into the stage that precedes it). We're not likely to look for grace, or the lack of it, in other life stages either – again with the possible exception of middle age, damned by its proximity to old age.

---

[4] For examples, consider the image of over-sixty characters in movies: 'Often, the characters were dying, which was either grim (Amour, Iris) or patronizingly fantastical (Cocoon). If they showed signs of life, they were reckless or desperate (Going in Style, The Bucket List, The Cool Kids). They were prudish about sex (Hope Springs, Book Club). Or, if they were still sexual, it was played for hooting laughter (The Golden Girls, Hot in Cleveland, It's Complicated)' (Schneller 2018, R1).

A second reason we would not likely ask, Is childhood good? Is adolescence good? Is young adulthood good? is that these stages of human life seem *inevitable.* The earlier stages of life appear natural, normal, to be expected, and, perhaps for those reasons, acceptable, desirable, and even keenly anticipated. This is the case even though adolescence, and even childhood itself, are relatively recent social creations, which are frequently reinvented (e.g., Fass 2016), and even though what we now call middle age is a stage that was not reached by a lot of people in the distant human past, and that even today, in large parts of the world, remains unattainable (World Bank 2019).

But by contrast, old age is usually not keenly anticipated, and may not even appear to be inevitable. For some people, old age is *literally* not inevitable; they will not live that long. Poverty, racism, misogyny, and hard, dangerous, boring, tedious, or dirty jobs, contamination of water and air, lack of opportunities, and violence reduce people's survival rates and lower life expectancies. These conditions may be so exhausting and debilitating that they make life difficult to endure and reduce the desire to go on living.

For people living with greater wealth and privileges, the situation is different. Old age may appear not inevitable but rather, in a way, optional. And it may be perceived as optional for three very different reasons.

First, for some people, their lifestyle choices make ageing and old age less likely and hence a matter of choice. In this case I'm not referring to disadvantaged people living in poverty, but to people who make deliberate decisions about their bodies and their lives that affect their longevity. Enamoured of youth, they live hard and fast, they drink, they smoke, they overeat, they use recreational drugs, they take physical risks, they use up their bodies – and they die younger than they might otherwise have if they'd engaged in different behaviours. I make no judgement about this set of choices; it may in fact be rational, in some cases, to live intensely at the cost of dying early, or earlier.

Second, the possibility, in a few nations, of being able to *choose* to end one's life via assisted suicide or so-called medical assistance in dying (MAiD) gives people the opportunity to opt out of some parts of old age and hence appears to make ageing optional. Now that MAiD is legal in my own country, Canada, I have heard some colleagues and friends express relief that they will have a choice about how long they live; they will not necessarily have to endure what they take to be the worst parts of extreme old age.

Third, old age seems optional to many, perhaps especially members of the so-called Baby Boom generation, because of the illusions of unending youth retailed by corporate capitalism, which says that as long as you wear the right clothes, eat the right food, live in the right houses, do the right exercises, undergo the right cosmetic surgery, and buy all the right products, you will never grow old but remain 'youthful' until the end.

Obviously, although some behaviours may help to prolong one's health and life, the idea that biological youthfulness can be prolonged indefinitely is a serious mistake. Nonetheless, I suggest that, at least for people with socioeconomic privileges, old age appears to be avoidable, or at least not inevitable. And if people become convinced that old age is optional, they may not see any necessity to ask whether ageing is good. At the same time, the very fact that they see old age as optional and avoidable suggests that their covert answer to the question is no; ageing is not good.

Why the Question Is Important

So far I've suggested that, for three reasons, the question, Is ageing good? is an odd one. I've also suggested that, for a couple of reasons, we do not usually ask whether other life stages are good. Hence, to take the question Is ageing good? seriously is to swim against the prevailing cultural tide in the West, because it implies a possibility about old age that is not often recognized: that it might be good. Indeed, to ponder the possible value of ageing is to strike back against ageism, a viewpoint that sees ageing as little else than decline, a series of losses and diminishments from the supposedly healthy, strong, intelligent, competent, high-functioning status of youth. As Ashton Applewhite points out, an 'overarching characteristic of aging ... is that it is stigmatized. That stigma is rooted in denial – our insistence that we're "not old," even as we enter our final decades. "Us versus them" thinking underlies all prejudice; the greatest irony of ageism is that the "other" is our own future selves'. As Applewhite points out, to embrace ageing, and to challenge its stereotypical equation with decline, is a radical act (Applewhite 2017).

The question, then, is how to make a case for the value of ageing. Presumably one could argue either that ageing is good for individuals, or that it is good for society collectively, or both. I shall focus on the possible good of ageing – that is, its value – for individuals. I will not consider whether ageing is good for society, because I think such a question is close to, if not identical with, asking whether old people have an *instrumental* value or disvalue. As I pointed out earlier, we don't ask whether the life stages of infancy, childhood, adolescence, young adulthood, or even middle age are good, and we don't ask whether these stages are good for society collectively. We don't try to evaluate whether babies, children, teenagers, young adults, or middle-aged persons are collectively beneficial for society.

By contrast, this culture does, unfortunately, frequently weigh in on the question whether older people are collectively good for society. And – despite some nods to older people's paid work, caregiving work, volunteer work, and contributions as citizens and taxpayers – the typical answer is, No. Some commentators who worry about global over-population and the so-called greying of developed societies claim that increasing life expectancies pose potential or actual problems for nations becoming top-heavy with elders. 'The aging of baby boomers means that within just a couple decades, older people are projected to outnumber children for the first time in U.S. history. By 2035 there will be 78 million people 65 years and older compared to 76.7 million ... under the age of 18' (Jonathan Vespa, quoted in National Population Projections 2018). This landmark – older people outnumbering children – was passed in Canada in 2016 (Statistics Canada 2017). Old people are categorized as burdens; as being in conflict with young people; as withholding jobs and housing from other members of society; as costing too much; as being 'bed-blockers' who use up too many health care resources; as being dangerous drivers; and as failing to contribute to society (Bennett 2018). In Ezekiel Emanuel's words,

living too long is ... a loss. It renders many of us, if not disabled, then faltering and declining, a state that may not be worse than death but is nonetheless deprived. It robs us of our creativity and ability to contribute to work, society, the world. It transforms how people experience us, relate to us, and, most important, remember us. We are no longer remembered as vibrant and engaged but as feeble, ineffectual, even pathetic (Emanuel 2014).

No other age-demographic is assessed for usefulness or uselessness in the way that old people are. But assessing any group of people in these terms is morally execrable. I do think ageing persons contribute enormously to their society in a myriad of ways, as citizens and participants in an interconnected society – through paid work, paying taxes, volunteer work, and care for family members. It has also been argued that they contribute in other, less tangible ways, through 'intellectual, emotional and motivational expressions of productivity' (Kruse 2016, 404). But I will not try to defend the value of ageing in this way.

Instead, I wish to place ageing persons in the centre of my discussion by asking whether, and how, ageing is good for *them*. Yet to say what exactly is the value of ageing for individuals is difficult, mainly because it is difficult to generalize about ageing people. As Applewhite remarks,

stereotyping lies at the heart of ageism: the assumption that all members of a group are the same. It's why people think everyone in a retirement home is the same age – old – even though residents can range from 50-year-olds to centenarians. (Can you imagine thinking the same way about a group of 20- to 60-year-olds?) And the longer we live, as more experiences inform our uniqueness, the more different from one another we become. Think about it: Which group is likely to have more in common, a bunch of 17-year-olds or of 77-year-olds? As doctors put it, 'If you've seen one 80-year-old, you've seen one 80-year-old' (Applewhite 2019, 8).

I will confine my comments to ageing people in developed nations, since that is the context I know. But ageing people in the developed world vary, at minimum, by socioeconomic class, sex/gender, race, ability and health status, sexuality, education, and geographical location. The process of ageing for an Indigenous gay man in Canada's far north is likely to be very different than the process of ageing for a middle class heterosexual white woman in California, and different also from the process of ageing for an impoverished person of any race or location who is struggling with poor health. Moreover, ageing is a process, not a steady state. As Kate De Medeiros notes, 'Since rates of biological and functional change are not universal across people but are instead affected by genetics and by environmental exposures and opportunities – including factors sometimes characterized as "social" – age reveals little about individual people's lives, health, or needs' (De Medeiros 2018, section 11). That is, the material and social conditions in which individuals live and work, along with their personal identity, help to define what the experience of getting old is like. So my argument about the value of ageing must proceed cautiously, with an acknowledgement of how presumptuous it can be to generalize about an entire cohort of people who are so variable. The challenge is to identify answers to the question, Is ageing good? that have some plausibility despite the variations among people who age.

Why Ageing Can Be Good

My first thought, a tart one, in response to the question of whether ageing is good is simply this: It's better than the alternative. Few people are eager to die, and especially not to die young. Despite pop songs celebrating eternal youth or dying before getting old, I suspect most people would reject early death in favour of ageing. Recently a dear friend, only sixty-three, died of a virulent lymphoma. She was a vital, active, energetic woman who contributed creatively and powerfully to her profession and who loved and was loved by family members and a wide circle of friends and colleagues. Surely it would have been better for her to have had the opportunity to age.

But why is ageing better than the alternative? It is worthwhile to ask whether there are *experiences, characteristics, or relationships* that are attainable only by virtue of ageing. This is, in part, an empirical question about what actually happens to people as they age. But it is also a normative question, because what we are seeking are experiences, characteristics, or relationships that are both desirable and good.

One possibility is that extended longevity is valuable simply because it gives us the opportunity for *more* of what we have already experienced: more time with family members, more time with friends, more time for work (if we value our work), more time for the projects we regard as worthwhile, more time for cultural and social and political participation, and more time for leisure activities. If spending time with one's daughter is a good thing when one is thirty, then probably it will remain a good thing when one is sixty or ninety. If playing the clarinet is worthwhile in middle age, perhaps it will remain worthwhile in old age.

The continuing value of such experiences, activities, relationships, and goals depends in part on the persistence of one's ability to pursue them. Some pursuits may become impossible, tedious, or painful. Running marathons, for example, may decline in importance in old age if one's knees no longer permit high-impact physical activity. But in addition, some activities may just lose their allure. In his *A History of the World in 10 ½ Chapters*, Barnes imagines a man who wakes up, after his death, in his own version of paradise. It is a paradise where he gets to play golf (among other activities) as much as he wants, for as many years as he wants, until he gets so good at it, and so accustomed to the courses, that he can complete a course in just eighteen shots. But then the problem for the man is that golf is 'used up' (Barnes 1989, 296).

The question, then, is whether there are activities and experiences that will not get 'used up' in old age and are worth repeating over and over again. The answer may largely be a matter of individual psychology. It baffles me that some people can watch NHL hockey year after year, and always regard it as worthwhile. But for aficionados the fascination of hockey is renewed every season. For me, on the other hand, it looks as if reading novels could be an undiminishing source of pleasure, at least for as long as my eyesight and my mind are functioning. We could say that probably, for most people, there are activities whose rewards are *renewable*; their benefits do not diminish despite repeated indulgence.

Ageing is good, then, to the extent that it permits the enjoyment of renewable activities. But in addition, aside from renewable activities we already enjoy, there is also the possibility, for many ageing people, of undertaking new experiences, new activities, new relationships, and new goals. And this is an important point. Part of the lie of ageism is the idea that old people are 'stuck in their ways', not willing to try new things, limited in their vision. This is no truer of old people than it is of any other group.

For many older individuals, there is the opportunity to give up difficult, stressful, repetitive labour, to cease working as hard as they did when they were younger. They may then have the chance to work at a more comfortable pace, to do different kinds of work, or to engage in volunteer work. They may become involved in political projects, or new businesses, or creative activities, or caring for or mentoring people in a way they have not previously done. They may have the chance to keep learning, whether through formal courses, or informally, developing new skills and trying new activities. They may make new friends. They may begin, or renew an attachment to, a religious or spiritual identity. Or they may just rest and enjoy their leisure, possibly for the first time in their adult lives.

Another possible answer to the question of the value of ageing is that there may be features of getting old that are both unique to old age and profoundly valuable, such that they make ageing good. One unique and valuable feature of living into old age – widely touted and for good reason – is having grandchildren. Not everyone gets to have grandchildren (since their existence depends partly on one's choices as a younger self, and partly on the decisions of other people), and not everyone gets to have good relationships with the grandchildren they may have. However, there is something important and almost irreplaceable about connecting with members of younger generations. The opportunity to have relationships with one's children, nieces and nephews, grandchildren, and maybe even great-grandchildren is a joy and a learning experience only attainable by living a long time.[5] Of comparable value is the opportunity to interact with present or former students, mentees, young athletes, neighbours, or the children or grandchildren of friends. Andreas Kruse refers to this activity as 'generativity', which he defines as 'social cohesion between generations' (Kruse 2016, 407).

The sheer endurance of some relationships is also important. Ageing provides the opportunity to sustain long-lasting relationships – with family members, friends, or colleagues – that may flourish and deepen with longevity. A relationship such as a friendship, partnership, or marriage that lasts forty years or more may be of special value, since it has all the richness of a shared history. There can be something deeply comforting about a connection with someone who knows one's personal history and values, and shares at least some of them. In such a relationship the other person may know one's strengths as well as one's weaknesses and vulnerabilities, and can be a cheerleader for the former and a support for the latter. There's a country song performed by real-life friends Dolly Parton and Kenny Rogers that captures this richness: 'You Can't Make Old Friends'. The singers say it was the two of them since way back when. They ask each other what they will do when the other is gone – who will tell them the truth, who will finish their stories? As Martha Nussbaum writes, 'Aging is bound to contain tragedy. It is not bound to contain comedy, or understanding, or love. What supplies both of these is friendship' (Nussbaum and Levmore 2017, 83).

What about wisdom; does it make ageing good? Western society pays lip service to the idea that old people possess special insights and irreplaceable experience, although it seldom accords old people much respect as a result. But just as negative stereotypes about older people are unjustified, so also is sentimentalizing about them. I suggest there is no more reason for supposing that old age *inevitably* brings wisdom than there is for believing that old age inevitably brings diminishment.

Nonetheless, there is no doubt that a lifetime of experience makes a difference to who one is and how one sees one's life. '[A] human person is a historical being, in whom the past remains immanent in the present, and whom the wear and tear of time enhances rather than diminishes' (McClay 2018). Getting old affords the opportunity to take the long view about one's

---

[5] On the other hand, as Lynne Segal points out, 'the demands of caregiving on grandparents are sometimes stressful and exhausting, perhaps exacerbating existing health problems' (Segal 2014, 189).

schooling, jobs, relationships, illnesses and disabilities, and participation in community. There is something important about one's personal history, pattern of relationships, efforts made, and successes and failures. There is the time, and the perspective, to try to make sense of oneself and one's life and one's situation with respect to others – 'accept[ing] one's life as a whole, including lost opportunities and unfulfilled aspirations and expectations' (Kruse 2016, 410). Years of observing and participating in personal relationships, social inter-actions, and political processes provide a perspective that is not possible for younger people. More broadly, while history may not repeat itself, it is valuable to see the social and political events of the current time within the larger context of sixty or seventy years of observation and participation.

Thus, an important potential value of ageing is the development of an enriched outlook on life (Pipher 2019a). As people age, what they take to be significant and valuable may evolve and develop. Goals are reached – or are set aside. New values, or reasons for living, come alive. Former obligations fall aside, while fresh responsibilities offer fulfilment. Geoffrey Scarre suggests that old age is a time when new virtues may be developed:

Age may or may not bring wisdom, but it can at least be a more fertile ground than earlier phases of life for the development of certain virtues, among them patience, fortitude, compassion, humility and tolerance. Older people often have more time on their hands than younger ones to weigh matters up, ponder their priorities, reassess their values and reach, often through painful first-hand experience, a deeper understanding of the 'thousand natural shocks that flesh is heir to' (Scarre 2016, 96).

Old rules that seemed inviolate can now be questioned. Women, especially, sometimes report that getting old can build confidence and autonomy, and be liberating in certain ways. Perhaps sexist stereotypes, or ageist ones, reveal themselves to be frauds: certain social limits no longer are compelling. Barbara Ehrenreich writes, 'Being old enough to die is an achievement, not a defeat, and the freedom it brings is worth celebrating' (Ehrenreich 2018, 13).

Indeed, there is significant empirical evidence that as people get older and the time left to them shortens, they may develop new values or attitudes towards their life and their place in the universe. A study of over 300,000 adults in the United Kingdom, released in 2016 by the UK Office for National Statistics, showed that people between sixty-five and seventy-nine had the 'highest level of personal wellbeing'. People who were ninety or older 'reported higher life satisfaction and happiness compared with people in their middle years' (Office for National Statistics 2016). And according to the English Longitudinal Study of Ageing (ELSA), 'nine-in-ten respondents agree that a lot can be learnt from old people; three-quarters of them do not think of themselves as old; three-quarters think of retirement as a time of leisure' (Demakakos, Hacker, and Gjonça 2006, 343). Similarly, according to

Statistics Canada, Canadian 'seniors' are strikingly 'more satisfied with their lives than [are] adults in younger age groups. Men and women in their 60s, 70s and 80s had higher average life satisfaction scores than men and women aged 20 to 59' (Statistics Canada 2018).

This study of life satisfaction revealed in Canadians the same U-shaped curve of life satisfaction that is found in members of other nationalities: that is, people tend to report a high degree of life satisfaction in their teens; their life satisfaction then declines in later decades, and begins to rise again in their sixties. According to Carol Graham and Julia Ruiz Pozuelo, 'Happiness declines with age for about two decades from early adulthood up until roughly the middle-age years, and then turns upward and increases with age. Although the exact shape differs across countries, the bottom of the curve (or the nadir of happiness) ranges from 40 to 60 plus years old' (Graham and Pozuelo 2017, 226). Their extensive data analysis, across countries ranging from Denmark and Bulgaria to South Africa and Peru, indicates that the specific point at which the happiness level begins to improve depends both on factors within the individual and on factors within the individual's society:

Naturally cheerful or happy respondents seem to navigate the aging process – and the stress associated with the middle-aged years – more easily than those who are lower in the well-being distribution. And navigating the aging process is likely easier for all respondents who live in happier environments because of the associated factors, such as the better (and more broadly shared) environments, health care, social safety nets, and governance structures that characterize the countries with the highest levels of aggregate happiness (Graham and Pozuelo 2017, 262).

When Ageing Isn't Good

Of course, the story of ageing is not all sunny. Not everyone feels happy in old age, and not all life aspects, even for those who are happy, are upbeat. For example, a majority of the subjects in the ELSA said they would prefer to be younger than their perceived age (Demakakos, Hacker, and Gjonça 2006, 339); more than two-thirds of them 'worry that their health will worsen as they grow older; and almost two-thirds believe that old people are not respected in society' (Demakakos, Hacker, and Gjonça 2006, 343). And the Office for National Statistics study notes that 'average ratings of life satisfaction, a sense that what one does in life is worthwhile' decline after age seventy-nine (Office for National Statistics 2016).

For some, getting old may mean 'mourning the roads not taken' (Segal 2014, 183). For others, the growing proximity to death may make ageing uncomfortable, especially for individuals who have a great fear of death and dying. The story of ageing as loss, while it fuels ageism, also has roots in some people's experience. Some may miss the work – paid, volunteer, or domestic – that they did previously, and feel bereft for no longer having a recognized role. And while people may acquire new family members and friends later in life, they may also lose loved ones, through the ending of relationships or through death.

It is also possible, as a person ages, that their life may be or become materially impoverished. Some people face a lack of money and resources, such that merely having enough to pay for food and lodging becomes a struggle. Rampant ageism, expressed in society's failure to provide respectful support and care that promotes flourishing, could make death better than continuing to age.

Some people must deal with disabilities as they age. I'm not going to deny the hard parts: the loss of vision or hearing or both; the potential cognitive decline; the bodily weaknesses, loss of balance, loss of strength and endurance, and greater vulnerability to illnesses.[6] 'Acknowledging old age means knowing that we are unlikely to remain the autonomous, independent and future-oriented individuals most of us once liked to imagine we were, and in Western cultures are encouraged to think we should remain' (Segal 2014, 184).

Probably there are, for most people, upper boundaries on how long living is good and how much ageing is desirable. One obvious limit is irremediable suffering. People vary in terms of how much they are able and willing to tolerate, but if major conditions such as cancer, heart disease, arthritis, or Alzheimer's take too much of a toll, some people may welcome death as an end to further distress. Some may simply become too tired to go on living. Partly this feeling may be a physical sensation; partly it may be an intuition that life lived for much longer is not going to offer enough of the features that the person regards as worthwhile. The rewards of even renewable pleasures may shrink in comparison to the demands and trials of carrying on in extreme old age.

Thus, given our biological vulnerabilities, there may come a point where more ageing is not necessarily better than death (although that point may arrive later, perhaps much later, than younger people anticipate).

Some Concluding Thoughts

Part of the answer to the question Is ageing good? is: It depends. Whether ageing is good depends in part on the physical, cognitive, and psychological health of the individual. But it also depends on the social environment in which the individual lives, on factors that the individual cannot control. These include

---

[6] Of course, one may also encounter such things at thirty. But it does seem true that more health challenges are likely to come up as we age – although I suspect that the standpoint of people who are temporarily non-disabled grossly underestimates the joys and rewards that can still be experienced in a life lived with disabilities.

the availability of high quality health care; comfortable, safe housing that is easily accessible for individuals who may have or develop various impairments; social services and amenities such as libraries, schools, and universities for continuing education; parks, and conservation areas; efficient and available forms of transportation; environments that are safe and healthy; and the absence of oppressive conditions that undermine well-being, such as racism, sexism, heterosexism, ableism, and ageism.

As I've acknowledged, ageing can be or become bad. But it is equally, or even more, important to recognize the good of ageing: renewable pleasures; new activities, relationships, and goals; and features distinctive of old age, such as connections with younger generations, long-lasting relationships, and an enriched outlook on life. But ageist social tendencies prevent us from seeing what can be good about ageing. For that reason, I believe, there are three *moral and political* reasons for affirming that ageing is or can be good.

First, an individual's belief, especially if shared by others around her, that ageing is good may help to make the process of ageing a better one for the individual.[7]

Second, affirming that ageing is or can be good, given at least minimally supportive material and social conditions, can remind everyone how important it is to try to create those conditions,[8] so that as many older people as possible can experience ageing as good.

Third, affirming the goodness of ageing is a deliberate way of counteracting ageism, and the neglect of and disrespect towards old people that ageism countenances. In the words of Wilfred M. McClay, 'Aging is not a problem to be solved ... It is a meaning to be lived out' (McClay 2018).

---

[7] The 'power of positive thinking' in respect to age is supported by recent findings that while 'a cultural construct, age beliefs, may contribute to the development of dementia in older individuals', 'positive age beliefs [are] a protective factor against developing dementia', even in individuals who carry the gene for dementia (Levi et al. 2018).

[8] See 'What Makes a Good Life in Late Life? Citizenship and Justice in Aging Societies' (De Medeiros 2018) for extensive discussion of the ways in which states and communities can contribute to making the environment for older persons more 'age friendly'.

6 Mental Health in Old Age

Simon Keller

Introduction

Lanfen often forgets where she has left things. She can only stay alert for a couple of hours at a time and she needs a nap every day. She is sometimes unaware of her surroundings; she cannot be left alone near a busy road because she might wander into the traffic. If she finds herself alone in a supermarket or a shopping center, she is likely to become disoriented and worried.

If Lanfen is aged one, then, as far as can be told from the description, there is nothing wrong with her. She is a normal growing child.

If Lanfen is forty, then she has a mental health problem. She might suffer from a cognitive disability or from some other condition that significantly restricts her mental functioning.

What if Lanfen is ninety? For a ninety-year-old, Lanfen, as described, is not unusual, and she might be perfectly happy. She might be comfortable, clever, and funny, and she might enjoy rewarding relationships with friends and family. From one point of view, considering only what we know from the description, Lanfen might be a normal or even thriving ninety-year-old. She might be a picture of mental health.

Still, the fact remains that Lanfen is slow and dependent. Her mental acuity and cognitive functioning have presumably deteriorated significantly since she was a young adult. Most adults, including the younger Lanfen, would not want to swap their mental capabilities for those of the ninety-year-old Lanfen; to do so would be to suffer a mental decline. From a second point of view, then, Lanfen is not a picture of mental health. From this point of view, the fact that she might be doing well for a ninety-year-old serves only as a reminder that most ninety-year-olds are not mentally healthy.

Prevailing theories of mental health tend to take one or the other of those two points of view. Some imply that an elderly person has good mental health so long as she is about normal for her age. Others imply that the model of mental health is the productive, alert, well-functioning young adult, and hence that the mental health of most elderly people is poor.

I am very grateful for helpful comments and research assistance from Snita Ahir-Knight, and for helpful comments from Nicholas Agar, Monika Betzler, Don Locke, Edwin Mares, John Matthewson, and Christopher Wareham.

Each of these two points of view is too simplistic. It is a mistake to measure an old person's mental health just by looking at what is normal for her age, but it is also a mistake to measure an old person's mental health using the standards you would apply to someone younger. That means that many prevailing theories of mental health struggle to explain mental health in old age. To get a better account of mental health in old age, we need to rethink the nature of mental health and also to ask about the significance of old age in the story of a human life. Those, at least, are the claims I will defend in this chapter.

"Mental," "Health," and "Old Age"

To talk of *mental* health is to apply broadly medical terms – "health," "disease," "disorder," "illness," "pathology" – to the mind. Mental health is concerned with the health of mental states and processes. Whether you are mentally healthy depends upon whether you have healthy emotions, feelings, beliefs, and appetites; whether you have healthy ways of reasoning and responding to evidence; and so on. It may be that mental states and processes can all be reduced to physical states and processes, and it may even be that to have a healthy mind is, ultimately, to have a (physically) healthy brain, but still, in talking about mental health we begin with the mental. If you say that someone is depressed, and I say that she has a chemical imbalance in her brain, then you are talking about her mental health and I am talking about her physical health, even if there is a sense in which we are talking about the same thing (Arpaly 2005).[1]

Mental *health*, as I will speak of it in this chapter, is a substantive positive condition of the mind. I am talking about what is sometimes called "positive mental health." So understood, mental health is not the absence of mental disorder but rather the presence of certain mental goods.[2] You could suffer from poor mental health, in the relevant sense, without suffering from a mental illness or disease. If you are constantly stressed and distracted, for example, or if your memory or reasoning processes are not working well, then you have poor mental health, even if you do not have a disorder.

That noted, mental disorder usually has implications for (positive) mental health. Usually, if you have a mental disorder then you thereby lack some of the goods that constitute a positively healthy mind. If you suffer from a depressive disorder, for example, then you probably have a disposition to feel excessive sadness, which probably means that you have a diminished disposition to find enjoyment in everyday life, which in turn means, plausibly, that you lack one of the goods that contributes to positive mental health. Still, to talk of mental health,

---

[1] See especially Arpaly (2005, 282–290).
[2] See the use of the term mental health in, for example, Huppert and So (2013, 838) and Keyes (2009, 89–90).

in the sense at issue here, is not to talk only of conditions that would warrant medical diagnosis or treatment.

There are many conceptions of old age. Whether we describe you as "old" might depend variously on whether you are near the end of your expected lifespan, whether you are older than most of the people around you, whether you have reached the age of retirement, or whether you require certain kinds of care, among other possibilities. My concern here, though, is with a set of mental changes that people tend to experience in later life. You have entered old age, as I will conceive of it, if you have reached the age at which a significant proportion of people in your society have begun to show the mental signs of ageing. In societies like mine, I take that age to be about eighty-five; by eighty-five, most people have begun to undergo mental changes characteristic of old age. If I can put it this way: if you are about to meet someone and all you know about her is that she is eighty-five or older, then you can reasonably expect her mental capacities to be different, in certain respects, from those you would expect to find in a one-year-old or a forty-year-old. That is what it means, for my purposes, to say that the person you are about to meet has entered old age.

Mental Health Problems in Old Age

Many of the mental changes associated with old age are negative. As a person enters old age, she is likely to become less energetic and to tire more quickly. She is likely to become mentally slower, taking longer to think things through and finding it more difficult to follow everyday conversations. She is likely to have poorer short-term memory. She is likely to find it more difficult to perform demanding mental tasks and to learn new mental skills. All these changes would cause serious concern if seen in a forty-year-old, but they are common among the elderly.

There are mental diseases of ageing, most obviously dementia in its various forms and degrees. Dementia afflicts many people over eighty-five – perhaps as many as half, though estimates vary – but is rare in people under sixty-five (National Institute on Aging 2019). Dementia can involve severe memory loss, as well as paranoia, depression, confusion, insomnia, emotional instability, and changes in personality, and it can involve the loss of the abilities to think and speak clearly, to recognize loved ones, and to carry out simple tasks (Verdelho and Gonçalves-Pereira 2017).

In addition, there are mental health problems that are seen at all ages but seem disproportionately to affect elderly people, or at least to take a distinctive character among elderly people. Elderly people are often lonely, often feel neglected and undervalued, and often struggle with motivation. Some forms of depression and anxiety are common among elderly people, but do not appear to be symptoms of dementia or to be straightforwardly attributable to the physical process of ageing (Royal College of Psychiatrists 2018, 2–3; Skoog 2011).

Some mental health problems in old age appear to be results of the physical ageing process. Others are due to the treatment of elderly people within particular societies.[3] Still others are predictable results of the changes in a person's circumstances and attitudes as she approaches the end of her life. An elderly person is likely to have seen friends die, to have a frail body and to be unable to engage in activities that once brought happiness, and to see the limits of her life's achievements, all of which may lead to sadness, loneliness, and loss of motivation.

Some of the mental health problems common in old age are compatible with subjective happiness. An elderly person who has suffered memory loss and mental slowing may yet have a very pleasant life. Problems like depression, loneliness, anxiety, and paranoia, however, are different. They make a life less pleasant and less happy at whichever age they are experienced.

Mental Health as Good Functioning

According to one approach to defining mental health, a healthy mind is a mind that performs its natural function. In the literature, this idea is most commonly expressed by way of a theory of mental disorder, in which a mental disorder is a certain kind of impediment to the mind's natural functioning.[4] But much of the history of thought about positive mental health, too, is influenced by the idea that a healthy mind is one that works as nature, in some sense, intends.[5]

There are varying stories about where to find the natural function of the mind. As a representative example, Christopher Boorse says that a mental function is "some species-typical contribution to survival and reproduction . . . characteristic of the organism's age" (Boorse 1976, 63). For Boorse, the explanation of why certain states and processes are parts of the evolved human mind is that they allow individual humans to perform certain tasks that historically helped humans to survive and reproduce. Fear, for example, might serve its function when it provides warning of danger, and memory might serve its function when it provides information that leads to more effective action (Boorse 1976, 64).

However, exactly, the functionalist approach is expressed, and as Boorse's definition makes explicit, it can explain why different standards should be used in assessing mental health at different points in human life. It is very likely that the human mind has different natural functions at different ages. A young child might exhibit a well-functioning mind when she forms emotional bonds with her parents and develops language and social skills, while a young adult might

---

[3] For a description of some extreme cases of the poor treatment of elderly people, see The Standing Committee on Health, Aged Care and Sport (2018).

[4] Two well-known examples are Boorse (1976) and Wakefield (2007). For a thorough argumentative survey of various functionalist accounts of disease (both mental and somatic), see Griffiths and Matthewson (2018).

[5] On the role of this idea in the history of thinking about mental health, see Dowbiggin (2011).

exhibit a well-functioning mind when she takes opportunities to reproduce and raises healthy children.

Applied to elderly people, though, the functionalist approach is implausible. It is not clear that the human mind has a natural function in old age, or that if it does have a natural function, then fulfilling it would be healthy. Elderly people are past the age at which they can reproduce and are often unable to contribute much to the survival of individuals who share their genes. It is plausible to think that humans were not designed to survive into old age, or at least that evolutionary selective pressures applied only to characteristics that promote survival and reproduction in earlier life. Perhaps the elderly body and mind are merely what remain once the natural human functions have been discharged.[6]

In any event, an assessment of the mental health of an elderly person should not be made to depend on discoveries about the natural function of the ageing mind. There is no good reason to expect that a person who displays excellent mental health well into old age will thereby live as nature intended. We should not presume, for example, that being content and well-adjusted in old age is, in this sense, "natural" (Garson 2019, chapter 11).

This weakness of the functionalist approach is likely to arise for any theory that tries to account for mental health in old age just by describing the natural, normal, typical, or characteristic elderly mind. Memory loss, confusion, long-term sadness, and loss of motivation might be normal, and might even be selected for, in old age, but they still count as deficits in mental health.[7] In some respects, plausibly, to age normally or naturally is to suffer a decline in mental health. An account of mental health in old age should be able to hold people to standards of mental health that elderly people do not naturally, normally, typically, or characteristically meet.

Mental Health as Well-being

In talking about mental health, as I said earlier, I am talking about "positive" mental health, a substantive positive condition of the mind. Many theorists, especially within public health and positive psychology, take that substantive positive condition to be equivalent to "well-being," so that a person has a healthy mind if she enjoys well-being; and they take well-being to consist in certain objective goods, which they go on to specify.[8]

---

[6] See the overview in chapter 1 of Nesse (2019).

[7] See the discussion of osteoarthritis in Griffiths and Matthewson (2018, 320–323). Griffiths and Matthewson argue that statistically normal health problems in old age raise problems for a "biostatistical" functionalist account of disease, but not for a "selected effects" account.

[8] The approach on which well-being is defined through a list of substantive goods is only one of many possible approaches to defining well-being, but is the one that dominates in this field. On the wider project of identifying mental health with well-being, see Keller (2020).

One high-profile definition of this kind is given by the World Health Organization (WHO). It says, "Mental health is defined as a state of well-being in which every individual realizes his or her own potential, can cope with the normal stresses of life, can work productively and fruitfully, and is able to make a contribution to her or his community" (WHO 2001).

The WHO's definition of mental health implies that there are no mentally healthy one-year-olds. One-year-olds are not able to cope with everyday life – they cannot look after their own needs or navigate the world independently – and they are not able to work productively and fruitfully or to make contributions to their communities.

The same goes for most elderly people. The mental, physical, and social changes that mark old age tend to restrict the ability to be a productive worker and contributor, and they tend to leave elderly people relatively dependent upon others in everyday life. Normal ageing, according to the WHO's definition, is a mental health problem.

Similar implications flow from other definitions offered by authors who define mental health as well-being. Corey L. M. Keyes' list of the goods that make for positive mental health, to give a further example, includes such items as "Feels that one's life is useful to society and valued by or valuable to others," "Exhibits capability to manage complex environment," and "Exhibits self-direction" (Keyes 2009, 91). As with the WHO's definition, Keyes' definition pictures the mentally healthy person as an active, useful, autonomous adult at the peak of her cognitive powers. A mentally healthy elderly person, according to this approach, is an old person with the mind of a young person.

The approach captures something plausible about mental health in old age. As we enter old age, we tend to become more dependent upon others, to be less productive, and to feel less useful to society, and some mental health problems in old age are results of these changes. To some extent, old age by its nature brings problems with mental health. The implications of the approach for the mental health of children, however, are obviously implausible. Mental health cannot be a matter of being independent, productive, and useful – not, at least, when you are a child. And the approach's failure to explain the mental health of children gives reason to think that it fails to explain the mental health of the elderly too.

When you imagine an elderly person with good mental health, you do not need to imagine someone who thinks and behaves as though she is still forty. You do not need to imagine an independent, useful, productive worker. As it can be healthy to have the mind of a child when you are a child, there are at least some respects in which it can be healthy to have the mind of an elderly person when you are elderly. Perhaps a mentally healthy elderly person, compared to a mentally healthy forty-year-old, will be calmer and less driven, will have a greater sense of perspective, will be better at enjoying quiet time, or will be more focused on enjoying the smaller things in life. Even if old age often or usually brings mental health problems, surely it also, like childhood, presents its own way of being mentally healthy.

If that is right, then to understand mental health in old age we need to say why old age is special. For the reasons mentioned earlier, it is doubtful that we can find the specialness of old age in its natural function, but we can look elsewhere.

Mental Health as a Resource

Here is my version of a third approach to defining mental health, which I will call the "resourcist" view.[9] On this approach, the elements of mental health are the mental resources that make an individual more likely to live a good human life, in one form or another. The idea is that there are some mental characteristics that help almost any human, in almost any situation, to live a better life, and those are the characteristics that constitute the healthy human mind.

As an analogy, consider the value of having good nutrition, and the value of having a basic education. Whichever path you take in life, you will probably live a better life if you enjoy good nutrition and if you have been given a basic education. Poor nutrition and a lack of education will hold you back whether you aim to have a family, become a musician, or work as a travel agent. If you want your child to live a good life, then you will want to give her good nutrition and a basic education, even if you do not know what kind of life she will pursue. Good nutrition and a basic education do not guarantee a good life; plenty of well-nourished and well-educated people live awful lives. And they are not necessary for a good life; plenty of undernourished and poorly educated people live wonderful lives. But still, good nutrition and a basic education are valuable resources in the quest to live a good human life. Almost always, they help. In my resourcist view of mental health, the mental characteristics that constitute mental health are in this respect similar to good nutrition and a basic education.

One such mental characteristic, plausibly, is patience. Another might be the ability to form cooperative relationships. Whether you aim to have a family, become a musician, or work as a travel agent – and whether you live as a surfer, philosopher, banker, parent, explorer, or husband – you will probably live a better life if you are patient rather than impatient and if you have the mental

---

[9] The resourcist view of mental health is not prominent in the literature, but it is defended or touched upon by a number of authors. I sketch my version in Keller (2020). Per-Anders Tengland (2001) argues that mental health consists in the abilities required to pursue vital interests. See especially chapters 6–7. Within a larger discussion of mental disorder, George Graham (2013) suggests that mental health may consist in having the faculties and capacities that we would recognize as important from behind a veil of ignorance – that is, in ignorance of our particular conceptions of the good life. See especially chapter 6. Sam Wren-Lewis and Anna Alexandrova (2021) argue that mental health consists in the mental resources that give a person access to well-being.

skills and capacities that enable you to cooperate with other people. Patience and the ability to form cooperative relationships are then elements of mental health, according to the view in question. Other elements of mental health might be impulse control, perseverance, the ability to moderate your use of alcohol and other drugs, a reasonably happy disposition, a tendency to let go of past resentments, and the habit of forming beliefs based on the evidence. These are all things that make you more likely to live a good human life. As with good nutrition and a basic education, they are not sufficient for a good life; a person who is patient and good at cooperating with others can still live an awful life. And they are not necessary for living a good life; you might be impatient and bad at cooperating with others, and also live a wonderful life. But still, mostly, they make the good life more attainable. They are mental characteristics that you would probably want your child to have, if you want your child to live a good human life but do not know what path in life she will take.

Good human lives come in many different forms, and the various forms of the good human life are often mutually incompatible. You can live a good life as a celibate monk or as a polyamorous popstar, perhaps, but the two lives involve different goods and you cannot live both at once. There are some forms of the good human life, presumably, that you and I cannot imagine. The life of a hunter-gatherer, a Viking, or a solitary traveling mystic might be a very good human life, though many of us could not say how or why.

While the good life comes in many different forms, not just any human life is good. There are many forms of the bad human life too. A life can be unhappy, immoral, or deluded; it can be a life of failure, can be lived in fear or pain, and can be tragic or stunted. Some mental characteristics make a person less likely to live a good life, and in the view I am expressing, they are the characteristics that constitute poor mental health. Plausibly, you are less likely to live well as a human, whatever your circumstances and goals, if you are susceptible to delusions, suffer from depression or anxiety, lack empathy, cannot control your temper, have poor memory, are constantly tired and distractible, have poor reasoning skills, or are unaware of your surroundings, to give just a few examples. It is possible, again, for a person who has some of these characteristics to live well – a person who suffers from anxiety can live a wonderful life – but for the most part, they make the attainment of a good life less likely.

To see what it means for a particular person to be mentally healthy, according to the resourcist approach, we need first to ask what good forms of human life are available to her in principle. (The answer will be different for a person living in a city today as compared with a person living in a hunter-gatherer community long ago.) Then we need to ask what mental characteristics will make her more likely to live one or other of those good forms of life: which mental characteristics will be useful to her whichever of the available forms of the good human life she pursues. Insofar as she has those characteristics, she enjoys good mental health.

The Story of a Human Life

When we ask what forms of a good life are available to a person, we will have reason to ask not only what it would take for her life to contain good moments, but also what it would mean for her life to go well when considered as a whole. Many of the values that characterize a good human life are manifested across parts of a life or across a whole life. A good human life has a structure, its value coming partly from the relationship between its different episodes and parts. It is not simply a collection of good moments.[10]

Consider a few relevant values. A human life might be good because it is a life of integrity, but to live with integrity is to live by sincerely held principles over time. A good human life can be built on good relationships, but to enjoy a healthy personal relationship – to be a good parent or sister or friend – is to participate in a relationship that persists and evolves over time. A good human life might be a life of achievement, but to live a life of achievement is to set goals and work toward them over time (Bradford 2015). Your life might be a good life partly because you learn from your mistakes, or overcome obstacles, or show loyalty, or live as a philosopher or a doctor or a scientist. Whether your life manifests any of these values depends upon the story of your life. It depends on how the different moments within your life are connected with each other, not just on their quality, each considered in isolation.

The mental resources that make you more likely to live a good human life, then, are not just the resources that allow you to enjoy pleasant or otherwise good moments. They include the mental resources that make you more likely to live a good human life story. Such resources might include memory, a persisting sense of identity, the ability to make plans and stick to them, and the capacity to form adaptable, constructive, loving, long-term relationships.

Exactly what resources make you more likely to live a good human life, and in exactly what form they may best help you to live a good life, will vary, depending upon your age.

Mental Health in Childhood

As humans, we all begin life as children. Childhood plays a special part in the good human life, in part through its role in a human life story. There are many distinctive goods that you can only experience as a child. They include the goods associated with innocence, imaginative play, and a child's sense of wonder and adventure. Childhood is, by its nature, a time of rapid development, so living well as a child involves learning quickly, acquiring new skills, experimenting, and adapting. In addition, it is often in childhood that you forge the traits, interests, values, and relationships that come to inform your

---

[10] For defenses of this claim as it applies to well-being or welfare, which is plausibly a component of the good life, see Velleman (1991) and Keller (2009).

life and to give it meaning and structure. Often, the story of a good human life is a story of living by values learned in childhood, or overcoming trauma and other obstacles encountered in childhood, or coming to self-knowledge and peace through a better understanding of childhood experiences.

You will be more likely to live a good life when you are a child, and to live a childhood that contributes to a good life overall, if you have the mind of a child. In comparison with an adult, a child may be more likely to live well, as a child, if she is less skeptical, more open to new experiences, and more willing to change her habits; and if she has a more vivid imagination, a more malleable sense of identity, and the cognitive skills that allow her more readily to seek and absorb new information. As childhood steadily progresses, different mental resources will be useful at different ages and stages. That is why, according to my resourcist view of mental health, the standards by which a child's mental health is measured are different from those by which an adult's mental health is measured, and those standards change as childhood progresses. There are special ways in which you can live well as a child and there are special mental resources that make you more likely to live well as a child – and so there are special standards by which a child's mental health should be assessed.

Old Age and the Good Life

As there are special goods of childhood, there are some special goods of old age. Old age can bring perspective and wisdom. As an elderly person, you are likely to have fewer responsibilities and face less pressure to work hard and to be productive, which can bring a new kind of freedom. Old age can offer extra time to think and to pursue your interests, and to do what you want to do without being so answerable to others. While old age brings difficulties, it also offers new possibilities for enjoyment.

Too often, however, as it seems to me, we focus only upon the momentary goods of old age. We can imagine the good life in old age as a life of contented inactivity, as though old age is valuable only insofar as it is pleasant. We can think of the thriving elderly person as one who enjoys nice meals, quiet walks, visits, good books, and sleep-ins, who follows the news of her younger relatives and spends time chatting with friends. Advertisements for retirement communities, as they strike me, tend to emphasize the provision of comfort and entertainment, as though the highest aspiration in old age is to avoid pain and boredom. These things are all important, of course, but if we focus only on goods of this kind – goods that have to do largely with having good moments – then it is easy to think that the best that can be hoped for in old age is a pleasant time as we wait for it all to end.

Compared with childhood and young adulthood, old age can seem to have little to add to a human story. If you think about the prospect of dying at sixty-five rather than eighty-five, you may well feel that you will be deprived of a crucial part of a human life; if you think about the prospect of dying at eighty-five rather than one hundred and five, you may feel that you would be deprived only of twenty years of hanging around. To understand living well in old age through a closer analogy with living well in childhood, we need to say something more constructive about how old age can make a distinctive contribution to the story of a good human life.

An explanation of the place of childhood in the story of a good human life can have some grounding in the natural role of human childhood as a time of growth and formation. For reasons given earlier, though, it is relatively difficult to identify an attractive natural function for human old age. Old age is natural, insofar as it comes at the end of every human life that lasts for long enough, but what we are supposed to do with old age is not given by the very nature of old age. What place old age takes in a good human life story is, to a far greater extent than is the case for childhood, up to us.

Old age can be a time at which a human life story is drawn to its conclusion. In old age, you might look back at your life and find its meaning or moral. You might bring closure to relationships or episodes within your life, perhaps offering gratitude to those who have been good to you, perhaps recognizing your mistakes and apologizing or seeking forgiveness. You might find ways to ensure that the story of your life continues beyond your death; you might pass your wisdom on to others, provide help for those who will survive you, or make sure that you leave a positive legacy. You might do things to make it more likely that your life story is complete, or that it is a story with a good ending.

Depending upon the society in which you live, you might add to your life story in old age by attaining a status that is reserved for the elderly. In a society that venerates old age, the elderly can become leaders, keepers of wisdom, and tellers of stories. As an elderly person you might come to have a status, an audience, and a kind of respect that you would not be granted as a young adult.

Those are a few thoughts about the possibilities for living a good life in old age. As I see it, there is good reason to think that living well in old age is not simply a matter of resisting old age for as long as you can; there are special momentary goods of old age and there are special contributions that old age can make to a human life story. Exactly how old age can add to a good human life story is partly a matter of what social roles are made available to the elderly. Where a society sees the human life story as essentially finished by the time you reach old age, and where it sees a good old age as little more than the accumulation of additional good moments, it makes old age worse; it makes it more difficult for elderly people to manifest a distinctive kind of human good. What it means to live well in old age, and the extent to which living well in old age is possible, depend to a large extent upon the social significance that we grant to old age and the social roles that we make available to the elderly.

Assessing Mental Health in Old Age

The good life in old age is different from the good life in childhood and different from the good life in young adulthood. As a result, there are different mental characteristics that can make a person more likely to live a good life as an old person. According to my resourcist view of mental health, there are hence differences between the mental characteristics that constitute mental health in old age and those that constitute mental health at earlier stages of life.

There are of course similarities. Like a younger person, an elderly person will be less likely to live well if she suffers from anxiety, is impatient, cannot form cooperative relationships, or cannot control her anger. For living well in old age, though, it is perhaps less important to have social and professional ambition, the skills that enable you to deal with raising children, or the ability to deal simultaneously with multiple demands on your time. It is perhaps more important in old age to have the grace to tolerate physical frailty and to accept physical dependence on others, the motivation to stay active and engaged when you do not have others relying on you, and the sense of perspective that better enables you to make sense of your life so far.

It is a sad fact about old age that the mental changes that characterize the ageing process often serve to diminish the mental resources that most help an elderly person to live well. Some mental changes in old age are quite compatible with some of the distinctive goods of old age, and some may make the elderly person more likely to attain such goods; some aspects of mental slowing in old age, for example, might make the elderly person more likely to relax and to enjoy her relative freedom from responsibilities. But in other respects, having the mind of an old person makes it more difficult to live well as an old person.

As an elderly person, you have lived for longer than most people around you, and so you have a greater capacity to hold first-hand memories of the relatively distant past and to draw lessons for the present. But old age often brings both memory loss and trouble in following changes in the contemporary world, the effect of which is to undermine that capacity.

In old age you can reflect on your life, mostly already lived, and then draw meaning from your life, bring closure to episodes and relationships, bring projects to fruition, and pass on a legacy. Manifesting this good is difficult, however, when you have less energy, feel undervalued, have trouble concentrating and following conversations, and find it difficult to adopt new styles of thinking.

Speaking generally, much of the story about what happens to the mind in old age is a story about why it is difficult to hold on to the resources that help you to live well in old age. My resourcist account of mental health can explain why mental health in old age should be assessed by special standards and informed by the special possibilities available for living a good human life as an old person, but also why many of the normal mental signs of ageing are such as to detract from mental health. Mental health in old age is different from mental health at other stages of life, and the natural and social realities of ageing often make it difficult to attain.

Conclusion

If you want to be mentally healthy in old age, then you do not need to see old age as something to fight. It is possible to be unashamedly old and also to enjoy good mental health. Enjoying a good life in old age takes a different kind of mind from the mind that helps you live a good life when you are younger. There is a difference between the mentally healthy ninety-year-old and the ninety-year-old with the mind of a forty-year-old.

Yet, there are some mental aspects of ageing that are unambiguously bad, and that you should resist, if you can, for the sake of your mental health. Dementia, no matter how common or natural, is awful, and it would be wonderful if it could be prevented or cured; the symptoms of dementia are obstacles to the living of a good life, in old age as much as at any age. Similarly, you should not embrace memory loss or the inability to keep up with fast-moving conversations; these are aspects of ageing that you might be able to tolerate, within limits, but they do not tend to make old age any better.

None of this is especially reassuring, but it gets things right. It also gives some guidance as to how we can improve the mental health of the elderly. Improving mental health in old age is not just a matter of such things as finding the right medical interventions, providing comfort and entertainment, and fighting loneliness, though these are all important. We can also improve mental health among the elderly by offering greater possibilities for adding to a good human life story in old age, and by making sure that those possibilities are available, as far as possible, to a person with an elderly mind.

7 In Defense of a Semi-Stoical Attitude about Ageing and Death

David DeGrazia

Human beings generally fear death, considering it a terrible harm to the decedent, the individual who dies. Some assume it is the worst of all possible harms. Others acknowledge that some fates—involving what is literally or figuratively torture—can be worse than death. But nearly everyone agrees that death is ordinarily a terrible harm and that mortality is a very sad feature of human existence. Consistently with this attitude, most people seem to believe that getting older (at least once we have grown up) is regrettable insofar as it brings us closer to death. Is it sensible to fear death and the ageing process that brings us closer to it? After rejecting one philosophical strategy for stoicism about death, I will contend that it is most reasonable not to fear death and ageing *if we reach, or are likely to reach, the age of life expectancy with a decent quality of life.*[1] My first argument for this thesis appeals to what we can reasonably expect out of human life. My second argument appeals to the wisdom of overcoming what I will call our tendency toward "cosmic narcissism."

Preliminaries about the Ontology and Harm of Death

An important assumption underlying my reflections is that there is no afterlife. That is, death ends our existence. When one of us dies, she does not continue to exist in some other realm such as heaven, hell, or purgatory; nor does she exist in this realm, as a corpse or pile of ashes. I assume that a necessary condition for our existence is being biologically alive. This assumption was shared by an ancient Greek philosopher whose strategy for justifying stoicism about death merits our brief consideration.

Work on this paper was supported, in part, by intramural funds from the National Institutes of Health Clinical Center. The author thanks Christopher Wareham for suggestions and encouragement. The ideas presented here are the author's own. They do not necessarily reflect the policy or position of the National Institutes of Health or any other part of the US federal government.

[1] Although I will describe my approach as "semi-stoical," I do not intend to tie it in any formal way to the tradition of the ancient Stoics. I am using "stoical" in its everyday sense of facing pain or (more relevantly here) loss calmly and without complaint.

Epicurus argued that we should not fear death because nonexistence negates the possibility of being harmed.[2] As he reasoned, when we exist we are alive and our death is not a reality; and once death occurs we do not exist. Why fear what cannot touch us? A widely accepted rejoinder to his reasoning is that it misconstrues death as *intrinsically* harmful—as a state that is bad to be in. Epicurus is correct that, if there is no afterlife, death is not a state that a human being (or any other creature) can ever be in; rather, death is one's no-longer-existing. But this cogent piece of reasoning neglects the most plausible way of conceptualizing the harm of death, namely, as *instrumentally bad in entailing a deprivation or loss*: Death harms the decedent by depriving her of the prudential good or well-being her life would have contained had she continued to live.[3]

This instrumental conception of the harm of death is counterfactual. That is, it focuses on what would have happened had some actual state of affairs not obtained (so expressing this conception requires the subjunctive mood). For example, one might reason that if Fuki had not caught the coronavirus and died at age thirty, then she probably would have lived about another half century with a decent quality of life. The harm of her death is a function of the good in her life *she would have had* minus the good in her life she *actually did have*: she lost out on about fifty years of human life worth living.

A notorious oddity about this counterfactual conception is that there seems to be no time at which the decedent is harmed by death: not while she "is dead" because she doesn't exist then; and not while alive because she hasn't died yet. But we can conceptualize the harm of, say, Fuki's death by considering her actual life *as a whole* and comparing it to the whole life she would have had, had she not caught the coronavirus. In this way, a person's premature death may be intelligibly regarded as an instrumental harm involving a loss to her. If one insists on pressing the question, "When, exactly, did she incur this loss, this harm?" I suspect there is no satisfying answer and that, in a sense, the harm she incurs is timeless.[4]

In addition to this oddity about timing, there is another major challenge to conceptualizing the harm of death in counterfactual terms. We are to understand the harm, or loss, as the difference in the overall good in life that one actually had and the overall good in life that one would otherwise have had, had one not died then. But, if one had not died then, when and under what circumstances *would* one have died? There are, in principle, infinitely many

---

[2] Epicurus' thesis that "death is nothing to us" is defended in his Letter to Monoeceus (see translation by Robert Drew Hicks, available at http://classics.mit.edu/Epicurus/menoec.html; accessed April 30, 2020).

[3] For a classic statement, see Thomas Nagel (1970).

[4] Steven Luper proposes, to the contrary, that death harms us just as we are about to cease existing (Luper 2009, chapter 6). Some contend that the harm of death to the decedent occurs posthumously. See, e.g., Ben Bradley (2004).

possibilities. If Fuki had not died from complications of the coronavirus when she did, she might have died from complications of the coronavirus the next day, in which case she only lost one day of life. Or, if we imagine counterfactually that Fuki never caught the virus, she still might have died from a car accident on the day on which she actually died from the virus. Or, instead, maybe she would have died from cancer two years later. Or perhaps she would have lived for decades and died of more ordinary causes.

As Jeff McMahan notes in a probing investigation of this problem, in dealing with such uncertainty we intuitively consider what seems *most likely* to have happened, had a particular death not occurred; we also zero in on some salient factor such as whether or not the victim acquired a particular fatal disease or was involved in a particular accident or kind of accident (McMahan 2002, chapter 2). I will adopt this general way of thinking about the relevant counterfactual associated with a particular death (while acknowledging that it leaves many questions unanswered). In the case of Fuki, I imagine that she is a generally healthy person with an ordinary life expectancy who never catches the coronavirus and does not have terrible luck. On that basis, I assume that, had she not died from the virus' effects at the age of thirty, she would have lived about fifty more years—suggesting that her premature death constitutes a terrible instrumental harm to her.

Note that in Fuki's case I am assuming that, had she not died when she did, she would have lived to about the age of life expectancy, roughly eighty years. That seems to be a reasonable guess or stipulation. But what is an appropriate counterfactual for someone who reached that age, or beyond, before dying? That will depend on the circumstances. Someone who reaches age eighty in excellent health while living in a safe neighborhood might have a life expectancy of ten or more years. Such a person who dies in a car crash at age eighty might lose out on a decade of life, much of it of good quality—a fairly sizable loss. By contrast, someone who has several significant health problems who dies of cardiac arrest at eighty might not have missed much had he avoided that particular heart attack. Such reflections as these can illuminate how much harm a particular death involves.

A distinct issue, one central to the present discussion, is normative: What is the *appropriate attitude to have about one's own eventual death* on the assumption that one will reach (or already has reached) life expectancy? Just as we need some baseline for determining how much one has been harmed by a particular death, it would help to have a baseline for determining what one's attitude should be about one's own death. The baseline I will suggest in the next section is normative and therefore distinct from the descriptive matter of what is most likely to have happened, counterfactually, had a particular death not occurred.

One more assumption before advancing to my principal arguments. Although I appreciate that human life can sometimes be of very low quality and that some people do not value their continued existence, for the purposes of this discussion I assume what I take to be the more typical situation: That a given person values her continued life for her own sake and that it is good for her to continue living. The point of this assumption is not to overgeneralize from what I take to be typically true, but rather to address only those cases that are typical in the respect just mentioned. It is about this category of cases, I think, that my position has something interesting to say.

A Normative Baseline

Suppose Mario has reached age eighty-five with a very decent quality of life but far from perfect health. He knows there is a fair chance of dying, one way or another, in the next five years and a very high chance of dying within the next decade. What should his attitude be toward his own inevitable death? To answer this question, it will help to have a standard, or baseline, by which to evaluate his situation and, thereby, his attitude toward his situation.

I suggest, as a general baseline, what we can reasonably hope for as human beings, given the actual state of the world (including human physiology and the current state of medical technology) at the relevant time. On this basis I suggest, more specifically, that we should not fear a death that occurs after one has lived a life of good overall quality that reaches or surpasses life expectancy.[5] (Here, in referring to quality of life, I remain largely agnostic as to how particular subjects will, or should, construe what constitutes a good life for them. Some, for example, might understand a good life primarily in terms of enjoyments and satisfaction; others might give a greater place to achievement and meaningful relationships whether or not they bring enjoyment or satisfaction.) The approach I favor implies that Mario should at least try not to fear his own death. I don't mean that he shouldn't take care to stay alive by living in a healthy, relatively safe manner; I mean, rather, that he should not regard his mortality with despair, as something terrible. Yes, he is in a position to live longer with a decent quality of life. But it doesn't follow that he should regard the possibility that he will die sooner rather than later as a terrifying monstrosity captured in the image of the Grim Reaper. Death, for someone in a position like Mario's, is something to be accepted more than railed against.

My reflections suggest a thesis that may strike the reader as highly counter-intuitive: A younger person, say in middle age, who is living a life that is of good quality by her own lights should *welcome ageing*. Why? Because with the passing of time she moves closer and closer to attaining all she may reasonably hope for from a prudential standpoint. Her overarching prudential hope, if she

---

[5] Cf. the ideas of Jeffrie Murphy, who argues that it is rational to fear "premature death" rather than death in general (Murphy 1976).

is sensible, is to live a life of good quality and of a decent length. If her life is going well, then with each birthday she steps closer to achieving this overarching goal. So, instead of fretting over having less time left, as we get older, we should increasingly appreciate the good life we are having. We should be pleased to age and advance closer to a full life of decent quality.

There are a couple of ways to challenge my claim that the appropriate normative baseline for comparing any actual life that ends is a life of decent quality that reaches life expectancy. Both claim that accepting this baseline involves settling for too little. One challenge asserts that the *quality* of human life is objectively bad, contrary to my aforementioned assumption that our lives are often of good quality and something to be satisfied with. The other challenge agrees with my assumption that human life can be good but rejects my setting the baseline of reasonable *quantity* at life expectancy: the more good life, the better, according to this view, so we have reason to fear any death that ends a life of good quality. I take up these very different challenges in turn.

Against the Invocation of Super-Human Standards of Evaluation

In his fascinating book, *Better Never to Have Been,* David Benatar advances two major arguments for the thesis that it is always a bad thing to bring a new human being into the world (Benatar 2006). One argument, which appeals to various alleged asymmetries of value pertaining to population ethics, concerns the ethics of procreation and is not directly relevant to the present discussion.[6] The other argument, which focuses on the quality of human life, is quite relevant.

According to Benatar, while most people value their lives and generally prefer their continuation to dying, it would be a mistake to infer that their lives are prudentially good. Only if they fail to pay sufficient attention to what is happening to them in hedonistic or desire-satisfaction terms or use overly low standards, he argues, can they believe their lives are going well (Benatar 2006, chapter 3). The portion of his argument that most interests me here is the idea of using overly low standards. Benatar thinks that, when people evaluate their own well-being, they often compare themselves to other people and think they are doing well if they are meeting typical *human* standards—involving such factors as close personal relationships, achievement, enjoyment, and self-determination. But to invoke such human-typical standards is to remain mired in human mediocrity, as it were, to the extent that if we want to assess our well-being in terms of an objective list of goods, we should consider what a good life is sub specie aeternitatis—from the point of view of the universe (Benatar 2006,

---

[6] For my detailed replies to Benatar's arguments, see DeGrazia (2010) and DeGrazia (2012, 143–50).

82). According to Benatar, we should distrust our collective human sense of what makes a human being well-off.

In my view, this approach to evaluating our well-being is misguided. First, it may well lie beyond our capacities us to conceptualize value from the point of view of the universe, utterly divorced from a human perspective. If so, then the present approach affords us no tools with which to engage in prudential evaluation. Second, why should we even try to think of our well-being from the point of view of the universe? It strikes me as so much more sensible to evaluate how we are faring by reference to standards that *resonate* with us, that are responsive to what sorts of creatures we are. When we do so, it makes sense that we ordinarily value our lives and prefer their continuation over their termination. We tend to find prudential value, sources of well-being, in various aspects of our lives; and, even when we don't, we often value the opportunity to turn things around and get closer to where we want to be.

Recall our context: we are looking for an appropriate normative baseline for evaluating one's own inevitable death to determine whether, or to what extent, it is something to be feared, desperately staved off, resented for its inevitability, and so on. I contend that one should not have such negative attitudes about death if one has already lived (or expects to live) a life of decent quality that has reached (or will reach) life expectancy. Benatar's reasoning suggests that, because human life is never really of good quality, we are never in a position to feel satisfied with our lives. My reply is to reject the super-human standard of evaluation that underlies the pessimistic assertion about the quality of human life.

Against an Avaricious Attitude about the Quantity of (Decent) Life

A second challenge to my proposed normative baseline accepts that human life is often decent and well worth continuing, but denies that reaching life expectancy is good enough: Because more life of decent quality is always better than less life of decent quality, we have reason to regard death as a dreadful harm whenever it occurs in circumstances in which more good life was a possibility. A possibility by what standard? Let's assume, for the sake of discussion, this standard: A possibility given some of the actual lives that people are having at the time in question. So, even if Kai has had a very decent life as he lies comprehendingly on his deathbed at age 85, instead of being stoical about his impending demise he has good reason to lament that he isn't one of those lucky few who live to 100 with a decent quality of life.

To my mind, such an attitude is avaricious, overly grasping. I find it considerably less reasonable, and wise, than the semi-stoical attitude that says, "Having had a very decent and relatively long life, which is all I could reasonably hope for, I'm content for this good life to end soon." Why is this attitude more reasonable than the avaricious one? Part of my answer is that its standard is within the reach of many people, given the sorts of beings we are as well as our present technologies and circumstances.

One might reply that my reasoning is circular, or question-begging, in assuming that some widely accessible standard is preferable to one that only a few people can meet. Maybe so. Perhaps it will help to point out that those who have already reached life expectancy with a good quality of life can hardly count themselves unlucky—at least in comparison with most people—and that to be satisfied only by being among the exceptionally lucky is to embrace a standard that, logically, cannot be universally adopted. In other words, there is something very odd in advocating for a standard so high that it would make no sense for most people to adopt it (since most people cannot be among the lucky few).

This, however, hardly settles the matter. One might reply, "Just as an Olympic athlete can hope to be among the best at her event, and a lottery ticket buyer can hope to win a massive payoff, I—who am now 85 and in strong health—can hope to live to 100 with a high quality of life, and may consider any earlier death to be a dreadful misfortune." At this point, my only response to such an attitude is to say that it seems, to me anyway, very unwise. Adoption of such a standard would predictably lead to disappointment and perhaps despair for the vast majority of people who adopt it. What a waste of psychological energy. Better to set a more modest standard in keeping with the sorts of beings we are and with our present circumstances so that one has a decent chance of arriving at death's doorstep without railing against one's fate.

But what if someone has surpassed life expectancy—let's say she's eighty-five—but is on the verge of completing her magnum opus when she dies? In fact, she knew she would die a few days before she did. Compare her with her cousin, who only lived to seventy-five but achieved all he wanted to achieve before dying. Assume both enjoyed lives of decent quality. Can we really claim that she should accept her impending death, having surpassed life expectancy, whereas he would have had more reason to fear his death because he never reached life expectancy? Many would find this counterintuitive.[7]

Several points are worth making here. First, both individuals lived fairly long lives even if one fell short of life expectancy. Second, if the man who lived to seventy-five was quite satisfied with his life whereas the woman felt that her life was incomplete unless she finished the magnum opus, then we should seriously consider the possibility that, while both lives were of decent quality (as stipulated), the quality of his life was significantly higher. (This seems especially likely if one accepts a broadly subjective account of well-being according to which happiness or life-satisfaction is central.) If so, this higher quality of life can compensate to some extent for a smaller amount of decent-quality life. Notice that I have not argued that everyone with a decent

---

[7] Thanks to Christopher Wareham for bringing this issue to my attention.

quality of life who might not make it to life expectancy should fear that prospect. Rather, I argued that those who make it to life expectancy with a decent quality of life should not rail against death but should, instead, be relatively accepting of it.

The challenge that remains is the idea that the eighty-five-year-old facing her demise without finishing her magnum opus has good grounds for fearing, dreading, or resenting her death. Maybe a properly developed account should accommodate this judgment. One might say that while her death at eighty-five is hardly tragic—considering her many years of decent-quality life—it is disappointing given what was just slightly out of reach. I leave that possibility open— along with how, precisely, one might amend my account to make room for such a judgment. But I would also recommend that, if possible, people not hinge their hopes for a deeply satisfying life on something that might not come to fruition until a very old age. In cases in which someone has already enjoyed great achievements and has a grasping attitude toward *just one more* great achievement, he is probably aiming for more than one can reasonably hope for, contrary to my normative baseline.

Suppose one is sympathetic to my arguments thus far. One might wonder why I defend a *semi-stoical* standard, which favors contentment with a decent-quality life that meets life expectancy, rather than a *thoroughly stoical* standard that recommends contentment with a decent-quality life of any length at all—or maybe even a life of any quality of any length! One might, after all, emphasize that we are mortal creatures who are necessarily vulnerable to accidents, disease, and the evil others would do to us no matter how much we attempt to protect ourselves. This depiction of us, I must admit, is accurate. Yet, while we could be radically stoical and accept anything bad that happens to us that we cannot control, as Epictetus and other ancient Stoics recommended, I am inclined to concede somewhat more to human nature and, in particular, to our nearly universal desire to live a complete life.[8] Such a life creates opportunities for us to do much that we value. And hoping for a life that reaches average life expectancy seems reasonable rather than either avaricious or, like the radically stoical approach, overly guarded.

Allow me to admit that I am not entirely confident of my position. Sometimes I suspect that Epictetus was right that we should not vex ourselves about anything that is beyond our control, meaning, in his view, anything outside our own attitudes.[9] Indeed, it may be optimistic of Epictetus to think we have all that much control, ultimately, over our own attitudes! Nevertheless, I am only prepared to defend the more modest, semi-stoical attitude that we should hope for no more than a life of decent quality that reaches life expectancy.

[8] Here my attitude is more in keeping with Aristotle's view of human flourishing (Irwin 1999).
[9] See Epictetus (2008).

Overcoming Cosmic Narcissism

In the previous section I defended my semi-stoical position by reference to what we can reasonably hope for in living a life and forestalling death. If it is on the right track, this argument suggests that many of us should be more relaxed about the prospect of dying in our advanced years than people often are. It also suggests that, in the meantime, we should welcome ageing if our lives are going well because, by ageing, we move closer to having a good and full life.

My second argument for a semi-stoical attitude about ageing and death appeals to the wisdom of overcoming our tendency toward "cosmic narcissism." Natural selection made human beings, by nature, extremely keen on surviving. Our psychologies encourage this thought: "I am enormously important, so important that my survival is imperative."[10] From a cosmic perspective, this is implausible.

If you doubt that this is implausible, consider that astronomers learned in 2016 that there are at least 2 trillion galaxies (Conselice et al. 2016)—and our galaxy alone contains 100 billion stars (Howell 2018). If our galaxy has an average number of stars (a reasonable working assumption, as far as I know), then there are at least two hundred thousand thousand thousand thousand thousand thousand thousand stars. Currently, on our planet, there are about seven and a half billion living human beings and probably trillions of other sentient animals. Given how many stars there are in the universe, even a very conservative estimate of what proportion of stars have planets with conscious life on them is likely to entail that the universe is teeming with conscious, intelligent, meaning-seeking creatures. This may induce us to accept a more realistic view of our cosmic unimportance.

So, instead of thinking, "I am extremely important," each of us should think more realistically, "I am not the center of the universe, and everything of value in life and existence will continue on without me, even if not within me." For example, human life will continue when one of us dies. So will an enormous variety of nonhuman animal and plant lives. There will still be, in addition, beautiful mountains, and canyons, and rainbows, even if one is not around to see them. But what if the Earth is destroyed by an enormous collision or some other destructive event? Even then, presumably, intelligent and conscious life will continue in other parts of the universe, and there will continue to be keen minds, loving affection, beautiful settings, and whatever

---

[10] Of course, not all human beings have this attitude. My claim is that human nature, as fashioned by natural selection, includes a very strong tendency to think in these egoistic terms, since such thinking generally increases the likelihood of survival and passing on one's genes. It is noteworthy both that people suffering from depression often do not maintain this egoistic attitude and that depression is a mental disorder that departs from human-typical functioning.

else we think has value. From an egoistic perspective, one's own life and flourishing are extremely important. But the egoistic perspective is not exactly objective; nor is it broad. It is as subjective and as narrow as one can imagine. Those observations seem to recommend the adoption of a bigger-picture perspective from which the demise of one of us is not such a big deal.

Concluding Reflections

If we step out of our egoistic perspectives, overcoming our tendency toward cosmic narcissism, each of us can see that she is not the center of the universe and that her death is not that big a deal in the scheme of things. "But wait," one might respond. "Doesn't abandoning the egoistic perspective, while possibly liberating us from the notion that our deaths are terrible misfortunes, also suggest that the goods in our lives aren't very important? And, if that's correct, how can you support your thesis that we should welcome ageing if things are going well for us?"

Good questions. My response is that I do not recommend entirely abandoning the prudential perspective from which our well-being necessarily matters, and replacing it with the most objective, cosmic perspective of which we are capable. Rather, I recommend embracing both perspectives, which are, after all, both real. When thinking about our own lives and deaths prudentially, we should not hope for more than what we can reasonably expect. Therefore, I think, we should be content if we have good lives that reach life expectancy and not fret if we can't have more. We should also remember and sometimes adopt, I suggest, the broader perspective from which one's own life is just one among many, just one instantiation of stuff that matters, so that the extinguishing of this life has little effect on what matters in the universe, including the varieties of life within it. If we work with both perspectives, it may be fairly easy to achieve the semi-stoical attitude about ageing and death that I have championed. And, if we achieve that, we may be able to enjoy what time we have more fully and with greater contentment and peace.[11,]

[11] Cf. Gregory Pence (2019).

Part II

Ageing and Morality

8 Personhood across the Lifespan

Søren Holm

Introduction

Human beings are biological organisms who come into existence as definite entities with a numerical identity[1] at fertilisation and exit existence as living biological organisms at the time of death. However, human beings are typically more than mere biological organisms. They are persons with an inner psychological life, and they are social and narrative actors enmeshed in, and co-creating a complex social network, a social world, and a personal narrative. All of these aspects of a human being have potential implications for the 'moral status' of that human entity, where moral status is shorthand for describing the totality of the moral implications that flow from the characteristics of a particular entity in relation to how other moral agents should consider the entity.

In the bioethical literature emerging since the 1960s in the analytical and pragmatist traditions,[2] it has become common to link *full moral status*, the status possessed by the average adult human being, to the possession of (full) personhood. Let us call this position 'personhood theory'. Because of the prominence of personhood theory in contemporary bioethics, it becomes important to analyse how personhood changes across the lifespan and the implications of such changes. This is complicated enough in itself, but is further complicated by the intersection of questions about personhood and questions about personal identity, which has been present and problematised from the very beginning of personhood theory. Can someone who has become a person, in terms of personhood theory, change personal identity and become a different person, in terms of personal identity, and what are the implications of such changes?

This chapter will first outline the main elements of personhood and discuss the main complications and criticisms of personhood theory. It will then outline the main approaches to the question of the basis of personal identity. Because of the size of the literature on these topics, the exposition will

---

[1] See the section 'Personal identity' for a slight complication in relation to this claim regarding numerical identity.

[2] When used without a modifier, 'bioethics' means 'bioethics in the analytical and pragmatist tradition' in this chapter.

necessarily be selective and not exhaustive. The latter part of the chapter will then proceed to analyse different possible approaches to personhood across the lifespan and the ethical implications they raise.

Personhood Theory

The idea that what matters in ascribing rights to a human being or defining our obligations towards a human being, the basis for ascribing such rights and obligations, is whether or not that being is a 'person' can be traced back in the history of philosophy to John Locke, or earlier.[3] But, given Locke's position in the Canon of Anglo-American moral and political philosophy, the line of 'apostolic' philosophical succession is usually anchored in Locke's definition of person as a forensic term and his linkage of 'the self' to personhood:

... to find wherein personal Identity consists, we must consider what Person stands for; which, I think, is a thinking intelligent Being, that has reason and reflection, and can consider it self as it self, the same thinking thing in different times and places; which it does only by that consciousness, which is inseparable from thinking, and as it seems to me essential to it: It being impossible for any one to perceive, without perceiving, that he does perceive. (Locke 1975, E.II.xxvii.9)

Self, the first-person aspect of personhood, is defined as that conscious thinking thing, (whatever Substance, made up of whether Spiritual, or Material, Simple, or Compounded, it matters not) which is sensible, or conscious of Pleasure and Pain, capable of Happiness or Misery, and so is concern'd for it self, as far as that consciousness extends. (Locke 1975, EII.xxvii.17)

In its modern form, a recognisable personhood theory is probably first put forward by the Episcopal moral theologian Joseph Fletcher in his book 'Morals and Medicine' in 1954 (Fletcher 1954), and later expanded into the 1972 article 'Indicators of Humanhood: A Tentative Profile of Man',[4] published in the second volume of the *Hastings Center Report*, one of the first bioethics journals (Fletcher 1972). Fletcher's fifteen positive and five negative indicators of personhood are complex, and do not follow straightforwardly from any particular ethical theory.

Fletcher's complicated approach to personhood does not seem to have any direct descendants in the literature, but the underlying idea was taken up by a number of influential early bioethicists developing personhood accounts based on a variety of ethical theories, or in ways that are ostensibly theory agnostic or theory independent. We thus have slightly different accounts, such

[3] Hobbes might be claimed to hold a (proto-)personhood theory, and questions of what we would now conceptualise as 'moral status' are important in the general development of the concepts of autonomy and self-determination and their importance as ethical concepts (Schneewind 1998).

[4] At which time Fletcher had left Christianity and become agnostic.

as the ones developed by Jonathan Glover (1977) and Peter Singer (1975) based on preference consequentialism, Michael Tooley (1983) based on an interest theory of rights, H. Tristram Engelhardt (1986) based on a version of secular libertarianism,[5] and John Harris (1985), ostensibly simply from the question, 'what makes it wrong to kill an adult human being like you or me?'[6] The different theoretical starting points give rise to different accounts of exactly why personhood is connected to moral status, but the accounts of the state of personhood itself and the criteria for personhood are remarkably similar. All the accounts claim that the basis for ascription of personhood to an entity has to be something that is intrinsic to that entity and that it has to be a particular cognitive state or ability that the entity possesses at the time of ascription. This may be valuing future life, having an interest in future life, choosing continued life, understanding oneself as the subject living a life, or having an understanding of moral agency.

Personhood theory has potentially controversial implications across the lifespan, but significant initial attention was paid to questions about the moral status of the human embryo and foetus. At the time of the development of modern personhood theory, the question of the ethical permissibility of elective abortion was an active area of philosophical investigation, and the question of the legalisation of elective abortion a live political issue in many countries. The personhood approach seems to offer a definite and straightforward answer to the philosophical question, and an answer which has immediate legal applicability. The answer being that embryos and foetuses do not intrinsically possess the characteristic(s) necessary for full moral status, and that it is therefore not intrinsically wrong to kill an embryo or foetus (Kuhse and Singer 1985).[7]

Personhood theory also seems to offer relatively straightforward, albeit potentially controversial, answers to important questions about the ethical permissibility of infanticide, treatment withdrawal in cases such as patients in persistent vegetative states, voluntary euthanasia, resource allocation in health care, research without consent, and may other core bioethics questions.

Personhood Theory Questioned

The criticisms of personhood theory arise from at least three different concerns about the theory and its implications: 1) its focus on *full* moral status to the

---

[5] Although in the second edition of his book he laments not being able to say more on a secular basis, since he knows that these secular conclusions are fundamentally wrong following his conversion to Orthodox Christianity.

[6] This is not an exhaustive list of personhood theorists, but it does contain some of the most influential early proponents of the personhood approach to moral status.

[7] It might still be seriously wrong for reasons relating to factors extrinsic to the embryo or foetus, e.g., that the parents value the embryo or foetus and that killing it would harm and/or wrong the parents.

exclusion of other levels or kinds of moral status; 2) its counter-intuitive implications in certain cases; and 3) its theoretical underpinnings. The last two concerns are often combined, and the counter-intuitive implications are seen as being caused by problems with the theoretical underpinnings. It does, for instance follow straightforwardly from personhood theory that early infanticide is not intrinsically morally problematic (Kuhse and Singer 1985), and this has been claimed to be both highly counter-intuitive and a strong indication that the personhood approach is deficient. Some have even claimed that the defence of infanticide as not intrinsically wrong constitutes a *reductio ad absurdum* of personhood theory (Langerak 1979; Rodger et al. 2018). In the following, I will concentrate on the first and third concern, since an enumeration and explication of putative counter-intuitive implications is not likely to be particularly philosophically illuminating.

The first concern about and criticism of personhood theory is that it largely ignores the possibility of gradations in moral status both below and above the level of 'full moral status'. Even if we accept that the basis for moral status has to be an intrinsic property of the entity in question, there are arguably many different intrinsic properties that can give rise to a claim for moral consideration. And it is therefore conceptually possible that there can be levels or types of moral status that are lower than the full moral status possessed by persons, and levels or types that are higher. There could also be types of moral status that would not fit into the same hierarchy of statuses as the full moral status of persons. Lower moral status is not completely ignored by personhood theorists, either because they also work on the ethical issues around our relation to and use of animals (e.g., Peter Singer), or because they refer to animals in their arguments to exemplify the kind of entities that might have moral status of some kind, usually derived from sentience, but are not persons and therefore lack full moral status. The moral status of animals does receive sustained philosophical analysis in animal ethics, but this field of enquiry has gradually diverged from 'human bioethics' and cross-fertilisation of analysis and argument is now limited.

The issue of the (claimed) neglect of a full, in-depth analysis of the implications of 'lower moral status' also highlights the problem that it is not obvious that the kind of moral status that, for instance, arises from being sentient is less important than full moral status. This raises two questions. The first is whether the same set back to interests is ethically more important if it happens to a person. For instance, is it less important to protect a sentient non-person from experiencing severe suffering than protecting a person from experiencing the same suffering? The second is how to compare detriments to interests where one of these can only be held by persons, and the other interest is one that can also be held by non-persons. For instance, do interests of persons in self-determination always outweigh the experiential interests of sentient beings in not experiencing severe suffering? Some of these worries about taking proper account of all levels of moral status are not directed at the theory itself, but at the way it is commonly applied, because there is a tendency to elide full moral status and moral status, and write as if only those entities that have full moral status have any moral status.

The possibility of some entities having higher moral status than full moral status has been raised in relation to potential post- or transhuman entities with vastly superior cognitive abilities than humans have, but primarily in relation to the possible implications for political equality, or as a warning that such entities might treat humans as we treat animals or conceptualise their obligations to us primarily in terms of benign, paternalistic oversight (Wikler 2009). But the details of what *more than* full moral status might consist of and entail have not been the subject of sustained philosophical analysis.

There are many critiques of the theoretical underpinnings of personhood theory. They can be divided according to whether or not they accept the premise that moral status depends solely on properties that are intrinsic to the entity. Almost all of the critiques argue for an expansion of the set of entities that have full moral status, or sufficient moral status to make it wrong to kill them, beyond the entities identified by personhood theory.

The first set of critiques accept the premise that moral status depends solely on properties that are intrinsic to the entity, but argue that the set of properties that personhood theorists rely on is either too narrow a set, or the wrong properties. A common feature of this line of critique is the argument that the focus in personhood theory on presently occurring higher order cognitive abilities is too restrictive, for example the ability to know that you have a life and having a subjective interest in continuing that life. Many other properties have been argued to be intrinsic and sufficient for full moral status. They include properties like being human, having the potential for becoming a person (Holm 1996), having 'a life like ours' (Marquis 1989), and many others. Analysing each of these in detail is beyond the scope of this chapter, but it is important to note for present purposes that some entail that full moral status begins much earlier in the life of a human entity and some entail that it persists longer in cases where someone is alive but no longer a person according to personhood theory. The argumentative back-and-forth between this set of critics and personhood theorists is still ongoing, despite both sides believing that they have compelling, knock-down arguments against their opponents. Recent philosophically highly detailed contributions to the debate include books by McMahan (2002) and Eberl (2020).

The second set of critiques reject the premise that moral status depends solely on properties that are intrinsic to the entity. There are again many variants of this line of argument, but the common core of the critical aspect of the arguments is that personhood theory is far too simplistic in its focus on strictly individual properties. Human beings are not rugged, solitary individuals living in splendid isolation, and even fully solitary hermits will necessarily, given the inability of human infants and young children to sustain their own life, have been part of complex relationships before withdrawing into solitude and will have a personal narrative that is shaped by these relationships. What makes us persons, both in the literal, biological sense and morally, is, at least partly, our relationships. On the positive side of the argument, the idea that moral status and personhood is at least partly based in relational properties can be given a number of interpretations, either focussing on giving an account of those relational properties and their importance, or alternatively by developing a narrative account of human life. Both of these approaches can further be linked to arguments about the moral importance of (mutual) recognition. These approaches have intersections with feminist bioethics, care ethics, and com-munitarianism. It is impossible to give an exhaustive account of all of the different ways in which this can be worked out, but a good recent exemplar is Hilde Lindemann's book 'Holding and letting Go' (Lindemann 2014). In this book, she analyses issues of personhood and personal identity from a feminist, relational, and narrative perspective. According to Lindemann, our status as persons, our moral status, and our personal identity are not nearly as clearly defined or definable as much of the bioethical literature claims, for example in claims about personhood and full moral status being decidable according to one or a few criteria of cognitive function. Moral status and personal identity are necessarily complex, and one main factor of the complexity is that the status of a particular human being is influenced, and to some degree deter-mined, by how other actors act towards and interact with that human being. They can shape, support, promote, preserve, but also damage personhood and personal identity, partly through their ability to affect the personal narrative of the person. Lindemann argues that this creates ethical obligations to hold others with whom we have relationships in personhood by engaging construct-ively in the formation, development, or repair of their personal narrative. In the concluding chapter of her book, she describes her account in the following way:

Healthy specimens of our kind are inducted into personhood through the same social interactions by which we acquire our linguistic, rational, and moral agency. It's of the utmost importance that this be done, as we would otherwise be damaged, stunted, misshapen, unable—recall Kaspar Hauser—to live a human life.

To be held in personhood is to interact with other persons who recognize us as persons and respond accordingly. Much of this holding therefore has to do with the narratives we create or borrow from the common stock to make depictions of who a particular person is. These depictions are our personal identities; what they depict is the self, understood as the embodied locus of idiosyncratic causation and experience. Identities are the personae we perform in our dealings with others; they indicate how we are supposed to act and how we wish or expect to be treated. All persons have personal identities, even if they are incapable of contributing their own, first-person stories to the narrative tissue that represents them. But those who are capable of full participation in personhood act on the basis of the stories by which they understand who they are, the stories others use to make sense of who they are, and the stories they themselves contribute to others' identities.

Holding someone in personhood doesn't necessarily involve what I have been calling identity-work, as sometimes the simple recognition that someone is a person who is expressing a facet of her personality is enough to prompt a response. (Lindemann 2014, 202–3)

An important aspect of Lindemann's argument is that just as we have ethical obligations to hold others in personhood, we also have obligations to let them go. The dying must let go of the still living and the living must allow the dying to let go and to leave. She also points out that obligations to hold and to let go extend beyond death. The dead person still has a narrative and is still part of and entwined with the narrative of the living. In relation to the role of proxy decision-makers for the dying, she writes:

On my analysis, among the many tasks that a patient might have appointed a proxy to perform, one is holding onto the patient as the person they have known and cared about, making decisions that reflect that understanding of who the patient is. Presumably, it has mattered to the patient that his prehospitalization identity be maintained, since otherwise it's hard to see why he would have appointed a proxy in the first place. It can't be solely because he wants his experiential interests to be safeguarded, as those are the responsibility of the professional health care staff. And while it's true that prudence dictates having a family member or friend on hand to make sure the professionals are neither overzealous nor negligent in their care for the patient, that's not the proxy's primary duty. She is charged with making decisions, and even if the patient doesn't articulate it in so many words, he may have chosen her to do it or trusted her to do it because she is one of the people—perhaps the most important person—who has been holding the patient in his identity all along.

Holding, as we have seen, doesn't kick in just in case the patient is permanently incapable of exercising his own autonomy, which is when, under the law, the proxy is empowered to make decisions for the patient. Holding has usually been going on for years, and it can be a matter of great moral importance to patient and proxy alike that the proxy makes sure it continues to go on to the very end of the patient's life. (Lindemann 2014, 176–7)

There are also hybrid accounts of moral status that take elements from both personhood theory and the critiques of that theory. The most prominent and worked-out is probably the multi-criterial account presented in great detail by Mary Anne Warren in her 1997 book *Moral Status: Obligations to Persons and Other Living Things*. Warren presents a multi-criterial analysis of moral status that takes account of both intrinsic and extrinsic properties of a particular living being (Warren 1997). She argues that there are seven principles that determine the moral status of a particular entity and that these principles are linked to both intrinsic and relational properties of the entity in question. The seven principles and the properties that justify their role in determining moral status are:

1. The Respect for Life Principle – Life
2. The Anti-Cruelty Principle – Sentience
3. The Agent's Rights Principle – Moral agency
4. The Human Rights Principle – Being a sentient human being
5. The Ecological Principle – Ecological importance of species
6. The Interspecific Principle – Being a non-human member of a mixed human and non-human social community
7. The Transitivity of Respect Principle – Respecting the moral status attributions made by other moral agents

Let us call this 'Warren's scheme'. Adult human beings would usually score highly on criteria 1–4 and 7 in Warren's scheme, but criterion 6 would not be applicable and they might score quite low or perhaps even zero on criterion 5 since the ecological impact of the human species is probably negative overall. However, fulfilling the criteria 1–4 will ensure that the typical adult human being possesses the rights[8] that are entailed by full moral status according to personhood theory, for example the rights not to be killed, not to be tortured, to have self-determination, etc. And, fulfilling criteria 1, 2, and 4 will entail possession of basic human rights, even though it does not amount to personhood according to personhood theory. According to Warren's scheme, many animals will have a very significant moral status that is not just derived from their being sentient and thereby able to have positive and negative experiential states. It is important to note that Warren's scheme is multi-dimensional. It is not a simple step-wise scheme where moral status is purely additive and where there is a fixed sequence of 'moral status development'. The moral status of a human entity at a certain state of development is, for instance, not fully accounted for by a sequence of life–sentience–moral agency, where each step adds a little more moral status.

Personal Identity

According to most accounts of identity, a human being has numerical identity as a biological entity across the lifespan from fertilisation to death, and potentially even beyond in those cases where the body is preserved. There are complications to this simple relationship of numerical identity at the very beginning of individual life, since monozygotic twinning, which involves the

---

[8] I am making the point in terms of rights, but it could be made using different moral vocabularies, e.g., in terms of protection of interests, or claims to be considered morally.

fission of the early embryo, can occur up to about fourteen days after fertilisation, leading to two individuals emerging from one fertilised egg[9] (Mauron 1996). And, there are complications when slightly later fission of the early embryo occurs, leading to the birth of Siamese twins. Let us set these complications about numerical identity aside for the moment, since they are less relevant to the potentially problematic intersection between accounts of personhood and accounts of personal identity. The problems caused by the intersection are caused not by uncertainty about numerical identity, but by uncertainties about personal, qualitative identity. What are the identity criteria for a person at time t and a person at time $t+x$ being the same person? In daily talk we are perfectly conversant with the idea that someone's personality can change to such a degree that they are no longer the same person as they were before, and in the literature there are a number of ostensible real life examples discussed, perhaps most prominently the case of Phineas Gage, who changed personality after surviving having a tamping iron shot through his brain in 1848. Apparently, 'his mind was radically changed, so decidedly that his friends and acquaintances said he was "no longer Gage"'[10] (Harlow 1868, 340).

In bioethics, much of the discussion of personal identity has taken its point of departure as that in Derek Parfit's analysis in *Reasons and Persons*, where he argues, through a number of thought experiments involving brain splitting and mishaps during tele-transportation, that what matters for qualitative, personal identity is not biological or bodily identity, but overlapping chains of memories (Parfit 1984). A person at point t is identical to a person at a previous point $t-x$ if, and only if, we can trace unbroken chains of memories through all of the time point between $t-x$ and t. The person does not now have to have any memories of $t-x$, but the overlapping chain of memories linking $t-x$ and t must be such that, if we take only one intermediate point ti into account, the person at ti must have at least one memory of $t-x$ and the person at t at least one memory of ti or an earlier timepoint.

A Parfitian account of personal identity means that it is possible for one biological human entity to successively instantiate several different persons in the sense that they fulfil the criteria for personhood, but at the same time have different personal identities. This can happen when the overlapping chain of memories is broken, but the entities on both sides of the break possess the characteristic(s) that make them persons, for example both entities understand that they have a life and want to continue that life. The Parfitian account, however, also entails that it is possible that a change in personal identity coincides with a change in moral status, in cases where the change involves such changes in cognitive function that the entity before the change was

---

[9] Fusion of two early embryos into one chimaeric embryo can also happen, but is rarer.

[10] The precise nature, extent, and persistence of the changes to Gage's personality are disputed (Damasio 1994).

a person with full moral status, but the entity after the change is no longer a person in this sense but is still what we could call a 'social person', that is, someone who is part of reciprocal, personal social relationships. In the literature this is, for instance, claimed to happen in some cases of dementia.

The issues that arise for personhood theory if it is possible for a human being to change personal identity after they have become a person are primarily around what authority decisions made by the past person A have in relation to decisions to be made about the current person B, where these have different personal identities. This question has some practical importance in relation to whether or not advance directives should be seen as binding or not, and in relation to whether decision-makers should take account of preferences previously expressed by someone who is no longer competent to make decisions about themselves. In the literature a focal point for this discussion has been Ronald Dworkin's discussion in 'Life's Dominion' of variations on the case of Margo (Dworkin 1994),[11] based on a real case first reported in the *Journal of the American Medical Association* (Firlik 1991). In Dworkin's retelling and repurposing of the case, Margo has dementia but is happy in and with the life she leads and the pleasures it contains. She develops pneumonia and a decision has to be made concerning whether she should be treated with antibiotics. But, Dworkin's Margo has previously executed an advance directive that specifies that she does not want treatment in this kind of situation. Should we decide to treat Margo or not?[12] Dworkin argues that what he labels the 'critical interests' of the competent Margo about how she wants her life to go should outweigh the merely 'experiential interests' of the current Margo who can no longer form critical interests because of her dementia, and that we should therefore follow the advance directive and withhold treatment. But this conclusion is problematic if Margo is still a person with full rights despite her cognitive decline, which many of the critics of personhood theory will hold. And also, perhaps paradoxically, problematic if the current Margo with dementia is no longer qualitatively identical with the former Margo who had the critical interests. Whether or not the current Margo is a person, it is not clear why the former Margo should have any special decision-making powers in relation to the current Margo if they are not identical.

Personhood across the Lifespan: Issues and Implications

According to what is now the standard approach to personhood in bioethics, all human beings begin life as non-persons and most go on to become persons some time after birth, with the exact time differing between the different variants of personhood theory according to when the theoretically derived criteria for

[11] A Google Scholar search with the keywords 'Dworkin Margo' produces about 1,700 results.
[12] For an insightful and very influential critical discussion, see Dresser (1995).

personhood are fulfilled. Some human beings never become persons, either because they cease to exist before personhood can be attained or they never develop sufficiently to fulfil the personhood criteria. According to some conceptions, it is possible for a human being to live a long life without ever becoming a full person, despite in some cases developing a recognisable personality.

At the other end of the lifespan a human being may lose personhood, or enter a state of uncertain personhood, but still keep on living. As discussed above, a human being may also possibly retain personhood, but change personal identity and become a different person.

As outlined above, many of the alternatives to personhood theory entail one or more of the following conclusions that are at variance to personhood theory: that human beings become persons some time before birth or at birth, that all born human beings are persons, that no human being who is a person stops being a person before death, or that a person who experiences themselves as losing their personhood can be held in personhood by others.

In the following, we will focus on what can be said about the personhood and moral status of the old. Personhood theory and the concept of a person seem to have major implications for how we should treat the old.

Let us begin by considering the case of someone who follows the typical human trajectory and becomes a person early in life and maintains that personhood into adulthood. The first thing it is important to note is that most humans never lose the intrinsic cognitive abilities that are criteria for full moral status according to personhood theory, or only lose them very shortly before they die, in the agonal phase of dying. Even among the very old it is a minority that experience such a severe cognitive decline that the question of whether they still meet the criteria for being persons arises. The UK prevalence estimate of severe dementia is, for instance, only 24.2% for those aged 95 and over (Alzheimer's Society 2014, 34). So, most old people are persons with full moral status, irrespective of which particular account of personhood we find most philosophically defensible and compelling, and discussion about the rights of the old or the protection of their interests, for instance in relation to rights to health care, have to proceed on the basis that their rights are equal to those held by the young.

However, some people will lose personhood as defined by personhood theory and will therefore no longer have full moral status. Their moral status therefore very significantly diminishes according to personhood theory. It may no longer be intrinsically wrong to kill them, and their moral status might be on a par with other merely sentient beings. Here personhood theory diverges from many of the critical accounts, which either entail that all of these people continue to be persons with full moral status, or that we have an obligation to hold them in personhood, or that although their status is no longer that of full moral status they still have very significant moral status. This divergence has implications for those end-of-life decisions that involve intentional killings or withholdings of treatment with the primary intention of letting the person die. The alternative accounts entail that intentionally killing or letting die is a no less serious moral issue for this class of persons, and that the main factors involved in making such a decision continue to be the best interests of the persons themselves.

The divergence also has implications for how we should account for their interests when these interests are balanced against the interests of others. As described above, many applications of personhood theory proceed as if the interests of non-persons are less valuable than the interests of persons. This is not in any way obviously true if the interests are the same, but it is nevertheless often implicitly assumed or explicitly stated in argument. However, if these people are persons just like you or me, their interests cannot be discounted a priori but must be given equal weight.

If personhood and full moral status are threshold concepts, there may be situations where someone's personhood and moral status fluctuates because their cognitive state fluctuates. This problem is usually circumvented by claiming that those who are persons do not lose personhood as long as their *capacity* for personhood is intact; for example, a person does not lose personhood when they are sleeping or anaesthetised, because their capacity to surpass the criteria for personhood is intact and can be actualised when they wake up. This is perhaps a convincing answer for sleep, anaesthesia, and perhaps even temporary unconsciousness, but it becomes problematic in two situations both involving uncertainty. The first is when there is uncertainty about whether a person with diminished consciousness will wake up, and if so in what state. We can perhaps solve this with a reliance on some principle of precaution, but it is not always obvious what way precaution lies. The second is when the fluctuations are part of a downward general trend in cognitive function, where we cannot be certain about whether any particular fluctuation is the one that will finally end in permanent loss of personhood and full moral status.

The underlying philosophical problem in both situations is that because 'capacity' is used in these arguments to point to something the person intrinsically possesses at all relevant time points, in contradistinction to a 'potentiality' that points to possessing something in the future, the presence or absence of the capacity can only be detected in a situation where the person can be brought (back) to a state where they ought to be able to show evidence of a particular cognitive function and either can or cannot show that functioning. There will thus be many situations where we can only determine the point at which someone became a non-person retrospectively, and only long after it happened, because we cannot ascertain whether their *capacity* for personhood still persists. Brief episodes of lucidity can occur in patients with severe dementia (Normann et al. 2006), and research has shown that even patients diagnosed as being in a persistent vegetative state may still be conscious.[13]

---

[13] See Owen (2019) for a review of the literature.

The issues in determining with reasonable certainty when someone ceases to be a person while they are continuing to live indicate that even if personhood theory is correct, it might be less useful as a way of understanding and deciding on moral status at the end of life than it is at the beginning of life. The old are also typically participating in many more and more complex relationships and narratives than the embryo or the foetus, and therefore typically possess many more extrinsic value-conferring attributes than human beings at the very beginning of life. Even if, according to personhood theory, some of the old may no longer possess the intrinsic properties that make them persons, they may therefore still be valuable and valued in themselves. Which, again, tends to indicate that the implications of personhood theory and its focus on full moral status may, if all that is morally relevant is taken into account, significantly underestimate the moral importance of the old, whether or not they are strictly speaking persons according to personhood theory.

Coda

It is perhaps worth noting that although almost all bioethicists are committed to the formal equality of the old, or at the very least the formal equality of all old *persons*, and thereby to the in-principle view that they have equal moral status to the young (persons), this does not necessarily entail that the old are valued equally. The implicit anthropology of bioethics undoubtedly sees the young adult at the peak of their power as the paradigm moral agent, and old age as a negative deviation from that state (Holm 2013, 2016, 2020). The old are often lumped together in a group and argued to have less of what matters in relation to a particular ethical issue: less life, fewer life years, less quality of life, less social contribution, etc. When conceived of in that way, it does not help the old much that 'everyone counts as one and no one as more than one' if the counting is in reality a counting of items that intrinsically devalue the old, their lives, and their contributions.

9 African and East Asian Perspectives on Ageing

Thaddeus Metz

Introducing Two Ethics from the Global South

The cultures that inform the thought of most contemporary English-speaking moral philosophers are known for being WEIRD. This acronym is meant to signify not only the traits of being Western, Educated, Industrialized, Rich, and Democratic, but also ones that are amongst the least representative of the world's population (Henrich et al. 2010). When it comes to moral philosophy, as two scholars have pointed out, neither utility nor autonomy is characteristically considered to be the ultimate good for non-western peoples or those from what is now often called the 'Global South'; instead, they tend to believe that harmony is the 'mother of all values' (Bell and Mo 2014). What might considerations of harmony entail in respect of ageing? How might their implications differ from those of utilitarian and Kantian ethics and modern western values more generally? Do the differences provide any reason to reconsider the western approaches?

I seek to answer these questions in this chapter by considering two different long-standing moral traditions from the Global South, representative of more than two billion people. Specifically, I address classical Confucianism in East Asia (especially China, but also Korea, Taiwan, and Japan) and what is often called '*Ubuntu*' in southern Africa (literally 'humanness' in the Nguni languages there) but that is conceptually characteristic of much of the sub-Saharan region. Both traditions have been frequently interpreted as placing harmony at their centre, and I demonstrate that there are many overlaps between them entailing similar orientations towards those who have aged, ones that contrast with what salient modern western moral thought supports.

After expounding conceptions of harmony in Confucianism and *ubuntu* (first section), I apply them to three major topics pertaining to age, namely virtue (second section), the value of life (third section), and care (fourth section). Roughly speaking, indigenous East Asian and African values of harmony entail that only older adults[1] can be truly virtuous, that they have

For substantial comments on a prior draft, I am most grateful to Nancy Jecker.

[1] I do not analyse the concept of the elderly, old age, and related ideas, working with intuitive ideas that I presume overlap substantially amongst readers. See Jecker (2020a) for careful discussion.

a strong claim to life-saving resources, and that they are entitled to care from their children, views that I show are not characteristic of moral thinking in the contemporary West, neither for prominent philosophies nor the cultures out of which they grew.

This project will unavoidably involve making some large generalizations, in terms of both geography and philosophy. Africa is a huge continent, with some fifty-four countries and thousands of linguistic and ethnic groups, while Confucianism has a history going back at least 2500 years. While I appreciate the desire for particularity, there is also a place for making bird's-eye characterizations of places and ideas, particularly in philosophy. In the following, I focus on what has been *salient* in African thought about values, East Asian Confucianism, and modern western philosophy, that is, what has been prominent in these belief systems that has not been so prominent in other ones. Hence, to describe something as, say, 'Confucian' is not meant to suggest that all Confucians, or even only Confucians, hold the view; instead, it means that the view has been recurrent in Confucian thinking in a way it has not been in many other philosophies.[2]

Note, too, that this is principally a work of comparative philosophy, with its central aim being to expound some non-western ethical approaches to ageing and to contrast them with western ones. Just because many readers are WEIRD does not, of course, necessarily mean that their views are incorrect or unjustified, and I do not try to convince them to adopt a harmony ethic and its implications for older adults. I merely suggest that many Anglophone moral philosophers should be given pause by the existence of different perspectives on the part of at least two long-standing philosophies, and conclude by briefly proposing some ways that cross-cultural debate might be undertaken in the future.

Some Basics of *Ubuntu* and Confucianism: Two Conceptions of Harmony

Many African philosophers sum up their worldviews with a maxim such as 'A person is a person through other persons' (*Umuntu ngumuntu ngabantu* in the Nguni dialects of southern Africa (Mokgoro 1998, 16–18; Tutu 1999, 34–5; Mkhize 2008, 40)).[3] While the maxim has descriptive and specifically metaphysical connotations, to the effect that one's identity depends on others, it also has prescriptive and ethical senses. Specifically, it instructs an agent to become a real person, that is, to display *ubuntu* (humanness). Common in indigenous sub-Saharan thought is the idea that one has a higher, distinctively

---

[2] For an analysis and defence of this way of construing these labels, see Metz (2015a).

[3] Somewhat more common in western and eastern Africa is 'I am because we are' (Menkiti 1984, 171; Mbiti 1990, 106), which has similar connotations.

human nature that one's foremost aim in life should be to perfect.[4] Failing to do so would lead in stark ways to one's being labelled a 'zero person', a 'non-person', or even an 'animal', metaphorical judgements to the effect that one has not realized one's *telos* (Nkulu-N'Sengha 2009, 144; Murove 2016, 185).

This normative ethic is of course reminiscent of Aristotelianism. However, in contrast to Aristotle, who prized theoretical wisdom and practical temperance (amongst other individualist virtues), one leading understanding of our valuable human nature in the African tradition is strictly relational. One is to become a real person by relating to others in certain harmonious (or communal) ways or to develop a true self by being part of a harmonious network (or a community). As two South African theologians note, *ubuntu* is 'an inner state, an orientation, and a good disposition that motivates, challenges and makes one perceive, feel and act in a humane way towards others … and is best realized or evident in harmonious relations in society' (Mnyaka and Motlhabi 2005, 218; see also Paris 1995, 43 and 56; Murove 2007, 181).

Generally speaking, a 'harmony framework has to do with balancing … aligning and smoothing', remarks one of the first scholars to have compared the African and East Asian relational traditions (Anedo 2012, 16). These relational concepts are, on the face of it, markedly different from characteristically western and individualist ones of autonomy, authenticity, creativity, pleasure, desire satisfaction, and liveliness. As should become clear below, neither the African nor the East Asian conception of harmony sketched below is reducible to peace, conformity, or sameness; indeed, one of the most influential quotations from *The Analects* is 'The gentleman seeks harmony not sameness, the petty person seeks sameness not harmony' (translated by and quoted in Chan 2014, 91).

There have been various conceptions of harmony (community) amongst African philosophers, some more religious and 'spiritual' than others. However, the following characterizations constitute some empirical common ground. I focus on those in the southern African or *ubuntu* tradition, but note that their remarks would resonate with much of the rest of the continent.

- Yvonne Mokgoro, a former South African Constitutional Court Justice, says of an *ubuntu* ethic that 'harmony is achieved through close and sympathetic social relations within the group' (Mokgoro 1998, 17).
- Desmond Tutu, renowned former chair of South Africa's Truth and Reconciliation Commission, remarks of indigenous Africans, 'We say, "a person is a person through other people." It is not "I think therefore I am." It says rather: "I am human because I belong." I participate, I share … Harmony, friendliness, community are great goods. Social harmony is for us the *summum bonum* – the greatest good' (Tutu 1999, 35).

---

[4] For discussion in the context of several peoples, see Nkulu-N'Sengha (2009).

- Nhlanhla Mkhize, a South African academic psychologist, remarks in an essay titled '*Ubuntu* and Harmony' that 'personhood is defined in relation to the community ... A sense of community exists if people are mutually responsive to one another's needs ... [O]ne attains the complements associated with full or mature selfhood through participation in a community of similarly constituted selves ... To be is to belong and to participate' (Mkhize 2008, 39 and 40).

Consider how these characterizations of how to relate so as to exhibit *ubuntu* or live harmoniously mention two logically distinct ways to do so (first distinguished and reconstructed in Metz (2013; 2017a)). On the one hand, there is being close, participating, and belonging, which centrally involve enjoying a sense of togetherness and engaging in projects on a cooperative basis. On the other, there is being sympathetic, sharing, and responding to others' needs, which involve doing what will improve other people's quality of life and doing so for their sake. Such ways of relating involve virtues such as generosity, hospitality, compassion, and related kinds of benevolent dispositions (Gyekye 1997, 50; 2010; Tutu 1999, 34; Mnyaka and Motlhabi 2005, 227; Masolo 2010, 251 and 252).

These are ways that family and friends relate to one another, or at least intuitively should, meaning that one way of understanding the African tradition is in terms of a prescription to prize friendliness or a broad sense of 'love'. In addition, 'family first' and 'charity begins at home' are common maxims, meaning that those with whom one has had long and strong harmonious ties have some priority in principle when it comes to whom one should aid (Appiah 1998). To be sure, ideals of human dignity and hospitality towards visitors are also salient in African thought, but alongside those impartial considerations is the partial thought that one normally must do more for intimates. It is not just adherents to an *ubuntu* ethic who believe that one usually owes family more than others and that familial relationships should serve as a model for how to live more generally. Those in the Confucian tradition, or at least those particularly inspired by two classic exponents, Confucius and Mencius, are well known for thinking the same (Fan 2010).

Interestingly, Confucian ethicists tend to interpret ideal interaction between family members and harmony more generally in ways that differ from *ubuntu* ethicists, but I start by noting some similarities. Consider the following quotations, which could have been composed by African thinkers, but instead are expressions of mainstream classical Confucianism:

- Xinzhong Yao, in a scholarly introduction to Confucian philosophy, remarks, '(T)he potentiality within individuals that enables them to be finally differentiated from birds and beasts is yet to be developed and cultivated as actual qualities of their character ... [The goal of self-cultivation] is to fully develop original moral senses, is to become fully human, while to abandon or neglect it is to have a deficient character which is not far from that of an animal' (Yao 2000, 154).

- Roger Ames, who (along with Daniel A. Bell and Chenyang Li) has done the most to expound Confucianism for western audiences, says, 'One *becomes* human by cultivating those thick, intrinsic relations that constitute one's initial conditions and that locate the trajectory of one's life force within family, community, and cosmos. 'Cultivate your person' (is) the signature exhortation ... If there is only one person, there are no persons' (Ames 2010, 143).

- Tongdong Bai, who has drawn on Confucian values to address contemporary debates in political philosophy, says of Mencius' thought: 'If one can develop his or her distinctively human nature (compassion and wisdom that helps to apply his or her compassion to all) more fully than others, he or she is more human, or a greater human being than others' (Bai 2019, 45).

As one readily sees, like *ubuntu*, for much Confucian thought there is a distinctively human and higher part of our nature, and a lower, animal self, where both can be realized to various degrees. That is, one can be more or less of a human or person, understood as an individual with certain desirable traits, and one's basic aim in life should be to develop one's humanness or cultivate one's personhood as much as one can. Still more, for both Confucian and African ethics, the principal way that one can become a greater human being or person is by relating to other human beings in certain positive ways. It is not just that relating to others is a necessary condition of cultivating personhood, but, more strongly, that relationships are what *constitute* one's higher self. To be in relation with others *is* (at least in large part) to be a real person.

And the similarities continue, as it is also common for Confucians to encapsulate the right ways to relate in terms of 'harmony' (*he*). Harmony has been variously labelled 'the highest virtue' for Confucians (Yao 2000, 172), 'the most cherished ideal in Chinese culture' (Li 2006, 583, 593), the 'cardinal cultural value' that is of 'paramount importance' in China (Wei and Li 2013, 61), and the Confucian 'grand ideal' (Chan 2014, 2). As the influential Chinese scholar Wei-Ming Tu remarks, 'If someone is able to uphold the harmony in family relations, neighborly relations and in the relations between the upper and the lower ranks ... then we can call him a Confucian' (Tu 2010, 254).

Like harmony in *ubuntu*, Confucian harmony prescribes interacting with other persons in sympathetic, compassionate, caring, and more generally beneficent ways (often captured with the term '*ren*'). However, these commonalities are set in the context of fairly divergent overall conceptions of the nature of harmony. Confucian harmony is essentially a matter of different elements coming together, where differences are not merely respected, but also integrated in such a way that the best of them is brought out and something new is created. 'Harmony is an active process in which heterogeneous elements are brought into a mutually balancing, cooperatively enhancing, and often commonly benefiting relationship', remarks Chenyang Li, who has studied Confucian harmony more than anyone in the contemporary era (Li 2014a, 1). Aesthetic analogies are often used to illustrate this concept of creative tension between disparate properties; think of different instruments that make music together, or diverse moves that form the unity of a dance, or a variety of ingredients that constitute a tasty soup.

Now, one key kind of difference for the Confucian tradition is position in an interpersonal hierarchy. That is, a desirable kind of harmony often comes in the form of there being superiors who are highly qualified (say, in terms of education and morality) and who guide the lives of inferiors who are not qualified to the same degree. For classical Confucianism, harmony is to be realized within, and by means of, the Five Human Relationships of parents and children, rulers and citizens, elders and youth, friends and friends, and, traditionally, men and women, though the last site is rarely advocated in twenty-first-century Confucian works of philosophy. Aside from the interaction between friends, these relationships have been conceived in terms of hierarchical roles; harmony is present when those in the lower position are respectful of those in the higher one *and* when those in the higher position work for the benefit of those in the lower one. Then, differences are brought together such that a productive relationship is realized. Consider that two of the Five Constant Virtues in Confucianism are righteousness – conduct befitting a social role (*yi*), and propriety – rituals expressing respect for the position of others (*li*).

Although interpersonal hierarchy is a quite prominent way in which differences can and should be integrated for Confucians, it is not essential to their conception of harmony. As above, harmony can exist between friends amongst whom there is no difference in power. In addition, Confucians tend to recognize the ability for a single individual to harmonize her own mental states, although this intrapersonal dimension is not relevant for the purposes of this chapter.

Although the *ubuntu* and Confucian conceptions of harmony differ, they have some moral-political implications that make them similar in comparison to what it is common to encounter in western philosophy. For example, thinkers from both non-western traditions usually reject competitive, majoritarian democracy of the sort found in the West as being incompatible with harmony. Confucians generally favour meritocracy as being what would facilitate a politics that fosters people's virtue (representative texts are Bell and Li 2013 and Bai 2019), while Africans often defend consensus amongst elders or elected representatives as a way to advance the common good (Gyekye 1992; Wiredu 1996, 172–90; Bujo 1997, 157–71). For another example, consider the way that Confucians and indigenous African philosophers have conceived of freedom. Although talk of 'freedom' or 'autonomy' rarely appears in Confucianism, there have been recent philosophical works advancing Confucian conceptions of them (e.g., Johnson 2009, 57; Li 2014b). Basically, freedom is understood as self-governance, with one's highest, distinctively human self being in charge of one's life. From this perspective, one is more free, the more one is virtuous for relating to others harmoniously. This is also the dominant view amongst African philosophers (e.g., Bujo 2005, 432–3; Ikuenobe 2006, 80; Chachine 2008, 288, 290) (even if their conception of harmony differs), and it contrasts with the common western view that one is more free, the less interference there is with one's ability to act as one pleases.[5]

There is of course much more to say about the nature of *ubuntu* and Confucianism as ethical philosophies, including their conceptions of harmony and its attendant virtues.[6] I have downplayed discussion of 'spiritual' conditions that have traditionally been associated with ethics,[7] of self-regarding virtues or duties to oneself, and of what it might mean to relate harmoniously to non-persons such as animals or nature more generally. This sketch of empirical ways that human persons can interact harmoniously should, however, be enough for us to make headway on understanding key implications of *ubuntu* and Confucianism for the ethics of ageing.

Age and Virtue

One idea that stands out in the African and East Asian moral traditions is a close association between age and virtue. The thought that it is ordinarily older rather than younger individuals who exemplify substantial personhood is prominent in these two philosophies from the Global South, while it is not in contemporary western philosophy (Bell and Metz 2011, 90–2).

Amongst African philosophers and their peoples more generally, age is usually considered a necessary, but not sufficient, condition for moral wisdom, with 'elder' the term often used honorifically to indicate those who are both old and wise. It is possible to be old but not an elder and hence not to deserve the deeper respect that elders merit. That said, most sub-Saharan ethicists also maintain that it would be difficult, if not impossible, for someone in his or her twenties to exhibit a high degree of personhood. Ifeanyi Menkiti, an influential Nigerian philosopher whose work in ethics is amongst the most widely read in African philosophy, recounts his Igbo people's proverb, 'What an old man sees sitting down, a young man cannot see standing up' (Menkiti 2004, 325). Menkiti points out that 'although we would not have a great deal of difficulty talking about an 18-year-old mathematical giant, we would have a great deal of difficulty talking about an 18-year-old moral giant' (Menkiti 2004, 325).

---

[5] For additional respects in which *ubuntu* and Confucianism are closer to each other than to salient western approaches, see Metz (2015b).

[6] For additional comparisons of *ubuntu* and Confucianism, see Bell and Metz (2011), and Metz (2015b, 2017b).

[7] In particular, I set aside the view, found in both philosophies, that genuine elders are those who have become ancestors meriting respect from their human descendants.

Why think that age is essential for substantial virtue? For many African ethicists, harmonious or communal relationships of togetherness, participation, sharing, and compassion are crucially realized in a familial context. For many, acquiring substantial personhood or humanness is a path demanding that one go through various rites of passage, such as marrying, bearing and rearing children, and participating in a clan's way of life. 'The extended family is probably the most common, and also the most fundamental, expression of the African idea of community . . . The importance of this idea for ethics is that the family is something that is valued for its own sake . . . a microcosm of the community persons create as they develop and in which they find fulfilment' (Shutte 2001, 29).

Creating and sustaining a family might be thought to be doable in one's thirties and forties, but a greater investment in family roles and relationships is expected from someone to live a genuinely human life, requiring more time. For one, substantial personhood includes contributing to the upliftment of a person's extended family and the broader society in which she lives. For another, a person is expected to learn her society's folkways so that its culture can be passed on to future generations. Still more, someone with *ubuntu* evinces skilfulness at resolving conflicts and more generally exhibits moral wisdom.

The latter dimension of personhood, viz., of moral wisdom, is what particularly supports the claim that old age is necessary for substantial virtue. Dilemmas are often complex, requiring restraint and sophisticated understanding that is gained only through direct experiences of learning and coming to appreciate more fully the range of relevant considerations, including how to reasonably satisfy diverse desires and make needed trade-offs. In addition, cultivating character by living harmoniously or communally with others requires not merely judgement, but also nurturing within oneself certain emotional responses such as compassion and related dispositions that mark maturity. For example, it takes a long time to: become comfortable with an awareness of what motivates oneself and others; release resentment and forgive missteps; listen well and feel true empathy; and set aside one's own pressing desires and be patient with others.[8] With age, 'the heart does grow increasingly wiser, morally speaking' (Menkiti 2004, 325).

Confucians are similar in deeming age to correlate with virtue. One of the most widely quoted sayings from Confucius' *Analects* is the account of his own process of moral growth: 'At fifteen, I set my mind upon learning; at thirty, I took my stance; at forty, I was no longer perplexed; at fifty, I realized the "ways of the universe"; at sixty, my ear was attuned; at seventy, I followed my heart's desire without overstepping the boundaries' (Bell and Metz 2011, 90). The primary reason for Confucian ethicists to make virtue dependent on age is

---

[8] The last few sentences are paraphrased from Bell and Metz (2011, 91).

similar to a point made above in the context of *ubuntu*: Confucianism is a relational ethic, and relationships are complex, taking time to learn how to build, sustain, and enrich. For example, a manager of a business should strive to learn from mistakes in the ways she has engaged with her employees or supply chain stakeholders upon dealing with a wide range of them. She should also study written educational materials and confer with other managers. The time it would take to learn in these ways and become a truly wise leader would be substantial, particularly when one considers that a virtuous person would strive to act similarly in all her roles, including as a child to parents, parent of children, friend, and citizen.

However, there are other features, somewhat more characteristic of Confucianism than of *ubuntu*, that also entail that it is older adults who normally exhibit real virtue. One is the centrality of filial piety (*xiao*) in Confucian thought, which many scholars maintain is the most important virtue for at least Confucius and Mencius themselves (e.g., Liu 2003; Richey n.d.). Filial piety consists of upholding one's duties in respect of one's (grand)parents, with one scholar summing it up as 'respect for the elderly' (Mengxi 2018, 30). It has traditionally included continuing the family line (Jianxiong 2018, 98–104) and being deferential to one's (grand)parents and other people older than oneself (Sung 2000, 198–9). However, it has also included looking after one's (grand)parents when they are frail (as discussed below) and observing certain rites when they die (Mengxi 2018, 29). Normally, only a person of a certain age would be able to care for the needs of parents of an even greater age and to mourn them in the appropriate ways when they have passed on. While adherents to *ubuntu* certainly believe that one has weighty obligations to one's parents (see section on age and elder care), upholding these obligations is rarely, if ever, described as 'the fountain-head of the morality of the people' (Yu-wei 1959, 56), 'the summit of all virtues' (Yao 2000, 203), or 'the supreme principle of human life' (Liu 2003, 234).

Another fairly Confucian reason for thinking that virtue tracks age concerns the importance of book learning. Whereas nearly all sub-Saharan societies had oral cultures until the twentieth century, China has had a massive written corpus going back more than 3000 years. Both *ubuntu* and Confucianism prize wisdom, but adherents to these philosophies tend to have different views about how to acquire it. According to African wisdom, speech and tradition are the sources of knowledge. Oral tradition is 'the Great School of Life' (Nabudere 2006, 22; see also Mutwa 1998, 568). In contrast, for mainstream Confucianism it is essential to read what many others have thought about a certain matter; virtue consists to some degree of having obtained written knowledge. 'Since reading and studying is a time-consuming process, the elderly are more likely to have had the time to read and study with a view to improving their lives, where such improvement is in part constituted by this very reading and studying' (Bell and Metz 2011, 92).

The claim that substantial virtue requires age is not salient amongst modern western moral theorists;[9] it is not what stands out, and does not seem entailed by prominent accounts of the nature of good character. For example, Immanuel Kant's well-known view is that virtue consists of doing one's duty because it is one's duty, and having the strength of will to do so in the face of inclinations that would lead one astray, where one's duty is to act in ways that can be universalized. Lawrence Kohlberg, the extremely renowned psychologist influenced by Kantians such as John Rawls and Jürgen Habermas, believed that some graduate students in their twenties were able to display the highest forms of moral judgement and motivation, which roughly involve impartial reasoning (Kohlberg 1984, 272–3). In addition, there seems to be nothing particularly age-related about loving or being for the good and hating or being against the bad, which is one influential virtue ethic in contemporary western philosophy (Hurka 2001; Adams 2006). Similarly, it does not appear that older adults would be noticeably more able to advance the four ends of individual survival, continuance of the species, characteristic enjoyment and freedom from pain, and a group enabling its individual members to live well (Hursthouse 1999, 197–216). Roughly speaking, it is the differential focus on interpersonal relationships between western accounts of virtue and the non-western ones[10] that plausibly explains the differential emphasis on age as a prerequisite for substantial virtue.

Age and the Value of Life

For *ubuntu* and Confucianism, since virtue tends to track age, older individuals (or at least elders) merit greater respect than younger ones in a number of ways (e.g., Abraham 1962, 63–7; Paris 1995, 85, 90; Sung 2000; Chabal 2005, 79–80). In both African and East Asian cultures, respect might be expressed by serving elders first at a meal, avoiding initiating interaction with them, not speaking much or very loudly to older persons, using honorific language when speaking to or about them, offering a seat to those of a certain age, being deferential towards them, according (male) elders the authority of being head of a household, and upholding specific burial rites when they have died.

Many of these practices have been in decline, with the influence of the modern West, which is well known for prizing youth, according no special status to the aged, and, at least in recent times, for being somewhat less sexist. Morally speaking, though, there is something to the idea that wisdom merits

---

[9] A sociological explanation of this point probably includes the idea that, since Enlightenment developments, many societies are less reliant on older adults for information (see Jecker 2020a, 240).

[10] Slote (2001) does address familial relationships, although he believes one's devotion to family must be heavily tempered by political concerns, and his virtue ethic has not been as influential as other theories mentioned.

acknowledgement and appreciation in some way or other (depending in part on social conventions), and it is plausible, as per the previous section, to contend that normally older adults are the ones who are wise, at least in respect of relational values.

An interesting question is whether the substantial virtue exhibited by an older person provides good moral reason to save her life relative to a younger life in cases where not all can be saved; whether that is at least one factor to be balanced against the longer expected life of the youthful. Note that the question of whether to rescue your mother or your girlfriend from a burning building has been part of China's national judicial examination; the answer deemed correct is that one ought to save one's mother, if forced to choose (Hatton 2015).

Relatedly, consider Moral Machine, a large-scale study undertaken in which people around the world were asked whose life should be sacrificed if a self-driving car had to strike either a young person or an old one. The researchers note that globally there tended to be a preference for saving the life of the young, except for those in Eastern or what they call 'collectivist' cultures (Awad et al. 2018, 61–2). The researchers remark that 'participants from collectivistic cultures, which emphasize the respect that is due to older members of the community, show a weaker preference for sparing younger characters' and that the differential preference at the global level is so pronounced that 'the split between individualistic and collectivistic cultures may prove an important obstacle for universal machine ethics' (Awad et al. 2018, 62).

Africa did not feature in the Moral Machine experiment, aside from Egypt, where Arabs have had substantial influence, and South Africa, where Europeans have. However, my suspicion is that if enough of those influenced by indigenous sub-Saharan cultures had been surveyed, their judgement would have aligned with that of East Asian respondents. Suppose one had to choose between the life of Nelson Mandela *qua* elder and that of an average eight-year-old. The decision for many from African cultures would at least be difficult, with Mandela's accomplishments and standing as a moral leader counting in his favour to some real degree.

While Moral Machine is an empirical study about people's moral beliefs, it raises important normative questions about whose beliefs are true or more justified or about how to make morally right decisions when not all lives can be saved. The ethical philosophies that have grown out of people's cultures by and large entail the specific judgements reported above. Nancy Jecker (2020b) has done a nice job of showing how dominant western ethical theories of how to allocate scarce life-saving resources have the implication that younger lives are to be prioritized. Roughly speaking, utilitarian perspectives favour the young because of the greater amount of happy experiences that are on average expected to come, while Kantians tend to make judgements about a purportedly fair allocation of healthy life, the thought being that it would be unfair to confer benefits on those who have already had a reasonable share.

My suggestion is not quite that, by *ubuntu* or Confucianism, the lives of older age groups are normally to be prioritized. There could, of course, be some readings of them entailing that judgement. Vide this remark from an adherent to traditional African religion, who, holding that there is a correlation between virtue and strength of life, says: 'Causation flows all directions to maintain life in the universe, but the seriousness and depth of its effects normally depend on the quality of life and primogeniture. The force of the older and animate creatures is always perceived to be the stronger, and is understood to claim allegiance of the younger' (Magesa 1997, 46–7). However, in contrast to the claim that according to *ubuntu* and Confucianism there is usually the strongest reason to favour the lives of the old, I believe they most clearly differ from salient western ethical reflection for denying that there is usually the strongest reason to favour the lives of the young. The principal ground of potentially favouring the old is a requirement to respect elders,[11] counterbalancing reasons that support rescue of the youthful. For these two philosophies from the Global South, virtue is of paramount importance, such that while there is of course reason to enable people to become virtuous who have not yet, there is also reason to protect those who already have realized substantial virtue. On the one hand, virtue deserves recognition, and, on the other, those with virtue promise to sustain and enhance relationships in ways that others cannot (Jecker 2020b, 37).

Age and Elder Care

In this section I discuss not so much life and death matters that pertain to older adults, but rather care for their day-to-day needs. In particular, the issue considered is the morality of letting a public or private institution assist one's parents in lieu of oneself undertaking the labour. Must one be the agent who cooks for one's mother and father, cleans up after them, and tends to their medical concerns?

Virtually no one disputes the claim that an adult can be, all things considered, justified in not looking after his or her parents. The debate is instead about whether not looking after them is wrong to *some real* degree and how burdensome such care has to be before one may, on balance of considerations, permissibly decline to look after them.

For both *ubuntu* and Confucianism, there is pro tanto strong reason for a person to be the one to care for his or her parents, even if the burdens of doing so are substantial, where traditionally it has been daughters or step-daughters who have carried out such perceived obligations. African and East Asian older people have traditionally lived with their adult children as part of

---

[11] And probably, in the case of African cultures, also a principle of inherent human dignity, on which see Metz (2014).

an extended family, where, as I now explain, the moral frameworks for both prescribe that arrangement (beyond any prudential considerations involved such as grandparents helping to look after grandchildren).

Confucianism is frequently understood to be particularly adamant that it is not enough to ensure that parental needs are met by someone else, and that one must instead be the one who meets them. 'While his parents are alive, the son may not go abroad to a distance' is a line from *The Analects* (Book 4) that is ascribed to Confucius and is frequently mentioned. Filial piety, which, recall, is widely taken to be the supreme virtue for Confucianism, is standardly understood to require caring for one's parents when they need help (Fan 2007; Fan 2010, 95–102). Indeed, such a perceived moral obligation is also a legal one in China. According to the Chinese Constitution,[12] 'children who have come of age have the duty to support and assist their parents' (Article 49), and the Protection of the Rights and Interests of the Elderly, a Chinese statute adopted in 1996, says that 'family members shall care for and look after' (Article 10) the elderly as well as 'cater to their special needs' (Article 11).[13] Even in fairly westernized Hong Kong, two scholars report that 'the Confucian notion of filial piety where caregiving for the elderly is seen primarily as a responsibility of the kin still runs deep' (Wong and Chau 2006, 601).

Although not particularly enforced, there is also a legal obligation on an African individual to 'respect his parents at all times, to maintain them in case of need', as per the African ('Banjul') Charter on Human and Peoples' Rights that is binding on all member states of the African Union (Article 29).[14] Such a law grows out of the perceived moral obligation of family members to take care of one another. As one commentator remarks, 'Talk of the Western practice of placing ageing relatives in nursing homes makes most Africans shudder with horror. The duty of the young is spelt out in a Ghanaian proverb: "If your elders take care of you while cutting your teeth, you must in turn take care of them while they are losing theirs"' (Maier 1992). Appealing to the conception of harmony sketched above, it is not enough to be sympathetic and share resources with one's parents; in addition, part of relating harmoniously is being close, participating with others, and cultivating a sense of belonging, which naturally prescribe living with one's parents or at least visiting them enough to meet their needs, particularly given a long history of having related harmoniously in intense ways.

Over the past twenty years or so, adult offspring in East Asian and African societies have been doing less for their parents on average, and hence older persons have been relying on public institutions (when available) and private institutions (when affordable) for care in ways they had not before. The most

---

[12] https://bit.ly/3qon2D9
[13] For some related laws in Taiwan and Singapore, see Jecker (2020a: 188).
[14] www.achpr.org/public/Document/file/English/banjul_charter.pdf

common explanations for the changes include a lower birth rate, urbanization, women entering the workplace, and the rising cost of living, especially in respect of housing and education (Maier 1992; Croll 2006; Zhang 2006; Alber et al. 2010; Fan 2010, 89–95). As some social scientists have remarked of an African context, 'there has been no visible qualitative change in the shared idea that the younger generation is obliged to care for the older generation ... The only thing that has changed is the quantity of support they receive' (Alber et al. 2010, 59).

In contrast, in western cultures a quite common view is that it is optional for adults to live with their parents or otherwise take care of them on their own. Studies of Americans who provide care to their parents reveal that they normally do so because they elected to, not because they judge themselves to have an obligation to do so (cited in Jecker 2020a, 194). In addition, the salient moral philosophies that have grown out of western cultures appear to support the judgement that caregiving is supererogatory and not required by duty. In accordance with utilitarianism, it could well be that pleasures or satisfied desires are maximized in the aggregate when one older person is in a nursing home, allowing the rest of the family to have more time to pursue more rewarding pursuits. For Kantianism, duties to aid others are standardly viewed as discretionary in the absence of a promise or voluntary participation in a cooperative scheme, where few people in Euro-American-Australasian societies have promised to care for their parents when they cannot do so themselves, and having been brought into the world as a needy being and reared in a particular family as a child is hardly a voluntary choice. One can of course find some western *philosophers* who argue that grown children are obligated to look after their parents, but they generally appeal to relational values that are not central to modern western moral *philosophies* (e.g., English 1992).

Conclusion: Towards Intercultural Debate about Ageing

One major aim of this essay has been to expound some important ethical judgements pertaining to older adults that follow from philosophies salient in sub-Saharan Africa and East Asia. I spelled out how *ubuntu* and Confucianism both make harmonious relationships central to their moral frameworks, and explained how considerations of harmony plausibly entail the views that virtue tracks age, that the lives of the virtuous and hence of those who are older are not to be discounted when rationing scarce life-saving resources, and that adult offspring have weighty duties to take care of their older parents, with institutionalization being morally insufficient.

Another aim of this essay has been to contrast these ethical judgements pertaining to older adults with what is salient in modern western moral thought. Here, it is in contrast prominent to encounter the views that old age is not necessary for real virtue, that the young are to be prioritized when it comes to whom to rescue from death, and that there is no obligation to care for parents oneself (even if there might be to ensure their needs are met).

The differences between the two traditions from the Global South and that of the modern West raise the question of which side is closer to the truth. In practice, when those from differing cultures encounter one another, it would be natural to look for negotiated compromises (on which see Jecker et al. 1995). However, there would remain the philosophical matter of what is true or justified in the face of reasonable disagreement. Can people generally be substantially virtuous in their twenties? Do children have a greater claim to be saved from death? Would it be merely supererogatory to have one's older parents live with one and to take care of their needs oneself? These questions admit of 'yes' or 'no' answers, and, supposing relativism is off the table, defending specific answers that have some universal justification will require careful and sustained cross-cultural engagement.

One might be tempted to suggest that since the WEIRD cultures are in the minority, they are likely to be incorrect. However, the WEIRD cultures have made clear contributions to areas of human life pertaining to science, technology, economics, and the arts, and one might suggest in reply that this provides reason to adopt their ethics.

Beyond these 'meta' or 'external' rationales, it would be revealing for philosophers from different traditions to speak to one another in search of common ground and even change of mind. It would be natural for friends of *ubuntu* and Confucianism to appeal to intuitions about the moral importance of family that westerners themselves hold, and to draw out from them principles that might put pressure on modern western moral thought. Conversely, modern western ethicists might show that even those in the Global South have some strong impartial intuitions about what is owed to strangers that are central to morality, suggesting best explanations of them that pull in a direction away from considerations of harmony, at least as normally interpreted. Such bilateral intercultural debate has yet to be undertaken in any sustained way, but the diversity of views portrayed in this chapter ground compelling reasons to pursue it.

10 Special Obligations in Long-Standing Friendships

Diane Jeske

Who ought to care for the elderly? Who is responsible for covering the cost of elder care? These questions have become pressing in recent years as highly expensive medical interventions have led to longer lives for more people. The public policy issues regarding the extent to which the collective, through the agency of the government, ought to provide quality elder care at reasonable cost are some of the most important issues facing us as a society.

There are also issues that we, as individuals, face as our loved ones age. While we might welcome government assistance in covering the cost of caring for our loved ones, we may not welcome having (all of) the actual work of caring for our loved ones done by agents of governmental welfare agencies. Care itself comes in many forms, ranging from assistance in getting up from a chair to companionship and emotional support. But even providing aid in getting up from a chair can be done in a caring manner or a non-caring manner. Further, the caring manner of a friend or family member is often perceived and received in a very different way than is the caring manner of, for example, an employee of a nursing care center.

Much as we might like to be the ones providing care for our loved ones as they age, doing so can demand great sacrifices from us. The elderly often need care with simple daily tasks, and their emotional needs can increase as they become less a part of the outside world. If we ourselves are in a position to provide care, we are also likely to have other projects and demands upon us. It may, in the end, be impossible to avoid remorse as we trade-off some demands in order to meet others.

So it is important for us to determine what we owe our loved ones in terms of care as they age. While much has been written about the filial duties of adult children to care for their elderly parents, less has been said about the reciprocal duties of friends to care about each other as they age.[1] For those of us who are single and childless, after having cared for our parents, we will ourselves be in

---

[1] I do not intend to imply that adult children cannot be friends with their parents. But, for the purposes of this paper, I am going to be using the term "friend" to refer to persons who are friends but who are not also family members, whether biologically or legally defined. For a discussion of the view that filial duties are in fact based upon the friendship between adult children and their parents, see Nicholas Dixon (1995), "The Friendship Model of Filial Obligations."

need of care and are likely to have friends as some of, if not the most, important people in our lives. But even for those who are married and/or have children, there is no guarantee that their spouse or child will be in a position or be willing to provide care. Some people regard it as inappropriate to put the same demands of care upon friends as they would put upon children or spouses. What is the strength and range of obligations friends owe one another as they age?

And, many people will insist, no matter what our obligations to our friends are, nobody wants to be cared for by someone who is motivated by the thought that she has an obligation to do so. Many philosophers have argued that friends ought to be motivated by love and concern, not by thoughts of duty or obligation.[2] They claim that acts of care done from a motive of duty are not done in an appropriately caring way, particularly when the persons involved are friends or other loved ones. Especially as we become vulnerable and near the end of our lives, we want to be cared for by people who act from a personal motive of love, not from an impersonal motive of duty.

In this chapter I will argue that one of the great joys and benefits of ageing is the possibility of being in very long-term friendships – such friendships, by their very nature, are not available to the young. These friendships ground strong reciprocal special obligations. Such long-term friends have very strong obligations to care for each other as they age and as they become vulnerable as a result of declining mental and/or physical strength. These long-standing intimate relationships, insofar as they ground strong special obligations, are precisely what a friend ought to be thinking about as she is moved to care for her friend. Thus, in thinking about a duty, one is thereby thinking about the valuable relationship that has bound one to one's friend over an important and extended portion of one's life. Acting from a special obligation to a long-term friend is to act in precisely the right sort of caring way.

In the first section, I will discuss the value and meaningfulness of long-term friendships, and how they enhance and add joy to the ageing process. In the second section, I will present the relationships theory of special obligations, according to which it is the special relationship in which we stand to an intimate such as a friend that grounds our special obligations to care for them. In the third section, I will show why certain considerations that might suggest a weakening of obligations as we age do not actually support the claim that our obligations weaken in such circumstances. In the fourth section, I will show why, given the relationships theory of special obligations, acting from duty or obligation to care for a friend is in no way objectionable and is, in fact, precisely how we would want a friend to act in caring for us.

---

[2] For the classic statement of such a position, see Michael Stocker (1976), "The Schizophrenia of Modern Moral Theories."

The Value of Long-Standing Friendships

All genuine friendships are valuable, but there are features of very long-standing friendships that give them a unique significance in our lives.[3] In examining some features of friendships, we will see how these features are enhanced the longer the friendship lasts. Further, we will see that there are certain features that only a friendship of long standing can have, and given that we can only have such long-standing friendships as we age, these features bring a unique joy to and help to ease the pains of ageing.

Friendship is an intimate relationship that is characterized by some cluster of the following features: (i) the parties to the relationship care about each other more than they care about just any person, (ii) the parties to the relationship desire to spend time together, (iii) the parties to the relationship have a special knowledge of each other, (iv) the parties to the relationship love or like each other, and (v) the parties to the relationship have a history of interaction that displays or embodies the care that they have for one another. While some cluster of (i)–(v) is constitutive of the friendship relationship, there are further features, such as trust and emotional dependence, that often piggyback on some combination of these constitutive features.

Consider feature (iii) – the parties to the relationship have a special knowledge of each other. This special knowledge that friends have of one another is not to be understood as the kind of knowledge a biographer or a reader of a biography would acquire, no matter how comprehensive is the research that lies behind the biography. The knowledge that we have of our friends is acquired through our interactions with them. Sometimes this knowledge results from explicit confidences, at other times it is acquired through inferences from behavior. Often this knowledge is experiential in nature: we know what it is like to share a joke with a friend, to be comforted by a friend, to be hugged by a friend, etc. We are familiar with small eccentricities or gestures, and come to understand their significance when placed in a larger picture. It is not unusual to say of a friend, "She knows me better than I know myself," because our friends can often see our self-deceptions or understand the patterns in our behavior that we ourselves can miss. While a therapist can also come to read us in this way, our relationships with our friends are reciprocal and caring in a way that a therapist-to-patient relationship is not: we know our friends as they know us, and this two-way knowledge deepens and develops the mutual caring between us.

It is obvious that this reciprocal special knowledge is particularly wide-ranging in very long-term friendships. Consider a friendship begun when the

---

[3] I have left the concept of a long-standing or very long-standing friendship vague. I am primarily thinking about relationships that extend into old age and which began at some point before middle-age. Such friendships have lasted over significant episodes of maturation and change and have persisted into the last or near-to-last phases of life.

parties to it were in their early twenties that then continues into old age when the parties are in their sixties or seventies. People change a great deal from their twenties into old age, and when someone has known us throughout all of those changes, that person has a comprehensive perspective of us. This allows her to understand how we came to be the way that we are, and to put our present self into the context of our past choices and circumstances. Further, she herself has been an important catalyst in creating our present self, given our long history of concerned interaction. Thus, as my older self reflects on who I am, my old friend understands that self in a way that only someone who has known me for a long time could understand me and plays a significant role in the explanation and understanding of who I am.

This comprehensive perspective allows my friend to care for me in a way that others cannot. She is aware of decisions I have made in the past and how my ideals and values have changed over time. She can help me to remember my past and to integrate that past into my present and my future. She can share with me the joys of reminiscence. Further, I can reciprocate all of this, because I play a similar role in her life to the one she plays in mine. Our friendship is a shared project that helps to constitute our life courses. Our very self-understandings are in part created and sustained by the ways in which we view each other: we cannot help but understand ourselves through the lens of a friend's conception of us. But, unlike seeing ourselves through the lenses of strangers or acquaintances, when we see ourselves through the eyes of a friend, we are seeing ourselves from a caring and comprehensive perspective. However, a caring perspective is not necessarily an uncritical one, but it is one in which critical judgment is aimed at promoting well-being.

So the special knowledge unique to friendship is particularly deep in long-term friendships, and plays a significant role in constituting the friends' understanding of themselves. And this peculiarly deep special knowledge allows the concerned interactions between friends (feature V of friendship) to be particularly effective in ways that the concern of others simply cannot be. These intrinsic features of long-term friendships impact the features that are often parasitic upon friendship itself. Being able to trust a friend, not only to help us and to keep our confidences, but also to remain a friend, is an important good. As we age, we will inevitably lose loved ones to death, and fear of such loss can create a very profound sort of loneliness. Having people whom we can trust to remain at least figuratively by our side as long as such is within their power can do a great deal to ease that fear and that loneliness. When someone has been with us through thick and thin, when that person has seen us at our worst, we become more confident that they are there for the long haul, even when that haul gets difficult, as it inevitably does as we age.

Friends want to be together (feature ii of friendship). Often, over the course of a long-standing friendship, friends are forced to live geographically separate lives. But the longer the friendship lasts, the more firmly friends are embedded in each other's lives, regardless of physical proximity. We now have so many ways of staying in touch that previous generations never even dreamed of (email, text messages, Zoom meetings, and various social media), and these tools allow us to 'spend time with' our friends in new ways. While some of these tools have their downsides with respect to friendship,[4] with firmly established friendships they are able to cement people's places in our lives. And the longer a friendship lasts, the more secure we feel in our implicit acceptance of the fact that our friend will always 'be there' for us.

This is only a sketch of some of the ways in which long-standing friendships add value and meaning to our lives and ease some of the burdens of ageing. Before moving on I need to point out that not all long-standing friendships provide the same benefits to the parties to them. While all friendships have intrinsic value,[5] they do not all have the same instrumental value: some contribute more to our happiness and well-being than do others. Some long-term friendships can lay heavy burdens on those party to them, and it is not the case that these burdens are always outweighed by the benefits. It is also the case that there are some long-standing friendships such that the parties ought to have terminated them. Sometimes we cling to relationships that are such that all parties to them would have been better off if they had ended, or even never begun in the first place. When it comes to human relationships, there are always contingencies involved that make it difficult to make universal generalizations beyond the necessary truths regarding the intrinsic constituents of relationships of those types. So it is important to note that I am focusing on some subset of long-term friendships in this chapter.

The Grounds of Special Obligations

Most people take for granted that they have special obligations to friends and other loved ones. But, for philosophers, the claim that we have such special obligations is controversial. After all, we all seem to accept that all persons are of equal moral worth and have equal claims to be cared for. So how can we justify devoting a good portion of our time, energy, and other resources to caring for a small set of people distinguished only by the fact that they happen to stand in some special relationship to us? How can I justify giving special care to my friend when there are so many people who are so much more needy than she is?

I will present two opposing theories about our reasons for caring for our friends: the consequentialist theory and the relationships theory. I do this not because I intend to argue for the relationships theory against the consequentialist

---

[4] This is, I believe, particularly true of some ways in which social media gets used. See Diane Jeske (2019).

[5] See Diane Jeske (2008) for the defense of this claim.

theory here – I have done that extensively elsewhere. Rather, I start by presenting the consequentialist theory for two reasons. First, contrasting the relationships theory with the consequentialist theory helps to clarify the former. Second, the contrast with the consequentialist theory will help to highlight the nature of the motivations involved in acting from duty as conceived by the relationships theory. These are not, of course, the only two theories about the grounds of our obligations to care for our friends, but, as my goal here is not to provide a comprehensive argument for the relationships theory, I will not provide an extensive discussion of the range of views on this issue.[6]

Very roughly, consequentialism holds that right action is action that produces the best consequences. The type of consequentialism that I am considering is a universalistic moral theory, in the sense that right action is determined by the effects of one's actions on all persons.[7] One is not allowed to consider only oneself and one's loved ones, nor is one allowed to give oneself and one's loved ones any extra weight in deciding how one ought to act. If one has the choice of providing a certain benefit to a friend or a certain slightly larger benefit to a stranger or acquaintance, and there are no other consequences of one's action, then the right action, according to consequentialism, is to give the slightly larger benefit to the stranger or acquaintance. Who receives a particular benefit is, in and of itself, of no moral significance for consequentialism. A quantum of value is the same quantum no matter whose life it lands in, and, given that no person is more morally significant than any other, what we ought to do is to produce the greatest net sum of value (positive value minus negative value) that we can.

It is important to emphasize that, for the consequentialist, *the mere fact* that some person is my friend gives me no reason to benefit her over anyone else. However, consequentialists since Mill and Sidgwick have argued that special relationships have an instrumental or derivative significance. As we deliberate about how to expend our resources, we have to recognize our limitations, both causal and epistemic. None of us has a god's-eye view of the world that would allow us to always distribute resources in the most efficacious way. So we need to take into account the fact that we know our intimates better than we know other people and we causally interact with them on a regular basis. Thus, our efforts to benefit our intimates are more likely to be efficacious than if we were to be more indiscriminate with our benevolence. Consequentialists have thus argued that we are justified in exerting greater benevolence with respect to our

---

[6] For a discussion of the relationships theory as well as what he calls the projects view and the individuals view, see Simon Keller (2013). For a more complete discussion of the relationships theory, and a defense of it against the consequentialist theory, see Jeske (2008).

[7] There are non-universalistic versions of consequentialism. For a discussion of such and of their implications for special obligations, see Jeske and Fumerton (1997) "Relatives and Relativism."

intimates than we are with respect to non-intimates, because doing so has a greater likelihood of bringing about the best possible consequences.[8]

We can see why, for a consequentialist, long-term friendships provide particularly good derivative reasons for parties to such relationships to care for one another. In particular, as we saw in the previous section, long-term friendships provide the parties to them with distinctive epistemic outlooks on each other's wants and needs. Further, those wants and needs are likely to involve being cared for by someone to whom one stands in a reciprocal loving relationship. Thus, the most efficient way to distribute benevolent labor is to have friends care for friends, especially when those friendships are of long-standing.

The relationships view differs from the consequentialist view insofar as the relationships view sees intimate relationships as directly rather than indirectly grounding special obligations. As a result, the relationships view understands special obligations to care for intimates as fundamental reasons that compete with whatever reasons we have to promote the overall good, rather than as reasons derivative from our reason to promote the overall good. Thus, according to the relationships view, a special obligation to care for an intimate might outweigh the reason to maximize value, while according to the consequentialist view that is impossible, given that the former reasons are derivative from the latter reasons. So if the relationships view is true, then in a situation where saving a stranger would produce more good than saving a friend, our special obligation to save a friend might trump the reason to promote value.

According to the consequentialist, the strength of any reason to perform an action is a function of, and only of, the value of the consequences of that action. And how much stronger my reason to perform action A is, is determined by how much more value A produces as opposed to B. But according to the relationships view, the strength of the reasons that are grounded by our special relationships are a function of the nature of the relationship. Determining the strength of our reason to care for an intimate is not always going to be a straightforward matter because an intimate friendship has more than one component, and so relationships can vary across more than one dimension. For example, while my knowledge of my friend Polly may be deeper and richer than my knowledge of my friend Paul, my fondness for and desire to spend time with Paul may be more intense than my fondness for and desire to spend time with Polly. So if, in a given situation, I can only care for one of Paul or Polly, it may be difficult to determine for whom my reason to care is stronger.

However, it is quite clear that in very long-standing friendships that involve love, strong desires to play a part in each other's lives, a long history of caring

---

[8] There are newer and more sophisticated attempts to accommodate special obligation-style reasons to care for intimates in the recent consequentialist literature, beginning with Peter Railton's (1984) "Alienation, Consequentialism, and the Demands of Morality."

interaction, and a deep and wide-ranging knowledge of each other, the parties' reasons for caring for each other are very strong. And this is true regardless of the legal or biological status of the relationship. So just considering the relationship in and of itself, my reason to care for a friend may be no weaker than and may in fact be stronger than another person's reason to care for her partner or spouse. In the latter case, there may be additional reasons in play, such as those created by vows or legal contracts, but friendships may also involve promises and commitments, even if those commitments are not as explicit and are not legally binding.

It seems, then, that long-standing friendships give the parties to them strong reasons to care for one another, and such caring, in old age, will involve providing aid in handling diminishing or altering mental and physical capacities. And, as we noted in our discussion of consequentialism, long-standing friends are particularly well placed to provide such care and to do so in a caring manner. It is all too easy to stereotype elderly people, seeing them only in terms of their frailties and their disabilities. All too often, even well-intentioned persons will condescend to and patronize the elderly as a result of weakening memory or even hearing loss. But long-standing friends know each other's histories and so can understand the ageing person as who she is: a long-standing friend sees the ageing friend as the latest incarnation of someone whom she has loved and had as part of her life for a very long time. So she will know the person who has the fading memory and the hearing loss and so will see, for example, how those afflictions impede her friend's ability to engage in the witty banter that has always been so characteristic of her. Knowing the person behind the affliction can make it easier to be patient and to empathize. Further, friends who have seen each other through many changes will be better placed than others to take further changes in stride, seeing all changes, for the better or for the worse, against the larger picture.

As I said in the introduction, much has been written about the obligations of adult children to care for their parents as they age, while much less has been written about the reciprocal obligations of friends to do so. The caring of adult children for their parents is, as it were, symmetrical: parents care for children when the latter are young, and then children care for parents when the latter are old. The caring of long-standing friends for each other is, on the other hand, reciprocal: as friends age together, they provide mutual support through life stages. For friends who are within ten or even fifteen years of each other, then, the care and support that they can provide for each other is different from that provided either by parent to child or by adult child to ageing parent. Friends will traverse their lives together, and so the sympathy gained from a friend will be different from that gained from an adult child, regardless of the friendship that exists between the adult child and her parent. So friends can accept aid from each other without feeling like burdens: the challenges of old age that they face together will be one more set of challenges to add to the list. The reciprocity characteristic of friendships that are not between parent and child makes such long-standing friendships particularly apt for the type of caring we need as we age.

Ageing's Effect on Friendship

According to the relationships view, it is the special relationship in which one stands to a long-term friend that grounds one's special obligations to care for that friend. It might be argued, then, that certain factors that occur with ageing can weaken bonds between long-term friends and, thus, if the relationships view is correct, weaken, if not entirely undermine, the reasons that such friends have to care for one another as they age. In particular, ageing is often accompanied by some form of dementia. Such dementia can take extreme forms, such as Alzheimer's disease. Individuals suffering from such forms of dementia in their later stages will fail to recognize their intimates and may be unable to recall entire swaths of their lives, and thus may be unable to remember any interactions with a friend even if the friendship is very long-standing. With milder forms of dementia, there will still be some memory loss and confusion that can thereby alter a person's attitudes, desires, and personality. So dementia might very well affect the factors that constitute the friendship: it can wipe away or make inaccessible special knowledge of the friend, it can erase desires to spend time together, and it can severely alter attitudes of love and care. It would seem an odd consequence of the relationships view that our strong special obligations to care for our long-standing friends cease to exist when our friends most need care.

But drawing the conclusion that such changes in one's long-term friend undermine or weaken one's reasons to care for her is unwarranted. According to the relationships view, what grounds special obligations to an intimate is the relationship in which I stand to them, and relationships are temporally extended entities. My relationship to my friend is not constituted merely by current facts, but by facts about the entire course of our relationship. In long-term friendships there is a long history of love and care and of interactions that embody that love and care, and it is that history that grounds the reasons that long-term friends have to care for one another. We cannot look merely at the current state of a relationship in order to determine the nature and strength of the reasons grounded by that relationship.

Long-term friendships are usually such that they have survived and traversed significant changes in the persons involved in them. One of my closest friends is someone I met in graduate school thirty-two years ago. Both she and I were very different people then than we are now. Those changes in us are ones that we have observed in each other and suffered through together. In fact, many of those changes are such that the other person has either played a role in causing them or played some other role in their evolution. So our current friendship is constituted not only by current shared interests and attitudes, as some short-term friendships are, but by that long history of interaction and developing attitudes. Our friendship has not been a straight course: it has had its ups and downs, times at which we were very close, others at which we were more distant. But moving past the more distant times back toward a more enriched closeness is part of the strength of the relationship and bond: we know that we might move apart but will always gravitate back to a strong intimacy. And that long history remains even when some memory loss occurs or desires change. So when that occurs in old age, our special obligations to care for each other remain.

I do not want to be taken here as saying either (i) that long-term friendships will always give parties to them strong obligations to care for one another, or (ii) that changes such as those occurring with certain forms of dementia can never undermine the presence of special obligations grounded by an intimate long-term friendship. With respect to (i) I think that there is an interesting question as to whether the fact of a relationship having existed continues to ground obligations even if the relationship does not continue into the present. If I break from a friend, do she and I still have reasons to care for one another in virtue of the fact that we were once friends? I think that one plausible answer to the question is to understand friendships as generating reasons for at least some time after they cease to exist, and, the longer the friendship lasted and the closer it was, the longer those reasons will continue to exist. So for close long-term friendships, the reasons they generate will continue to hold for quite some time. I think such an answer is both philosophically plausible, given the relationships theory of special obligations, and also intuitive: I think most people will feel a pull to care for someone who was a friend over a twenty-year span much more strongly than they feel such a pull to care for someone who was a friend over a five-year period. So very long-term friendships that last into old age are quite plausibly seen as generating reasons that last a lifetime.

With respect to question (ii), there are very difficult and important questions about personal identity in the offing. If, for example, memory is necessary for personal survival, it is quite possible that severe forms of dementia amount to the cessation of the person.[9] So if my friend's dementia progresses to a certain point, she may cease to exist: her body will continue to function, but it will house a new person (or, if the dementia is severe enough, what remains may fail to constitute a person at all). In such a case, I will no longer have special obligations to this person, because she is not my friend.

But that does not mean that I do not have obligations to care for the person who now inhabits my friend's body. First, I may still owe it to my friend to care for this person. Most of us, for whatever reason, will feel concern that our bodies, and the mental life animating those bodies after the onset of dementia, are cared

---

[9] For a full discussion of these issues, see David DeGrazia (2005).

for, whether or not we view ourselves as continuing in those bodies. One way of caring for a friend is to carry out her wishes even after she is dead, and so we may very well have obligations to our friends to care for their bodies and the mental lives animating those bodies even after our friends cease to exist. I will also have other sorts of reasons to do so, reasons having to do with my own desires and attitudes. For the vast majority of us, it is nearly impossible not to continue to feel attached to a friend's physical form even after she ceases to occupy it. For the still living friend, it will be a way to honor her friend's memory and her attachment to that friend to continue to care for her body and its animating mental life even if that mental life no longer constitutes her friend.

What I have said so far supports not only the claim that long-term friends have strong obligations to care for one another in old age, but also that others have very good reasons to include them and perhaps even defer to them in deliberations about how to take care of someone who may not be competent to make such decisions for herself. Priority is usually given to family members, particularly to spouses/partners and adult children, in deciding how to care for the elderly who are unable to make rational decisions on their own behalf.[10] But long-standing friends, as I have pointed out, have comprehensive perspectives on each other's lives that adult children may lack. They also may know aspects of a person that a spouse or partner does not. Family members need to understand and respect long-standing friends' obligations to care for one another. Further, family members ought to, in carrying out their own special obligations, consult with long-standing friends: doing so will allow them to have the fullest information possible to provide care in the most caring way.

Long-term friendships, then, both add great value to our lives and provide strong reasons to the parties to them to care for each as they age. In fact, parties to such long-term friendships can care for one another in old age in ways that no one else can, given the commanding perspectives they have on each other's lives. But in what way, if at all, do we want our friends to integrate a recognition of their obligations to care for us into their motivations to do so?

Love and Obligation as Motivations to Care

We often think that the ideal motivation behind the caring actions of friends is love, pure and simple. If a friend says that she is driving us to a doctor's appointment or going grocery shopping for us because she recognizes that she has an obligation to do so, many of us will feel let down. We will regard the appeal to obligation as motivation as cold and impersonal. We prefer that a friend say, "I'm doing this because I want to. I love you, and your happiness means so much to

---

[10] But see Amber Rose Comer et al. (2017), "Physician Understanding and Application of Surrogate Decision-Making Laws in Clinical Practice," for a discussion of how physicians sometimes deviate from legal policy.

me!" It seems that recourse to thoughts of obligation to motivate one only occur when one's desires to help a friend, desires that result from care and love, have worn thin. Thus, we think that when a friend aids us from thoughts of duty, she is in a situation where she has to dredge the bottom of the motivation barrel in order to force herself to do what she really would rather not do. And doing something from such motivation hardly seems like doing it in a caring way.

This picture may be the correct one if the person acting from duty is acting from what we can think of as a bare thought of duty, where a bare thought of duty is a thought that involves no underlying conception of why one has the duty or of on what one's duty is grounded. For many people, when they have such a bare thought of duty, it amounts to nothing more than thinking something like, "I'm supposed to do this," "I have to do this," or even "It is expected of me that I do this." Such thoughts in the context of helping a friend do seem like the sort of motivation that we hope our friends are not acting on: when a friend takes care of us from such motives, we naturally feel relegated to the category of tasks such as paying taxes or wiping down our equipment after use at the gym.

I do not think, however, that most people, when acting from duty in caring for a friend, are acting from a bare thought of duty. In thinking about their reasons to aid a friend, they will reflect upon the bond between them, upon the mutual love and concern that has characterized their interactions over the years, and upon how much joy they have received from being a part of each other's lives. In other words, they will reflect upon the nature of the relationship they have had with each other, and, in doing so, they are reflecting precisely upon the grounds of their special obligations to care for one another. Of course, people who are not philosophers will not think in terms of special obligations and their grounding in special relationships, but in being motivated by thoughts of the nature of their friendship, they are being motivated by what gives them special obligations.

It is important to see how, as we age with our long-term friends, our motivations to care for each other, insofar as those motivations are guided by a robust understanding of the grounds of our special obligations, will involve a rich grasp of the long history between the two of us. In being motivated to care for our ageing friend, insofar as our motivation is rooted in the grounds of our obligations, we are not being moved by the sorts of responses that professional caregivers will have. Even the most caring of such professionals will be unable to put an aged person in the same sort of context that a long-term friend can. Unfortunately, this often leads to a conceptualization, on the part of the most well-meaning of caregivers, of the person for whom they are caring that highlights the fact that they are elderly. Of course, this is natural, because the individual needs the professional care in virtue of difficulties that are the result of her age. But long-term friends, even though they of course grasp the fact that their friend (and likely they themselves) are elderly, do not highlight that fact in their understanding of their friend and of their reasons to care for her. They have known each other at various life stages, each of which has called for care of different sorts. The latest stage in which they find themselves may provide new challenges, but they are viewed as challenges their friend is facing, not 'the challenges faced by the elderly' understood generically. My friend is the same person I knew when we were twenty, and she just happens to be old now and thus has new needs. Thinking in this way generates a very different sort of caring response than can be drawn from someone who only knows my friend as an elderly person.

I do not intend to fault professional caregivers here, but only to show how the care given by a long-term friend will be different. Our society stigmatizes, patronizes, and demeans the elderly, while extolling and idolizing youth. These attitudes are extremely detrimental to our well-being as we age, and having long-term friends who have known us as people across the life course provides a very important reminder that we are not just old people, that we are not to be reduced to our age. And this sort of corrective cannot usually be provided by adult children, who do not have the same sort of perspective on our lives, as I have previously pointed out. Thus, given that long-term friends can provide a uniquely valuable sort of concern, they have further obligations, grounded in the promotion of value, to care for their ageing friends.

Conclusions

If the relationships theory of special obligations is correct, long-standing friendships provide ageing friends with very strong reasons to provide care for each other. These relationships, in addition to grounding such reasons, can bring great joy and value to the ageing process. Insofar as they are a good that, by their very nature, is only available to us after a certain age, reflection upon them provides an important corrective to our society's devaluing of the later stages of our lives. Further, long-standing friends, given their commanding perspectives on each other's lives, can provide for each other a unique and highly valuable form of care that cannot be given by professional caregivers or even by adult children.

In a way, my philosophical arguments serve to highlight something we all know but perhaps don't take as seriously as we ought and often find tiring in the elderly. The older we get, the more we love to reminisce. When older relatives or those we have volunteered or are paid to care for reminisce, it is usually one-sided: we feel forced to listen to this older person going on and on about their glory years. But with long-term friends, reminiscence is an entirely different activity: it involves a review of a rich and valuable mutual history that has helped to shape us both into the people we now are. In reminiscing, we grasp the bond between us that undergirds our mutual obligations, making those mutual obligations something other than mere burdens to be endured: those obligations are a reflection of a valuable history and in being motivated by them in our actions we further enrich and carry forward that deep and lasting bond.

11 Forgiveness and Ageing

Geoffrey Scarre

Introduction

Forgiveness has been succinctly defined by Trudy Govier as 'a process of overcoming attitudes of resentment and anger that may persist when one has been injured by wrongdoing' (Govier 2002, viii). Some writers have emphasised a more positive side to forgiveness, whereby the elimination of negative attitudes is accompanied by the development of feelings of goodwill towards the wrongdoer (e.g., Garrard and McNaughton 2010, 24). While forgiveness responds to offences committed in the past, it bears significantly on the future when it enables the parties to a former act of wrongdoing to make a fresh start. The forgiveness of wrongdoers by their victims, as Desmond Tutu remarks, 'give[s] all the chance to begin again' (Tutu 1999, 228), and this restorative function of forgiveness is certainly amongst its most important. Charles Griswold likewise recognises that forgiveness has 'diachronic and perspectival dimensions'. He proposes that forgiveness should be understood within a 'narrative conception' of a life that regards instances of forgiveness as important not just when they happen but for the long-term future; by forgiving, a person 'projects her own narrative into the future' and incorporates within it 'a view about the sort of person [she] would want to be' (Griswold 2007, 98, 103).

To claim, with Archbishop Tutu, that there is 'no future without forgiveness' presumes that both the forgiver and the forgiven have a future before them. But what about forgiveness at, or approaching, the end of life, when the future is at best a limited one? Even philosophers who, like Griswold, have plausibly sought to define the place of forgiveness within a 'narrative conception' of human life (where the significance of particular events and experiences is estimated by reference to their place in the life-story as a whole) have had little to say about what forgiveness may look like, and what special roles it may play, at different points in the life cycle. Granting or requesting forgiveness may be as worthy at ninety as at nineteen, but it cannot be assumed that its occasions, forms, motives, practical expressions and impacts will be exactly the same in youth and age. People who have many more years behind them than in front may feel a keener need to bring moral closure to unfinished business, heal fractured relationships, and ease their own consciences by asking forgiveness for previously unrepented or unacknowledged faults. Assessed from the perspective of advancing years, offences that once seemed unforgivable may diminish in magnitude, and relationships with parents, children, lovers, friends or others that once seemed terminally broken present a less hopeless appearance. For people in their senior years who wish to tie up the moral loose ends in their life story, it might even be said that there is 'no past without forgiveness'.

Forgiveness in regard to ageing raises many intriguing questions, not all of which can be discussed within the limits of this chapter. The main focus will be on the situation of the older person against whom serious offences have been committed in the (maybe quite distant) past, and that continue to bear a sour fruit of ill-feeling, indignation, mistrust, a sense of thwarted opportunities or other negative feelings. Should ageing people be prepared to forgive, or at least consider forgiving, old offences that it might not have been (so) appropriate for them to have forgiven at an earlier date? Could they be accused of 'bearing a grudge' if they fail to do so? Or does moral consistency require that the amount of time that has elapsed since an offence was committed is irrelevant to deciding whether it should (or can) now be forgiven? In deciding whether to forgive, should the older person think about the original impact of the offence, its continuing effects over the years, or its residual impact at the present time? To what extent should recognisable changes over time in the personalities and outlooks of both offenders and victims affect the decision whether to forgive? And is a desire for mental ease and comfort in old age a morally respectable reason for desiring to find forgiveness for old injuries that may still rankle, or does it smack too much of self-interest?

Of course, it would be unattractively self-righteous for persons in their later years to recall only those instances in which they had been offended and ignore those in which they themselves had been at fault. Offenders of any age should be prepared to apologise and ask forgiveness for their wrongdoing, however long ago an offence was committed; where the victim's subsequent death makes this impossible, an offender should at the very least regret that he has delayed his apology too long. If the offering of apology rather than the requesting of forgiveness is, strictly speaking, the more dutiful act here, it would be odd to offer an apology yet be indifferent as to whether the victim was disposed to forgive or not; to be careless about the victim's response would suggest that the apology was, if not insincere, less than fully heartfelt. Delay in offering an apology should not by itself be taken as evidence of insincerity, since changes of heart can happen at any stage in life. A victim who receives an apology for an offence committed years earlier may be surprised, but she ought not to reject it simply on the ground of its lateness; to refuse forgiveness 'because the apology should have been made earlier' would be ungracious, if not curmudgeonly.

The plan of this chapter is as follows. The first section provides further analysis of the nature of forgiveness in the light of recent philosophical literature, looking in particular at the role that forgiveness may play in the evolving narrative of a life. The second section discusses how the impact of offences on victims can shift and alter in the course of time, and what this implies for the practice of forgiveness, morally and psychologically, particularly in the case of old offences. In the third section, the focus moves to worries about the intelligibility of forgiveness arising from concerns about personal identity and continuity over time. It is argued that forgiveness has a valuable role to play despite the changes that happen to people as the years pass. Finally, the fourth section considers the topic of self-forgiveness, paying specific attention to the question of whether an offender may forgive herself for an offence committed against someone who is now dead. It is concluded that although this would be out of order, an offender may legitimately consider forgiving herself for the harm she has done to *herself* through her wrongdoing.

Forgiveness: Changing One's Heart in a Narrative Context

Unless an offence is very trivial, forgiveness is rarely instantaneous; more commonly, forgiving is a process rather than an act, taking time to complete. To feel moral indignation when one has been treated disrespectfully is both natural and proper, and forgiveness that is granted too quickly may indicate that the victim is deficient in self-respect. According to Bishop Butler, resentment is neither 'faulty' nor 'blameable', provided it is proportionate to the offence (Butler 1970 [1727], 81), while Jeffrie Murphy has argued that resentment 'stands as a testimony to our allegiance to the moral order itself' (Murphy 2003, 19). In Margaret Holmgren's view, forgiveness involves a 'change of heart' away from such (justified) resentment towards a kinder, more generous attitude towards the offender, which reframes him as a person 'subject to various needs, pressures, and confusions in life, and vulnerable to error' (Holmgren 2012, 32–3). She agrees with Pamela Hieronymi that forgiveness must have a 'cognitive' as well as an 'affective' component, some change of judgement about the offender being needed to justify the replacement of resentment with softer feelings (Hieronymi 2001, 529–30). Griswold similarly contends that, in order to forgive, a victim needs to be able to 'see the injurer in a new light' (Griswold 2007, 103). Yet this line of thought should not, perhaps, be pressed too far: for while forgiveness may *commonly* turn on a reconsideration of the offender as a flawed and error-prone human being against whom continued resentment is 'unworthy' (Holmgren 2012, 32–3), it might also consist in an unusually gracious relinquishment of resentment and a willingness to afford another chance to an offender of whom one's original judgement has not significantly altered and who entirely deserves one's indignation. In such a case, what makes forgiveness possible is more likely to be the thought that none of us is perfect, a proneness to error being natural to our species.

Forgiveness that was felt by the victim but not communicated to the offender would remain unfinished business; in ideal cases, 'I forgive you' is the prelude to the restoration of active good relations and the renewal of mutual trust. But the level and type of restoration produced by forgiveness varies. Carl Reinhold Bråkenhielm notes that forgiveness sometimes achieves a 'full reestablishment of personal relationships', at others a lesser restoration of 'the moral community', where people express some practical good will for one another but withhold their friendship (Bråkenhielm 1993, 30). It is doubtful whether forgiveness may ever be demanded by an offender as a right, and the granting of forgiveness is more often thought of as being like the giving of a gift than the fulfilment of a duty. Even if forgiveness is more gift-like than dutiful, it is reasonably regarded as subject to certain norms, as Griswold has noted (2007, xv), so it would be inappropriate to forgive an offender who laughs in the victim's face, and ungenerous to refuse forgiveness to one who was truly repentant and eager to make amends. Some people are naturally more forgiving than others. If a disposition to forgive ('forgivingness') is an appealing trait of character, to count as a virtue it must be guided by sound judgement and avoid both excess and defect (Roberts 1995). A person who is never or rarely prepared to forgive can be written down as hard-hearted, but one who is ready to forgive anyone and anything is merely soft. While many, if not most, instances of forgiveness spring from forgivingness, alternative origins are also possible: thus, a person not especially imbued with forgivingness may forgive an offender because he thinks he deserves to be forgiven, all things considered.

Through its role of repairing relationships that have been damaged by wrong-doing, forgiveness benefits not just offenders but victims as well. Both parties profit from the restoration of mutual trust and good will, and where victim and offender make the effort to know and understand each other, each may find sources of value in the other that were hitherto overlooked. It is important, however, that those who grant forgiveness do not glory in their own gracious-ness. Griswold writes that 'The forgiver must not only see the injurer in a new light, but see himself in a new light' (Griswold 2007, 103). The victim who forgives an injury because he recognises that he, too, although a valuable human being deserving of respect, is fallible and prone to error, advances in self-knowledge. Forgiveness, said Bishop Butler, flows most readily from the person who, 'conscious of many frailties' in himself, has learned the fitness of being 'meek, forgiving, and merciful'. For Butler, this knowledge deepens with experi-ence, as we discover how prone we all are to moral error. It is the 'good man' at the close of life who sees most fully the 'amiableness' of forgiveness, because he recalls how often he has needed it himself (Butler 1970 [1727], 88–9).[1]

---

[1] Butler also remarks that the 'good man' who forgives others improves his prospects of receiving divine forgiveness for his own offences after death. Considered as a motive for forgiving others, this must be accounted a somewhat heteronomous one.

Age does not invariably bring wisdom, but older people have had longer to learn that all human beings are frail and fallible, and also that motives for action are often a good deal more complex than they may appear at first sight (including to their agents themselves). In the words of T. S. Eliot in *East Coker*:

> As we grow older
> The world becomes stranger, the pattern more complicated

Of dead and living. (Eliot 1970, II. 189–91)

It would be too much to hope that our former judgements of people and their motives were always sound. Too often, as Eliot observes, 'We had the experience but missed the meaning' – our templates of interpretation did not really fit the (all too elusive) facts (Eliot 1970, l. 93). As social animals, we could not exist without attempting to understand and appraise others' actions and motives, but judgements should always be considered as provisional and open to review. Older people may not always be better than younger ones at evaluating others' actions, but their longer experience should have taught them how easily human motives can be misread. This knowledge should make them more cautious in passing judgements, and more prepared to give the benefit of the doubt – and perhaps to forgive – when motives are obscure.

Narrative conceptions of life construe the meanings of particular acts, episodes and experiences by reference to their place in a life-story as a whole. They emphasise that human lives do not consist in random series of unrelated happenings but are structured (to a greater or a lesser degree in individual cases) by the formation of plans, projects, ambitions and relationships that link past, present and future in significant sequences. The metaphor of lives as 'narratives', however, should not be stretched too far, because individuals as the 'authors' of their lives do not enjoy a wholly free hand in the construction of their stories, but face constraints imposed by their social, economic or geographical circumstances; they also have to adapt their narratives to take account of the interacting and often conflicting narratives of other persons. Nevertheless, thinking of the ways in which all but the most disordered lives resemble narratives points attention to the purposive structures and the patterns of growth and development that form the framework of experience and provide it with existential meaning. People are differentially competent at learning from experience, but, as we grow older, our perspective on life changes (or at any rate, *ought* to change) in what David Carr has characterised as a continuous 'creative process of self-formation and self-interpretation' (Carr 2016, 184). Such self-interpretation requires that we should step temporarily outside the protagonist's role and attempt to look at ourselves from a more 'external' or objective viewpoint; from this viewpoint we candidly acknowledge our successes and failures and project not simply the future we wish to have, but the self who is to have it.

Questions about the granting or requesting of forgiveness are ideally considered from an external viewpoint ('How, long-term, did that offence affect me?') which, by placing offences in a broader narrative context, escapes being influenced by the mood of the moment. And as our self-evaluations change, so too do our evaluations of others, so that offences that once seemed very hard to forgive may later present themselves in a fresh light. Where resentment once ruled, the passage of years enables a narrative recontextualisation that situates former offences in a new setting. A previously unrepentant offender may in the course of time have been brought to a more remorseful attitude by the means of her own self-evaluations; or, as Griswold notes, communication with others may have enabled the victim to 'narrate her story differently, as she looks at self-past and self-now from a different "external" perspective, viz., one consonant with that of others who were not part of the [original] story-world' (Griswold 2007, 103). There are certainly cases in which no amount of narrative recontextualisation will persuade a victim that her original reading of the offence and the offender was too harsh; and where the offender remains unrepentant, forgiveness may never be appropriate. A victim who longs to be able to cast her past in a more positive light should not force herself to forgive, or persuade herself she has forgiven, solely in order to gain peace of mind. That way lies a fool's paradise.

Forgiveness and the Passage of Time: Knowing When (and When Not) to Let Go

When a person considers whether to forgive an offence committed against him long before, should he focus on the initial impact it had on him, its resonances over the intervening years or its residual impact at the present day? An injury that hurt very much when it was inflicted long ago may have ceased to be more than a mildly unpleasant memory today. Given its shrunken role in his past narrative and its unimportance for his future, then absent any request from the offender for forgiveness, the wisest thing may be to let bygones be bygones and think no more about it. Raking over the ashes of the past in the name of a quest for moral closure may be in the interests of neither victim nor offender. Knowing when to let go even of justified grievances is a form of practical wisdom that recognises that excessive focus on the faults of the past can hinder progress towards a better future. The victim who is willing to overlook past offences reveals, besides practical wisdom, a magnanimous spirit that is lacking in the victim who perpetually dwells on her injuries.[2] Although letting

---

[2] Preferably this should not be the kind of magnanimity ascribed by Aristotle to the 'great-souled' man (*megalopsuchos*), who disregards injuries and affronts done to him out of a sense

bygones be bygones may be considered a privilege of victims, it may occasion-ally do more harm than good for an offender to apologise and ask forgiveness for an offence committed long ago, if this revives the victim's memory of painful incidents that she would have preferred to forget. Such cases may be exceptional, but sometimes forgetting *is* better than forgiving.

The passage of time can reduce the impact of offences on the narratives of victims, but some injuries have a searing effect on victims that lasts a lifetime. Hence, there can be no statute of limitations on offences beyond which forgiveness is necessarily redundant. An elderly person who remains indignant at an injury that was inflicted on her in her youth may still hope for an apology, and be prepared to grant her forgiveness should the offender offer it. One difficulty about the forgiveness of ancient offences is that memory is fallible, and victims and offenders may not recall 'what really happened' in the same way. Where narratives conflict about the facts, or about their significance, the best the parties may now be able to do is to wish each other well while agreeing to disagree about the putative offence. Not every lasting sense of grievance is warranted, and offences are sometimes inflated in memory. Where that is the case – or the offender sincerely believes it to be – he is not obliged to accept forgiveness on the terms on which the victim (real or self-styled) is ready to grant it. Both offenders and victims should recognise that memory can be unreliable, especially in regard to the distant past. They should also take care to avoid creatively revising their narratives in their own favour, representing their actions as more innocent, or their sufferings more serious, than they actually were.

People who in their later years re-evaluate their past narratives need to be alert for errors of memory and for the natural desire to interpret their narratives in ways most favourable to themselves. But they should be careful, too, to avoid softening or sanitising their recollections of a painful past, diminishing the magnitude of crimes or the horrendousness of suffering. Some ageing people can look back on terrible things that either they did themselves or endured at the hands of others in their younger days. To suppose that the mere passage of years reduces the need for forgiveness, as if time itself could wash sins away, insults victims and lets offenders off the hook too easily. But it would be wrong to assume that a person who has suffered great injuries must finally be able to find forgiveness for her offender(s) if her narrative is not to end imperfectly. Where someone has experienced truly shattering injuries, abandoning her resentment in the evening of her life, far from tying up the moral loose ends, might threaten her narrative with incoherence. After such resentment, what forgiveness? 'People who forgive too readily', David Novitz has argued, 'do not

of lofty disdain for those around him, holding it beneath him to harbour resentments against lesser men, but rather the generous spirit that humbly acknowledges our common human fallibility (see Aristotle 1954, 94 and 1125a).

manifest the right degree of self-respect; they underestimate their own worth and fail to take their own projects and entitlements seriously enough' (Novitz 1998, 299). Attempting to subdue justified resentment in order to achieve closure in one's final years is morally and intellectually dishonest if it turns on distorting the facts or faking one's ethical judgements. Because a person's moral judgements may quite legitimately change as she ages, forgiveness that comes late may not always sound a jarring note; it could even signal the start of a new chapter in her story. But in the case of some very bad injuries, preservation of moral integrity may require the retention of resentment until the close of life.

Holocaust survivor Eli Wiesel, speaking in 1995 at the fiftieth anniversary commemoration of the liberation of Auschwitz, prayed, 'O God: do not have pity on those who established this place. God of forgiveness, do not forgive the murderers of Jewish children' (cited in Bash 2007, 48). For Wiesel, no degree of repentance by the perpetrators could warrant the forgiveness of such heinous crimes. Some writers have found this outlook too intransigent, though it is generally conceded that any personal criticism of Holocaust survivors by those who never experienced such horrors would be impertinent. Trudy Govier finds in the human capacity to change and improve a potential ground for victims to forgive even the most terrible offenders whose hearts are not fixed irremovably on evil (Govier 1999, 2002). Eve Garrard, in an essay on forgiveness and the Holocaust, goes further in suggesting that the fact that the Nazis do not *deserve* forgiveness is not a compelling reason why they should not be forgiven: forgiving, in the sense of wishing the perpetrators well, she thinks, is possible even in the case of some very bad agents (Garrard 2003, 237–8). Garrard stresses that such forgiveness in no way implies endorsement of them or their values; rather, it acknowledges their status as 'our fellow human beings', capable, as we all are, of 'both good and evil' (Garrard 2003, 238, 241). Citing the historical researches of Christopher Browning and others, she reminds us that many of the Nazi torturers and killers were neither sadists nor insane but 'ordinary men' – people very much like ourselves (Garrard 2003, 241; Browning 1998).

The fact, assuming it to be one, that all or most human beings are capable of doing terrible things in suitably impelling circumstances does not imply that there are no unforgivable acts or agents. Griswold considers that although perpetrators of terrible atrocities may not be 'absolutely unforgivable', they are unforgivable so long as they show themselves 'incapable of reason, choice, and moral transformation' (Griswold 2007, 93). But even when the doers of awful things sincerely repent, there is no obligation on the victim's part to let go of resentment against gross injury, early or late, if doing so would be at too great cost to her self-respect. Griswold's view may be more realistic than the somewhat idealised positions of Govier and Garrard, which, by focussing so heavily on the positive benefits of forgiveness, risk overlooking the fact that forgiveness can itself be costly – and even injurious – to the victim. Graciousness can come at a price to the gracious.

Forgiveness: Taking Care of the Self – and Others

Life-narratives typically display both continuity and change. According to the standard view, which is firmly rooted in our self-reflection and taken for granted in our everyday transactions and for forensic purposes, people remain numerically identical throughout their lives, whatever physical and psychological changes they undergo. The standard view has occasionally been challenged by philosophers (notably by Derek Parfit [1984] and Galen Strawson [2009], who propose that human beings are rather series of connected but discrete selves), but rejecting it would seem to undermine the idea that forgiveness for an injury can be granted long after the event – for by then the original offender and victim will have ceased to exist, having been replaced by successor selves who at best can only be doubtful proxies for their predecessors. Yet even assuming the standard view to be correct, some of the inevitable *qualitative* changes – in beliefs and judgements, attitudes and values, desires and ambitions, plans and projects – that take place in people over time can give rise to similar worries about the intelligibility of granting forgiveness once significant changes have taken place in the offender, the victim or both. One particularly intriguing version of this argument holds that even on a short timescale, sincere repentance on the wrongdoer's part is itself sufficiently transformative to ensure that forgiveness must miss its mark, since the original offender is no longer there! Thus, Aurel Kolnai has argued that where a former offender has 'revoked and disavowed the offence in point', thereby disconnecting himself from 'his past in the given context', that very fact that he now deserves forgiveness makes forgiveness superfluous (Kolnai 1973, 95–9). Chester Calhoun has likewise been sceptical about the value of forgiveness that follows the wrongdoer's remorse and repentance, suggesting that by coming to 'deserve' it, he reduces it to being 'cheap' and 'minimalist' (Calhoun 1992, 80–1). Most radically of all, Jacques Derrida proposes that forgiveness is 'mad, and that it must remain a madness of the impossible', because if the victim is prepared to forgive 'on the condition that the guilty one repents, mends his ways, [and] asks forgiveness', he would then 'no longer be exactly the same as the one who was found to be culpable'; forgiveness must inevitably target the wrong person (Derrida 2001, 38–9). According to views like these, forgiveness granted in old age for offences committed long before would appear to be especially liable to the charge that it is redundant, if not incoherent.

Derrida's critique of forgiveness may trade on conflating the notions of numerical and of qualitative identity, but even when it is conceded that the repentant recipient of forgiveness is still numerically identical with the offender, the admission that he is a 'changed person' in a qualitative sense (he is at least now sorry for his actions) may threaten to make forgiveness idle at best. To make matters worse, questions about qualitative change arise also in regard to the person who forgives. The angry and indignant victim of an injury at time t who finds herself at a later time, $t+1$, ready to replace her negative attitudes with good will, has also undergone some internal transformation. Particularly (but not only) where the interval between t and $t+1$ is a long one (as when an elderly person forgives an offence committed against her in her youth), the internal changes in attitudes, beliefs, expectations, even in values, may be extensive and profound. Seemingly, then, this forgiveness relationship has the 'wrong' person at both ends.

To respond to these worries, it is necessary to reconsider the dynamics of forgiveness. It is profoundly mistaken to think that because an offender has come to deserve a victim's forgiveness, forgiveness now becomes superfluous. For on the contrary: the offender who repents shows herself to be ready and willing to make a new start in her relations with the victim, and by forgiving her offender, the victim demonstrates a reciprocal willingness. Forgiveness facilitates the forward development of both the victim's and the offender's narratives after they had become stalled. (Griswold [2007, 109] remarks on the way in which forgiveness assists personal *growth*). The fact that people can change in qualitative aspects while remaining numerically the same individuals, far from making forgiveness 'impossible', as the critics contend, is exactly what gives forgiveness its importance in their personal stories. Anger, indignation and suspicion are replaced by positive attitudes enabling the recovery of mutual trust and respect. To be sure, the repentant wrongdoer may retain some painful feelings of guilt, and victims may require time to feel fully reconciled with the offenders they have forgiven, but forgiveness marks the start of the process by which both parties transcend the disruptive events of the past. Calhoun concedes that victim-forgiveness would not be 'minimalist' and 'risk free' were it to target the *un*repentant, rather than the repentant, wrongdoer (even if forgiveness in the absence of repentance might seem 'repugnant' [Calhoun 1992, 93, 76]). But forgiveness is also very far from being trivial when a victim and a *repentant* wrongdoer agree to transcend a difficult past and begin their relationship anew. Far from being easy and risk free, this can take real guts.

Whether the offences they forgive are recent or ancient, forgiveness enables people to come to terms with the past while making provision for a better future. And rather than being undermined by personal change, forgiveness is a form of personal change that is valuable at any time in life. There is little empirical evidence that people become significantly more forgiving as they age, and the longer that injuries rankle within human breasts, the harder it can be for forgiveness to overcome entrenched resentments. The popular belief that people become more tolerant of human faults and foibles as they age probably owes more to wishful thinking than to experience, and the flexibility of response required for forgiveness does not always come easily to people who have become set in their ways of feeling and thought. Older people may also find it hard to come to terms with changes in social behaviour that cause offence where none is intended (for example, an elderly person who is used to a more formal style of conduct may object to being called by her first name by a young teenager). Forgiveness can be difficult where the 'offender' and the 'victim' differ as to what constitutes an offence. But on the positive side, where the value of forgiveness has been learned though a lifetime of practice, a willingness to forgive is unlikely to desert a person in old age.

Because the harbouring of grudges and resentments is inimical to the achievement of inner peace, popular 'self-help' literature has seized on the therapeutic potential of forgiveness 'to reduce or get rid of psychological states that distress the victim, or make it hard for him to get on with his life' (Garrard and McNaughton 2010, 66–7). This approach values forgiveness primarily as a 'coping strategy' for people who are suffering from depressive conditions brought on by the consciousness of injury. A victim might feel impelled to have done with memories of old injuries by performing 'a piece of mental hygiene: a spring-cleaning of unwanted lumber from the mental attic' (Garrard and McNaughton 2010, 68). The problem with this, as Garrard and McNaughton point out, is that while no one disputes that making people feel better is generally a good thing, '[a]dvocating forgiveness as a form of self-help therapy leaves out a huge part of the moral dimension of forgiveness because it leaves the wrongdoer out of the picture' (Garrard and McNaughton 2010, 67). By putting forgiveness on a level with such self-improving endeavours as losing weight or taking up a hobby, the self-help approach ignores several important questions: Does a particular offender *deserve* forgiveness? Is he repentant? Ought he first to apologise, or to offer some reparation, before forgiveness should be granted? What kind of relationship with the wrongdoer is possible or desirable in the sequel? What can then be expected from him? And what from oneself? Forgiveness cannot do what Garrard and McNaughton term its proper 'moral work' unless such questions are posed. Forgiveness is a moral transaction, not merely the elimination of an upsetting attitude (which might anyway be more effectively achieved by the use of hypnosis or an amnesiac drug). The satisfaction that is felt when one forgives an injury comes, or should come, from the consciousness that one has acted in the morally fitting way, and that one has done so because it *is* the morally fitting way. The offender relieves his troubled conscience by apologising to the victim and receiving his forgiveness; the victim is happy that good relations have been restored with the offender. The peace of mind produced by genuine forgiveness is thus quite different from the superficial relief attained by a moral-lite expulsion by the victim of distressing thoughts and attitudes for the sake of feeling better.

Mental ease and release from the pressures and stresses of life being conditions naturally desired by people in their later years, the prospect of acquiring them by means of the 'forgiveness' touted in some self-help manuals may look especially tempting to the elderly. But those siren attractions ought to be resisted. To be the genuine article, forgiveness must involve a concern for the offender's well-being as well as for the victim's own. This is more likely to be felt by those older people who have learned to say, 'There, but for the grace of God, go I', than by those of a more self-righteous disposition who are less alert to their own faults (or who even enjoy bearing grudges).

Self-Forgiveness

A repentant offender of any age may seek to assuage his troubled conscience by apologising to his victim and asking to be forgiven. But for older people who have unforgiven offences on their consciences, the quest for forgiveness takes on particular urgency if the sands of time are running out for themselves or for their victims. A life-review conducted by anyone but a saint will disclose a multitude of fallings-out, disputes, quarrels, betrayals, failures of trust, acts of selfishness or meanness that remain unresolved by apology and forgiveness. Sometimes repentance, and with it the desire for forgiveness, arrives too late. That letting-down of a friend, or the family quarrel in which one behaved badly, or the hurtful remark made in a moment of anger, returns to haunt one when it is no longer possible to do anything about it because the victim is now dead or has passed out of one's life.

Where requesting forgiveness is no longer possible or practicable, there may still be relatives or friends of the victim who would appreciate an expression of remorse, however belated. But it is – to say the least – very doubtful whether they or anyone else can forgive on behalf of a deceased (or any other) victim. The principle that only victims are entitled to forgive the injuries they have suffered is intuitively compelling, and writers on forgiveness have mostly rejected the idea of vicarious or 'third-party' forgiveness on the ground that it infringes a moral prerogative of victims.[3] Even if vicarious forgiveness *were* possible and proper, it could never be more than a distant second-best form of forgiveness, since it could do nothing to heal the damaged relationship with the victim. The offender who leaves it too late to ask forgiveness will never know whether his request would have been granted by a now-deceased victim, nor can he offer any compensation or begin their relationship anew. Making his

---

[3] Many offences and injuries hurt other people besides their primary victims, and there is nothing to prevent co-sufferers from forgiving their own share of harm. The parents of a child killed by a careless motorist may consider whether to forgive him for their own pain at the loss of their child, even if they cannot forgive him on behalf of the child. For critiques of third-party forgiveness, see, inter alia, Griswold (2007, 117–19), Holmgren (2012, 36–8), Scarre (2004, 66–70) and Walker (2013). For a dissenting view, see Pettigrove (2009, 2012).

peace with the victim's descendants, however desirable that may be, will never adequately replace receiving the victim's forgiveness.

If a victim is no longer alive to grant forgiveness to an offender, might it ever be appropriate for the offender to perform an act of *self*-forgiveness? Not if this means that the offender takes on the role of proxy for the victim, and grants himself forgiveness on the victim's behalf: this is plainly ruled out by the principle that only victims can forgive their own injuries. An individual who grants herself forgiveness for harm done to another would resemble a competition entrant who awards herself the prize or a college student who determines his own course grades. Forgiving oneself for harming another should not be confused with reflecting on the quality of one's own past deeds, subjecting them to the tribunal of conscience – a form of self-appraisal that is both permissible and meritorious. Looking back over her life as objectively as she can, an elderly person may conclude that some of the things she did in her younger years were worse than she then thought they were, others not so bad. Hindsight provides a long-term perspective in which past acts appear more clearly in context. But self-forgiveness goes beyond self-appraisal in that it involves an illicit reconfiguring of the roles of victim and offender: in self-forgiveness, the offender assumes the victim's privilege of determining whether and on what conditions forgiveness should be given, and when resentment may appropriately be replaced by good will. This can never be legitimate.

There is, however, another side to wrongdoing that needs to be considered, besides the harm it does to the victim. Many ethical writers have plausibly contended that wrongdoing injures wrongdoers themselves as well as victims. According to Kant, because agents ought always to act 'in keeping with the worth of man', someone who behaves immorally lets himself down: by acting in an unworthy manner, he is 'then in contradiction with the essential ends of humanity in his own person, and so with himself' (Kant 1963, 124). If in harming another person an agent also harms himself, treating himself without the respect he owes to his own humanity, then he is an ancillary victim of his own misdoing. This appears to let a form of self-forgiveness back into the picture. A person who is sorry for the harm he has done himself by offending – provided that he does not regret his act for that reason alone, ignoring the harm he has done to his victim – may seek to heal that self-inflicted wound by facing up to his fault, (possibly) performing an act of penance, resolving not to do the same thing again, and wishing himself well in his future endeavours.

A possible objection here, that the notion that wrongdoers can forgive themselves for the harm they do to themselves implies a fissile view of the self, may be answered by the observation that our capacity to view ourselves objectively enables us, as Nancy Snow remarks, to look on some of our 'beliefs and motives, ... traits and dispositions' as providing 'standards by means of which others can be checked or corrected' (Snow 1994, 76). No splitting of the self is involved here. Still, the idea that we are entitled to determine when we merit our own forgiveness, and are justified in 'letting go' of the self-directed moral indignation that we might rightly feel, may appear to run foul of the jurisprudential principle that 'no person should be judge in his own case'. There is also a danger that in estimating our own faults, we succumb to self-complacence, or even hypocrisy. Notwithstanding these doubts, a number of recent writers have urged that self-forgiveness, or something closely akin to it, does have a role to play where the consciousness of wrongs done is sufficiently distressing to have a cramping effect on an agent's present and prospective actions. Where it is felt that nothing can be done to wipe the slate clean, the result can be a mood of hopeless despondence which, it is suggested, only self-forgiveness can cure. As Robin Dillon observes, shame, self-contempt and self-loathing can combine with remorse to undermine the agent's self-respect (Dillon 2001). An older person with unforgiven major offences on her con-science may judge her narrative to be irretrievably flawed and incapable of being brought to a morally satisfactory conclusion. To restore her self-belief and a sense that her life has been worthwhile, she needs to come to terms with her own failures and weaknesses just as she does with those of other people she forgives. 'The affective component of an attitude of self-forgiveness', suggests Holmgren, 'consists of a basic feeling of self-respect and self-acceptance' (Holmgren 2012, 106): the agent decides she must put up with herself, warts and all. Govier sums up self-forgiveness succinctly: 'When we forgive our-selves we make emotional shifts away from blame, guilt, and shame; ... we reframe ourselves as capable of a fresh moral start; and we reaffirm relevant values – the acts in question were wrong and we resolve to do better' (Govier 2002, 133). Self-forgiveness of this sort can be an existential life-preserver.

Self-forgiveness can also complete what forgiveness by the victim has begun but not fully accomplished because the forgiven offender retains a sense of shame or self-contempt; and it may be the only form of forgiveness available where an unusually curmudgeonly victim has ungraciously refused to forgive a repentant offender. For the elderly person who seeks to put her house in moral order before she departs the scene, settling her debits and credits may necessi-tate some acts of self-forgiveness along with the forgiveness of others and requests for their forgiveness.

In 'Little Gidding', the last of Eliot's *Four Quartets*, what are ironically described as 'the gifts reserved for age' include:

> At last, the rending pain of re-enactment
> Of all that you have done, and been; the shame
> Of motives late revealed, and the awareness
> Of things ill done and done to others' harm
> Which once you took for exercise of virtue.
>
> (Eliot 1970, II. 129, 138–42)

Although painful awareness of the things that one has got wrong is not an experience peculiar to the elderly, older people have had more time in which to get things wrong, and so potentially have more to regret. Self-knowledge is instrumentally valuable (we learn from our mistakes), but also desirable in itself, and the arrival in age at an unblinking recognition of our past bad acts and corrupt motives is appositely termed by Eliot a 'gift'. But it would be a sad thing if that were inevitably the end of the story. The cited passage from 'Little Gidding' appears premised on the pessimistic assumption that regret, remorse and self-disappointment, once they have entered the soul, are there to stay. That is not true, because there is always the prospect, up to our last hour, of making our peace with others and also with ourselves through the medium of forgiveness. To bear grudges till the end and forgive them on one's deathbed is certainly to leave things very late, and some deathbed acts of forgiveness are probably less than wholly sincere. Even so, forgiveness is a gift that, if not exclusively 'reserved for age', may play an especially significant role at the close of a life-narrative.

12 Life-Extending Treatments for People with Dementia

Nancy S. Jecker

Introduction

In Jonathan Swift's novel *Gulliver's Travels*, struldbruggs are fictional people that look just like ordinary human beings save one difference. Struldbruggs live forever. While it might be considered a great blessing to live forever, it might also be considered a great curse, because struldbruggs never stop ageing. At age eighty, they are legally dead and lose their rights under the law, even though they are biologically very much alive, growing increasingly decrepit. Swift's satire makes a mockery of the quest for immortality and the case of the struldbruggs suggests that more than staying alive matters.

If more life is not necessarily good, how do we tell when it is? What features must a human life have or not have to qualify? Philosophers have offered up various answers to this conundrum, claiming that the features that matter most to a good life are having a pleasant life, having one's preferences satisfied, being conscious, retaining the capacity for rational thought, or the life mattering to the person whose life it is. According to some analyses, the more good features a life contains, the higher its quality. Presumably, if life's quality dips below a certain threshold, being alive may not be a good, or may even be worse than death.

This chapter examines different views about the conditions under which life is worth continuing. The first section examines the view that whether living longer is good or bad is contingent upon the kind of experience life is. The metaphor of life as an experience machine brings out the philosophical assumptions inherent in variations on this theme. Limitations of the experience view of life's value lead us to formulate alternative accounts, which refer to objective human capabilities, authenticity, or being in synch with reality. The second section explores how various assessments of life's value inform judgments about whether to provide lifesaving interventions for persons with dementia, focusing on decision-making for individuals with Alzheimer's disease.

Life's Experience

What are we to make of the quality of life of an older adult with advanced dementia? Consider the case of Margo, widely discussed in the literature.

The Case of Margo

> Margo develops Alzheimer's disease, yet it turns out she is content most of the time. Previously, she executed an advance directive specifying that if she develops dementia, she should not receive treatment for any potentially fatal condition. When Margo develops pneumonia, should we treat her with antibiotics? Since she is content most of the time, what is the significance of her past desires?
>
> (Dworkin 1994)

Positive experiences. Margo is content. Is that enough? One way to gain insight on this is by comparing Margo's case to the situation of the person in Nozick's experience machine.

Nozick's Experience Machine

> Imagine a machine, perhaps something akin to a virtual reality machine, that could give us whatever desirable or pleasurable experiences we want. The machine stimulates a user's brain to induce pleasurable experiences that are indistinguishable from the kind that the user would have apart from the machine. If the machine's settings manufactured positive experiences, presumably we would prefer to stay connected and if it produced negative experiences, we would prefer to exit the machine.
>
> (Nozick 1974, 42–45)

Nozick maintains that no one would want to be plugged in to his experience machine. Assuming that is right, he goes on to argue that the experience machine discredits the philosophical stance known as hedonism, which is the view that the sole thing of value is pleasurable experiences. Analogously, in the case of Margo, although she has positive experiences while she is plugged in, she does not have the life that she really would want, if she could step outside and see her life from her previous capacitated perspective. Like the plugged-in person in Nozick's experience machine, Margo has lost that perspective. However, before her Alzheimer's disease took hold, when she still retained capacity, she made it clear that the experience machine kind of life was not for her.

Margo's prior preferences, as expressed through the advance directive, converge with what many philosophers who have commented on Nozick's experience machine have to say, namely, living plugged in to a machine is not a good life for a human being (Anderson 1993, 129; Kraut 1994; Kagan 1998, 38–39; Adams 1999, 87; Feldman 2004, 16). What is it that renders Nozick's experience machine so undesirable? A key concern Nozick expressed was that having our brains stimulated by a machine is an entirely passive experience. Someone plugged in lacks agency.

Agency. To address this concern, consider a variation of Nozick's experience machine concocted by Greene.

Greene's Experience Machine

> You wake up in a plain white room, seated in a reclining chair, with a steel contraption on your head. A person in a white coat is standing over you. "The year is 2659," she explains, "We at IEM interrupt our client's programs at ten-year intervals to ensure client satisfaction. Our records indicate that at your three previous interruptions you deemed your program satisfactory and chose to continue. As before, if you choose to continue you will return to your life with no recollection of this interruption. Your friends, loved ones, and projects will all be there. Of course, you may choose to terminate your program at this point if you are unsatisfied for any reason. If you terminate your program, your life will abruptly end because in your other life you are dying. Do you intend to continue with your program?"
>
> (De Lazari-Radek and Singer 2014, 257)

Does Greene's experience machine avoid at least some of the objections that Nozick's raises, since it adds an element of agency, allowing the user to select from a menu of options, and since it includes a range of different types of pleasures? Presumably, in Greene's machine, a user could decide to hug a friend or learn a language. Even if Margo, before she became ill, would have preferred not to stay plugged in to some kinds of experience machines, such as Nozick's, perhaps she would have agreed to other types of experience machines, such as Greene's, that create greater agency and enable choosing higher-end experiences. If so, then the pertinent question for deciding what to do in the case of Margo would be to ask which kind of machine is she in. As her disease progresses, the answer we give to this question will shift as her agency diminishes and the range of pleasures she enjoys narrows.

Experiences connected to reality. Nozick raised three further objections to the experience machine: actually doing something matters, actually being a certain kind of person matters, and actually having contact with reality matters. As Nozick puts it, the lesson we learn from his (or any) experience machine is that "something matters to us in addition to experience" (Nozick 1974, 311) Unger expresses a similar point (Unger 1992, 301). According to Unger, we care deeply about many things independently of the experiences those things secure for us. For example, I care about my children's lives going well after I die. It is not that I imagine looking down upon my children's lives from heaven and feeling good about them; it is, instead, that I want their lives to be happy for their sakes, irrespective of whether I derive any personal pleasure from it.

If we care about the way things really are, not just having pleasant experiences, this has practical implications for a case like Margo's. While she is not in a machine experiencing simulated experiences, her experiences are false in another sense, namely, they are a product of her disease. Absent the disease,

Margo would perceive her life quite differently. If she grasped her true predicament, she would cease to find her life pleasant. In this sense, her desire for sensory experiences is *ill-informed*, because she can think only of Margo-now. If this is correct, it is better not to plug in to Nozick or Greene's experience machine. Although both generate positive subjective experiences, we care about more than what is in our head. We care about having a life connected to reality.

Heathwood distinguishes several additional respects in which a person's desires can be defective: being *pointless*, *being irrational*, or *making a person badly off* (Heathwood 2005). It could be argued that in addition to being ill-informed, Margo's desires are defective in each of these ways. Like the person who derives pleasure from engaging in the pointless activity of counting blades of grass (Rawls 1971), Margo's pleasures serve no larger purpose. Her desires are irrational in the sense of being inconsistent with her prior desires, before dementia set in, as reflected in her advance directive. Finally, Margo's desires make her badly off in the sense that they are contrary to her prior wishes. Living with dementia is a bad ending to the story of Margo's life, because she did not want her life to end this way.

If Margo's contentment is ill-informed, pointless, irrational, or makes her badly off, then perhaps her contentment is defective. To say this, we need not specify a full-blown account of objective human flourishing. Instead, all we need to say is that Margo's life falls sadly short of what a human life can be. For example, she has lost central human capabilities she once had, such as the ability to reason and think about her life.

Yet in reply to defective desires type objections, it might be argued that they miss the point. In Margo's case, this is the only life she has. She cannot decide to exit the experience machine and go back to some other life, such as her former life before disease. She cannot choose higher desires or desires that are more connected with reality. In light of this, a more accurate depiction of Margo's predicament might be as follows.

Margo's Experience Machine

Imagine a machine, perhaps something akin to a virtual reality machine. The machine is giving us pleasurable experiences of the sort we share with non-human animals, such as satiation of hunger. It simulates positive sensory pleasures, such as the tactile pleasure associated with stroking a piece of fur or watching fish swim in a tank. Life plugged into the machine is the only life we have. Once we unplug, we will not have any experiences at all.

If this is what Margo's experience machine is like, then perhaps the right answer for Margo is to stay connected as long as her machine makes her feel good. For now at least, Margo's life is pleasant.

A still stronger reply to the defective desires series of objections would be to make the only experiences Margo can have better and less defective. For example, suppose a technology of the future is developed for people with dementia that offers them simulated experiences of various types. Suppose further that the options are fully explained to a person who has decisional capacity at the time they complete an advance directive. They are given the chance to specify in their directive if they would like to be connected to a virtual reality (VR) device to ensure that the quality of their experiences remains high and includes the things that matter to them, such as spending time with grandchildren, listening to opera, reading a book, or being with friends.

Such a suggestion is not far-fetched. It has been piloted in competent older adult populations using 360-degree VR scenes that included mildly calming scenes from nature (Appel et al. 2019). The results showed that, despite limited mobility and range-of-motion, ninety percent of participants were able to move their heads side-to-side and up and down in order to observe VR surroundings and seventy-five percent of those who used a swivel chair felt comfortable rotating the chair, with wheelchair-bound participants able to request a caregiver to turn their chair. Participants expressed interest in seeing a variety of scenes, including social scenes with people and animals, and familiar real-world scenes such as places from their history. Post-VR, participants were eager to share their feelings about what they saw, the memories the VR evoked, and to involve others in viewing the same scenes they did.

Suppose that at the time Margo completes her advance directive, she can elect for a VR experience machine.

The Virtual Reality Experience Machine

A virtual reality machine is available that simulates high quality experiences for persons with dementia. At the time an advance directive is completed, a person specifies whether they want to be hooked up to it and what kinds of experiences they would like to have in order to ensure that their life is meaningful for them in the event that they have progressive dementia.

Before she was diagnosed with dementia, would Margo choose this for her future self? More generally, can offering a VR experience machine to persons with dementia adequately address the concerns of those who think that the quality of life with dementia declines unacceptably? Would it better satisfy the preferences of competent adults prior to dementia by offering them a wider array of options from which they can choose?

One objection to introducing a VR experience machine to enhance Margo's experience is that there is an objective sense in which Margo's life would still fall short. Even though Margo's life would be pleasant, and the VR experience machine would enhance the range of pleasures she enjoys as well as her prior agency, having these experiences in these ways is not equivalent to leading a flourishing human life. For example, according to some interpretations,

Aristotle held that "the notion of eudaimonia (happiness) is primarily the notion of the ethical quality or value of the life, not of the way this life feels" (Rabbas et al. 2015). This rendering of a human life worth living points beyond the person's subjective state and draws a distinction between having a pleasant state of mind and having a life go well (Haybron 2019). Having a pleasant state of mind, as Margo would with all the experience machines discussed, is descriptive and refers to certain psychological states obtaining, such as pleasure or prior preference satisfaction. By contrast, having one's life go well is normative and refers to the occurrence of valuable activities. Even if Margo has a pleasant state of mind, if her life includes nothing but machine-induced experiences and she can no longer engage beyond herself in valuable activities, what's the point? Sumner claims that even when life is going agreeably for someone, it might nonetheless be "unworthy of a human being" because welfare tracks only one narrow dimension of a human life (Sumner 1992, 217).

Yet it might be argued that to tell whether or not Margo has a *valuable* human life, one which she desires to extend, we should ask Margo-now, because Margo-now is the one who is actually having the subjective experiences and knows what it is like to be in this situation. The significance of this point is strengthened by evidence showing that healthy and able-bodied people are unreliable judges of what quality of life is like for other people living with disease and disability (Walasek et al. 2019). In Margo's case, there is every reason to think that Margo before she became ill was a poor judge of what life is like for Margo-now.

Social scientists have observed a related phenomenon occurring in later life. *The paradox of ageing* describes a body of observational evidence that, as people age, their self-ratings of pleasure in life improve; people sixty-five and over are more likely than people at younger ages to see their life as meaningful, and to report that they are achieving the goals they set for themselves. What makes such findings paradoxical is that older adults at the same time report generally worse physical and cognitive functioning compared to younger years. In other words, as people's minds and bodies decline, rather than feeling worse about their lives, they generally report feeling better. Empirical evidence shows that subjective well-being is approximately U-shaped over the life course, with well-being hitting its lowest mark during middle age (Blanchflower and Oswald 2008). Specific diagnoses, such as stroke, dementia, and cardiac disease, that are more common in people age sixty-five and over are unrelated to life satisfaction (Enkvist et al. 2012).

Evidence of increasing well-being correlating with disease and disability suggests that implicit biases, such as ableism and ageism, may cloud judgments people make when they execute advance directives and attempt to imagine themselves as future persons with disease and disability. One possible explanation for the gap between judgment and reality is that people who experience gradual functional loss with age develop resilience (Jeste et al. 2013).

According to Harpham, a person has resilience to the extent that their experiences match their expectations and that their routines help them navigate their days. When people with disease and disability develop resilience, they acclimate by altering expectations and routines to align with their situation (Harpham 2019).

If the above analysis is correct, which measure should we use to assess the value of life for a person with dementia? Should we measure the value of Margo's life on the basis of the values she articulates in her advance directive? The concern here is that Margo's prior preferences could reflect implicit biases, and she might have made erroneous predictions about what her subjective well-being would be like in future health states, such as dementia, that she had not experienced. Perhaps, the best measure of Margo's life is not how her experience now compares to a prior "normal" life (without Alzheimer's disease), but instead finding out if Margo's remaining capabilities are supported and her present needs met. This strategy recognizes that across the life course, human beings display different needs and abilities. Even when a person remains healthy throughout life, their desires and needs shift from birth to death, as do the values they hold most dear (Jecker 2020a). A good childhood is not the same as a good mid or later life. Perhaps, when we say that Margo's life with dementia "falls short," we are using a midlife, healthy yardstick to measure it. Why suppose this is the gold standard for judging Margo now?

A better approach for someone in Margo's situation is to ask if their needs and capabilities receive reasonable support. For Margo, we might ask, is she reasonably safe and healthy, which might include being nourished, clean, and engaged in some form of activity? Does she have bodily integrity, in the sense of being able to move freely from place to place, at least some of the time? If Margo is inclined to wander, can she do so safely during some period of the day? If she enjoys going outdoors, is she able to be outside? Other relevant capabilities might include: being able to express oneself through music or movement; hearing the sounds and sights of television; enjoying a meal she likes; affiliating with others through shared activities.

When all is said and done, is what is left for Margo enough? It seems that Margo still retains many capabilities that make life good for her. One way of spelling this out is to consider a list of central human capabilities and ask which of these Margo still has and to what extent. One possible list, which I develop and defend in greater detail elsewhere (Jecker 2020a), is the following:

10 Central Human Capabilities

1. *Life*: having an unfinished narrative
2. *Health*: being able to have all or a cluster of the capabilities at a threshold level

3. *Bodily integrity*: being able to use one's body to carry out one's desires and goals
4. *Senses, imagination, thought*: being able to sense, imagine, and think
5. *Emotions*: being able to feel and express a range of emotions
6. *Practical reason*: being able to form and reflect on plans and goals
7. *Affiliation*: being able to live for and in relation to others
8. *Nature*: being able to live in relation to nature and other species
9. *Play*: being able to laugh, play, and recreate
10. *Environment*: being able to regulate the immediate environment

We might determine that Margo has some degree of each capability remaining. For example, while Margo has significantly diminished practical reason, she still knows what she likes and gravitates toward it. While she has less ability to affiliate, she still enjoys a touch on her shoulder, holding hands, or singing. While the range of emotions she can feel and express are reduced, the emotions that remain are less inhibited and more forcefully expressed. Margo may still enjoy going outdoors, playing, and being able to go where she wants to go and do what she wants to do. When we focus more on what is physically, emotionally, and socially possible now, instead of the past, we gain a deeper appreciation of the value and significance of Margo's life for Margo now.

Life's Length

The above analysis suggests that despite its tragic components, a person with dementia can have a good life in old age, judged by both subjective and objective measures. If a person in this situation is content and well cared for, we can say that, judged by the measures appropriate to their life, it is going well. Yet a further question remains, namely: How long should such a life last?

One way of approaching this question would be to say that the same strategies that apply in other cases apply to a person with dementia. For example, if having more positive experience is good, then Margo should continue living as long as she has positive experiences. If being connected to reality is good, then Margo should continue living as long as she stays connected to reality and refuse life-sustaining treatment if this connection is irrevocably lost. To explore these suggestions further, let us ask what light the various considerations we have been discussing might shed on the question of whether to use antibiotics to extend Margo's life.

Happiness. If having happy experiences is the measure of whether a person's life should continue, it could be argued that the case of Margo, as a "happy person with dementia," is a partial picture. As Margo's Alzheimer's progresses, various indignities and sufferings will inevitably be visited upon her. Even living in a VR experience machine will not change that. For example, her speech may become limited to just a few words; she may become totally functionally dependent, incontinent, and unable to ambulate (Mitchell et al. 2012). Further complications of advanced Alzheimer's disease typically include infections, eating problems, pneumonia, difficulty swallowing without aspirating, and decubitus ulcers. When these conditions set in, Margo may reach a point where more life is not an unqualified good. Even if all we cared about is pleasure, Margo's present state of contentment will not last.

If we use the same yardstick to judge Margo's death as we use to judge the death of someone without her diagnosis, then death from a treatable pneumonia would be bad, because it deprives her of possible future goods (Nagel 1979). However, when we think in terms of the future possibilities Margo truly has, we might conclude that if Margo were to die, this would not deprive her of future goods, but of great suffering and a worse life which, at some point, might become unbearable. The relevant comparison for a person with progressive disease is not to die or to live *well*, but rather to die this death now or another death, at some later time, that would be *worse* (McMahan 1988, 50; McMahan 2002). If Margo dies now of pneumonia, she bypasses disease progression. This might be the best course for her, all things considered.

Prior wishes. The prospect of inevitable disease progression provides a strong reason for a person diagnosed with Alzheimer's disease to execute an advance directive during an early stage of the disease, prior to cognitive decline, and to indicate when (if ever) in the course of their disease they prefer not to have steps taken to extend their life. Dementia-specific advance directives can be especially useful in this regard. These directives track goals of care to disease advancement and ask people to specify wishes about the use of life-extending interventions during mild, moderate, and severe stages of disease (Gaster et al. 2017). Other advance planning strategies, such as holding conversations with and educating family members, also enhance outcomes by helping to ensure a patient's wishes are reflected in surrogate decisions. For example, nursing home residents with advanced dementia whose proxies understood the clinical course and poor prognosis of the disease were less likely to receive aggressive interventions, such as hospital transfer, tube feeding, or intravenous therapy, during the last three months of life (Mitchell et al. 2012).

It might be thought that advance directives are of limited value in cases of dementia for the reason discussed already; namely, people are poor judges of what the quality of life is like in a future impaired state that they have never experienced (or even come close to experiencing) (Davis 2004). However, this concern does not necessarily establish that prior preferences carry no weight. Instead, the objection gives grounds for taking other considerations into account alongside advance directives, such as the patient's own perceptions of benefits and burdens.

Impersonal value. An alternative approach holds that Margo's prior wishes should be heavily discounted, because Margo's life has a superlative value. The staunchest supporters of this view are those who hold that people's lives have an impersonal value or worth in all cases and should be continued for this reason. Finnis (1995), for example, maintains that every human life has an impersonal value and dignity, irrespective of the personal value it has for the person. According to some interpretations, Kant held a similar view, implying that a person's life could not have a value below worth continuing (Kant 2005). Withholding simple treatments, like antibiotics, from a person with Alzheimer's disease would be difficult to justify according to this view and might only be allowed in extreme cases, such as forced trade-offs under resource constraints.

However, even if there is always an impersonal value to human life, who's to say that this impersonal value takes priority over life's personal value? An alternative view, championed by McMahan, holds that in some instances, such as a decision about whether to act to save a person's life, personal value should override impersonal value (McMahan 2002, 465). According to this analysis, even if Margo's life has impersonal value, if it does not (or cannot) matter to her, then she cannot morally make a claim to be kept alive. It does not follow that Margo's life ought to be ended, but it does follow that the (impersonal) value of her life is not a reason to prescribe antibiotics for pneumonia and override her view about her life's value. The more relevant consideration would be whether Margo finds her life meaningful and worth having.

Narrative lives. Another way of understanding how to make a decision on behalf of Margo draws on the metaphor of life as a story that unfolds over time, from birth to death. So understood, later life is not just a chance for more experiences added to the ones that came before, but the closing chapter of a story. Thus, a central question becomes: What is a good ending to the story of Margo's life? In answering this question, it might still be relevant to think about pleasure versus pain, being connected to reality, and having our capabilities supported. However, the answer to such questions would be framed with reference to the larger goal of bringing closure to the whole narrative of a human life. Reasoning along these lines, Velleman argues that the pattern of a life matters, over and above the aggregate good (Velleman 1991). For example, it is better if the narrative of a person's life includes struggles that lead to life improving than if a person's life starts off well, then deteriorates, even if the aggregate good is the same.

If Velleman is right, we cannot simply add together the constituent moments of a life to decipher its value as a whole. Yet, how can we judge? Elsewhere, I argue at greater length that narrative conceptions of persons include a normative component, which guides decisions in the direction of values such as prudence, integrity, and fairness (Jecker 2020a, 115–116). Prudence requires tempering present desires in light of future needs. More broadly, it demands people to base their decisions on a whole-life assessment, rather than a moment-to-moment one. Integrity is "the condition of having no part or element taken away or wanting," an "undivided or unbroken state," and "material wholeness, completeness, entirety" (Oxford Dictionary 2020, "Integrity"). A human life shows integrity when its constitutive parts work together harmoniously. Fairness rounds out this trio by requiring people to treat each stage of their life equally and to avoid arbitrary bias in favor of one life stage over others.

A person serving as a proxy decision-maker for an individual with dementia upholds prudence, integrity, and fairness by considering the larger story of the patient's life, rather than just the patient's present medical story and the patient's immediate desires. Honoring a person's life in this way requires gaining a fuller understanding of a patient's history and what their life has been like over time. Relevant questions might include, what are the patient's abiding values? What have been their central aspirations? What kind of ending would be a good ending for this particular person's life? Although these questions do not admit of easy answers, someone who knows a person well can better answer them (Jecker 1990).

Conclusion

When thinking about whether to extend life in old age for a person with dementia, there is both a subjective or personal value to life and an impersonal or objective value to life. The relevant considerations for objective value might include having central human capabilities, being in touch with reality, having more pleasure than pain, and having a life that is better than not existing. The relevant considerations for subjective value might include some of the same features, judged from the standpoint of the individual at a particular moment in time, or from the perspective of their life as a whole.

When thinking about extending the life of a patient with dementia, a relevant question to consider is what postponing death would mean in light of their prognosis. During early stages of dementia, for example, postponing death might afford an individual many more years of life that they would enjoy. For someone at a later disease stage, future prospects might be bleak. This approach avoids both midlife and ableist bias, by avoiding comparing a person's present situation with their midlife state.

In closing, I began this inquiry with Swift's struldbruggs, fictional beings cursed to live forever while they grow older and increasingly decrepit. That fate is not Margo's. Yet she could share an analogous fate if she lives beyond the point where life offers her experiences she can enjoy. The "right time" for someone in Margo's situation to die is when their disease progresses to the point that what is possible for them in the future would be worse than the alternative of dying or would be a very bad ending to their particular story.

13 'Half in Love with Easeful Death': Rational Suicide and the Elderly

L. W. Sumner

Gillian Bennett had a long and successful career as a psychotherapist, but by the time she reached her ninth decade she had begun experiencing the progressive memory loss and disorientation characteristic of dementia. In the lengthy farewell letter she left behind, Bennett said that what lay ahead for her was 'the state that all dementia patients eventually get to: not knowing who I am and requiring full-time care' (Bennett 2014). She explained that she had therefore decided to take preemptive action while still able to, 'before the day when I can no longer assess my situation'. She discussed her plan with all of the members of her family and, in August 2014, at the age of eighty-five, dragged a mattress out to one of her favourite spots outside her home in western Canada, where she ended her life by swallowing a lethal dose of pentobarbital (washed down by a shot of whisky).[1]

In his best-selling book *Being Mortal*, Atul Gawande has sketched how the trajectory of later life changed over the course of the last century with advances in both medicine and public health (Gawande 2014, chapter 2). Statistically, you are still most likely to succumb to one of the major killers: cancer, heart disease, stroke, lower respiratory disease, etc. Many of us, however, will manage to dodge these bullets. Instead, like Gillian Bennett, we may just slide slowly into the fog of dementia, or struggle instead under the burden of multiple minor ailments: hypertension, osteoarthritis, tooth loss, osteoporosis, loss of dexterity, diabetes, decline in bowel function, neuropathy, muscle weakness, fatigue, loss of appetite, and so on and on. For those on this track, as Gawande puts it, 'the curve of life becomes a long slow fade' (Gawande 2014, 27–8).[2]

Whichever path we come to find ourselves on, unless we die suddenly from a devastating illness or accident, we are likely to have an extended period in which to contemplate our current condition and future prospects. Some of us – hopefully only a minority – will reach the stage where we begin to wonder

---

[1] https://bit.ly/3m5dlYJ. Accessed 14 December 2021. There are many striking similarities between Bennett's suicide and that of Sandra Bem, which took place just three months earlier (Henig 2015).

[2] Compare Lynn (2005) and Nicholson et al. (2012).

whether there remains any point in carrying on further. In addition to the burdens of illness – or perhaps in place of them – we may simply come to suffer from 'life fatigue': the sense that our life is complete, that we have accomplished everything we set out to do, especially with respect to career, family, and friends, and therefore have nothing left to strive for. Whatever the cause, for those of us who end up feeling that life is no longer worth living, the next step may be to consider ways in which we might speed up its inevitable end.

There are a number of options available to anyone who wishes to hasten their own death, or at least not to postpone it. One is to decline further treatment of a life-threatening medical condition. One of the prominent themes in Gawande's book is overtreatment of the elderly: the continuation of therapies, or the trial of new therapies, long past the point of expectable medical benefit for the patient.[3] Sometimes the imperative to 'do everything you can' comes from patients themselves, or from their families, but equally often it is doctors who make unrealistic estimates of patients' survival times and feel the need to suggest just one more intervention to further extend life (Gawande 2014, 167). It can be challenging for elderly patients to resist the medical imperative to stave death off by all available means. Research has shown that preferences by older patients to receive such potentially life-extending treatments as resuscitation, artificial nutrition and hydration, antibiotics, and artificial respiration are followed much more frequently than preferences to forego such treatments (Pasman et al. 2013). One thing seems clear: many elderly patients who have been hospitalized with serious and potentially life-threatening conditions regard some states of functional and cognitive debility as worse than death (Rubin et al. 2016).[4] If they wish to avoid ending their life in such a state, one means at their disposal is to aggressively assert their right to refuse treatment, or have family members do it on their behalf.

Hastening death by treatment refusal presupposes suffering from a condition serious enough to be life-threatening. It was not an option for Bennett and will do little for the infirm elderly whose misery stems from a constellation of more minor afflictions. For them it may come down to the choice that Bennett made: taking matters into their own hands by actively seeking means to end their lives. It is this option of suicide that will be the focus of the discussion to follow. The first question to address is whether it can be a rational choice.

Rational Suicide

In the abstract it is easy to make a philosophical case that suicide can be rational. Practical rationality, in the relevant sense, is instrumental: the choosing of effective means to achieve a desired end. One end that all individuals desire, and pursue, is their own interest or well-being. Ordinarily, dying is

---

[3] See also Kaufman (2015).   [4] But see also Nothelle and Finucane (2017) and Rubin (2017).

contrary to our interest – bad for us – because of the valuable future life of which it deprives us.[5] But suppose that future life will no longer be so valuable. Perhaps instead it promises to be grim, either more of the same old or, worse, an accelerating downhill slide. Then death can come to seem not an enemy but a friend, not a tragedy but a welcome escape. So it seemed to Bennett. Under circumstances in which death can be a benefit and not a harm it can surely be rational to actively seek it, including by suicide.

This abstract model of the rational suicide has little traction among mental health clinicians, who tend to regard suicide as a product, and symptom, of mental illness. According to one researcher, 'Suicide is generally a complication of a psychiatric disorder. More than 90% of suicide victims have a diagnosable psychiatric illness, and most persons who attempt suicide have a psychiatric disorder' (Mann 2002, 302). The accompanying psychiatric conditions can be as varied as schizophrenia, alcoholism, substance abuse, and personality disorders, but by far the most common are mood disorders, above all depression. The effect of serious depression is to colour subjects' perception of their life circumstances, magnifying everything that is going wrong and undermining any hope that it could ever be better in the future. Because the depressive person's deliberative processes are distorted in this way, the argument goes, a decision to end it all is seldom, if ever, based on a rational calculation of the benefits and burdens of continued life. Furthermore, since depression is often a treatable condition, the clinical emphasis should rightly be on finding effective treatment and, thereby, effective means of suicide prevention. Nelson and Ramirez nicely summarize the prevailing ethos:

The orthodox view among mental health clinicians is that suicide is an important and largely preventable public health problem that is inextricably intertwined with and usually caused by mental illness. This view holds that because suicide arises out of mental illness, it is irrational, contrary to the interests of the individual, ethically wrong, and ought to be opposed and prevented in all cases. (Nelson and Ramirez 2017, 1)[6]

This approach to the issue, which is applied to suicides at all ages, takes on a particular urgency with respect to the elderly, who tend to have higher suicide rates than any other age group (Conwell et al. 2002, 2011).

The orthodox view is doubtless a good fit for many – perhaps most – suicides. But it cannot be the right story for all. This becomes clear when we look at jurisdictions that provide legal access to medical assistance in dying (MAiD). I will use my own country – Canada – as an example. Under current Canadian

---

[5] For a fuller explication of this deprivation account of the badness of death, see Sumner (2011, Section 1.1).

[6] Citations in Nelson and Ramirez (2017) omitted. Nelson and Ramirez do not themselves endorse this view.

law, in order to qualify for MAiD you must have a grievous and irremediable medical condition causing physical or psychological suffering that you regard as intolerable. If you have nothing to look forward to except further suffering, then hastening the end by requesting MAiD would seem to exemplify the philosophical case that death can be a benefit rather than a harm. But there is more. The process of accessing MAiD requires that you be assessed as decisionally capable and that your request be free and voluntary. The assessment process acts as a safeguard against both cognitive distortion due to mental illness and the impulsivity that marks many suicides (Mann 2002, 304). Requests for MAiD seem a bad fit for the orthodox view that suicides are standardly irrational.

Just to be clear, MAiD is not, for either legal or clinical purposes, suicide.[7] The American Association of Suicidology has found fifteen points of difference between MAiD and conventional suicide and has stated emphatically that the two are 'conceptually, medically, and legally different phenomena', though they may in some cases overlap (American Association of Suicidology 2017). But MAiD does share two essential characteristics with suicide: in requesting it you are seeking a medical intervention that (a) is intended to cause your death and (b) will cause your death. Furthermore, like conventional suicide, MAiD skews old, with an average age in Canada of 73.[8] Statistics collected in Oregon, where a form of medically assisted dying is also available, give us an idea of the concerns that usually motivate patient requests: (in order of frequency) loss of autonomy, loss of ability to engage in enjoyable activities, loss of dignity, loss of control of bodily functions, concern about being a burden to others, and pain (or other disagreeable physical symptoms).[9] It is scarcely worth pointing out that these are among the conditions that frequently compromise quality of life among the infirm elderly. Some of them defined the future that Gillian Bennett was so determined to avoid. If a request for MAiD for these reasons can be rational – as it appears it can – then why cannot opting for suicide be equally rational, especially in a jurisdiction in which a medically assisted death is not legally available as an alternative?[10]

---

[7] The Oregon 'Death with Dignity' Act (Oregon Health Authority, Public Health Division 2017) contains a clause stating that the practice authorized by its provisions does not constitute suicide or assisted suicide. The Annual Reports issued by the Department of Human Services for the first eight years of the Oregon policy nonetheless used the language of 'physician-assisted suicide'. This practice was abandoned in 2006, largely at the behest of families who wished to avoid the stigma of suicide.

[8] https://bit.ly/3pHtTao. Accessed 14 January 2019.

[9] Oregon Health Authority, Public Health Division (2017). See also Ganzini, Goy, and Dobscha (2009).

[10] At the time of her death in 2014, MAiD was not yet legally available in Canada. But even under the current law (in 2020) Bennett would probably not have been eligible.

The foregoing considerations are enough to at least suggest that there is logical space for rational suicide by the infirm elderly. Bennett's suicide appears to occupy that logical space. So do some others:

Kim Teske

In 2008 Teske discovered that, like her older brother Brian, she had inherited from her father the gene for Huntington's disease, whose symptoms combine elements of Parkinson's, Alzheimer's, and schizophrenia. Six years later, having watched the progression of the disease in her brother, who had to be placed in a nursing home in 2012, she resolved that she would find a way to end her life before she reached that stage. She considered going to Switzerland for a physician-assisted death but finally hit on another option: Voluntarily Stopping Eating and Drinking (VSED).[11] She discussed her plan with her mother and her sisters, who agreed to support and care for her during her fast. After a final reunion with all of her siblings and extended family, she began the fast in April 2014 and died twelve days later, just before her fifty-third birthday (Martin 2014; Martin 2016, 21–2).

Cecilia Chmura

By the time she reached the age of fifty-nine, Chmura had suffered from unbearable pain from fibromyalgia for more than twenty years. In the most recent five years, her condition had deteriorated to the point where her pain was excruciating and she was spending most of her time in bed. Medical marijuana and opiates provided some measure of relief, but also left her feeling 'loopy'. In the autumn of 2017 she requested MAiD under Canada's law but was refused because of the stipulation in the law at that time that her natural death be 'reasonably foreseeable'. Following the refusal she decided to take her own life, a plan that she discussed with her husband and their children. In January 2018 she ground up her morphine pills and downed them with some pudding, washing it down with vodka and orange juice. She died in her bed a little more than two hours later in the arms of her husband.[12]

Lester Angell

Marcia Angell tells the story of her father, who in 1981 was diagnosed with prostate cancer. For a few years he managed quite well until the cancer began to spread and cause him excruciating back pain. The pain was managed with radiation and medication whose side effects included nausea and vomiting. In March 1988, at

---

[11] VSED is one option of choice among the infirm elderly for hastening death (Wax et al. 2018).

[12] https://bit.ly/3pMcTzK; https://bit.ly/3lSrSHj. Both accessed 16 January 2019.

the age of 81, he suffered a fall and was scheduled to be taken to hospital the next day to determine whether he had fractured a bone. Lester Angell was, as his daughter put it, 'a man of great dignity for whom independence was enormously important' Angell (2004, 20). He realized that if he was taken to hospital he might lose his last opportunity to end his life on his own terms. So instead he shot himself that night with the pistol he kept in his bedside table. He did not discuss his decision with his wife for fear that she would stop him from carrying it out.

The commonality among these stories (and Bennett's) is that in each of them a decisionally capable adult intentionally ends their own life as a means of escaping a present and/or future condition that they regard as intolerable. However, there are also significant differences. One of the most obvious is the choice of means. The three women all found a peaceful way to end their lives, while Lester Angell had to resort to an act of violence. The cases also differ in terms of the subject's location in the trajectory of their disease. Gillian Bennett and Kim Teske were in the relatively early stages of a degenerative illness and did not yet find their condition unbearable; their decisions were preemptive, intended to forestall a worsening of their condition that would rob them of the capacity to act.[13] Cecilia Chmura, by contrast, wished to put an end to intolerable suffering that she had already experienced for more than twenty years. Angell's suicide had elements of both motivations: serious occurrent suffering plus the prospect of his situation getting worse in his view of it (through loss of independence) and of missing his last opportunity to take action. Finally, the three women all took care to involve those close to them in their planning, while Angell felt unable to do so for fear of intervention by his wife.

The important question for our purposes is whether these might be examples of rational suicides. While it would be presumptuous to come to a final verdict on this point without knowing a great deal more about these four people and their circumstances, we may nonetheless be in a position to draw some provisional conclusions based on the information we do have. To do so we must first take a closer look at the conditions of practical rationality. Margaret Battin (1999) has suggested five criteria for determining whether a suicide is rational:

> *Ability to reason.* The person must have the ability to move from premises to practical conclusions without making mistakes in logic, and the ability to foresee the consequences of plans of action adopted.
>
> *Realistic world view.* A suicide decision must not be based on bizarre beliefs about the nature of the world, due to conditions such as schizophrenia.[14] It must also not be based on a picture of the person's own life situation – including their identity, position in the world, and

---

[13] For a discussion of preemptive suicide in the face of Alzheimer's disease, and the rationality thereof, see Davis (2014).

[14] As Battin (1999) notes, this condition raises questions about suicides based on religious beliefs, such as belief in an afterlife.

talents, abilities, and disabilities – that is distorted by conditions such as severe depression.

Adequate information. The person must be fully informed about both their present circumstances and future prospects. In cases in which someone contemplates suicide due to one or more medical conditions, the information in question must include current diagnosis, likely future prognosis, the risks and benefits of possible treatments, the availability of alternative means of alleviating suffering, such as palliative care, and the consequences of choosing suicide.

Avoidance of harm. As previously discussed, under the person's circumstances it must make sense to think that death could be a benefit to them and not a harm.

Congruence with fundamental values. The decision must accord with the person's own deepest values and convictions.[15]

At least on the surface of it, there seems no reason to think that a decision for suicide by the infirm elderly could not satisfy all five criteria and therefore qualify as rational. So how do the four cases cited so far measure up against these standards? In none of them was there any reason to doubt the subject's decisional capacity. Nor had any of these people been diagnosed with a psychiatric disorder, including severe depression.[16] Each was pretty fully briefed on their current medical condition and future prospects. Bennett and Teske each knew full well what would lie in store for them if their illness was allowed to progress; in Teske's case she had the example of her older brother close at hand. Cecilia Chmura's pain had endured for over twenty years and appeared to be untreatable, though it is impossible to fully rule out finding more effective ways of managing it. Lester Angell's suicide might seem more problematic on this informational ground, since better means might have been found of managing both his pain and the side effects of his treatments. Furthermore, he elected to kill himself before finding out just how much damage had been done by his fall, since it was the hospitalization itself that he wished to avoid. Both Bennett and Teske faced the cruel dilemma of finding an exit while they still had some decent quality of life in front of them, in order not to wait until they were no longer able to do it. If Chmura's pain could not otherwise be relieved, then it is not difficult to understand how she might regard her suffering as making her life no longer worth living. Again, Angell is a more ambiguous case, but if what mattered most to him was his independence then its loss could well have been a greater harm to him than loss of his life. At least it seemed so to him, since he appeared to have been motivated by the fear that once he was institutionalized he would come to regret not having taken action when he

---

[15] I have edited, paraphrased, and somewhat modified Battin's criteria. See also Werth (1999) and Nelson and Ramirez (2017, 13–16).

[16] Some may, of course, have been depressed by their condition and their prospects. But depression of this sort need not compromise rationality. I return to this issue below.

could. Finally, it seems clear that each of these four people acted in accordance with their own deepest values, whether these were rejection of a future as a demented person, the desire to escape further physical suffering, or a high value placed on dignity and independence.[17]

It is noteworthy that each of these four people would probably have elected for a physician-assisted death had one been available to them (recall that Chmura actually requested one). The eligibility criteria and assessment procedures for MAiD are structured so as to ensure that patient decisions will satisfy all five conditions for rationality. As noted earlier, only patients who are decisionally capable can request MAiD, and where capacity is in question, or where a psychiatric disorder such as severe depression is suspected, patients can and will be referred to professionals for assessment. Patients requesting MAiD must be fully informed of their current condition, their future prognosis, the risks and benefits of further treatment (if any is available), alternative means of end-of-life care, and, finally, the implications of choosing MAiD. Since the eligibility criteria (in Canada) require a grievous and irremediable medical condition causing intolerable suffering, there seems little doubt that MAiD will qualify as conferring a medical benefit rather than inflicting a harm. Finally, the process itself provides patients with ample opportunity to ensure that their decision reflects their own deepest values for their life. Had any of Gillian Bennett, Kim Teske, Cecilia Chmura, or Lester Angell qualified for MAiD, their decision would have been uncontroversially rational. It is hard to see why it would be less rational for them to take action themselves.

Despite these cases of seemingly rational suicides, some may still have a niggling worry about the relationship between suicide and depression. If it is true that most people who choose suicide are depressed, and if depression significantly impairs cognitive functioning, then won't most suicides be irrational? We could, of course, respond simply by pointing to subjects like Bennett et al., who were not depressed and who did not suffer from any other psychiatric disorder.[18] But instead let's take a closer look at clinical depression itself. According to the American Psychiatric Association's (2013) *DSM-5*, a major depressive disorder (MDD) can be diagnosed when 'five (or more) of the following symptoms have been present during the same 2-week period and represent a change from previous functioning':

1. Depressed mood most of the day, nearly every day.
2. Markedly diminished interest or pleasure in all, or almost all, activities most of the day, nearly every day.

---

[17] I want to emphasize that any or all of these conclusions about the four cases could well be amended in light of further information. But I see no reason to think that any such information could suffice to rule out the possibility of a rational suicide.

[18] Corna et al. (2010) present evidence to show that 'Although suicide ideation is associated with depression and anxiety disorders, many older adults with suicidal thoughts do not meet the criteria for these clinical disorders.' For an example of an elderly patient with suicidal thoughts but no diagnosable psychiatric disorder, see Balasubramaniam (2018).

3. Significant weight loss when not dieting or weight gain (e.g., a change of more than 5% of body weight in a month), or decrease or increase in appetite nearly every day.
4. Insomnia or hypersomnia nearly every day.
5. Psychomotor agitation or retardation nearly every day.
6. Fatigue or loss of energy nearly every day.
7. Feelings of worthlessness or excessive or inappropriate guilt.
8. Diminished ability to think or concentrate, or indecisiveness, nearly every day.
9. Recurrent thoughts of death (not just fear of dying), recurrent suicidal ideation without a specific plan, or a suicide attempt or a specific plan for committing suicide (American Psychiatric Association 2013, Chapter 5).

What is striking about this list of symptoms is how common many of them are likely to be among the elderly afflicted either by a single serious condition (Alzheimer's, Huntington's, fibromyalgia, cancer) or by a constellation of more minor ailments, and who feel that there is no realistic prospect of improvement. It will scarcely be surprising if they are feeling depressed, that they lack interest in daily activities, that they are losing weight due to loss of appetite, that they feel fatigued, and that they have recurrent thoughts of death. Not everyone will, of course, react in this way; many will remain relentlessly cheerful through all this adversity until the end. But becoming depressed would seem to fall well within the range of normal and realistic responses to such significantly diminished life circumstances and would hardly qualify as cognitive distortion. If so, then we have two ways to respond to the *DSM-5*'s list of indicators of MDD: either the manifestation of five or more of these symptoms is not always evidence of a psychiatric disorder or some psychiatric disorders do not necessarily impair cognitive functioning or decisional capacity. In either case it is possible for you to be depressed and to make a rational decision for suicide; indeed, sometimes depression is itself a rational response to one's life conditions.

Assisting a Rational Suicide

From this point I am simply going to assume that some suicides by the infirm elderly can be rational and, absent further information, that the four aforementioned cases are examples of them. Our attention now shifts from the primary actors to second parties: if a suicide would be rational then would it be ethical for someone to assist it? One way to approach this question is to invoke an ethical principle along the following lines: if an act would itself be ethically justified, then it would also be ethically justified to assist it. But this approach requires us to answer a prior question about the ethics of suicide itself: if a suicide is rational, then is it also ethical?

In general, the fact that a course of action is rational does not entail that it is also ethical. Rationality is a matter of efficiency in achieving one's ends or promoting one's interests. It can therefore sometimes be rational to cheat or to lie, but that does not make it ethical. More to the present point, the fact that suicide can sometimes be rational for the infirm elderly leaves open the possibility that it is nonetheless wrong. One possibility is that suicide is always and intrinsically wrong. Since I have dealt with them extensively elsewhere (Sumner 2011, section 4.1), I will give only brief consideration to arguments purporting to show the intrinsic wrongness of suicide. Suicide is a special case of the intentional taking of human life. If you want to make a case that it is morally wrong, then the obvious argumentative strategy would be to include it within the scope of broader ethical principles prohibiting wrongful killing. Leaving aside special justifications, such as self-defence, we all think that it is wrong to kill another person – wrong, say, to commit murder. But what is wrong with it? Two ethically salient features of wrongful killing immediately come to mind. The first is the harm or injury it does to the victim. What makes murder the most serious offence against the person seems to lie in the special seriousness of the harm – the deprivation of life – that it inflicts on the person. The second feature is the violation of the victim's self-determination or autonomy. By taking the life of another without their consent, the killer denies the victim sovereignty over their own life, thereby demoting them to the status of subordinate or chattel.

If this is (more or less) the right account of the wrongness of wrongful killing, the problem with extrapolating it to rational suicide is then glaringly obvious: neither of these features seems to apply. Taking them in reverse order, when a suicide is genuinely rational then it would appear to be an exercise of autonomy on the part of the subject, not a usurpation of it. And when it puts an end to a life that the subject has come to find intolerable, or forestalls further decline into such a condition, then it would appear to confer a benefit rather than inflict a harm.

There seems little prospect, therefore, of finding a convincing secular argument that will show rational suicides to be wrong in principle.[19] However, that is not the end of the ethical question. Even when a rational suicide is not self-harming, it can still be devastating for surviving family and friends. The ethics of rational suicide is therefore a matter, not of the intrinsic nature of the act, but of its manner, means, and consequences for others. Suicides can be attempted, or even completed, for the worst of reasons, including spite or revenge. They can be designed to inflict maximum trauma on whoever first discovers the body or to guilt family members by leaving a message pinning the blame on them. Whether a suicide that is rational could also be intentionally hurtful in

---

[19] Traditional theistic arguments for the wrongness of suicide are beyond the scope of the current discussion.

these ways is a nice question, but also one that we need not discuss. For it is clear that a rational suicide can be carried out in a way that will hurt loved ones, whether it is intended to or not. There is here a clear difference among the suicides cited earlier. Gillian Bennett, Kim Teske, and Cecilia Chmura all discussed their plans with family and friends and were fully supported by them when the time came to carry those plans out. They also found a non-violent means of ending their lives, one likely to cause the least trauma for survivors.[20] By contrast, Lester Angell's wife was in the adjacent bedroom when, with no prior warning, she heard a gunshot and then found her husband's bloody corpse in his bed. I am not suggesting that, all things considered, Angell was wrong to take his life in the way he did (for one thing, his options at that point were severely constrained). It suffices to make the point that in virtually no suicides are the interests of the primary actor the only ones in play. The ethics of suicide can therefore get very complicated, with an overall verdict sometimes quite unclear. However, it is also worth remembering that no one else's interests are impacted by the act quite as seriously as those of the person committing suicide themselves. If a suicide is rational then the fact that it is in the subject's interest is already a strong, though not necessarily conclusive, argument in its ethical favour.

I will venture the view that rational suicides by the infirm elderly are *pro tanto* ethical: absent any evidence of avoidable harm to others, their ethical status becomes conclusive. The suicides by Bennett, Teske, and Chmura are all, I would argue, clear cases, while Angell's suicide is arguably one as well. So back to our principle: if an act is itself ethical, then it is also ethical to assist it. Unfortunately, this principle is vulnerable to decisive counterexamples. It may be entirely ethical for me to sit an examination but that doesn't mean that it is ethical for you to assist me (by feeding me the answers). Some things just have to be done solo. So the fact that an act is ethical does not entail that assistance in it is also ethical. But what about a rational suicide? If it is ethical, could assistance in it fail to be ethical as well? Again, there is no straightforward entailment.[21] For one thing, suicide stays (largely) within personal boundaries: the life you take is your own. But assistance crosses those boundaries: you are affecting not your life but that of another. In many ethical contexts this boundary-crossing matters (think of sex, for example), so maybe it matters here too. However, it is hard to see how this might play out in the case of a rational suicide. Because the suicide is rational, we are entitled to assume that the plan is that of the primary actor themself, with no undue influence from any other parties. The role of the latter is limited to helping provide the means to carry out that autonomously determined plan. In that case, it is hard to see

---

[20] There are organizations in many countries that will provide information on peaceful means of 'self-deliverance', based on Humphry (1991), but no active suicide assistance.

[21] For further discussion of this issue, see Sumner (2011, section 4.2).

anything ethically problematic about them playing this role, since the primary actor is still very much in control.

As it happened, none of the aforementioned suicide cases involved any assistance from second parties. Actually, that statement requires some qualification. Lester Angell's suicide was clearly unaided, since as far as we know no one had any prior knowledge of it: he used his gun in the privacy of his bedroom. But Gillian Bennett's plan to end her life by ingesting pentobarbital was common knowledge among her family, as was Cecilia Chmura's decision to overdose on her pain pills. Furthermore, each of these women died in the company of their husband, who presumably could have intervened to prevent the act. Where do we draw the line between active assistance (say by supplying the drugs) and passive allowance (by not intervening)? And why is the latter not itself a form of assistance? Bennett dragged her mattress out of the house herself, despite her weakened condition, rather than allowing her more robust husband to do it. But if he had taken on the task, would that have been assistance in her suicide? David Dunn, husband of Cecilia Chmura, was briefly detained by the police after reporting her death, despite having done nothing to assist her except holding her until she died. He was not subsequently charged with assisting her suicide, but you can see the point. And what about Kim Teske? Her fast lasted twelve days, during which time she was cared for by two of her sisters who, among other things, ensured that she got enough water to take her medication. This looks even more like assistance with her plan.

Leaving this assistance/non-intervention boundary issue aside, we can also ask how much it would have mattered ethically if Bennett's or Chmura's husband had been more actively involved. Bennett secured her pentobarbital herself, without her husband even knowing how she did it, while Chmura used her own prescribed opiates. But suppose that Bennett's husband had instead sourced the drug or that Chmura's husband had given her his medication. That would have been assisting a suicide (by providing the means), but do we really think it would have made any ethical difference?

I see no way of arguing that assistance by a second party in a rational suicide would be invariably unethical. On the contrary, it seems likely that it is at least *pro tanto* ethical, though this conclusion might be defeated in particular cases by further factors, such as suspicion that assisting the suicide had crossed over into counselling or encouraging it. At any rate, the time has come to confront the elephant in the room in this ethical debate: the fact that assisting a suicide is unlawful in virtually every jurisdiction and carries the risk of a serious legal penalty.[22] This remains the case in those jurisdictions that have legalized forms of medically assisted death, since the exemption from prosecution there covers

[22] Switzerland is a partial exception to this generalization, since under Swiss law assisting a suicide is unlawful only when done for a 'selfish motive'. This exception in the law provides the legal space for right-to-die organizations to provide assisted suicides. For further discussion, see Sumner (2011, 158–60).

only health care providers who apply specified criteria and follow specified procedures. Assistance rendered by private parties, such as family or friends, remains a criminal offence.[23] That fact does not entail that such assistance would always be unethical. A blanket prohibition on suicide assistance may be justified on the ground that no narrower or more selective provision would be equally successful at protecting the vulnerable from coercion or manipulation.[24] But that does not mean that every particular instance of such assistance is unethical because it is coercive or manipulative, especially when the suicide is genuinely rational. It does mean, however, that it would normally be unfair for a person contemplating suicide to request assistance, since complying with the request would come at significant personal risk. That is why Gillian Bennett and Cecilia Chmura asked for no help from their husbands, except their presence to the end. But suppose that help had been volunteered; far from being unethical, taking that kind of risk to help a loved one in extremis might well be regarded as heroic (at least as long as the suicide was itself rational).

Where medically assisted death has been legalized, health care providers can act within the terms of the enabling legislation to help their patients to die, if they so choose. Where assisted dying remains unlawful they would place themselves at great personal and professional risk to comply with a patient request, since they would be vulnerable not only to a criminal charge but to disciplinary proceedings as well, including loss of licence to practice. But again, were a doctor to elect to assume these risks in order to respond compassionately to a patient's needs, I can see no ground for ethical condemnation (Quill 1991).[25]

MAiD and 'Life Fatigue'

We have so far been dealing with the relatively easy cases: the infirm elderly whose illnesses are sufficiently serious for them to qualify for MAiD, at least in some jurisdictions. As mentioned previously, the law in Canada requires that a patient's medical condition be 'grievous and irremediable'. In Belgium, patients requesting MAiD must be in 'a medically futile condition' resulting

---

[23] At least in Canada, it is unclear whether the sort of assistance given to Kim Teske by her sisters put them at legal risk, since it is unclear whether for legal purposes death by VSED constitutes a suicide. For discussion see Downie (2018) and the further references cited therein.

[24] Though that justification was rejected by the Canadian Supreme Court in Carter v Canada (Attorney General), 1 S.C.R. 331 (Supreme Court of Canada, 2015). However, the exceptions to the prohibition mandated by the Court applied only to health care providers, not to laypersons.

[25] An unknown doctor appears to have helped Sue Rodriguez to die in 1994, following her unsuccessful challenge of the Canadian law prohibiting aiding or abetting a suicide (Martin 2016, 167–71).

from 'a serious and incurable disorder', while under Dutch law there must be 'no prospect of improvement' in their condition. In all three jurisdictions, the patient's medical condition must result in 'intolerable' or 'unbearable' suffering. In the US states that have legalized MAiD, the patient must have a terminal illness – one with a life expectancy of no more than six months – but there is no requirement of suffering. In all of these jurisdictions, most patients who qualify for MAiD present with one of the major killers – cancer, heart disease, or lower respiratory disease – or with a neurodegenerative disorder such as Amyotrophic lateral sclerosis (ALS).[26]

The various legal jurisdictions differ considerably in their eligibility criteria for MAiD, with some much more expansive than others. But they all agree in their exclusion of the elderly who may or may not have a suite of debilitating medical conditions but who seek an assisted death primarily because of 'life fatigue'. To their predicament we now turn.

First we need another story:

Peter and Suzan

In the early months of 2014 this Dutch couple, both in their seventies, carried out their plan to die together in their home by taking lethal doses of medication. For decades they had been active members of two right-to-die organizations, which provided information on suicide methods. Peter had been an artist and lecturer in fine arts, but sometime after his retirement he lost his manual coordination, to the point where he was no longer able to paint or sculpt. He also suffered from a sensory disorder that robbed him of the ability to enjoy food, as well as cognitive decline that led him to doubt his ability to carry on with his research. On top of that, he had also become impotent. Suzan identified less with specific activities than with her commitment to her family and to the volunteer work she undertook on behalf of others. However, her ability to continue with these causes diminished significantly due to the pain and immobility inflicted on her by arthritis, to the point where she became housebound. Both Peter and Suzan felt increasingly alienated from their own bodies. Both also had very negative memories of the indignity, dependence, and lack of privacy experienced by Peter's parents when they were in a nursing home. Peter and Suzan had notified their children of their resolve to end their lives before they lost their independence (van Wijngaarden et al. 2016, 1068–9).

It should be obvious that this case differs in some important respects from those discussed earlier. Peter and Suzan have physical afflictions, to be sure, but none as serious as Alzheimer's, Huntington's, cancer, or even Cecilia Chmura's fibromyalgia. Instead, their suffering (and I do believe it is entirely

---

[26] The statistics in Oregon are typical: see Oregon Health Authority, Public Health Division (2017).

accurate to call it that) is of a sort often labelled 'existential' and characterized above all by an acute sense of *loss*, especially of the ability to engage in the activities and enjoy the experiences that previously gave their lives meaning. The other prominent theme in their story is one that we have seen before (especially with Gillian Bennett and Lester Angell): the expectation and fear of a further loss, namely of independence and autonomy.

The first question for us to ask about Peter and Suzan is whether their suicides could qualify as rational. As in the earlier cases, it would be presumptuous to offer a definitive answer to this question without knowing a good deal more about them and their situation. But this much we can say. There seems no doubt that both of them were decisionally capable. There is no indication that their assessment of their life situations was distorted by a psychiatric condition or otherwise uninformed or unrealistic; when they were tested they showed 'little chance of serious depression' (van Wijngaarden et al. 2016, 1064. Cf.1070). As far as we can make out, their decision to die was formed on the basis of their own deepest values. Peter's decision appears to have been driven primarily by the sense that he had outlived himself and was no longer capable of pursuing the interests that had shaped his self-identity. Suzan's case is a little more complicated. The timetable for their joint suicides was, we are told, very much driven by Peter. Left to her own devices, Suzan would have waited longer, but she did not want to carry on without her husband (van Wijngaarden et al. 2016, 1068-9). In Peter's case I think we can readily understand how he could have reached the conclusion that his life was no longer worth living, especially if his likely future lay in a nursing home. To see Suzan's prospects in a similar light we would have to construe her deepest values as including her devotion to her husband.

Peter and Suzan carried out their plan without the assistance of others. But as far as the ethics of assistance is concerned, I see no reason to depart from my earlier conclusion. If their suicides were indeed rational – or at least could have been – then no ethical wrong would have been committed by a second party – whether a family member, friend, or right-to-die organization – who assisted them, for instance by helping them to procure the medication they used.

At this point some may wonder why Peter and Suzan had to carry out their joint suicide on their own, rather than requesting MAiD under the terms of the Dutch policy. The answer to that question requires a little history. The criteria for MAiD established by the law passed in the Netherlands in 2002 require that the requesting party be experiencing 'unbearable suffering' with 'no prospect of improvement'. If we think that Peter and Suzan's suffering had risen to the level of being unbearable, and that there was no other way of alleviating it, then they would appear to qualify (perhaps Peter more clearly than Suzan). The text of the law does not stipulate that the suffering must stem from a serious or incurable medical condition, whether physical or psychological. It therefore looks as though it might accommodate the kind of 'existential suffering' manifested by Peter and Suzan. However, this appearance is deceptive, due to a judicial decision that predated the legislation. In April 1998 Dr Philip Sutorius assisted the suicide of Edward Brongersma, an eighty-six-year-old former senator. Senator Brongersma suffered from no physical or mental illness; his reasons for wanting to die were concern about further physical decline, a feeling that his existence was hopeless, and a general 'tiredness of life' (Lewis 2007, 99–101; Griffiths et al. 2008, 35–9). Dr Sutorius's acquittal at his 2000 trial was appealed by the Minister of Justice and subsequently overturned in 2001 by the Court of Appeals, which held that the patient's suffering must stem from a 'medically classified disease or disorder', and therefore may not be merely 'existential' in nature. This ruling was affirmed by the Supreme Court in 2002.

At least officially, nothing has changed in the Netherlands since that time, though in 2011 the Royal Dutch Medical Association (KNMG) did clarify that an accumulation of old-age complaints, including loss of bodily functions and dignity, could be legitimate grounds for MAiD. A year earlier, a 'Completed Life' campaign had been initiated by the Dutch Voluntary Euthanasia Society (NVVE), the country's largest right-to-die organization. This campaign led the way for a Citizen's Initiative called 'Out of Free Will', which collected over 100,000 signatures for a petition submitted in 2012 to the Dutch parliament calling for MAiD to be extended to people over seventy who do not have a diagnosable medical condition but are 'tired of life'. Though the petition resulted in no legislative change, NVVE continued to advocate that MAiD be available on grounds of 'completed life', which the organization defined (following the KNMG) as including persons 'suffering from the prospect of having to continue to live in such a way that there is little or no more quality of life, which leads to a persistent desire to end their lives, without the main cause for this being a somatic (physical) or mental condition' (NVVE 2016, 25). NVVE lists the following indicators for 'life fatigue':[27]

- Non-life-threatening conditions such as physical deterioration (trouble walking, seeing, hearing, tiredness, feeling listless, incontinence) resulting in an inability to perform activities that make life worthwhile;
- Loss of independence and personal dignity;
- Dependence on professional care and/or care from family and loved ones;
- Loss of status and control over one's own life;
- Loss of one's social network as a result of the death of a partner and/or children, friends, and neighbours;
- Loss of meaning and purpose;
- Detachment from society;
- Fear of the future;
- No prospects for the future.

[27] See also the indicators of a 'completed life' in My Death My Decision (MDMD) (2016).

Many, though not all, of these factors appear to have played a role in Peter and Suzan's decision for a joint suicide.[28] Most Dutch physicians will not agree to provide MAiD to persons requesting on the basis of 'life fatigue' or 'completed life', which may explain why Peter and Suzan did not take that route. However, at least some physicians working with the End-of-Life Clinic founded by Right to Die NL in 2012 appear to assume a more generous interpretation of the criteria for MAiD: one study found that in its first year of operation, the clinic granted eleven requests for MAiD (out of a total of forty) by patients who were tired of living (Snijdewind et al. 2015). However, the issue has clearly not gone away in the Netherlands. In one recent survey of the Dutch public, about one-quarter of respondents agreed that MAiD should be available to an older person who is 'tired of life' without having a serious medical condition (Raijmakers et al. 2015).

Had they been so inclined, Peter and Suzan might have been able to access a medically assisted death in Switzerland. While euthanasia remains a criminal offence in that country, assisting a suicide is permitted as long as it is not done with a 'selfish motive'. What this requirement amounts to in practice has been glossed by the Swiss National Advisory Commission for Biomedical Ethics in the following way: 'The reasons are deemed to be selfish if the offender is *pursuing personal advantage*. Such gains may be of a material nature ... but also non-material or emotional (e.g., gratification of hatred, a desire for revenge, or spite)' (Swiss National Advisory Commission for Biomedical Ethics 2005, 7). Nothing in the Swiss law requires that the person assisting a suicide be a physician, and the most distinctive feature of the Swiss situation is the role played by the various right-to-die organizations active in the country, including Dignitas, Lifecircle, and two branches of EXIT. Applicants for a medically assisted death must be examined by a doctor who, if satisfied that the criteria have been met, provides a prescription for a lethal dose of a barbiturate. Until recently, those criteria have required that the applicant be adult, competent, and be suffering from 'a fatal illness, a severe disability deemed unacceptable or unbearable pain for which there is no prospect of relief' (Baezner-Sailer 2008, 142). However, Lifecircle and both branches of EXIT have recently expanded their criteria to include the elderly who wish to die despite having no serious health problems. Lifecircle will also provide this service to foreigners.[29]

Since the Swiss seem to be going the route of permitting MAiD on the basis of 'life fatigue' and the Dutch are under pressure to do so as well, that leads us to

---

[28] Many of these indicators appear frequently as reasons underlying the wish to die among the elderly who are 'tired of life' (van Wijngaarden, Leget, and Goossensen 2014, 2015). See also Richards (2017). As noted earlier, they are also similar to reasons given by Oregon residents who seek an assisted suicide. However, the Oregon law restricts MAiD to patients with a terminal illness.

[29] See, for instance, the story of Gill Pharaoh: https://bit.ly/3rZ2Ny3. Accessed 8 February 2019.

our final question: is there a case for expanding the criteria for MAiD to include the elderly who are merely 'tired of life' without a serious underlying medical condition?

If there is such a case then it will inevitably lean heavily on the value of autonomy. Respect for autonomy acknowledges everyone's right to make their own decisions about their lives in accordance with their own deepest values. If respect requires allowing others to live their lives according to their own lights, then it must also allow them to manage their dying process in the same way. In medical contexts, respect for autonomy is embedded in the requirement of informed consent to treatment (and the allowance for informed refusal). It allows patients to choose for themselves which of the array of treatment options will best enable them to manage the last stage of their lives on their own terms. No one size fits all here; people just differ in the importance they attach to factors such as independence or dignity or some degree of control over their living conditions. They also differ on the living conditions they find burdensome or even intolerable.

Respect for individual autonomy is one of the foundational values of all existing regimes of legalized MAiD. It is embodied in some of the criteria for accessing MAiD: applicants must be decisionally capable, their decision must be both fully informed and fully voluntary, and a waiting period may be imposed between approval for MAiD and administration of the procedure, in order to ensure that their decision reflects their settled and stable wishes. As we have seen earlier, decisions in favour of suicide can be rational, and assistance with them can be ethical. From the point of view of autonomy, therefore, extension of legal MAiD to the elderly who lack a serious underlying medical condition but are 'tired of life' would seem to be relatively straightforward.[30]

Autonomy therefore provides a strong pro tanto justification for acknowledging 'life fatigue' as a legitimate ground for accessing MAiD. What case might then be made on the other side? Here is one way to go. In all existing legal regimes, MAiD has been heavily medicalised: doctors are the gatekeepers who determine who qualifies for the procedure and also usually the ones who administer it (except in regimes, like Switzerland and the various US states, that require patients to self-administer). Doctors, it will be argued, have the job of responding to medical conditions and, more particularly, the job of alleviating suffering caused by such conditions. But 'life fatigue' is not itself a medical condition, nor need it arise as a result of any such condition. So while it may be entirely rational for the elderly, like Peter and Suzan, who are 'tired of life' to turn to suicide, they are not entitled to the assistance of a physician in order to end their lives. MAiD is a medical procedure administered or enabled by medical practitioners and should be restricted to patients with medical problems.

---

[30] As is argued in Mathison and Davis (2018).

As we have seen, this was the position on the issue taken by the Court in the Brongersma case. It is also the position that I have previously defended (Sumner 2011, 171). Unfortunately, however, it rests on an untenable distinction between medical and non-medical sources of suffering (Mathison and Davis 2018). It would be arbitrary and discriminatory to require that requests for MAiD be based on a serious underlying *physical* illness. Consequently, it is established law in the Netherlands, Belgium, and Switzerland that patients presenting solely with a mental illness can be eligible for MAiD, and that intolerable suffering can be either physical or psychological in nature. But once this physical/psychological line is crossed then there is no way to keep 'life fatigue' from qualifying as a medical condition. Patients who consult their physicians manifesting symptoms on the NVVE list (above) will be standardly offered remedies ranging from talk therapy to medication. If we determine whether a condition is medical by its eligibility for treatment by a medical practitioner, then 'life fatigue' can be a medical condition. It can therefore, at least in principle, be eligible for MAiD as well as other forms of treatment.

If autonomy were the only value in play, then it would be difficult – perhaps impossible – to deny MAiD to the elderly who are 'tired of life'. But it is not the only value in play. Legal regimes of MAiD are based not only on respect for autonomy but also on beneficence. Doctors have a duty to prevent or alleviate suffering, when they can do so by means that are consistent with patient autonomy and do not cause greater harm. This duty of beneficence is also reflected in some of the eligibility criteria for MAiD: applicants must have a 'serious' or 'grievous' medical condition that is 'incurable' or 'irremediable' by other means, and it must cause them suffering that is 'intolerable' or 'unbearable'. These conditions have the function of ensuring that requests to die are not based on adverse medical conditions that are either trivial or transient and therefore that in seeking death patients do not do themselves irreversible harm. They are paternalistic constraints on the exercise of patient autonomy.

Might these beneficence-based constraints suffice to exclude the elderly who are 'tired of life'? Perhaps in many cases, but not entirely. These applicants for MAiD may not present with an underlying physical illness that is 'serious' or 'grievous' but, as we have seen, their 'life fatigue' itself can be a medical condition that rises to that level of seriousness for them. And while their suffering is not physical but 'existential', again, as we have seen, it can rise to the level of intolerability for them. It is often said that the suffering condition must be interpreted subjectively.[31] People's tolerance levels for suffering can differ dramatically, and so the question is always whether *this* suffering is intolerable *for this person*. In that case, it is not difficult to imagine cases in which 'existential' suffering can be intolerable to the one who is experiencing

---

[31] I have said this (Sumner 2011, 171).

it. In fact, we don't even have to imagine such cases: Peter is one of them, and perhaps Suzan as well.

But the popular view that suffering is subjective is at best a half-truth, or perhaps we should say, a myth. In actual practice doctors, who are the gate-keepers for MAiD, must certify that a patient's medical condition is sufficiently serious, and their suffering sufficiently intolerable, to qualify. What this means is that the doctor who is assessing a patient for MAiD must find the patient's view of their life as no longer worth living *comprehensible*. In effect, the doctor must be satisfied that the assisted death would be rational (in the sense explicated earlier), and therefore would constitute a benefit rather than a harm to the patient. All of this is so much paternalism, designed to screen out requests for MAiD that are impulsive, ill-considered, ill-informed, or distorted by transient circumstances. (And, yes, requests by the elderly can be irrational in these ways, just as suicides by the elderly can be.) In practice, therefore, the requirements of a 'serious' medical condition causing 'intolerable' suffering will set a high threshold for those who request MAiD on the basis of 'life fatigue'. But there is no reason to think that the threshold could not be surpassed. Like respect for autonomy, beneficence would lead us to permit at least some access to MAiD for the elderly who are 'tired of life'.

The standard justification for legalized MAiD rests on both of those values. The logic of that justification leads inexorably towards a principled case for expanding the eligibility criteria (or interpreting the existing criteria) to allow at least some cases of MAiD on grounds of 'life fatigue'. However, that is not the end of the story. A public policy that has a principled justification may still be a bad idea if it will have sufficiently bad unintended consequences. The most effective objections to expansion are therefore not principled but practical (Huxtable and Möller 2007). (Of course, it is itself a principle that we should not do things that have overall bad consequences, but I will set aside this nicety.)

So what might the unintended consequences be? One suggestion that is frequently heard is that allowing access to MAiD for 'life fatigue' will send the message to the elderly that their lives are not worth living. But I think this objection is overrated. Why should we think that this would be the message sent by allowing people like Peter and Suzan to end their lives at the time and in the manner of their choosing? Why would the message not be instead that the elderly can retain some degree of autonomy and dignity through the final stage of their lives, that they can be the ones to decide how it is all to end? That message is not demeaning or diminishing – it is instead empowering.

More important, I think, is the worry that allowing the elderly access to MAiD on the basis of 'life fatigue' will result in some of them dying prematurely and unnecessarily because they are not fully capable of making such an important decision (due to cognitive decline), because their decision is not fully voluntary (due to pressure by others), because it is distorted by a diagnosable mental illness (such as depression), because it is not fully informed (due to unexplored alternatives for coping with or overcoming the sources of their discontent), or because it is impulsive (a response to immediate but transient and remediable circumstances). The point being made by this objection is that while it might be acceptable to offer MAiD to those for whom suicide would be rational, in practice it would also be offered to many for whom suicide would be irrational. If so, then, all things considered, the harmful consequences of the expansion might outweigh the beneficial ones, despite its principled justification.

To assess the strength of this objection, we need to determine just *how* MAiD might be accessed by the elderly who are 'tired of life'. There are a number of possible policy options. The most conservative is the one we have been discussing so far: either expanding or reinterpreting the eligibility criteria for MAiD to include 'life fatigue' as an admissible ground. This is the direction indicated by the traditional justification for legalizing MAiD, since it continues to balance respect for patient autonomy against protection of patient interests. It would keep doctors involved as gatekeepers so as to ensure, as much as possible, that MAiD will be available to the elderly only for rational decisions to die.

The most radical alternative is exemplified by the proposal issued in 2017 by the Dutch health and justice ministers: that a 'completed life' pill should be available to anyone over the age of seventy, with no doctor's permission required (de Bellaigue 2019). The idea of such a pill was introduced into the Dutch debate as far back as 1991 and has since been advocated by NVVE (Griffiths et al. 2008, 29). This option assigns a preeminent justificatory importance to autonomy, since it entirely cuts out the paternalistic constraints imposed by the medical gatekeepers to MAiD. By eliminating all safeguards, it would leave decision-making solely in the hands of the elderly themselves.

Intermediate policy proposals are also imaginable. For instance, it would be possible for the 'completed life' pill to require a prescription, with the role of the doctor limited to determining patient decisional capacity.[32] Or the doctor's role might be slightly expanded to attest as well to the absence of distorting mental conditions. Or a 'cooling off' period could be mandated between request for the pill and delivery, so as to safeguard against impulsivity. No doubt other regimes could also be devised. Which of them we prefer will depend on how seriously we take practical concerns about the likelihood of abuse or mistake and where we think the balance should be struck between autonomy and beneficence. However this may be realized, the question seems to be not *whether* to recognize 'life fatigue' as a legitimate basis for accessing MAiD, but *how*.

---

[32] I owe this suggestion to Eric Mathison.

Conclusion

This is a good time to remind ourselves that the vast majority of suicides are tragedies, and often preventable ones. Where suicide is in question, it makes sense to expend our resources for the most part on detection and prevention. However, where the elderly are concerned, suicide can have its attraction as a way out when life is no longer worth living. This discussion has aimed to establish three salient conclusions: that suicide by the elderly can be both rational and ethical; that when it is rational, assistance with it can also be ethical; and that it makes sense for that assistance to take the form of access to MAiD, even when the sole ground is that the applicant has become 'tired of life'.

Part III

Ageing and Society

14 'To Grandmother's House We Go': On Women, Ethics, and Ageing

Samantha Brennan

Ageing is a topic that philosophers have largely ignored. We have had lots to say about death, some things to say about dying, but rather little to say about the life stage that usually, when all goes well, precedes it. Mirroring our lack of attention to children and childhood, we have preferred to focus our attention on idealized (rational, independent, autonomous) adults rather than adults in the last part of their lives. For much of the history of philosophy, philosophy has also ignored the lives of women. These two areas of philosophical abandonment may well be connected, for old age is much more the domain of women than of men. You cannot begin writing about justice, gender, and old age without noting that old age is gendered. Old age is gendered both in concrete terms, who the old are, and in conceptual terms, how we think about old age.

We can start with the basic fact that women, on average, live longer than men. In Canada, at age 65, there are about 125 women per 100 men and by age 80, 170 women per 100 men. Among centenarians, there are 500 women for every 100 men (Statistics Canada 2011). More than 70 per cent of the residents of homes for the elderly, nursing homes, or long-term care homes are women. So too are most of the staff. In Canada, more than 90 per cent of the staff working in long-term care homes are women (Estabrooks and Keefe 2020). Women are both the 'cared for' and are more likely to do the caring for. The caregiving of the elderly, as with children, is also gendered. Whether the elderly who need care are cared for by staff or by family, it is likely they are cared for by women. But old age is gendered in other ways too. Insofar as life's goods and their distribution is gendered, women usually lead different lives than men in their old age. What does an ethics that includes the elderly and the young look like? We are more likely to have an ethical theory that includes care and vulnerability as well as rights and autonomy (Tong 2014).

Finally, the association of old age as a life stage with vulnerability and dependence, traits more often associated with the feminine than the masculine, means that our very concept of old age may be gendered. Philosophical theories

Thanks to Alan Richardson for the title. As he notes, the missing old men are inscribed in kids' stories and popular songs.

of life's goods that focus on agency, autonomy, and independence likewise leave out understanding both childhood and old age as possible sites for well-being and human flourishing (Brennan 2014). At best they are seen as diminished states where life's goods only exist in weakened versions, if at all.

Of course, to say that gender is relevant to age and well-being is not to say that gender is the only variable that makes a difference. When we are thinking about the distributions of well-being and justice, then race, class, ethnicity, disability, marital status, sexual orientation, and geographic location also matter. In particular, disability and dependence are two factors associated with advanced age, but the link between the two is not a necessary one. Old age looks like many different things to different people. That said, very few people make it to late old age, say ninety plus, without some need for assistance in daily living. In a society that places a great deal of weight on independence and autonomy, the elderly are worse off for multiple reasons, only one of which is the association of age with dependence and femininity. Another is our societal stigmatization of disability.

What are we talking about when we talk about old age? Diane Jeske (2017, 331) makes an important distinction between 'merely getting older, that is chronological ageing, [and] the characteristic processes associated with human beings' getting older, what I will call the process of ageing'. Still, we tend to think of life stages in the chronological sense because of their strong association with the process of ageing. It is for that reason that, for example, young people in Canada can start learning to drive at sixteen even though only some may be developmentally ready at that age and others not. The same is true for markers of old age – such as having to redo one's driver's certification, receiving government assistance for drugs and health care, or getting the seniors' discount at the movie theatre. Carolyn Heilbrun (1998) suggests life after sixty is a unique life stage, while the normal retirement age of sixty-five might be another useful demarcation point. In our current environment, we hear a lot of old age denialism – sixty is the new forty, and so on. It's hard to define old age because sixty can look like so many different things, but what ninety looks like hasn't changed as much as one might hope; and one thing ninety definitely looks like is female.

Christine Overall (2016, 28) assesses old age in the following way: 'Oldness is a universal possibility, and if we are fortunate, we will all get old. There is therefore all the more reason not to stigmatize it, but instead to (re)claim oldness as a valued identity and stage of life.' The challenge is to destigmatize old age on its own terms. Much recent destigmatizing takes the form of an unrealistic rebranding of old age that sets unrealistic standards followed by disappointment. Martha Nussbaum's theory of the stigmatization of the aged is that it is, 'at its core, a stigma about our embodiment and our mortality' (Nussbaum and Levmore 2017, 121). We need to make big shifts in our attitudes towards our bodies and towards death if we want to combat the stigmatization of old age that fuels our discrimination against older persons.

This chapter explores five themes related to women's lives, ethics, and ageing, touching on issues in normative ethics and well-being, in justice and right action, and in applied ethics. These themes are meant to be more illustrative than exhaustive. I am afraid the chapter raises more questions than it answers, but my hope is that the chapter presents the reader with an idea of the richness of the philosophical terrain and a sense of the range and depth of questions under the heading of women, ageing, and ethics.

Welfare, the Plight of the Worst Off, and Elderly Women

The most common lens through which elderly women are seen, from the perspective of ethics and political philosophy, is through the lens of the 'worst-off persons'. It isn't the whole story, as we will see in other sections of this chapter, but it is part of the story. Contemporary political philosophy is, according to different political theories, centred on different moral concepts and measures, such as utility, rights, equality, and the plight of the worst-off persons. John Rawls (1971) famously argued that we evaluate justice across societies not by measuring and comparing total or average welfare but rather by seeing how well a particular society treats its worst-off members. Inequalities in the distribution of primary goods can only be justified by increases in the well-being of society's worst-off members. If we think Rawls is right, then in many societies we can judge justice in terms of comparing how older women fare. Even if Rawls is not right that the situation of the worst off is the only, or the most important, measure of justice, we can agree with Rawls that how the worst off are faring matters morally and politically.

In her book chapter 'Women: Eventually the Only Sex', Susan Jacoby (2011, chapter 6) looks at downside of women's longer lifespan. Old age is a women's issue, she writes, because two-thirds of those over age eighty-five are women. Eighty-five per cent of American centenarians are women (Jacoby 2011, 125).

One might be tempted to think of women's extra years of life as an injustice that ought to be of concern to egalitarians, the arguments of which will be taken up in the next section. Is it really fair that women live longer than men, that women get something that men do not? Should public policy tools try to address this inequality? If it were just a matter of extra years of life, it might be that the men's rights/lifespan egalitarians would have a point. However, old age for women is not necessarily the addition of extra good years of life. Women are two and a half times more likely than men to encounter disability in old age (Jacoby 2011, 127). Note that to say that the quality of life of those with disabilities and the quality of life of racialized persons is worse is not to say it is inherently worse. It is worse, when it is worse, because of political choices we have made about the distribution of wealth and of care.

More than half of Black and Hispanic women seniors in the United States live beneath the poverty line (Jacoby 2011, 127). Again in the United States, almost

70 per cent of women age seventy-five or older are widowed, divorced, or never married, compared to only about 30 per cent of men. Older women are much more likely than men to live alone. Nearly half (48 per cent) of women age seventy-five or older are living alone, compared to less than one-quarter (22 per cent) of men (AARP Public Policy Institute, 2007).

The philosopher Mary Mothersill (1999, 13) puts the costs of supporting older persons this way in her APA Presidential Address on 'Old Age':

We, the oldies, are very expensive. We do not pull our weight. We are mostly unemployed and assumed by those whose opinions count to be unemployable. We are unproductive. Some of us live off pensions and annuities; others (not everybody) have social security which, as we are reminded daily, is running out of funds. We have a disproportionate number of medical problems, many chronic and severe. Some of us need part-time caregivers; some need round-the-clock institutional care. Who is responsible for us? Who is supposed to provide for our housing and pay our medical bills? Who is to keep us from dying of boredom? Our children? But what if we have no children or if our children are supporting their children and finding it hard to make ends meet? Should wage-earning taxpayers foot the bill? Why should they get stuck with having to subsidize us?

Notably, Mothersill does not mention that it is mostly women who need care and financial support. Mothersill raises the issue of caring for the elderly primarily as a matter of distributive justice, where what is to be distributed is the cost of care, but it is also companionship and the care itself that plays a role in the well-being of the elderly. The old are subjected to social isolation in addition to economic hardship. Writing about the costs of caring for the elderly (in response to Daniel Callahan's (1987) work on setting limits) Nora Bell (1989, 170) puts it this way:

When one looks closely at the data, however, what one very quickly discovers is that there are many more elderly women than there are elderly men, and these older women are poorer, more apt to live alone, and less likely to have informal social and personal supports than their male counterparts. Furthermore, a disproportionate number of nursing home patients are women. Older women, therefore, are more likely to make the heaviest demand on health care resources.

In addition to our views on age and gender, our attitudes towards disability also play a role in how we think about old age. Christine Overall (2016, 16) writes,

In addition, ableism plays a role in the stigmatization of oldness. Ableism is prejudice, stigmatization, negative discrimination, and even oppression aimed at a particular person or group of people because of their impairment(s) or perceived impairments. Persons who have lived a very long time are likely to be dealing with a greater incidence of disease and impairments. However, unsurprisingly, societies valorize being able-bodied and free of disease and impairment. Hence, to be old is to be doubly devalued.

So how should we think about the problem of old women? Or to put it differently, why are old women a problem at all? If we focus on seemingly objective measures such as wealth and physical ability, it looks as if the situation of older women is very dire indeed. It seems clear that older women are very often the worst off. Much feminist work on ageing and justice makes this point: capturing the problem of women and old age is a problem of distributive justice. At the same time, describing women and old age in this way may miss out on key aspects of the lived experience of old age from the perspective of older women themselves. It also makes ableist assumptions about the connection between disability and well-being. These descriptions also centre on midlife, missing out on the goods of old age.

Diane Gibson (1996, 435) writes,

By focussing on issues of disadvantage, feminist analyses of old age have tended to obscure not only the heterogeneity of old women but also the aspects of being old and female that are a source of both celebration and strength. While there is no doubt that women face a number of adverse physical, emotional, mental, social, and economic eventualities in their old age, such eventualities do not adequately represent the totality of their experiences.

While older women may be the worst off from a certain perspective, it is also clear that the situation is more nuanced and complex in a variety of ways.

Is Women's Longer Lifespan a Grave Injustice?

Another perspective on women and old age does not look at women as the worst off. Instead, it looks to women's longer lifespan as an unfair advantage. Women live longer than men, on average six to eight years longer. The 'why' is complicated. Women's extra years of life are partly the result of biological factors, partly a result of environmental circumstances, and partly the result of gender impacting life choices. It is also not true that women live longer than men across the board, around the world. According to the World Health Organization (2009), 'notably in parts of Asia, these advantages are overridden by gender-based discrimination so that female life expectancy at birth is lower than or equal to that of men'. In other parts of the world, high maternal mortality rates bring down the average lifespan of women. What remains true is that in nearly all populations throughout the world there are substantially more older women than men.

The first philosopher to draw attention to this issue as a source of egalitarian injustice is John Kekes (1997). Kekes notes that there is a serious inequality with respect to life expectancy between men and women. He tells us that among American men and women born between 1970 and 2010, inequality is between seven and eight years, roughly one-tenth of the human lifespan. Egalitarians ought to take this difference seriously, argues Kekes, if they really care about equality regarding life's basic goods, as surely life expectancy has at least as strong a claim to count among the primary goods as any other candidate. Now it is important to note that Kekes is raising this as an issue for egalitarian positions in moral and political philosophy. He means it as a reductio of the egalitarian position that natural inequalities ought to be remedied by state solutions. But it might be true that if we care about inequalities, then lifespan differences between men and women are an important difference that ought to merit our attention.

Kekes (1997, 658) writes,

It is a basic egalitarian belief that serious unjustified inequalities are morally objectionable and that a measure of a just society is the extent to which it eliminates or at least reduces them. Inequalities are serious if they affect primary goods, which are necessary for living a good life ... All serious inequalities are unjustified unless they benefit everyone in one's society, especially those who are worst off ... Overcoming unjustified inequalities requires the redistribution of primary goods.

Since life expectancy is a primary good and is unequally distributed between men and women, egalitarians ought to be committed to making up for this gap.

Philippe Van Parijs (2015, 82) presents the problem in these terms: 'As long as most people would be willing to give up some income in order to live longer, women's higher life expectancy reduces the inequality between men and women.' If the different length of lifespans between men and women is an injustice, is there anything that public policy can do to address the inequality in lifespan between men and women?

Kekes argues controversially that what follows from an egalitarian commitment to reducing undeserved inequalities are policies to employ more women and fewer men in risky, life-threatening jobs. Men ought also to have longer vacations and shorter work days and make smaller contributions to government pension schemes since they are less likely to benefit (Kekes 1997, 661). These policies, however, strike many as absurd. The question arises, therefore, whether other policies favoured by egalitarians to overcome other inequalities are not similarly absurd. But likewise, one could take Kekes' starting point and egalitarian justice seriously and commit to the conclusions that follow. Should we?

In what follows I consider two different possible responses to Kekes' argument that egalitarians ought to care about and try to remedy lifespan egalitarianism between men and women.

Are the Extra Years Good Ones?

One explanation as to why egalitarians haven't risen up in arms over this sexual inequality can be found in the work of Christine Overall. Overall argues, in the course of a discussion of death's differential badness for women, that although women live longer than men, those additional years are often years of considerable poverty and ill health. In the United States, for example, women are twice as likely as men to end their later years in poverty (Overall 2003).

Suppose that two people – call them Jack and Jane – both live to the age of seventy-five with the same amount of well-being in their lives. Suppose further that Jack dies at seventy-five, and Jane lives for an additional five years but at a greatly reduced level of well-being. Whether or not Jane's life is better on balance than Jack's will depend on whether you think well-being over a lifespan is best assessed in terms of the total or the average view. The additional years of poverty and ill health (assuming they are years worth living) increase the total for Jane but bring down Jane's average.

So yes, the average lifespan of women exceeds that of men. Although women may have less of some goods in their lives, does a longer lifespan mean that it equals out in terms of total good at the end, or is average well-being the thing that really matters? The point here is that it is not just a commitment to egalitarianism plus the claim that women live longer than men that leads to the conclusion that the extra years of life for women are a concern for egalitarian theories of justice. You must also believe that the total view is the right way to determine well-being across a lifespan.

You must also think that we count goods equally across the lifespan without a preference for patterns. Many of us – for the same amount of total good in a lifetime – would prefer a life that starts out badly and ends well to a life that starts out well and goes downhill. We tend to like life stories with rough beginnings and good endings: think of memoirs by Jeannette Walls (2006), Augusten Burroughs (2002), David Sedaris (2004), and Tara Westover (2018). But no one wants to have reached peak well-being in high school and have it all be downhill from there, no matter how good the early years are. Again, if women's lives most often end in poverty and ill health, they also have the less-preferred distribution of goods across a lifespan even if they have a greater total amount of well-being. This shows it is not clear that egalitarian ethics regards women's longer lifespan as an unfair advantage. It might be that women's extra years of life do not make women better off.

What's the Cause of the Gap? Does That Make a Difference?

Another line of response to the lifespan gap between men and women looks to the causes of the gap. We might note that the lifespan gap between men and women appears to be closing as men shun smoking, turn to healthy diets and exercise, and make regular trips to the doctor. According to a Statistics Canada (2011) report, female life expectancy in Canada is now just 4.7 years longer than that of males. This suggests men's shorter lives may result from a series of bad choices. Many egalitarians think we need to equalize differences that are the result of brute luck but not necessarily those that follow from choices that we make. Indeed, the countries with the biggest gaps in male and female lifespans are those countries in which women's smoking and drinking is highly controlled but men's is not.

Does it make a difference if men's shorter lifespan is due to causes within men's control? Richard Arneson raises this option in a symposium on Keke's work. He writes,

Consider a simple conceivable scenario. The difference in life expectancy between men and women could be entirely attributable to anticipated differences in the lifestyle choices of men and women that affect longevity. Men might on the average consume more alcohol and tobacco products than women do, commit more acts that risk violent encounters, be less disposed to cooperate in interactions that are representable as single-play prisoner's dilemmas, and so on. On the face of it, an inequality in life expectancy attributable to these factors would be a shallow not deep inequality, and an egalitarianism sympathetically construed would be sensitive to this difference, so that the moral imperative of egalitarianism urges the elimination only of deep inequalities. (Arneson 1998)

Feminist philosophers, though, will not be so quick to assign responsibility to outcomes for acts that result from gender role socialization, whether it is masculine or feminine socialization that is at issue. The philosopher David Benatar explores the ways in which men's lives are worse than women's in his book *The Second Sexism.* Benatar (2012) notes that men's health is on average poorer than women's health. Men are more prone to alcoholism and drug abuse, and more vulnerable to violence. No doubt some of this is the result of choice, but not all of the ways in which men's lives are worse than women's are self-chosen. Male suicide rates are also considerably higher. In Canada, men are nine times more likely than women to be imprisoned. Men constitute about 85 per cent of homeless adults. Canadian men show higher dropout rates at every level from primary school to university. Men are more likely to be conscripted into military service, to be the victims of violence, and to lose custody of their children in the event of a divorce. Men also tend to work longer hours than women.

Paula Casal (2015, 93), in response to Van Parijs and the line of argument about choice and responsibility, writes,

Most feminists, and perhaps most liberal egalitarians, tend to hold social rather than biological explanations of gendered behavior, and so they may find the lifestyle explanation of longevity plausible. This, however, does not commit them to the view that if a man's behavior is gendered, he is not liable to bear the burdens arising from it.

Are the Goods of Old Age Gendered?

If the worries raised earlier about justice and old age look at the ways in which women's lives are worse than men's lives, on average, this section looks at accounts of well-being according to which old age is a particularly valuable stage of life for women, with its own unique goods. In the final section, I say something about how we might reconcile these views.

Philosophers who defend accounts of the good that give priority to autonomy and rationality are going to want to give less value to both old age and childhood. This is true for both Kantians and for consequentialists. Michael Slote (1982), for example, in the course of arguing against the view that goods in a life are to be treated equally no matter when they occur, defends the view that it makes sense to discount life-stage-specific goods that occur in both childhood and old age. Slote is presenting this view as an alternative to both 'neutrality across time' views and the view that the present counts for more. Slote (1982, 317) writes,

[T]he period known as 'the prime of life' is typically conceived as containing precisely those goals, strivings, miseries, and satisfactions that are to be taken most seriously in human life, and is thus largely an exception to what we have been saying about childhood and senescence. Indeed, the very expression 'prime of life' conveys the implication that the failures and successes of other periods are inherently less serious and less determinative of what one's life has, for better or worse, been like.

According to Slote's account, we can reject the view that the present counts for more without having to treat all goods equally across time. Instead, he thinks it makes sense to discount goods that occur in childhood and in old age. Partly I think Slote is wrong because he places too much value on 'the prime of life', and partly I think he is wrong because of the kind of goods he thinks childhood and old age contain. Slote writes about old age and shuffleboard trophies (Slote 1982, 319), but really he is thinking about 'achievement goods' when the goods of old age might be better located in relationships, the chance to read books, long walks, deep thought, and freewheeling conversations.

Margaret Walker (1999) notes that philosophers with otherwise quite divergent philosophical views share a certain conception of life. Walker calls this conception 'the career self' (1999, 83). A career self sees life as a unified field in which particular enterprises, values, and relationships are coordinated in the form of a 'rational life plan' (Rawls 1971). This conception of a human life puts a great deal of emphasis on agency, narrative unity, and planning. Life is viewed as coming in distinct stages, each stage with its own goods. Walker writes, 'The image of the fit, energetic, and productive individual who sets himself a course of progressive achievement within the boundaries of society's rules and institutions, and whose orderly life testifies to his self-discipline and individual effort, remains an icon of our culture' (Walker 1999, 102).

Note this is an interesting illustration of the tension between philosophers' theories of well-being over the lifespan and subjective well-being assessments in the psychology literature. For while many moral philosophers think of the adult years as the prime of life, psychologists believe that there is a U-shaped curve of happiness which puts midlife at the very bottom. The U-shaped curve of happiness suggests that middle age is the least happy time of life, across the world, and that happiness peaks in old age (Blanchflower 2021). It is also not surprising that most of the philosophers writing about the extra significance of 'prime of life' goods are themselves writing during those years. Gibson (1996, 438) writes, 'It is worth considering that the lack of fit between objective and subjective indicators of well-being in old age may be at least influenced by the midlife perspective of most researchers.'

How might feminist theories of well-being approach this issue? Some feminist work on well-being looks to close personal relationships as an important part of the good life. It might be argued that women's lives – traditionally more focussed on family than on work – include more of this particular good. However, since chosen goods are better than those one is forced or coerced to pursue, the lack of choice might offset the benefit to women. Writing about late-in-life goods, Gibson (1996, 438–9) writes that '[w]omen, with a lifetime of experience in maintaining and establishing social bonds within families, friendship networks, neighborhoods, voluntary associations, school associations, and so forth, are simply better equipped to maintain and redevelop their social networks when confronted with the vicissitudes frequently attendant on old age'.

But not all accounts of the value of old age look to relationships. Another important aspect of the value of the last stage of life for women concerns time for oneself. After a life of caring for others – often a husband and children – the later years represent a time in which women get to put themselves first. In some lives that means the ability to cook simple meals if that's what one feels like. In other, more affluent lives, the choices might be about travel or where to live. In *The Last Gift of Time: Life Beyond Sixty*, Carolyn Heilbrun (1998) describes this period of a woman's life as containing special goods. Heilbrun writes, for example, about her decision to stop wearing dresses, hose, and heels after turning sixty and her desire to have more time alone to write and live quietly. Strikingly, after her children and grandchildren kept returning to their country home on the weekends, Heilbrun bought her own house to live and write alone some of the time.

Mary Pipher (2019b), a popular psychologist, writes that describing older women as miserable results from a misogynistic misunderstanding of women's lives. Rather than being the worst off, Pipher writes that older women are among the happiest people. Older people are generally happier than people in midlife, and, according to Pipher, older women are happier than older men. Recent census data from the United Kingdom, cited in Pipher, finds that the happiest people are women aged sixty-five to seventy-nine.

How do we reconcile the two very different views of how bad old age is for women? When one focusses on material goods, women fare worse than men at most life stages. That is true also for access to political power and vulnerability to sexual violence. But feminist philosophers, in addition to raising the complaint of equality when it comes to career opportunities and equal pay for work of equal value, have also proposed alternative, feminist theories of well-being. According to many feminist theories of well-being, what is central to human well-being and flourishing are relational goods. It is in this respect in which many women's lives – again, at all life stages – are better than those of men. Men often suffer from lack of family connections and friendship.

Beauty and Old Age

Women's lives are often valued only for our role in childbearing and rearing, for our work caring for others, and, when present, for physical beauty. Once these goods are past, and women need to be cared for rather than providing care, and women are no longer attractive objects of desire, it is then that older women become a problem. Older women complain of feeling invisible or irrelevant. Many older women say they feel a deep shame in the changes their bodies go through as they age. Feminist philosopher Sandra Bartky conceptualizes this invisibility as a social disability of old age. In her 'Unplanned Obsolescence: Some Reflections on Aging', Bartky (1999) writes about the loss of the admiring gaze that comes with old age, the experience of being rendered invisible, as no longer being seen as sexually attractive or no longer seen at all. Through stories of her own experience and the experiences of relatives, Bartky lists the different kinds of loss that accompany old age, many of which follow from an emphasis on women's looks in the first part of life and a loss of regard for women's looks as we age.

In this section we will look at the age-related puzzles posed by the focus on women's looks. Insofar as women's value is based on physical appearance, and beauty standards tend to favour youth, older women are seen as less-valuable members of our youth-orientated culture. This cuts both ways, however. Older women are seen as less beautiful and so less valuable, and yet it's also true older women are under increasing pressure to keep up with beauty standards and not let themselves go. As Heather Widdows (2018, 65) notes, it used to be the case that beauty expectations decreased with age, but now women in their fifties, sixties, and seventies are expected to maintain beautiful youthful faces and bikini bodies. Eating disorders were once mostly found among adolescents but now are growing among women in middle age and older.

The extension of beauty culture into old age is a double-edged sword. On the one hand there is appreciation for beautiful older women. On the other there is a continued expectation of beauty as a normative ideal. A considerable amount of money, time, and effort must go into 'aging gracefully' even during the relatively young decades of old age, one's sixties and seventies, writes Susan Jacoby (2011, 143). Jacoby details the amount of work, time, and money in the areas of clothes, make-up, hair care, jewellery, and possibly cosmetic surgery an older woman must invest if she is to continue to be seen as beautiful.

One of the few philosophers to write about women's experience of old age is Simone de Beauvoir. She wrote *The Coming of Age* when she was seventy-two. Beauvoir's description of the loss women face in old age is tragic and striking. It is important to keep in mind that Beauvoir is not giving a normative analysis of the way women ought to be. Rather, her work is descriptive in the sense that she is describing the role concepts such as 'women' and 'old person' play in governing our lives (Deutscher 2003). Both are socially constructed categories, but the challenge for older women, according to Beauvoir's understanding, is that these concepts contradict one another. One can't be an older woman, since our under-standing of woman – created and not born – includes the concept of youthful beauty, which is missing in old age. To age, in her view, is to lose the status of 'woman'.

Another way of putting this is to say that the myth of femininity inevitably clashes with the myth of old age. Weiss writes,

Insofar as the myth of femininity offers us an image of a thin, beautiful, young, graceful, seductive, and nurturing woman, it might seem to have an advantage over the myth of old age where the image of the ugly old hag immediately comes to mind as the feminine woman's very negative counterpart. To the extent that old women are perceived to be beautiful in early twenty-first century Western visual media, their beauty is almost always associated with their miraculous ability to retain the youthful face and expression associated with the myth of femininity, that is, with their success in expressing what Beauvoir calls the 'Eternal Feminine'. (Weiss 2014, 48, quoting from Beauvoir's *The Second Sex* (1989))

For Beauvoir, ageing is both a personal and practical problem for women, as well as a conceptual challenge. It is not just about how others see or treat older women. It is also about how older women come to view themselves.

While it is evident, simply by virtue of individual bodily differences, that no two people will experience the ageing process in exactly the same way, the almost universal tendency throughout history to value men more for their intellectual achievements and women for the youthful beauty of their bodies makes it virtually impossible for most elderly women to remain unaffected by the societal association of a loss of youth with a loss of one's femininity. Of course, there are many different ways women can resist such an identification; however, as Beauvoir persuasively demonstrates in *The Coming of Age*, the internalization of such negative gendered stereotypes encourages a disidentification both with one's own and with others' ageing female bodies (Weiss 2014, 52).

There is the external pressure, but we also cannot ignore the amount to which beauty standards that include youth become part of our own identities. Women come to see ourselves as old and unattractive in ways that undermine our agency. While social scientists report that women who care the most about looks have the toughest time ageing, it may be that caring greatly about looks earlier in life is a rational response to the rewards and benefits of beauty. Once those standards are internalized, however, it can be hard to avoid emotions such as shame and sadness as one ages.

More recently, Martha Nussbaum has written about ageing in her part of the conversation with Saul Levmore in the book *Aging Thoughtfully: Conversations about Retirement, Romance, Wrinkles, and Regret*. Nussbaum pushes us to confront our disgust at ageing bodies. As feminists in the sixties and seventies urged women to take control of our bodies, Nussbaum asks us to extend that same activism, interest, and curiosity to our bodies as we age. Nussbaum strikes an interesting middle road in her thinking about age and beauty. She doesn't condemn cosmetic surgery as long as it doesn't take the place of exercise or diet and it doesn't use up all of one's resources that could go to altruistic giving. 'There is nothing wrong with wanting to look better', Nussbaum writes. 'It's what we all do every day' (Nussbaum and Levmore 2017, 120).

Of course, not all older women experience ageing in this way. Not all women experience being seen as attractive by others in their youth equally. Age can be a welcome equalizer among women. Once others were thought beautiful and you were not, and now no one is. Many do not care about being found attractive by men in the first place or find it troubling and bothersome at best. It might be worth noting that Nussbaum, Bartky, and Beauvoir are all beautiful women writing about ageing. That experience might be different among women who didn't benefit from the male gaze in the first place, either because they were not thought to merit it or they did not want it. Indeed, some women claim a feeling of relief in invisibility. The loss of the male gaze may be seen as positive change. Finally, for gender nonbinary female bodied persons, moving beyond the category 'woman' as one ages may also be a welcome shift. The decreasing significance of gender can be understood in positive terms. Older women of all orientations may seek to move beyond caring about appearance. In the controversial essay 'The Third Age', Francine du Plessix Gray (1996) writes, 'If the gaze of others wanes, one might choose to acquire instead a deepened inward gaze, or intensify our observation of others, or evolve alternative means of attention-getting which transcend sexuality and depend, as the mentors of my youth taught me, upon presence, authority, and voice.'

The Goodness of Old Age and the Badness of Death

This chapter began by noticing that philosophers have paid more attention to death and to dying than we have to old age. This final section of this chapter returns to the question of death. But it is not about death per se; rather, it explores the ways in which our views about how bad death is are connected to our understanding of old age. In particular, it looks to the ways in which a negative view of old age is connected to sexism and ableism, and to the view that death is not a bad thing for the very old.

On what has come to be the standard philosophical account of the badness of death, death's badness consists in the goods it takes away. Death is not bad intrinsically, according to this view. It is not an experience to be feared. Rather, what makes death bad, when it is bad, is that death deprives of us good experiences we would have had had we not died. One result of this view is that death is always a bad thing. When the next chunk of life of which death deprives us is full of bad experiences, when it is on balance bad, then death can be a good thing for the person who dies. For example, when someone dies rather than experiencing more pain and suffering, then their death is not necessarily bad.

Unsurprisingly then, apologists, who wish to claim that death in old age is not so bad after all, focus their attention on what old age is like. Daniel Callahan (1987), for example, looks at old age, or least advanced old age, as a time of ill health, loneliness, and disability. Or, even when things are going well, as a time when one has had the chance to experience life's goods and one has discharged one's responsibilities to others. As Bell (1989) points out, both of these claims may have gendered implications, as women may have had fewer opportunities in their youth and may have begun their careers later than men. In the time of the COVID-19 pandemic, one saw the practical implications of the view that death is not so bad for the elderly in our treatment of and callous disregard for the welfare and well-being of the residents in long-term care homes. Shelley Tremain (2020) makes an important distinction between the narrative that sees those in care homes as 'naturally vulnerable' and the narrative that sees their vulnerability as a matter of policy and choice, 'social vulnerability'.[1]

The richest discussion of old age and response to death apologism can be found in the work of feminist philosopher Christine Overall (2003, chapter 2) in her discussion of the badness of death and in particular in her discussion of arguments against prolonging the human lifespan. Many such arguments rely on seeing old age as a bad thing.

'The view that "I'd rather be dead than a disabled old person" reflects tremendous ignorance about disability', writes Overall (2003, 43). It is false that a life lived with disability is not worth living. In assessments of quality of

---

[1] See also Picard (2021).

life in old age, as with quality-of-life assessments of persons with disabilities, there is a real tendency to ignore self-evaluation of well-being in favour of objective measures. Overall points to a number of factors that give the lives of older women well-being and meaning. In particular, since women's lives are often front-loaded with responsibilities in caregiving, particularly the care of infants and children, it is sometimes only in later years that women have opportunities to pursue their individual interests and passions.

Likewise, when we look at some of the feminist theories of well-being that prioritize relationship goods such as friendship, by these lights older women's lives contain much of value. Certainly, by subjective measures many women thrive in old age.

Jamie Lindemann Nelson contrasts the goods of relationship with the goods of agency, arguing as well that we do better from the point of view of avoiding death's badness by focussing on the unexperienced goods of relationships. For example, Jill is invested in unexperienced goods when she cares a great deal about her children's flourishing. Jack, on the other hand, focusses his life on the goods of experience. Nelson (1999, 124) writes, 'People who manage to make the good of others central to their lives . . . are importantly invested in something robust enough to withstand their deaths.'

But to the extent that it is true that by some objective measures – say, for example, poverty and ill health – women do not fare well in old age, it also seems a double-edged sword to say that death is less bad for older women because of their lower quality of life. Now not only do women suffer an injustice, but it is made worse if we take actions or build policies based on the view their deaths are less bad. Clearly a better response, if we have choices to make, is to improve the quality of life of older women. Yes, this has the effect of making death worse, but that is a result of a particular account of death's badness. On this account we should all hope that our deaths are very bad for us, because their badness comes from living a life rich in goods.

Conclusion

When we begin thinking about women and old age, there is a lot of scope for ethical outrage because of the combined results of ableism, ageism, and sexism. Continuing to think about women and old age also reveals some important difficulties with the way moral philosophers, including feminist ethicists, fail to pay attention to women's first-person account of ageing and the good life. This chapter has briefly outlined some of the issues in ethics and value theory that arise in our thinking about women and ageing.

15 Ageing, Unequal Longevities and Intergenerational Justice

Axel Gosseries

Introduction

My goal in this chapter is to clarify the nature of some ageing-related problems of economic and social justice. The focus will be specific in four ways. I will limit myself to *distributive* justice, as opposed to, for example, corrective justice or justice in the judiciary sense. I will focus on distributive justice *between generations*, rather than, for example, across genders or borders. I will stick to issues of intergenerational distributive justice that are directly related to *population ageing*, rather than issues such as climate justice between generations or the fairness of letting a public debt grow. Finally, I will restrict myself to *institutionalized* interactions and transfers between generations, that is, those mediated through institutions such as the social security or education systems, rather than those going through the family channel. This fourfold restriction is not meant to reflect any factual or value judgment about the relative importance of the issues at stake. It merely flows from the need to make choices in order to allow for some depth.

I will also assume here the need for the democratic debate to select *normative principles* on such ageing-related economic and social issues. Otherwise, we run the risk of arbitrary decisions with no reference to, for example, impartiality or solidarity. Identifying such principles requires a precise formulation, one that goes beyond merely invoking "equality," "freedom" or "reciprocity" in general terms. We need to go and search for our deepest moral intuitions, put the right words on our values and then get concrete. I assume that it is both necessary and possible to argue on such matters with rigor and to feed a collective dialogue on our values, seeking to identify together what the general interest requires in specific areas.[1] We also need to confront our

I wish to acknowledge the financial support of the Agency of the Czech Academy of Sciences through the project "Taking age discrimination seriously" (grant ID: 17 – 26629S), obtained by the Institute of State and Law (Academy of Sciences of the Czech Republic, Centre for Law and Public Affairs [CeLAPA]). This chapter also benefitted from interactions as part of the ARC project "Sustainable, adequate and safe pensions" (2018–2023). I wish to thank P.-A. Deproost, Ph. Hambye, G. Ponthière, M. Valente, V. Vandenberghe and C. Vandeschrick. The ideas presented in this chapter have been published as an earlier version in Portuguese and Italian.

[1] On reflective equilibrium: Daniels (2003).

ideas with possible implications in other areas to check for consistency. And one ought to ensure that our principles could work as *political* principles, that is, principles that a pluralistic society could, and should, *impose* on all of us through legally binding instruments.

After a first section devoted to conceptual clarification, the text will proceed in three steps. For reasons of clarity, I will begin with a simplified world. At each of the next two steps, I will add *one* extra dimension. The purpose is to end up with a realistic description of the problem of population ageing. A description that does not disregard any of the three core components will allow us to understand the role played by each from the angle of distributive justice. This setting will allow me to show that the core intergenerational justice challenge when a population ages is already present *in the absence* of any population ageing. While the latter will only appear in the third step, intergenerational justice concerns obtain from the first step onward.

I will begin with a world with *high and homogenous* longevity, that is, in which longevity neither varies today, nor changes across time (section 2). In such a hypothetical world, there are no differences in longevity across, for example, genders, classes or countries. Also, I will assume at this stage that longevity remains constant across generations, and that other possible sources of population ageing, such as natality decrease or youth emigration, don't obtain. What is central at this first stage is that longevity is *high*. The next step introduces the dimension of unequal longevities *within* each generation (section 3). Hence, at this stage, I will not yet relax the assumption of a constant average longevity *across* generations. This step will allow us to see how our core intergenerational justice problem is already present in a society with a *high and intragenerationally heterogeneous* longevity, in the *absence* of any population ageing. The latter will only be introduced in the last step (section 4). I will add there the assumption that longevity tends to increase across time, each generation enjoying a longer life than the previous one. Hence, our three steps correspond respectively to a population with a longevity that is uniform and constant across generations (section 2), heterogeneous within generations while constant across generations (section 3), and heterogeneous within generations and increasing across generations (section 4).

The focus of this chapter will consist in crossing what (if anything) long-lived people owe to short-lived people *with* what a given generation owes to the previous and/or the next ones. I will also inquire about what long-lived generations owe short-lived generations, which I believe is a central dimension in understanding the demands of distributive justice in ageing societies.

Concepts and Framing

Before engaging in our three steps, a few words on concepts. First, we should avoid confusions about *ageing*. Even for those aware of the fact that we are dealing with *population* – rather than individual – ageing, it is worth considering connotations in other languages. In French – as in other Latin idioms – "ageing" does not translate as "âgement," but rather as "vieillisse-ment," which literally means "oldification." English is interesting in this respect: while pointing at progress in age, it does *not* focus on advanced age. In fact, it does not point at *any* specific *stage* of our life. In contrast, the French language stresses "elderhood" in its ageing concept.

This terminological point matters for two reasons. First, population ageing results from several causes that interact during the "demographic transition" (Ponthière 2017, 35). It can result from a decrease in natality, a decrease in child mortality, a decrease in mortality at advanced ages and/or an increase in youth emigration. If population ageing resulted exclusively from a decrease in natality, a population could become older on average without any increase in the absolute number of those reaching an advanced age. In contrast, in cases in which the main driver of population ageing is an increase in longevity – which is common – we could refer to population "lengthening" (or "stretching").

Hence, shifting from "oldification" to "ageing" and then from "ageing" to "lengthening" allows us to focus more explicitly on change in total life *duration* rather than on age *stages* or on age *shift* – even though "ageing" may admittedly have both connotations of "age shift" and "gain in length." To make an analogy, when our days get longer in spring, we don't refer to this phenomenon as "afternooning" or "time passing." Having longer lives can actually stretch *all* the stages of our lives, not only the latest one. And this relates to our second point. Population ageing refers to an increase in the average *chronological* age of a population through time. Such an increase in average chronological age does not necessarily lead to a proportional increase in average *biological* or *productive* age. The relationship between chronological ageing and healthy or productive ageing is complex. While we often tend to associate "elderhood" with reduced physiological or productive capacity, we should keep in mind the possibility of an *increase* in the average chronological age of a population compatible with a reduction in morbidity or a decrease in the share of retirees under certain social and technological arrangements (Ponthière 2017, 17–26).

Besides this twofold clarification of the concept of ageing, we should also distinguish between three concepts of *generation*: birth cohorts (or "birth groups"), period groups and age groups. A birth cohort refers to a set of individuals born between date x and y. It is an ephemeral group whose size starts shrinking through mortality as soon as the reference "birth period" is over. Every birth cohort ends up vanishing with the death of its last representative. The second, less usual concept, that is, "period group," refers to a group of individuals defined by the fact that its members have been alive during a given period of history, regardless of their date of birth or longevity. Again, the existence of this group is ephemeral, as for birth cohorts. The third concept, that is, "age group," refers to all those sharing the same stage of chronological advancement at some point in their life, regardless of whether they actually coexist or not. For instance, as long as there will be teenagers, this age group *will continue to exist*, even if its size fluctuates across time.[2]

While both birth cohorts and period groups are ephemeral, age groups can exist as long as humankind exists, possibly with interruptions if, for example, certain age groups are temporarily eradicated at specific points in history, be it through a disease or for other reason. In addition, while both birth cohorts and period groups involve coexistence within the group, age groups could still be referred to as groups – that is, sets of several individuals – even in the hypothetical scenario of lineages of a single individual per age group at a time, for it would be enough to have members from time to time in history to add to a given age group. Note that even in such a case, we could still have a coexistence between members of *different* age groups at a given point in time. This is the overlap circumstance that people usually have in mind when they express concern about justice between age groups.

One of the key challenges in addressing issues of population ageing from the perspective of justice between generations consists in assessing the *normative* importance of inequalities respectively between birth cohorts, between period groups or between age groups. The word "ageing" may suggest the centrality of justice between *age groups* here. Yet, if inequalities should be assessed in priority over people's *entire lifetimes* – that is, from a *lifetime perspective* (to which I will return) – wealth oscillations across periods or synchronic wealth differences across age groups might actually matter *less* than inequalities between birth cohorts over their entire lifetimes. The inclusion of the unusual notion of "period group" is meant precisely to help emphasize that idea. The lifetime perspective – a normative perspective not to be confused with "life-cycle" analysis – is more at home with cohortal analysis than with a focus on period groups or age groups. In fact, when comparing members of different "period groups" or "age groups," we tend to compare their situation, respectively, between periods ("were people better off *during period x* than during period y?") or within a period ("is age group x *currently* better off than age group y?"). This differs from what happens with birth cohorts, for which we do not tend to limit ourselves to looking at what happens "while they remain within the birth period."

Hence, I will show that a lifetime view commands a focus on justice between birth cohorts in assessing the challenges of ageing. To put it differently, if population ageing increases our concern about synchronic relations across the ages, there will of course be room for analyzing it from the perspective of justice between age groups. However, if the lifetime perspective claims that such synchronic relations matter *less* than what can be revealed through

---

[2] On these concepts and Lexis's diagram: Vandeschrick (2001).

a focus on entire lifetimes, then our primary focus may have to be on birth cohorts.

I just discussed various understandings of "generation," stressing the need to focus on inter-cohortal concerns rather than on justice between age groups or period groups. Of course, this does not mean that *non-generational* concerns are irrelevant. I would like to say something about this before we proceed. Population ageing also magnifies, for example, issues of gender justice. Here are two examples. On the informal care front, the assumption is often that women bear a disproportionate share of this. Ageing may tend to increase this burden. There is also the issue of differential longevity between women and men. This in turns raises the question of whether taking seriously the disadvantage suffered by short-lived people may call for policies privileging men, who tend to be shorter-lived. Another non-generational dimension is global justice. For example, what is sometimes referred to as "replacement migration" is meant to buffer the demographic effects of ageing. Up to a certain level, replacement migration may even benefit poorer countries of origin (Docquier and Rapoport 2012; Gosseries and Zwarthoed 2016). This again will be left aside here, despite the fact that it also connects with the issue of justice between short-lived and long-lived, poorer countries often experiencing lower life-expectancies.

I will also leave aside plenty of other philosophical issues such as the impact of ageing on the centrality of paid labor, on the need for human–machine substitution, on our relationship with sickness and death, etc. What will mostly interest me here is the issue of justice between short-lived and long-lived persons, crossing it with the *intergenerational* dimension.

High Longevity, Contribution Rates and Lifetime Equality

I begin this exploration with a world in which longevity is high. At the same time, there are no significant inequalities in life expectancy in that world, nor is there any increase across time. While longevity is high, it is also homogeneous and constant. The question is: what does an *age group* owe another in such a world? I will focus on that first, despite having suggested earlier that justice *between birth cohorts* is what should interest us in priority. In fact, I will even focus more specifically on what "active midlife adults" owe "retired older adults," leaving aside what adults owe young people, what young people may owe other age groups, etc.

One way of framing of our concern consists of looking at the issue of a *fair contribution rate*, through a succession of three questions:

Q1: Is there a justice-based argument against a *high* contribution rate in the absence of any inequalities in longevity?

Q2: Is there a justice-based argument against a *high* contribution rate in the presence of heterogeneous, while constant, longevity?

Q3: Is there a justice-based argument against a *high* contribution rate in the presence of heterogeneous and growing longevity?

In the present section, I focus on Q1, leaving Q2 and Q3 for the next two sections. In order to answer Q1, two things need to be defined. First, the concept of a contribution rate. A dependency ratio increases whenever the share of "dependent" people increases in relation to the so-called "active population." Societies with higher average longevity tend to be associated with a higher dependency ratio. This is a plausible assumption, despite the fact that it depends very much on the structure of the labor market and on people's health. The latter dimensions have a key impact on our ability to remain "active" at an advanced age (Ponthière 2017, 17–26). Now, whenever the dependency ratio increases, our expectations toward the active population also tend to increase, translating, for example, into a higher tax rate imposed on gross wages. Hence, in a society with higher longevity, with a higher dependency ratio, the rate of contribution of the active population will also tend to be higher. Pension regimes are a case in point.

Note here that under a funded pension scheme – as opposed to a PAYGO one – we may be under the impression that what is being put aside for our old age is our *own* money, as when we gather firewood for the winter. In that sense, we might have the impression that we are not imposing anything on the next generation and that whether we wish a high pension or a low one merely depends on what we are willing to put aside when we are younger. Yet, even in a funded scheme, it is misleading to believe that each generation takes its own decisions about its pension level without imposing anything on others: The value of the money we put aside – unlike the combustion power of our firewood – depends on the labor of the active population during our retirement time. Hence, even under a funded scheme, we do impose a given level of effort to the next generation, one that could turn out to be fair or not.

We then need to assess under which conditions a higher contribution rate can be more problematic than a lower one in terms of *justice.* Imagine that we approach this from an egalitarian angle of some form. By this, we mean a conception of justice that does not merely care about equality before the law, that is, the view that all those falling under the same legal category should be treated identically, hence avoiding an arbitrary application of the law. Here, I am rather referring to egalitarian theories of justice that are a bit more substantial. A theory of justice wants to go further than equality before the law. It cares about identifying which inequalities are unjust and which are not; it cares about how to articulate efficiency and equality; it tells us whether it is inequalities as such that should worry us; it cares about whether weight should be given to responsibility; etc. For instance, for some egalitarians, those inequalities that are necessary to improve the situation of the least well off may be seen as just. The same may hold for inequalities that result from specific exercises of one's freedom, the costs of which should not be imposed on others.[3]

What matters to me here is yet another dimension of what egalitarians may be concerned about. Often, we do not worry too much about instant-aneous inequalities as long as they do not lead to cumulative inequalities across people's *entire lives*. For instance, in a society in which longevities are equal, the political disenfranchisement of those below eighteen may not lead to any significant inequality in political power over people's entire lifetimes. This is so if all of us will have faced the same disenfranchisement, regardless of our actual age. I think that there is something right to this "entire lifetime" (or "complete life," or "lifetime") intuition, even though the challenge is to work out the details of what it consists in, of what drives it, of its degree of dominance over other intuitions, and of what it entails in practice. Space is too limited for a full account here.[4] However, we can formulate the general intuition as follows:

Lifetime Egalitarianism

"Spot inequalities" only matter from the point of view of justice if they lead to cumulated inequalities over people's entire lives. It is insufficient to limit ourselves to "spot inequalities" without knowing the distribution of what matters – for example, opportunities for well-being – between two individuals across their entire lifetime.

The intuition can be expressed with various intensities, leaving more or less room for competing intuitions. For some versions, lifetime inequalities are the *only* relevant inequalities. For others, they are simply *more important* morally speaking than spot inequalities.

Once we bridge the idea of a high contribution rate with the intuition of lifetime egalitarianism, the challenge is the following. Some of us may have the impression that in a society where a large share of the population has an advanced age, the contribution rate imposed on the "active" population is *unjustly high*. However, in what sense is it unjust if it is imposed on all of us in the same way when we are active? To put it differently, what's wrong, in such a society involving a homogenous and constant longevity, with an equal distribution of opportunities for well-being that would turn our active life a bit less profitable and our old age a bit less heavy, assuming that it would not necessarily lead to any inequality over entire lifetimes? And would it not actually follow that *any* contribution rate, including very high or very low

---

[3] On egalitarianism: Arneson (2002); Arnsperger and Van Parijs (2004, chapter 4).
[4] See McKerlie (2012) and Gosseries (2014) for fuller accounts.

ones, should be deemed acceptable from a lifetime egalitarian perspective in such a world?

Consider a first possible perspective on this. In the world that interests us here, lifetime egalitarianism challenges anyone concerned with the idea of a just level of *ascending* transfers, as when we care about setting a contribution rate to fund a pension system. Ascending (or upward) transfers are transfers from a later and currently younger generation to an earlier and older one. Descending (or downward) transfers are transfers from an earlier and currently older generation to a later and younger one, as when parents fund their children's education.[5] We could have the impression that ascending transfers mostly concern age groups while descending ones mostly concern birth cohorts. However, this does not need to be the case. Ascending transfers can perfectly be seen as part of what a birth cohort owes another, be it a later or earlier one, and descending transfers – as those aimed at education – could be assessed through the prism of age groups. Hence, both types of generational groups are potentially relevant to both transfer directions.

A general theory of intergenerational justice tends to give special weight to *descending* obligations between birth cohorts. This may be due to the relative importance of what we cumulatively inherit from earlier generations in comparison to what we are actually able to add ourselves as a single generation and what we are able to transfer to the previous generation through ascending transfers within our lifetime. One possibility consists in expecting each birth cohort to transfer to the next one *no less* – and of the relevant "stuff" – than what it inherited from the previous generation (Gosseries 2008). This will include natural resources, the quality of our education system, the efficiency of our technologies, the resilience of our political institutions, the wealth of our built heritage, the beauty of our landscapes, etc. Imagine that it were possible to assess all this through a single metric – for example, potential for well-being. Considering a birth cohort that inherited 1000 units of what matters, however you name it, from the previous generation, it would be expected not to transfer less than these 1000 units to the next birth cohorts.

The problem is that such a theory of *descending* obligations between birth cohorts does not tell us anything about our ascending obligations, that is, about the fair contribution rate to be expect from our children as a birth cohort or as an age group. One could of course envisage *consolidating* descending and ascending transfers. For instance, if the generation of our parents transfers us 1000 units, that is, the equivalent of what they inherited from their parents, and if we transfer them 10 units back as pension funding, we may conclude that they ended up transferring us only 990 units of what matters. We could also discuss whether this ascending transfer of 10 units should be considered as a gift. What all this indicates is that, once ascending transfers took place, there

---

[5] On this distinction in the context of intergenerational reciprocity: Gosseries (2009, section I).

may be room for consolidating them with descending ones for the sake of moral assessment. Yet, as such, it still does not tell us whether the pension-oriented ascending transfer *should* consist in 10 or 20 units. The descending-transfers-focused approach does not tell us that, because there are various ways of discharging our duties. We could very well argue that there is no problem if we do less for our parents and more for our children.

To wrap up things about this first perspective, I don't think that the magnitude and nature of our ascending duties could simply be *derived from* our core conception of descending duties. If we accept the plausible idea of consolidation, what we happen to do for our parents may of course affect what we owe our children. Yet, what we owe our parents is still left open. Hence, I would hypothesize that our ascending obligations should partly be defined on independent grounds if we want to give them a more definite content. This suggests that it is uneasy to end up with an integrated theory of intergenerational justice that covers both descending and ascending transfers.[6]

What are the alternative paths? One of them consists in comparing successive ascending transfers and using one of them as a reference point. *Parentiarchalism* is one of the options (in reference to the non-gendered version of "patriarchal"). The idea consists in looking at what the currently old generation actually did for its own parents, and to use this as a reference point. The rule could be "transfer to your parents at least as much as they actually transferred to theirs." In a sense, this means that one generation has some room to decide upon what it wishes to benefit from during its old age through transferring the equivalent amount to its own parents. While the next generation is expected to comply with this, if it does not, this will not affect in turn what the third generation owes the second one, as the rule is not compliance-sensitive. In short, it is what your parents did for theirs that defines what you owe them, not whether your parents did the right thing. This raises in turn two difficulties.

First, it is not straightforward to draw implications for what we owe them from what our parents did for their parents. This is so because what they did usually can't be uniquely described through the prism of a single normative principles, which then leaves room for a variety of accounts. If our parents transferred 100 dollars to their parents, we may still wonder whether, in order to assess what it would entail for us, we need to take demographic, economic or other evolutions into account. We need a rule through which we can retranslate these 100 dollars into an equivalent today. The rule needs to be inferred and

---

[6] Another interesting dimension – left aside here – has to do with the fact that an increase in longevity does not merely raise questions about our ascending duties. It also impacts on what we will as a matter of fact tend to transfer the next generation. This suggests possible interconnections between issues of ascending and descending duties in the presence of increasing longevity. See e.g. on the link between population ageing and economic growth, especially through the channels of savings and education, Ponthière (2017, 40–60).

several rules are probably worthy of consideration. The second difficulty is that it is not obvious why we should attach so much normative power to the decisions of a single generation, because even that reference generation may self-assess its own transfers as unjust. Hence, if what it did cannot straightforwardly reflect its own view about the right contribution rate, why should we take this specific transfer as our reference point at all?[7]

Alternatively, we may want to go for a "contractualist" account. The idea is one of a contract between successive generations such that each generation follows the same rule as the previous one to characterize and comply with its ascending obligations. However, either this is a hypothetical device aimed at putting us in the right frame of mind to derive a substantive rule, in which case it still does not provide us with a *substantive* rule, or we are talking about a real contract between real people. In that case, the difficulty comes from the fact that those initiating this chain of obligations are unable to involve future generations in their initial contractual deliberations. Because of this, it seems inappropriate to invoke real consent, which is central to any non-hypothetical contract.

Hence, neither the parentiarchal, nor the contractualist approaches seem satisfactory. A third possible approach to handle our worry about an *unjustly high* contribution rate in a world of homogeneous longevity is *sufficientarian* in nature.[8] Here, the idea is that besides inequalities as such, what also (or "primarily" under some views) matters is to ensure that persons are able to remain above a given living standard, defined in absolute terms. Such a level is not affected for its definition by what our parents did or by what we wish to do for our parents. A contribution rate such that the age group at stake would be unable to reach this minimum level could be unjust. Note here that this level is not simply defined on aggregate for the person's entire lifetime. It can actually be defined for specific moments in life, hence for specific age groups at any point in time. Yet, while this sufficientarian approach may tend to be helpful to address the case of a low contribution rate – one that would leave, for example, many elderly persons with too few resources – it seems to be less able to account for the intuition of a too-high contribution rate being imposed on

---

[7] This problem is less salient in a general theory of descending obligations between birth cohorts. The reason is that what we inherit is a stock resulting from the cumulated (non-) efforts of many generations, rather than from the previous one only. The more the destruction ability of each single generation increases, the more we should take distance from taking the level inherited from the generation that just preceded us as a reference point. A solution consists in looking at the average of what the last x generations inherited from their predecessors. Such a "multigenerational" baseline could admittedly also help attenuate the problem faced by the parentiarchal approach presented above. An alternative solution consists in dropping the reference to what we actually inherited as a baseline and to move to a view that defines what we owe the next generation independently from what we inherited. On cleronomic and non-cleronomic views, see e.g. Gosseries (forthcoming).

[8] On sufficientarianism: Casal (2007), Gosseries (2011).

the active population. This is so at least in cases in which the expected contribution rate does not put contributors in such a situation that they become themselves unable to reach the sufficient living standard that sufficientarians would set.

   This leaves us with a fourth possible account, one that has to do with the need to respect, in a pluralistic society, a certain diversity of visions about the good life, including preferences about the distribution of our activities along our lives. While some are jazz fanatics, others would not miss a single football match. Some want an intense and short career while others prefer an intra-life distribution of work and leisure that is more homogeneous along their existence. Each of us has a certain vision of what renders our lives valuable. A theory of justice should aim at preserving some degree of neutrality in this respect. A very high contribution rate during the most active part of our life potentially excludes certain distributions of work and leisure across people's lives. This leaves us with a possible option to account for the idea of an *illiberally high* contribution rate.

   Hence, here is our interim conclusion. In a world in which longevity is high and homogeneously distributed, it is far from straightforward to come up with a plausible account of why a given contribution rate should be regarded as too high. I began with the surprising and challenging claim that connecting the definition of our ascending duties with our descending ones is not straightforward at all. I then looked at four alternative accounts of what may render a contribution rate unjustly high. The parentiarchal one grounds the account on interpreting our parents' own transfers. The contractualist one relies on the idea of a hypothetical or real contract. The sufficientarian one focuses on the notion of a minimum standard of living. The liberal/neutralist one looks at the compatibility of a high contribution rate with a certain neutrality toward the conceptions of the good life and of how to distribute work and leisure along our lives. The two last alternative approaches seem to provide the most promising avenues. And yet, the sufficientarian one may have limited bite when it comes to excluding some contribution rates because of being too *high*, and the neutralist one it is still likely to remain open to a vast range of contribution rates.

Heterogeneous Longevity and the Core Dilemma

In the end, in our first type of setting, we seem to have little room for defining a just contribution rate in a sufficiently definite manner. Are things likely to change once we introduce heterogeneity on longevities? Here is our second sub-question:

Q2: Is there justice-based argument against a *high* contribution rate in the presence of heterogeneous, while constant, longevity?

We do live in a world with significant differences in longevity *within* each generation – understood as a "birth cohort." Longevity is significantly heterogeneous, not only between poor and rich countries, but also across genders or socioeconomic conditions. From a normative point of view, we could endorse the following twofold claim:

Ceteris paribus, having a longer life is an advantage *and* a significant one. We will take this axiological claim as given. Time and space are crucial to our lives. A farmer needs both space to seed her plants and time to let them grow. A musician needs both space to sit with her instrument and to communicate with the public and time to let her piece of music unfold. A human being needs space to move and time to develop her projects. There is a general sense in which having more time and/or space gives us more room to unfold what matters to us.

Now, the costs associated with a high dependency ratio – typical of any society with a high longevity – can be high, especially in terms of health care or retirement pensions. We can handle such costs in various ways. We can increase contributions or reduce benefits. First, we can increase the annual contribution of those who work, without necessarily increasing the duration of their career or worsening the condition of retirees in terms of retirement pensions or access to health care. Second, we can decide instead to reduce the annual benefits of the elderly (retirement pensions, health care, etc.). We can also increase the duration of contribution, which will also reduce the duration of benefits of the elderly, leaving transition issues aside. Such an increase in contribution duration can be achieved at both ends, that is, through retiring later, or through entering the labor market earlier. The latter idea consists in replacing the lengthening of our initial higher education investment with continuing education in the course of our career, without interrupting our work (Vandenberghe and Gosseries 2016).

Note a contrast. When considering an increase in the duration of contribution, we generally think about prolonging the end of our career (as opposed to starting earlier). And when considering a reduction in the duration of benefits, we generally think about delaying entry into the benefit period. However, would it be inconceivable to also shorten the benefit period at its end, for example through rendering certain benefits unavailable beyond a certain age? This is already being done for access to certain forms of health care and it raises important questions about a cut-off age that we will not address here.

Where does this leave us? There are basically three core elements at this stage:

– *Lifetime egalitarianism* invites us not to stick to comparing spot inequalities between age groups

- The axiological intuition of a *longer life as an advantage* and the fact that significant differences in longevity exist invite us to take such differences seriously
- Our menu of *policy options* includes increasing annual contributions, reducing annual benefits or both. Alternatively, lengthening the contribution period and shortening the benefit period accordingly is also an option. A mix of these options can be considered too.

Combining these considerations seems to lead to the following implication: Whenever a reform is needed, we should privilege policy options that put more weight *on more advanced ages*. Whenever we add further weight to younger contributors, we are actually adding further weight to short-lived people who are exclusively present among the younger among us. Consider the case of a person who contributed during part of her life to a pension system from which she will never benefit. Such a hypothesis should be taken into account in selecting the best policy option for pension schemes, health care funding, etc.

All entitlements that *automatically adjust* to the length of our lives actually increase inequalities between short-lived and long-lived individuals. This is so whenever benefits take the form of monthly installments that are not adjusted on an age basis and that go beyond covering the subsistence costs that the mere fact of running a longer life necessarily increases on aggregate – independently of the increase in subsistence costs associated with being older as such. And all this does not even take into consideration the fact that short-lived people also tend to belong to socioeconomically less advantaged groups, not to mention the gendered nature of longevity differentials. This raises a challenge:

Dilemma of a Society with High and Heterogeneous Longevity

Lemma 1. Given the demands of lifetime egalitarianism and the heterogeneity of longevities, we should avoid concentrating the burden associated with high longevity on the populations in which short-lived individuals are overrepresented, that is, younger age groups.

Lemma 2. If we take seriously the need to guarantee a minimum standard for each human being, independently of her age, we should not concentrate on the poorest elderly the weight of measures aimed at addressing the challenges of high longevity.

This seems to me the central dilemma that we are facing. The tension that it embodies reflects a deep tension between, on the one hand, a focus on lifetime equality that translates into a significant degree of concern for the short-lived; and on the other hand, a concern for dignity at any age that departs from an exclusive concern for lifetime equality. This concern for dignity at any age comes on top of the considerations that we have spelled out so far, and it can translate into a concern for the elderly poor in particular. While pension schemes understood as an insurance mechanism have traditionally aimed, to a significant extent, at addressing this elderly poverty alleviation concern, they have been less sensitive to the overrepresentation of the short-lived among younger populations. Yet, introducing the latter concern should not make us forget the importance of the former, even for those who give a significant importance to an approach of justice "over entire lifetimes" and who consider that being short-lived is a significant disadvantage.

Is the dilemma such that no policy can satisfactorily meet the demands expressed in each of the two lemmas? Taking seriously the problem of short-lived individuals may entail broader reforms in our socioeconomic systems, taking into account the uncertainty about who will end up being actually short-lived or not and the difficulty of postmortem compensation. It has been suggested that, for example, a lesser insistence on individual savings and further insistence on consuming early in life can reduce inequalities between long-lived and short-lived individuals (Fleurbaey, Leroux and Ponthière 2014; Ponthière 2017, chapters IV and V). While counterintuitive, it makes sense from the perspective we have developed. In addition, it is also clear that ensuring basic retirement benefits for all, and access for all to basic health services regardless of age, would tend to meet the demands of lemma 2.

At the level of funding, one option to be seriously envisaged is to reinforce solidarity *among the elderly*. If part of the pensions of those who are socioeconomically more fragile are paid by more wealthy pensioners themselves, then this will avoid further pressure on the short-lived. This means that we could rely on more solidarity within a given age group, provided that we are talking about solidarity among the elderly. Of course, increasing redistribution among the young may also actually reduce the risk of being short-lived in the first place. Yet, the increase in intragenerational solidarity route should mostly concentrate on solidarity between the elderly.[9]

There is a second set of conclusions we can draw at this stage. Introducing heterogeneous longevity into the picture has offered us one significant reason of justice – a concern toward the short-lived – to account for the intuition that a contribution rate may be too high. This concern is distinct from other possible concerns. Yet, this "merely" provides us with a pro tanto reason to care about this issue. It does not tell us about the possible weight of other considerations, including considerations other than longevity, for lifetime egalitarians. In addition, taking this seriously does not automatically tell us *at which level* in concrete terms a contribution rate starts being unjustly high. The idea of guaranteeing decent basic pensions to all may in contrast provide us with a criterion to define when a contribution is too low.

Now, two additional things should be said about the scope of the general dilemma. First, I conjecture that anyone worried about the idea of a too-high

---

[9] Thanks to D. Schwartz for having attracted my attention to this. For a related strategy in the gender context: Van Parijs and Vielle (2001).

contribution rate should see this dilemma as *the* core of this worry. Second, this dilemma is challenging us despite the fact that I *didn't* introduce the further complication of population ageing yet. Let me now proceed to this last step.

Increasing Average Longevity and a (Slightly) Softened Dilemma

Here is the final question:

Q3: Is there a justice-based argument against a *high* contribution rate in the presence of heterogeneous and growing longevity?

At this last step, we add one further element: *population ageing*, which is of particular relevance to this Handbook. It means that the average age of the next birth cohort tends to be higher than the average age of ours. This typically results from the conjunction of phenomena related to mortality, natality and migrations. In the context of this chapter, we will assume that ageing exclusively results from a decrease in mortality. This is a rather realistic assumption given that in, for example, European countries, the main driver of ageing is the increase in longevity. Hence, we are bracketing here fluctuations in birth rates that also play a certain role ("baby boom" followed by a "baby bust"). In addition, we shall also assume, as part of our reasoning, that this increase in longevity is constant, and consists in approximately a gain of three additional years of longevity every twenty years.

Population ageing adds a further source of heterogeneity in longevity. This means that there are not only differences of longevity *within* a generation, but also *between* generations. It thus seems that that the dilemma faced by an ageing society already obtains in a non-ageing one. It occurs as soon as heterogeneity in longevity obtains. This may suggest that the central problem of justice faced by an ageing society when it comes to worries about too-high contribution rates is actually not specific to it, albeit being perhaps of a larger magnitude since an additional source of heterogeneity in longevities is added. In short, while not adding any new dimension to our initial dilemma, the fact of population ageing could potentially render that dilemma more acute.

Yet, is that actually the case? On the one hand, inequalities in longevity within each generation invite us not to overburden its younger members (age group) since short-lived people are overrepresented among them. This entails, in an overlapping generations context, that members of the newest birth cohort should not be overburdened. On the other hand, inequalities in life expectancy in an ageing society are such that the newest birth cohorts are also those who will tend to have a *longer* life than those who are older today. Younger people belong to an age group in which short-lived people are overrepresented while belonging to a birth cohort in which people tend to be more long-lived.

Hence, the surprise is twofold. Not only is the core problem of justice faced by an ageing society already present in a non-ageing society. In addition, population ageing actually seems to attenuate rather than reinforce the magnitude of the central dilemma we face when taking seriously the gap between short-lived and long-lived people. Imagine, ex hypothesi, that the longevity gap within each generation is of ten years and that the longevity gap between the two generations at stake amounts to three years. In such a society, it will remain true that the short-lived are overrepresented among the young and that the currently old includes all the lucky members of their cohort that actually ended up being long-lived. But it will be less so than in a non-ageing society because the average longevity of the young as a birth cohort is still higher than the one of the elderly as a birth cohort. While the signs remain the same, the magnitude of the challenge is attenuated rather than worsened by population ageing. In a way, while population ageing seems to attract our attention to these issues, it actually also contributes to making them slightly less serious. Be that as it may, it only softens the problem because the currently old are all long-lived whereas only some of the currently young will turn out to be so, notwithstanding the fact that the newer cohort will have proportionally more long-lived people than the previous one.

Conclusion

In this chapter, I followed a pathway in three steps from which we can draw the following lessons. *First*, whenever differences in longevity don't obtain, the lifetime egalitarian intuition renders it more difficult to challenge high contribution rates on justice grounds. And this is actually a first lesson from this chapter. None of the tracks I have explored seem to deliver a strong case against a high contribution rate, even if the sufficientarian and the liberal ones should be taken seriously.

Second, once we introduce the idea of heterogeneity in longevities, the worry of justice toward the short-lived becomes salient. It leads in turn to a dilemma. On the one hand, a too-low rate of contribution would probably leave the basic needs of the elderly uncovered. On the other hand, a too-high rate of contribution would questionably worsen the disadvantage of short-lived persons. In that respect, we also stressed the importance of exploring avenues to increase redistribution *within the age group of the elderly*, in order to contribute to alleviating old age poverty while not burdening the young further, since the short-lived are overrepresented in this age group.

Third, it actually came as a surprise that population ageing softens the problem to some extent. This is so because the currently young (as an age group) include a larger proportion of short-lived people than the currently old, who are long-lived by definition. And yet, the currently young actually belong to a birth cohort that is likely to be more long-lived than the previous birth cohort, which softens the dilemma a bit, without eliminating it. Hence, population ageing confronts us with a dilemma of justice that is neither unique to it, nor stronger than in a non-ageing society. And yet, it remains a very serious one to consider.

16 Ageing, Justice, and Work: Alternatives to Mandatory Retirement

Daniel Halliday and Tom Parr

Introduction

Mandatory retirement is prohibited in a number of developed economies, with a few exceptions made for specific industries. While some jurisdictions have taken a more contested path to abolition than others, the trend in recent decades has been towards protecting an employee's right to keep working.[1] But mandatory retirement was once common – not because it was required by employment law, but because many employers included it in long-term employment contracts. Whether imposed by law or merely included by employers in contracts, it is easy to perceive mandatory retirement as arbitrary, unfair, and/ or discriminatory. And yet, it was present during an era (the mid-to-late twentieth century) when labour markets offered historically high potential for social mobility and the accumulation of wealth. Given these facts, we might wonder whether there is a case for mandatory retirement, or perhaps something approximating it. In this chapter, we aim to assemble some answers to this question.

In the first section, we briefly explore the issue of age discrimination. In the second section, we rehearse the most intuitive employment-based case for mandatory retirement, showing how it draws much of its force from the lump of labour fallacy. In the third section, we identify a different sort of argument for mandatory retirement, one based on enabling employers to incentivize employees in a controlled way. A specific version of this argument, associated

For useful feedback, we thank Sameer Bajaj, Juliana Bidadanure, Alycia Blackham, Christine Braun, Kasper Lippert-Rasmussen, and Christopher Wareham. Work on this chapter received funding from the European Union's Horizon 2020 research and innovation programme under Marie Skłodowska-Curie grant agreement 890434.

[1] Britain finally abolished employer rights to impose mandatory retirement with the Equality Act in 2010. See Blackham (2016, chapter 3). In the USA, employees have held this right since the Age Discrimination in Employment Act in 1967. Similar protections have existed in Australia and Canada for some decades, though their precise content varies across states and provinces. We note that there are significant exceptions to the trend towards abolishing mandatory retirement. For example, several member states of the European Union (EU) continue to practise mandatory retirement, as permitted under the EU's Employment Equality Framework Directive.

with Edward Lazear, sees mandatory retirement as a device for employers to structure wage payments over time to optimize workers' performance. In the fourth section, we argue that, in spite of Lazear's argument having force, some more modest proposals are more attractive. We defend one such measure, whereby employers have a right to reduce the number of hours of older workers. In the fifth section, we register some complexities relating to the fact that economic conditions are not constant across generations.

Mandatory Retirement and Age Discrimination

The most legally influential objection to mandatory retirement contends that we should rule it out on the ground that it wrongfully discriminates on the basis of age.[2] At the heart of this concern is that fact that this policy treats individuals differently on the basis of personal characteristics for which they are not responsible, and, in this way, involves ageist discrimination morally analogous to other forms that we take to be uncontroversially wrongful, such as sexism and racism. Proponents of this objection can acknowledge that the injustices of sexism and racism tend to be graver than those of ageism, but that is consistent with the conviction that all three practices are wrongfully discriminatory. We can call this the *discrimination objection* to mandatory retirement.

In addressing this objection, we can exploit a distinctive feature of ageism: since we all age, we are all subject to it at some point, at least unless we die young. The same is not true for sexism and racism. Norman Daniels explains the significance of this fact as follows:

If we treat blacks and whites or men and women differently, then we produce an inequality between persons, and such inequalities raise questions about justice. For example, if we hire and fire on the basis of race or sex . . . then we create inequalities that are objectionable on the grounds of justice . . . . But if we treat the young one way as a matter of policy and the old another, and we do so over their whole lives, then we treat all persons the same way. No inequality between persons is produced since each person is treated both ways in the course of a complete life. Thus the banal fact that we age means age is different from race or sex for purposes of distributive justice. (Daniels 1996, 259)

The upshot of this is that, since everyone ages, it is a mistake to invoke the discrimination objection to impugn mandatory retirement, at least under the assumption that mandatory retirement is maintained across generations consistently. Examining this assumption requires us to distinguish between

---

[2] For discussion, see Busby (2019) and Lippert-Rasmussen (2018). Blackham (2016, 46–51) provides a summary of the ways in which this argument has been both invoked and resisted in actual legislation.

discrimination between age groups, and the different idea of discrimination between birth cohorts. We return to this point in the fifth section.[3]

Critics might deny that a practice can be wrongfully discriminatory only if it produces inequalities between individuals. In particular, mandatory retirement may still prove wrongfully discriminatory if it disrespects older workers or because it involves prejudice against them. If this were the case, then the discrimination objection would not disappear merely because everyone is subject to this treatment at some point in their lives. In response to this concern, we note that, while it is possible that mandatory retirement policies might be presented in ways that signal a disrespectful judgement about the value or productivity of older workers, it is possible to offer a justification for mandatory retirement that works against this judgement.[4]

To be clear, these remarks fall some way short of establishing that a policy of mandatory retirement is justified. Indeed, the fact that everyone is subject to such a policy gives us by itself no reason to enact it. For example, we might object to the universal military conscription of young adults because it interferes too greatly in individuals' lives. Pointing out that everyone must go through conscription at some point is no rejoinder. The wrongness of military conscription does not consist in any ageist nature. Rather, if it is wrong, it must be wrong for independent reasons, like the interference invoked by the typical objection. It is in the light of this that arguments about the justifiability of military service must focus on our reasons for and against the policy, rather than on its ageist nature.

In a similar vein, it bears noting that two policies may treat individuals equally over their complete lives, without these policies being on a moral par with each other. For example, we can contrast mandatory retirement with laws that grant younger workers a lower minimum wage than that enjoyed by the rest of the population. Even if these two policies were to have an identical effect on individuals' complete lives, there may be weighty reasons to prefer the abolition of one of these policies over the abolition of the other. But such reasons will have to come from considerations that arise independently of a concern for equal treatment over a complete lifespan (Chandler 1996, 42–4).

If this analysis is correct, then, we should draw the same conclusions in the case of mandatory retirement. What matters is whether there are compelling justifications for it in the first place, not whether it treats individuals differently

---

[3] We are not the first to note how the reasoning in the passage from Daniels can be applied to rebut discrimination-based opposition to mandatory retirement. See Chandler (1996, 37–40). Wedeking (1990) also anticipates Daniels's reasoning.

[4] See our comments as to how some proposals (including the one we endorse) avoid claims about worker productivity declining with age, even if in most cases the proposal would gain some additional force from this being the case. We set aside any further discussion of this complication, which would require an investigation into the various reasons for which age-based discrimination would be wrongful. For discussion of these issues, see Bidadanure (2017).

at different points in their lives. We explore this issue in each of the next two sections, where we consider two distinct arguments in favour of mandatory retirement.

The Argument from Rationing

According to the *argument from rationing*, mandatory retirement is justifiable when and because it produces a more just distribution of employment opportunities. The motivating thought is that, without legislation of this kind, older workers will hog scarce employment opportunities, denying these opportunities to those who are younger. In the worst cases, the effect of this may be that a greater number of individuals (of pre-retirement age) persist in involuntary unemployment. Mandatory retirement combats this trend by forcing older workers to relinquish their jobs, creating employment opportunities that would otherwise be unavailable, for which those who are younger can compete (Kellaway 2012).

Advocates of the argument from rationing need not contend that mandatory retirement causes firms to hire more workers at any single point in time. Instead, what matters is that, because of the higher rate of turnover of workers that the policy produces, firms must share the same amount of work over a larger number of workers in the long run. To illustrate this reasoning, let us suppose that a firm has the need and financial resources to hire only one person to run its website on a day-to-day basis. In the absence of mandatory retirement, the firm may be able to make a new appointment to this position less regularly than with the policy in place. This is because there is some chance that the incumbent worker will continue in that position past the point at which she would have been forced out under the alternative regime. Crucially, if mandatory retirement were then introduced, there is no reason to think that the firm would suddenly increase the number of website specialists on its payroll. After all, the firm needed only one person to perform this role prior to mandatory retirement, and this change in legislation will not affect the demands of the role. For this reason, we should not expect this policy to cause this firm to hire more workers at any single moment.

Instead, the hoped-for effect of mandatory retirement is that the firm will hire a larger number of total workers across a longer time period. For example, it may mean that, over the course of a century or so, the firm hires four website specialists for an average of twenty-five years each, rather than three website specialists for an average of thirty-three years each. Of these four workers, three of them would have been employed for eight years more under the alternative system in which they were not forced to retire, or so we can assume, and therefore these individuals have been made worse off as a result. But one of them – we can call her Silvana – has been made substantially better off: whereas she would otherwise have never worked for the firm, now she enjoys twenty-five years of employment. Proponents of the argument from rationing plausibly maintain that it is better for each of four individuals to have twenty-five years of employment, followed by an earlier retirement, than it is for three of them to be employed for thirty-three years and one of them to be denied the offer of employment altogether.

There are comparative and non-comparative versions of this argument.[5] The first version rests on a *comparative* claim about the unfairness of some individuals suffering worse employment prospects than others, at least through no responsibility of their own. For example, we might worry about the fact that members of younger generations have less valuable prospects for success in the labour market than some members of older generations who have enjoyed decades of gainful employment. Again, we return to this idea in the fifth section. The second version of the argument appeals to a *non-comparative* claim about the moral and political importance of each individual having reasonable employment opportunities. According to this view, there is nothing disvaluable in itself about some individuals suffering worse employment prospects than others through no responsibility of their own. Rather, our reason to worry about members of older generations hogging employment opportunities is that this diminishes the labour market opportunities of members of younger generations. Though comparative and non-comparative versions of the argument from rationing offer distinct, though compatible, explanations for their conclusion, they unite behind the conviction that mandatory retirement is a tool whose use would make the distribution of employment opportunities more just.

One objection to the argument from rationing is that it risks misdiagnosing the problem that mandatory retirement is supposed to solve. In particular, the argument is appealing only when there is a surplus of younger individuals each seeking a position currently occupied by an older worker. But perhaps all this reveals is that there is an oversupply of labour for a particular industry, meaning that there are more individuals who have trained to enter an industry than the number of jobs in that industry. Returning to the example above, these remarks suggest that Silvana's real problem is not that the older workers are hogging their jobs. It is that she has trained to enter an industry with too few opportunities. Of course, the fault need not lie with Silvana here. For example, it could be that her society trains too many individuals to enter an industry that lacks a sufficient number of jobs.

There is something to this response. In fact, it might well be the case that a large problem with the academic labour market, at least in some parts of the world, is that universities train too many graduate students, given the employment opportunities available. Addressing this issue by reducing the supply of

---

[5] For this influential distinction, see Parfit (2000).

trained labour would relieve much of the pressure on older academics to retire in order to create new employment opportunities for younger generations. If that is correct, then the argument from rationing would lose some of its appeal.

However, this line of reasoning is a little too quick. To see this, let us suppose that, anticipating the oversupply of labour in the technology industry, the government successfully incentivizes young individuals such as Silvana to train for retail instead. The problem is that it is conceivable – indeed, perhaps even likely – that the employment opportunities in retail are less valuable than they would have been in the technology industry if mandatory retirement had been introduced. That is, the government has circumvented the need to introduce mandatory retirement by reducing the oversupply of labour, but only by acting in a way that risks worsening the employment opportunities of individuals such as Silvana. The implication of this finding is that, in order to know whether reducing the oversupply of labour in a particular industry is preferable to mandatory retirement, we need to know more about the quality of the employment opportunities that are on the table. The upshot is that, at most, the argument from rationing can provide us with only a highly qualified case for mandatory retirement.

Let us now turn to an objection to the argument from rationing that is more damaging.[6] It stems from the fact that the argument rests on a controversial empirical claim, namely that mandatory retirement improves the employment prospects of some individuals, mainly members of younger generations. This is indispensable to the example we discussed above, in which Silvana benefits from the fact that the firm's other three website specialists are forced into retirement. However, much of the appeal of this analysis derives from the lump of labour fallacy, which refers to the normally mistaken assumption that the demand for labour is fixed. In simple terms, it is often an error to assume that the total supply of employment opportunities is invariable such that we should conceive of older workers as reducing the labour market prospects of younger individuals.[7]

Of course, this assumption is plausible for some positions, such as that of president. Fairly obviously, a larger number of individuals hold the position of president over a specified time period in political systems in which there are limits on the number of terms that someone can hold office than in those without such limits.[8] However, the issue is that, for most positions in most industries, the demand for labour varies over time. For this reason, it is

---

[6] For related discussion, see section 2 of Bidadanure (2021, chapter 5).

[7] This fallacy, or at least the phrase 'lump of labour', was probably first introduced by Schloss (1891). For discussion, see Tom Walker (2007).

[8] We make this claim for illustrative purposes, acknowledging that the case for term limits in political office is not best justified by concerns about the just distribution of jobs, but rather concerns about uncapped political power.

typically unsafe to assume that a sensible way in which to create new employment opportunities for younger generations is to force out older workers.

As evidence for this, we can consider the post-war rise in women's labour market participation in most developed economies. If demand for labour were fixed, then what we would have seen is a huge increase in rates of involuntary unemployment, as more women entered the labour force to compete with men for a fixed number of posts. But this is not what happened. Instead, we witnessed a corresponding increase in the demand for labour. This is due to the rising levels of economic output and consumption that were made possible by this trend. We should expect something similar in the case of older workers. This is because, as a general matter, the demand for labour should be no lower when older workers are economically active than when they are retired and so more dependent on state benefits (Buttonwood 2012). Indeed, a recent study lends further support to this thesis, concluding that there is 'no evidence that increasing the employment of older persons reduce either the job opportunities or wage rates of young persons ... If anything, the opposite is true' (Munnell and Wu 2013).

To be clear, our view is not that the lump of labour fallacy applies to all industries, such that mandatory retirement can never create new employment opportunities for younger generations. We are open to the idea that, for some industries where the demand for labour remains stable, even if not fixed, then mandatory retirement might have its intended effects. This might include a number of public sector professions, such as in the judiciary. However, for the reasons we have mentioned, we are suspicious that this point generalizes across much of the labour market. As a result, the argument from rationing fails to provide a compelling justification for mandatory retirement in the majority of cases.

The Argument from Capped Rewards

Now we turn to the *argument from capped rewards* in support of mandatory retirement, according to which the policy is justifiable when and because it increases firms' economic efficiency. Viewed in this light, mandatory retirement is attractive because it allows firms to structure a worker's wages optimally over her lifetime without having to pay her high wages indefinitely. Firms will want to ensure that the rewards of higher pay in old age do not go beyond what is necessary to motivate workers earlier in life. One influential position, advanced by Lazear (1979), is that the promise of significant future rewards incentivizes individuals to work harder when they are young.[9]

---

[9] Lazear may have been influenced by the view that firms are generally organized to prevent workers from shirking. For example, see Williamson (1985). For further philosophical discussion of this view and competing views about the nature of firm hierarchy, see Singer (2019).

According to this view, rather than paying a worker according to her marginal product at any given time, a firm can increase productivity over the full term of employment by withholding benefits until later in life and making these conditional on satisfactory performance. This means paying a worker less than her marginal product when she is young, but offering to pay more than her marginal product when she is old, so long as her performance is strong up to that point. In a system in which there are fewer opportunities for a worker's wages to increase over time, there is less of an incentive for her to work hard during her younger years.

Mandatory retirement, then, gives employers the ability to delay rewards, *subject to an upper bound.* If a firm has no way of knowing when a promoted employee might leave, it takes a bigger risk when encouraging productivity in earlier years by increasing a worker's pay later on. Accordingly, employers have either to reduce the extent to which they structure wages over a long-term contract, perhaps by reducing the availability of promotion, or to cap payments in some other way, maybe by using indirect or bogus methods to lay off older staff, such as internal restructuring. Alternatively, employers might abandon long-term contracts altogether, leading to an increase in precarious employment, even for those workers disposed to maximize their productivity.

Strictly speaking, the argument from capped rewards does not depend on workers becoming less productive as they age, simply because they are *older.*[10] Instead, it merely depends on the claim that workers will be more productive on average, over a 'complete' working life, if some rewards are delayed. This means that it is possible to endorse the argument (or some weakened version of it, as we do below) with less danger of sending a potentially disrespectful signal about the lower value of older workers. Efforts to induce higher productivity earlier on may make it the case that productivity drops off with age, even if what is happening is merely that productivity 'returns' to a level no lower than what would have been present during younger years, had the incentives of later promotion and pay rises not been in place. This helps to show that any vague claim to the effect that older workers are less productive is in fact ambiguous with respect to the baseline against which productivity is measured. The claim that older workers simply work less productively in virtue of being old is distinct from the claim that they work less productively in virtue of having reached the point at which they have responded to and benefitted from incentives offered to them earlier in life. We think that it is clear that the second claim carries less potential for a disrespectful signal about the value of workers: if older works produce less than younger workers because they have merely run out of incentives to which younger workers are still responding, any argument that depends on this premise need not rely on any potentially disrespectful claim about the impact of age per se. The argument from

---

[10] For discussion, see Ash and MacLeod (2020).

capped rewards can draw force from either claim being true, but gets sufficient force from the claim about responding to incentives being true.

Nonetheless, the argument still has additional force if productivity does in fact decline with age in ways prior to, and that would occur in the absence of, any wage structuring aimed at incentivizing higher productivity early in a worker's life. Though it is widely accepted that older workers tend, albeit with numerous exceptions, to become less productive as they age, at least past some point, the causes of this are not well understood (Aiyar et al. 2016; Lee 2016). However, two factors stand out as potentially pertinent. First, at least in some industries, workers' productivity tends to decline as they age because of their deteriorating physical condition. This may be true for manual work, such as firefighting, construction, and some forms of nursing. Second, as technology changes, so too the skills of older workers become obsolete. The same is not true for younger workers, who, having trained more recently, are more likely to be familiar with the newest technology.

We emphasize that these two points hold independently of any tendency for younger workers to be more productive simply because the structuring of wages has been designed to incentivize this. That is to say, the physiological effects of ageing and changes in technology may render older workers less productive even if all workers were paid the same amount at all ages.

To be clear, advocates of the argument of capped rewards should acknowledge that mandatory retirement may involve considerable economic costs as well. As noted in the previous section, we have weighty reasons to prefer older workers to be economically active rather than retired and so more dependent on state benefits. But these reasons might not be decisive, especially if the benefits made possible by incentivizing individuals to work harder when they are young are sizeable.

The most serious worry with the argument of capped rewards, we think, is that there are measures beside mandatory retirement that deliver similar or greater economic gains and that have a range of advantages over that policy. This is the issue that we explore in the remainder of the chapter, though we pay special attention to one set of advantages, as well as to the fact that, since mandatory retirement has been legally prohibited for some time in most industries, feasibility concerns may favour something less than a full transition back to it.

Alternatives to Mandatory Retirement

One set of objections to the argument of capped rewards targets the empirical thesis that mandatory retirement enables firms to increase their workers' productivity. For example, if individuals tend to discount future rewards, as is widely believed, then the promise of higher pay in ten or twenty years' time may provide an ineffective incentive to work harder now. Though this is an interesting suggestion, we lack the space (and competence) to examine objections relating to the psychology of workers. Instead, we focus on two more general problems for any defence of mandatory retirement that draws on the idea of capped rewards.

First, as a method for improving efficiency, mandatory retirement has a clear heuristic character. This is because, since there are significant differences between workers, we should expect considerable variations in their optimal retirement ages. Moreover, these variations will not be transparent to employers until after the fact: it will be very hard, if not impossible, to identify any individual worker's optimal retirement age in advance when the clause is written in to a worker's employment contract.[11] If employers had the right to force a worker to retire from their firm, but they could choose not to exercise this right in the case of especially productive older workers, then the efficiency gains might be greater. This is because it would allow firms to structure a worker's wages optimally over her lifetime without having to pay her high wages indefinitely, and it would allow them to keep on those older workers who remain especially productive.

Second, the argument of capped rewards risks committing what we might call the *atomistic fallacy* regarding workers' productivity. The important point is that, when judging a worker's productivity, we must be sensitive to any interaction effects between workers. Workers are usually not isolated converters of inputs into outputs, especially not when employed in teams. Stated so generally, this is hardly a controversial claim, and is vindicated by core presuppositions in labour economics relating to the gains associated with the division of labour and specialization. More subtly, though, the collective productivity of workers might be enhanced by factors such as the presence of workers who have been in the same firm for a long time. These workers may possess valuable 'institutional memory' and other skills that accrue as a result of familiarity with the workplace and/or its industry. These skills and knowledge may endure in spite of, and might even offset, productivity reduction due to the physiological effects of ageing and changes in technology. These points can be easily overlooked in traditional economic analysis (Anton 2016).

In addition, a distinct worry with mandatory retirement arises from the fact that older workers who are shut out of the labour market altogether may have to bear some especially serious costs. Mandatory retirement can cut off an older worker from a social network on which she is highly dependent and, in the worst cases, this process can seriously damage her health (Wester and Wolff 2010). And, though it may be possible to integrate into new social networks, including through short-term employment contracts, this can be very costly.

---

[11] Though firms can mitigate this problem by promoting individuals at different stages, there remains potential for some workers to slow down sooner as they climb the ladder.

Because of this, we may have special reason for regulating labour markets so as to allow older workers to continue in their roles.

We acknowledge that the various deficiencies of mandatory retirement on which we have focussed do not apply with equal measure to all workers or workplaces. But we believe that the problems are sufficiently widespread to justify investigating some alternatives to the policy. We now turn to this task.

Though Lazear recognized the efficiency-based appeal of mandatory retirement, he was aware that it might be too blunt an instrument: 'one must ask why the productivity decline [of older workers] is dealt with by terminating the worker rather than by reducing his wages' (1979, 1262).[12] The suggestion is that, once we reach the point at which higher wages cease being necessary to incentivize harder work when someone is young, the appropriate response may be to reduce her wages rather than to force her to retire from the firm. Saul Levmore has recently discussed *rate-reduction* proposals of this sort (Nussbaum and Levmore 2017, 39–53). He speaks of a salary trajectory that follows 'an inverse U', whereby a mandatory retirement age is replaced by an age (perhaps earlier than the age at which retirement would have occurred) where employers can, if they wish, reduce a worker's wages.[13] Policies of this kind are attractive for several reasons. First, employers have the option of reducing wages, but there is no requirement for them to do so. This means that they may continue to pay high wages to older workers, say, in order to keep especially productive workers on the books. Second, the policy enables employers to retain less productive older workers with reduced pay, which may be preferable to forcing them to retire from the firm. This is not only because these workers remain somewhat productive but also because, as we have noted, we may have special reasons to allow older workers to continue in their roles.

While we agree with Levmore that rate-reduction proposals are an improvement on mandatory retirement, our sympathies lie with an alternative scheme. In particular, we propose a policy of *time-reduction* that gives employers the right to reduce the hours of older workers. Again, employers would have the option of reducing hours, but there would be no requirement for them to do so. This would mean that they may continue to employ older workers on a full-time basis if they wish to do so. In comparison with Levmore's proposal, what is distinctive about our view is that employers may not reduce the pay of older workers while requiring them to show up for the same number of hours each week or to complete the same number or kinds of tasks. Reduction in hours is not reduction in rate of pay per hour.

---

[12] Lazear went on to conclude that 'none of the so-called explanations [for preferring mandatory retirement] describes why it is optimal to terminate a worker at a certain age rather than reduce . . . wages accordingly and in a continuous fashion' (Lazear 1979, 1263).

[13] To save words, we suppress Levmore's observation that a mandatory 'inverse U' might be considered alongside a discretionary one.

In proposing a time-reduction scheme, we have in mind a broader set of arrangements than is common in many contemporary labour markets. More specifically, part-time employment normally occurs in a narrow range of ways, typically implemented over a short time span, namely the working week. Part-time workers tend to work between one and four days a week, rather than, say, for one week per month or for four months per year. Not working on Fridays may be fine for some kinds of employment, such as bus driving, where the rate of work remains pretty constant. But an office worker whose formal hours exclude Fridays may find that her employer and colleagues respond strategically by placing more demands on her earlier in the week. The upshot is that this worker may end up doing the same work as a full-time member of staff, but be paid for one day fewer.

This problem is exacerbated by the fact that work associated with computers, emails, and the like is hard to separate physically from the worker, as the capital often literally follows them around on their smartphone. Because of this, the demands of employment can easily spill into an individual's free time, and so the advantages of working only four days a week rather than five may turn out to be much less significant in practice than on paper. In these circumstances, part-time employment may be much more attractive if it operates over a longer time span, with employees working one week per month or for four months per year, for example.

Both time-reduction and rate-reduction schemes preserve the logic of the argument from capped rewards. In each case, the idea is that employers would prefer to pay older workers a higher rate than younger workers, but only so long as they have a means to limit the financial commitments they incur to older workers as a result. As with Lazear's argument, this does not depend on the judgement that older workers are simply less productive by virtue of being old. In both schemes, the goal is to give employers a means of avoiding having to pay older workers a higher wage indefinitely, but to introduce a degree of flexibility not secured by blanket mandatory retirement.

Why prefer time-reduction over rate-reduction? There are two main reasons. First, time-reduction policies serve workers' interests to a greater degree than rate-reduction policies. This is because, when a firm lowers the wages of an older worker but requires her to work the same number of hours, this makes her straightforwardly worse off, as the only change is that her income goes down. Changes of this kind are bad for workers in themselves and, beyond this, they may convey a message that older workers interpret as an affront to their worth.[14] But these concerns do not arise, at least not in the same way, when a firm reduces the hours of an older worker. In this case, the worker gets something in return,

---

[14] We are hesitant to put much weight on this point. This is partly because it is unclear that older workers would interpret a pay cut as an affront to their worth, and partly because, even if this is so, it is unclear that this gives employers any serious moral reason not to act in this way.

namely more time away from work, which effectively compensates (albeit perhaps only partially) for her reduced earnings. Because of this, reducing the hours of an older worker does not make her unambiguously worse off.

Second, earlier we noted that older workers tend to become less productive as they age, at least past some point. While this is true, we must be sensitive to the fact that productivity varies with the number of hours that an individual works. This is true for workers of all ages, of course, but we might expect long hours to take more of a toll on older workers than younger workers, at least in some physically demanding lines of work. Faced with these facts, it may be in everyone's interest for an older employee to work reduced hours at near-maximum capacity rather than for her to work full-time for reduced wages.

In addition to this, time-reduction policies avoid the problems that afflict mandatory retirement. In the first instance, let us recall the atomistic fallacy, committed by overlooking the interaction effects between workers and, in particular, by ignoring the fact that older workers may have an especially large institutional memory. Here it is significant that older workers can make distinctive contributions without being employed on a full-time basis. What matters is that enough of these individuals are around enough of the time, not that all or any of these individuals are around permanently.

Finally, we noted that we may have special reason for regulating labour markets in order to allow older workers to continue in their roles, given that employment can be a valuable source of social networks. Importantly, time-reduction policies meet this demand since access to these networks is normally not threatened by reduced hours. This is because the good in question has a satisficing character: what matters is that a worker shows up for a sufficient amount of time, which may be only one day per week or one week per month. This may be enough to access the relevant social networks (Wester and Wolff 2010).

A Note on Background Conditions

Much everyday talk of 'generations' obscures an important distinction between age groups and birth cohorts.[15] An age group refers to a group of individuals currently at a certain age. A birth cohort refers to a group of individuals born at a particular time. Talk of 'generations' is often ambiguous between these two different ideas. An age group can expect to become, or once was, another age group: teenagers will eventually become middle aged, for example. But this is not true for birth cohorts: millennials will never become baby-boomers. In the first section, so as to distinguish age discrimination from racist and sexist discrimination, we noted that inequalities between age groups are compatible with equality over individuals' complete lives. But it remains possible for a policy that formally treats everyone identically over their complete lives to

---

[15] For discussion, see Bidadanure (2021, chapter 1) and Bidadanure (Forthcoming).

treat different birth cohorts differently in practice. This is because of the simple fact that birth cohorts differ from one another in living out their lives through different periods of history, and under different social and economic conditions.

Writing thirty years ago, Gary Wedeking (1990) noted that the move to abolish mandatory retirement creates a problem of this sort. At the time of abolition, older workers in an earlier birth cohort had benefitted from decades of employment where firms structured wages so as to incentivize individuals to work harder when they are young, but with the expectation that the firm would not have to pay these wages indefinitely. However, with the abolition of mandatory retirement, firms then incurred additional costs, some of which were passed on to the next birth cohort of workers, who, in effect, were required to subsidize the prolonged occupancy of jobs by older, higher-earning workers. The economic contraction following the pandemic in 2020 may trigger something like the reverse of this process. Many older employees who have worked on the assumption that they would not be forced to retire may find themselves suddenly exposed to involuntary redundancies. (Perhaps the same goes for some younger workers as well, though employers may prefer to offload older staff with higher salaries and lower productivity.) Whereas a generation of workers was in a sense benefitted twice when mandatory retirement was abolished, this time a generation of workers may be hurt twice.

These episodes point to a more general issue with laws, such as retirement policies, that target specific stages of individuals' lives. Even if these measures formally apply in the same fashion to successive birth cohorts, their effect on individuals' opportunities may vary considerably depending on the background social and economic conditions. To this extent, arguably it is misleading to maintain that, since everyone ages, everyone is affected equally by policies such as mandatory retirement. We would stress, though, that the ebb and flow of economic conditions over time is a problem for *all* policies that remain in place from one generation to the next. This is important since it implies that our proposal regarding time-reduction for older workers faces *no special* difficulty owing to the tendency for some generations to have it better or worse than others merely because of changes in background conditions.

In the light of these considerations, one possibility is to enact policies that discriminate across individuals *within* birth cohorts rather than make adjustments *across* birth cohorts. For example, if economic conditions worsen in ways that lower the prospects of younger individuals to accumulate wealth through the labour market in comparison with the 'baby-boomer' generation, it may be appropriate to target wealth accumulation where it has occurred. Possibilities here include an increase in wealth taxes or an inheritance tax, perhaps with a reduction in income tax. Though these policies do not refer to age explicitly, in practice they are likely to impose a greater burden on the older generation, who have accumulated wealth through working during an era of prosperity. Moreover, tax policy can display sensitivity to age, for example by way of an increased income tax for older workers on very high salaries.[16] Again, the proposal we have defended in this chapter is compatible with various fiscal reforms of this sort, but it does not commit us to any of them. The main point is that, where one generation enjoys better or worse conditions than the generation before it, it may be best to address these inequalities through laws other than those that explicitly make an individual's age a determinant of her entitlements, as is the case with retirement policies.

---

[16] Levmore offers some support for the third of these ideas, namely an income tax sensitive to the earnings of older age cohorts (Nussbaum and Levmore 2017, 51–2).

17 Age and Well-Being: Ethical Implications of the U-Curve of Happiness

C. S. Wareham

Introduction

While many expect happiness to decline in old age, research into well-being and happiness suggests otherwise.[1] Represented graphically, happiness across a life – 'diachronic happiness' – is U-curved, with the bottom of the U, the unhappiest part, experienced in middle age. Against expectations, old age, with its accompanying decreases in health, tends to be as happy as youth, and substantially happier than midlife (Blanchflower and Oswald 2008).[2] I will refer to this surprising diachronic phenomenon as the 'U-curve of happiness', or the 'happiness curve'.

Given the central role of happiness in ethical theories and conceptions of the good life, as well as the urgent issues raised by population ageing, it is surprising that the ethical implications of the happiness curve have not received more attention. This chapter attempts to draw out some of these implications before focussing on an example in which the happiness curve influences a problem in the ethics of life extension and ageing societies.

Before beginning, it is important to point out a couple of limitations. First, I will not attempt anything approaching a full or fine-grained review of empirical and ethical issues concerning the happiness curve. Instead, I try to provide a general description of findings about the curve, and sketch some of the ethical implications stemming from this. Second, my aim in doing so is expository and I will not try to resolve the ethical problems that I raise. For instance, while I suggest that the curve plays an important role in the case of life extension I discuss, I will not claim that the issue is decided.

I am grateful to the participants in and organisers of: the Workshop on Ethics and Chronic Illness, Queen's University Belfast (2018); the Ageing, Suffering, and Despair Conference at the McDonald Centre for Theology, Ethics, and Public Life, Oxford University (2020); and the UC Louvain Hoover Chair Seminar (September 2021). Particular thanks to Ashley Moyse, Peter Singer, and Thaddeus Metz for helpful comments on this chapter.

[1] For the most part, I will not dwell on terminological issues and will, for instance, use the terms happiness, well-being, and subjective well-being interchangeably. While some distinctions are warranted, providing them is not necessary for my arguments here.

[2] In keeping with the broad-brush approach adopted in footnote 1, I will not try to nail down a definition for the terms 'younger', 'middle-aged', or 'older' people, 'later life', and the like.

The chapter is in three parts. First, I will say more about what the happiness curve is, and the reasons it is unexpected. Second, I outline some broad ethical considerations that the curve raises. Finally, I home in on a particular example of this kind of implication related to the ethics of life extension.

The Surprising Trajectory of Lifetime Happiness

To show why the happiness curve is remarkable, I begin by spelling out what I take to be the common view, or at least, *a* common view of ageing. This perspective is exemplified in the following, rather bleak biblical verses from the book of Ecclesiastes.

> Remember your Creator
> while you are young,
> before the days of trouble come
> and the years when you say,
> 'I find no pleasure in them.'
> When you get old,
> the light from the sun, moon, and stars will grow dark;
> the rain clouds will never seem to go away.
> At that time your arms will shake and your legs will
>   become weak.
> Your teeth will fall out so you cannot chew,
> and your eyes will not see clearly.
> Your ears will be deaf to the noise in the streets,
> and you will barely hear the millstone grinding grain.
> You'll wake up when a bird starts singing,
> but you will barely hear singing.
> You will fear high places and will be afraid to go for a walk.
> Your hair will become white like the flowers on an almond
>   tree.
> You will limp along like a grasshopper when you walk.
> . . .
> Everything is useless!
> The Teacher says that everything is useless.[3]
> (Ecclesiastes 12, 1–8)[4]

This pessimistic assessment of what is in store for us as we age continues for a number of verses. It exemplifies the common view that the years when we are old will be bad and perhaps useless, meaningless, futile, in vain, or not worth having (Lacey et al. 2006). Indeed, many people express the hope to die before

---

[3] This is also translated as everything is 'meaningless', or 'futile', or 'in vain'.
[4] www.bible.com/bible/105/ECC.12.NCV

they get old, from rock stars such as the Who's Peter Townshend (In the song 'My Generation') to prominent bioethicists such as Ezekiel Emanuel (Emanuel 2014).

The U-Curve

Flying in the face of prevalent, negative views about ageing is a phenomenon that has become known as the 'U-curve of happiness'. Rather than later years being unbearable and futile, as the quote from Ecclesiastes leads us to believe, happiness seems to increase in old age (Blanchflower and Oswald 2009). Summarising in *The Lancet*, Steptoe, Deaton, and Stone suggest that 'Older populations, although generally less healthy and less productive, might be more satisfied with their lives, and experience less stress, worry, and anger than do middle-aged people' (Steptoe et al. 2015).

This result contradicts the common view that the elderly phase is the worst phase of life, and the view that the curve of life is a long slow fade. Importantly, this finding about happiness in old age is not a small, isolated result by any means. It comes from a large number of data sets, involving millions of people (Steptoe et al. 2015). Moreover, the curve has been replicated in many contexts, though, as I discuss shortly, not all. Findings about the lifetime trajectory of happiness potentially have significant ethical implications. Before moving to these, it is important to give some depth to the understanding of the U-curve related so far by mentioning some of the methodological and conceptual debates about the curve.

Methodological and Conceptual Issues

Possibly due to its unexpectedly positive nature, the U-curve has generated an unusual degree of interest from the media and popular writers like Jonathan Rauch (2018). While Rauch gives an interesting and empirically sensitive discussion of the U-curve, often conceptual, methodological, and empirical nuances are overlooked in popular literature on the topic. It is important to point to some qualifications about the U-curve before considering its implications. For the remainder of this section, I will outline a few significant issues: how 'happiness' is conceived and measured in these studies; how prevalent the findings of a U-curve are; and the role of methodological choices in bringing about the curve. Thereafter, I will mention some prominent explanations for the curve. The purpose of this section is not an exhaustive discussion of empirical and conceptual issues related to the curve, but instead to provide context for a grounded discussion of the curve's ethical implications.

Conceptions and Measures of Happiness

There are age-old theoretical disagreements about what happiness is, what types of happiness there are, the relation between happiness and a good life, and whether happiness is something that can be accurately measured. Perhaps one of the earliest suggestions about how to measure happiness came from the utilitarian philosopher John Stuart Mill. In trying to distinguish 'higher pleasures', such as those of the intellect, from 'lower pleasures', like gorging oneself on food, Mill proposed that

[If one of two pleasures is,] by those who are competently acquainted with both, placed so far above the other that they *prefer* it . . . and would not resign it for any quantity of the other pleasure . . . we are justified in ascribing to the preferred enjoyment a superiority in quality (Crisp 1997, 28, my italics)

Mill's proposal is to use subjective preference as an *indicator* of happiness or well-being. This suggestion has been widely used and developed, to the extent that most common measures make use of subjective measures, and are typically referred to as measuring 'subjective well-being'. There are terminological disputes about the meaning of terms such as happiness and well-being, the extent to which they are interchangeable, whether they can be accurately measured through the use of subjective indicators, and whether such measures 'get at' the phenomena in which we are interested (Diener et al. 2002).

Theoretical disagreements and uncertainties about the meaning of happiness are often borne out in measures of happiness, such that different studies of happiness measure somewhat different phenomena with different ethical provenance and vintage. Steptoe and colleagues have suggested that empirical measures of happiness can be roughly divided into evaluative, affective, and eudaemonic measures (Steptoe et al. 2015).[5]

Evaluative measures ask participants to evaluate how well they perceive their lives as going. Cantril's ladder, a measure used in the Gallup World Poll, presents participants with an image of a ladder, with the top rung representing the 'best possible life for you' and the bottom rung representing the 'worst possible life for you'. The questionnaire asks participants to indicate where on the ladder they feel that they stand. Effectively, this evaluative measure gives an indication of how satisfied participants are with their lives at a particular point.

The ancient hedonists, such as Epicurus, saw pleasure as the absence of suffering and sought ataraxia – equanimity, or the end of worry and other negative feelings – as the ultimate ethical end of human existence (Oates 1957). Correspondingly, *Affective or hedonic* measures of happiness provide indicators of positive and negative affect. That is, they measure the presence of different feelings or moods, which gives an indication of subjective, or felt,

---

[5] In discussing these measures, I follow Steptoe and colleagues (2015). Interestingly, these three categories of measures could arguably map to Parfit's categorisation of theories of well-being into desire satisfaction, hedonistic, and objective list theories (Parfit 1984).

happiness at particular times. Affective measures might, for instance, ask how happy, anxious, or angry a participant felt the previous day.

Ancient virtue ethicists such as Aristotle took eudaemonia (roughly, meaning or flourishing) as the central aim of human existence (Crisp 2004). *Eudaemonic* measures, then, aim to capture aspects of well-being and the good life that do not neatly correspond to happiness as satisfaction with one's life or as having positive feelings. Instead, they aim at gaining an impression of how meaningful participants find their lives. The ONS Population Survey, for instance, asks, 'Overall, to what extent do you feel the things that you do in your life are worthwhile?' (Office for National Statistics 2021).

An important subject in normative ethics is how different sorts of well-being come apart conceptually and theoretically. For instance, a life with a high level of pleasure or positive affect might also be one spent in daily activities that are profoundly meaningless. John Rawls gives the example of a person who spends his days happily counting blades of grass (Rawls 1971). Such a life might be *happy* on hedonic measures, but it would be controversial to say this constitutes a good life. In this case, eudaemonic and hedonic views are likely to diverge. In practice, as in theory, different measures of well-being also sometimes lead researchers to draw contrasting conclusions. For instance, one large study found that there was a significant lack of correlation between negative life evaluation and the occurrence of stress and anger (Stone et al. 2010). While life-evaluative measures reported the U-curve, obeying the pattern of deeper middle age unhappiness, on hedonic measures, stress and anger sloped continuously downward throughout life and decreased more quickly after the age of fifty. That is, while life evaluation followed the pattern of unhappiness in middle age, negative affect peaked earlier and declined throughout life. Indeed, even measures of affect may come apart. People may, for example, feel less happy, but also feel less anger, and, conversely, they may tend to feel happier, but also experience anger more frequently (Steptoe et al. 2015).

There are significant differences between conceptions of happiness and different operational measures of subjective well-being. This provides one reason that it is important to be cautious in drawing conclusions about the shape of happiness across the lifespan.

The Prevalence of the Happiness Curve
A further reason to be cautious in drawing conclusions concerns contextual and geographic differences in findings about the happiness curve. In addition to not being replicated on all measures, the U-curve is not replicated for all contexts (Graham and Pozuelo 2017). Ulloa and colleagues usefully categorise a large number of conflicting and contrasting findings about the curve (Ulloa et al. 2013). Contextual variations in reports of happiness are valuable, since

they may provide information about the background conditions that contribute to happiness. For instance, some studies suggest that the curve is most robustly replicated in high-income, English-speaking nations (Deaton 2008). In countries of the former Soviet Union and Eastern Europe, by contrast, older people tend not to score as well on many measures. Similarly, in sub-Saharan Africa the happiness curve appears flatter. These findings could suggest that relatively strong social support for the elderly has an important role in increasing subjective well-being. Significantly, then, the U-curve is by no means ubiquitous across contexts or study populations. As I discuss shortly, different findings have important ethical implications depending on the evaluation of the curve.

Methodological Choices

A further significant area of controversy related to findings about the U-curve concerns methodological choices about controls. It is possible to adjust study data for the influence of numerous variables, such as health, income, etc. (Blanchflower and Oswald 2009). The use of such controls means that presentations of the curve should not be seen as presenting an unfiltered picture. In particular, studies may result in more prominent U-curves through flattening out the influence of health or income on happiness (Frijters and Beatton 2012). Given that health has a strong influence on happiness, and that health tends to decline in old age, this contributes to a more pronounced upward curve in older age than it would if the data was not altered. This kind of methodological step might appropriately be taken if, for instance, researchers were attempting to find underlying happiness patterns that are influenced only by age, and not by health. However, if the purpose was to give a more accurate representation of happiness in old age, this methodology would inappropriately distort the picture. This means that it is important to be aware of the controls used when interpreting findings about the U-curve.

Excitement about the U-curve should perhaps be modulated by these methodological and conceptual qualifications. Still, it remains surprising that studies of subjective well-being commonly arrive at the finding that people are happier in later life. Against expectation, this increase in different dimensions of happiness often occurs despite poorer health in old age.[6] Why should happiness in old age confound expectations in this way? How is the curve to be explained?

Explanations

There are various possible explanations of the U-curve, many of which may overlap in explaining the phenomenon. While I will not attempt

---

[6] It should be noted that there appears to be a strong decline in life satisfaction for the oldest old and from about a year before death (Mroczek and Spiro 2005; Gwozdz and Sousa-Poza 2010).

a comprehensive account of these, it is useful to indicate a few, since the ability to know and respond to the causes of the U-curve could affect ethical responses to it. The first possible explanation is that the curve has a biological origin. This hypothesis is given support by the fact that similar results have been found in great apes (Weiss et al. 2012). Unsurprisingly, unlike most studies, these were not based on self-reported happiness. Instead, people familiar with the apes observed the apes – chimpanzees and orangutans – and rated their well-being. It could be that the similar decline in middle-aged happiness could be due to similarities in biological changes, such as brain structure, across the life course.

A further explanation suggests causes with which many middle-aged people will be familiar. The middle of life is correlated with increased stress and burdens: one is more likely to have children and to have less leisure time; one is likely to experience deaths of very close loved ones such as parents; and there are additional work pressures and responsibilities. These factors suggest that the curve is due to a deficit in the happiness of middle age, rather than anything particularly good about old age.

An equally sobering explanation of the happiness curve is that happiness declines in middle age due to unmet aspirations, then increases in old age as we gradually adjust to expectations that will not be met (Schwandt 2016). In middle age we are resistant and disappointed, but as we get older, we come to accept that dreams of youth will not be achieved, and to enjoy present satisfactions. Put another way, younger people expect the future to be better than it is, resulting in disappointment. Middle-aged people expect the future to be worse than it is, and so are pleasantly surprised when they get there. Rauch suggests that

Middle-aged people tend to feel both disappointed and pessimistic, a recipe for misery. Eventually, however, expectations stop declining. They settle at a lower level than in youth, and reality begins exceeding them. Surprises turn predominantly positive, and life satisfaction swings upward. (Rauch 2014)

A more positive explanation, called socioemotional selectivity theory, points to the 'emotional wisdom' that one gains as one ages. Carstenson writes that 'as people age and time Horizons grow shorter, people invest in what is most important, typically meaningful relationships, and derive increasingly greater satisfaction from these investments' (Carstensen et al. 2011, 22). Ageing correlates with emotional wisdom, which allows us to select and pursue the experiences that we value more. Condensing these sorts of experiences increases the satisfaction we experience.

It is likely that these and other explanations of the curve overlap in bringing about later life happiness. The purpose of this section has been to give a brief and, of necessity, incomplete overview of conceptual and empirical investigations into happiness and potential explanations of the happiness curve. While there is much more of interest to say about studies on the measurement of happiness, and the explanations of the curve, this is not my main aim in this chapter. Instead, in the next section I turn to what I see as an important deficit, which is that the happiness curve has received very little attention in ethical literature.

Ethical Implications of the Happiness Curve

To illustrate why this appears to be an important oversight, in this section I outline potential ethical implications of the happiness curve, before concentrating on a particular consideration in the next section. By an ethical implication, I mean, narrowly, a consideration that should be of interest to the field of ethics and, broadly, a consideration that impacts on what actions or decisions societies *ought* to take. I suggest that the happiness curve has implications for the subfield of ageing ethics, and raises questions about our understanding of the role of happiness in the good life, the distribution of well-being across a life, the appropriateness of younger people taking end-of-life decisions for their older selves, and the distribution of goods between age groups.

While so far I have discussed what I take to be a common stance that there is a U-curved trajectory of happiness across the lifespan, some of the ethical issues discussed do not entirely rely on this. Instead, they can be seen as related to findings about the diachronic dimension of happiness, whatever its trajectory. The diachronic pattern of happiness should be of ethical interest, whether it is U-shaped or not.

The U-Curve and the Ethics of Ageing

An initial point of interest is that the happiness curve neatly maps on to the nascent field of the ethics of ageing. I have tried to delineate the scope of this field as follows:

The ethics of ageing is a field of normative enquiry encompassing ethical issues facing a person in her situation as an ageing person. (Wareham 2018, 129)

Significantly, a feature of ageing ethics is that it reflects the idea that 'ageing occurs, if not throughout the whole course of life, then at least through most of it' (Wareham 2018, 129). In other words, ageing ethics should capture the diachronic character of ageing, rather than having a narrow focus on ethical issues related to being old.

As such, the U-curve of happiness across a lifespan seems like a paradigmatic example of something that should figure in ageing ethics. It is an ethically relevant phenomenon that appears to closely track ageing. Moreover, it has potential relevance to the ageing person not just for the elderly but throughout the ageing process. It may guide expectations and choices in young and old, and could assist in understanding oneself and others, as well as seeking and providing guidance. The happiness curve thus appears to be an important focal point for a normative discourse about ageing that is ripe for expansion.

The Ideal Trajectory of Lifetime Happiness

The happiness curve also raises an important ethical question about which happiness trajectory makes a life go better. Arguably, one attractive feature of the happiness curve is that it appears to have an upward trend in the latter part of life. Some, like David Velleman, suggest that lives with this kind of upward narrative trajectory can be said to go better, even if they contained equal or somewhat less *total* happiness than another life with a downward trajectory (Velleman 1991). To see this, consider a person whose life contained a great deal of happiness but who gradually became more and more miserable as time progressed. We would be inclined to say that this person's life has gone worse than a person whose life starts off miserable, but ends happily.[7] That is, it appears that in judgements of the goodness of a life, it is not just the *quantity* of happiness that a life contains that matters. The organisation of happiness within the life is also relevant.

If this view about the trajectory of lifetime happiness is accepted, the upward curve is not just a curiosity. Instead, it is something that makes lives better than flat or n-shaped curves, something that individuals should prudentially aspire to and make efforts to achieve. It is also possible to be critical of happiness U-curves. Perhaps the shape of this trajectory is too radical, and individuals should aim for a more gradual increase of happiness across the lifespan, perhaps by taking some of the pressure off middle age.

The upshot is that considering whether the happiness curve represents a desirable trajectory may present considerations for the way we plan our lives. It may also influence how national happiness is evaluated: a diachronic picture, including population well-being at the end of life, becomes an important part of determining whether the lives of members of a population are going well.

The Role of Happiness in the Good Life and Society

Studies of the curve motivate questions about the centrality of happiness in a good life. Does the fact that middle-aged people are unhappier mean that their lives are going worse for them, such that there ought to be some corrective action? Or might it be claimed that the lives of middle-aged people, though unhappy, could be more valuable in another domain, such as the value of objective achievement or the meaningfulness of rearing children?[8] If the latter

---

[7] Daniel Kahneman (2011) has also found that happiness at the end of a process affects our evaluation of that process.

[8] Thanks to Thaddeus Metz for this point.

claims are correct, one could argue that the life of a person in middle age is going better despite the fact that they are less happy. This would complicate evaluations of the ethical significance of findings about the happiness curve.

Moving from the individual to the population level, findings about the happiness curve could impact on ideas about the desirable demographic make-up of a society. The rapid ageing of societies is commonly represented as a disaster, or 'demographic time bomb' (Loch et al. 2010). However, the happiness curve suggests that an older society may in fact be a happier one, other things being equal. This would be a particularly significant finding for population ethicists who endorse utilitarianism, the view that happiness is the greatest good, and that the aim of moral actions is to create the greatest amount of happiness (Crisp 1997). In this case, rather than something to be avoided, ageing societies may be something to be aspired to, assuming of course that externalities such as those related to dependency ratios could be overcome.

It may appear unlikely that these considerations would influence population level policies. However, welfare economists strive to incorporate welfare considerations into state and policy evaluations. The Kingdom of Bhutan famously shifted the evaluation of its success to be measured in Gross National Happiness (Bates 2009), rather than Gross Domestic Product. If these or similar moves became widespread, the tendency towards greater happiness in the elderly might be regarded as an important policy consideration.

End-of-Life Issues and Mistakes about Happiness in Old Age

Earlier I pointed to the common view that life in old age is bad and not worth having. Anecdotally, it is not unusual for young and middle-aged people to deplore the idea of getting old, and even suggest that they would rather die before they reach old age. The prominent bioethicist Ezekiel Emanuel has suggested that he *hopes* to die at seventy-five (Emanuel 2014).[9] However, studies indicating higher late life happiness suggest that this attitude may be deeply mistaken.

Given the prevalence of mistakenly devaluing old age, it is important to question decisions made about old age made by younger people, including those decisions one makes for one's older self. Nancy Jecker diagnoses some of this mistaken thinking as 'midlife bias' – a tendency to mistakenly superimpose the values of younger ages onto one's older selves (Jecker 2020a).

In the case of late life happiness, awareness of midlife bias might cause us to question the authority of advance directives and midlife decisions about end-of-life interventions. If the commonly held view about the badness of old age is so off-track, to what extent are we justified in making these sorts of

---

[9] See Wareham (2021), 'Between Hoping to Die and Longing to Live Longer', for a discussion and critique.

judgements for our future, aged selves? Note that I am not suggesting that advance directives, or decisions made for future selves, ought to be abandoned. However, the happiness curve at least suggests that decision-makers ought to approach those decisions with some epistemic humility about their future desires, values, and beliefs.

Age Group Justice

There is significant ethical controversy about criteria for just distribution of various sorts of resources (Williams 1997; Harris 2005). The role of *age* as a criterion is hotly debated in the distribution of health resources in particular, with some suggesting, and others denying, that it is justified to prefer younger people in the distribution of resources (Daniels 2007; Jecker 2013; Wareham 2015a). Findings about the U-curve could have some influence on these debates. On the one hand, one could argue, controversially, that later life happiness means that allocation decisions ought to accord greater value to older people. If one is to save a life, perhaps it is better to save a happier one.

On the other hand, though, one could claim that this distribution of happiness is *unjust*. Perhaps it is unfair that older people are happier while the middle-aged suffer. One might argue that it is more just to flatten the curve, by channelling resources from older people to 'level up' those in unhappy middle age. This might be done, for example, through provision of psychological therapy comparable in cost to the resources needed for physical care and the maintenance of agency in the elderly.[10]

While I do not aim to resolve this issue, or the others above, I have tried to indicate some intriguing directions concerning how the happiness curve may influence individual and social decisions and evaluations. These, in turn, may influence the way in which we react to findings about the happiness curve. The sorts of implications I have discussed mean that it is important that findings about the happiness curve should find their way into the broader debates above. In the next section, I focus more narrowly on a concrete example of an ethical debate concerning the social desirability of longer lives, in which empirical findings about the happiness curve can play an important role.

Superlongevity, Ageing Societies, and the U-Curve

The twenty-first century has seen a continuation of the substantial increases in longevity observed throughout the twentieth century. These increases have caused researchers to cast aside many predictions about maximum life expectancy for humans.[11] In 1928, for instance, James Dublin estimated that a life

---

[10] Thanks to Thaddeus Metz for this point.
[11] Life expectancy is the average amount of time a person can be expected to live.

expectancy of around sixty-five years of age represented the limit for humans. Other proposed limits have similarly been broken. While some continue to argue that life expectancy will eventually plane out as we reach a biological maximum expectancy (Olshansky et al. 1990), Oeppen and Vaupel (2002) argue that longevity increases are in fact roughly linear and that there is little reason to doubt that life expectancy will continue increasing indefinitely. Oeppen and Vaupel's predictions are given support by a tremendous amount of research into slowed ageing (Smoliga et al. 2011), the possibility of using engineering solutions to halt or reverse ageing (De Grey and Rae 2007), and massive investment into life extension by research and development companies, such as Google's Calico and pharmaceutical giants such as GlaxoSmithKline (Wareham 2016).

The prospect of substantially longer lifespans raises significant ethical questions. Would this be good for individuals? Is such a society likely to be substantially unjust? Would it result in population level problems that would otherwise not arise? While I will not aim to answer these questions here, I wish to indicate one way in which the happiness curve could have a bearing on the last question. I will briefly outline Peter Singer's argument that additional long lives may result in unhappier populations. Thereafter, I describe Mark Walker's response, in which he invokes findings about lifetime happiness to cast doubt on Singer's pessimistic conclusion. With some qualifications, I concur with Walker, and conclude concerning the implications of this for studies on the happiness curve.

'Singer Longevity'

In 1991, the utilitarian ethicist Peter Singer, at the time aged around forty-five, argued that, if only the latter part of people's life were extended, *total population* happiness would be reduced. This is despite the fact that *individuals* may be benefited by extra happy years. According to a version of utilitarianism known as 'total utilitarianism', the reduction of total happiness means that extending the latter part of life would be a bad thing overall, despite the gains to individuals.

Singer's conceptually complex argument stems from a thought experiment. He envisions a drug that increases life expectancy to 150. The drug has no effect until middle age. Thereafter, the period from middle age onwards is drastically extended, or stretched. Importantly, Singer suggests that the declines in health and youthful freshness that accompany middle age and old age mean that life will be somewhat less good from the time that the drug takes effect.

Despite this, individual lives will still be good and worth having. However, a longer time spent in the reduced happiness of older age across the lifetime entails that the less happy part occupies a greater proportion of a life. Consequently, the *average* lifetime happiness across extended lives will be lower. This becomes problematic if lifespan increases mean that it is necessary to limit population sizes. Singer suggests that in the hypothetical scenario in which it becomes necessary to restrict population growth, it would reduce utility to have people with extended lives, as their below-average happiness would reduce *total* happiness.

As a way of simplifying this idea, consider a 300-year timeframe. We must choose between populating this timeframe with

A) *two* people who live to 150 years and are individually better off, but who have slightly lower average happiness across their lives (the life extension scenario), or
B) *three* people who are individually less happy, who live to 100 years each, and have higher average happiness across their lives.

Total utilitarianism holds that all morality ought to be concerned with is total happiness, rather than the amount of happiness that individuals experience. In Singer's case, this may mean we should reject the life extension scenario and choose B, since, other things being equal, the higher average lifetime happiness would maximise the happiness gained in the 300-year timeframe.

As mentioned, this argument is complex and controversial, and I do not have space here to dissect all the ethical assumptions at work.[12] Instead, my response below focusses on the impact of empirical findings about age-related happiness on the argument.

Walker on the Happiness Curve and Longevity

Mark Walker has pointed out the questionable factual premise in Singer's argument, which is of course that, if studies indicating a U-curve are correct, happiness increases towards the end of life (Walker 2007). This means that, other things being equal, we should predict an upward curve in lifetime happiness, not the downward curve in well-being that Singer suggests. Substituting out the flawed empirical premise may mean that the longer life could have greater average happiness, *since more time would be spent in happier old age*. Findings about the U-curve suggest that Singer's life extension scenario could actually increase total happiness.

Walker concludes that utilitarians should be 'enthusiastic proponents' of life extension. However, even setting aside the methodological and conceptual qualifications discussed earlier, it is necessary to be a little more cautious about the drastically increased happiness that Walker predicts. Recall that in Singer's thought experiment middle age is similarly extended. While Singer incorrectly predicted that old age would lower happiness to a greater extent, the lowering of happiness by the extension of middle age should be factored in too. Moreover, it should be emphasised that this is a thought experiment: there

---

[12] See Wareham (2015b) for a more in-depth discussion.

are an indefinite number of imponderables in considering whether or not life extension would increase total utility. For instance, would this take place in the type of society in which the happiness curve was likely to be present? What would be the effect on happiness of limiting reproduction? Would the dependency ratio in this population become unsustainable? These and many other unknowns counsel against definitive conclusions about this problem in particular, and about the social impact of longer lives in general.

While I have not attempted to attend to the philosophical depth of Singer and Walker's arguments, this discussion is sufficient as a brief example of how findings about the U-curve can have a bearing on an applied ethical question. In this case, we should see that studies of happiness provide some grounds for reducing middle-aged 1991 Singer's pessimism about the value of longevity. I do wonder whether present-day Peter Singer, who has experienced some of the happiness that accompanies being older, might re-evaluate some of the conclusions that he reaches in this argument.[13]

Conclusion

Ageing is a ubiquitous biological process with tremendous implications for individuals, populations, and societies. Despite this, it has not taken off as a topic for ethical discussion in the same way that, for instance, reproduction has. This may be because ageing is typically construed as a troublesome period at the end of life when one is aged or elderly. Against this, it is plausible to view ageing as a process that occurs throughout most of, or perhaps the whole of, life. This observation has some significant ethical implications. One such implication is that we should consider ethical problems and dilemmas related to ageing across the entire lifespan.

An important example of this way of thinking is the so-called 'U-curve of happiness'. In the above, I pointed to some interesting and potentially significant ethical implications of the happiness curve. In presenting the curve as an optimistic contrast to the 'common view' of age as intrinsically connected to suffering, my aim has not been to downplay the negative aspects of ageing. Nonetheless, findings about happiness across the lifespan should at least challenge the common perceptions that well-being across time follows a downward trajectory in well-being and that later life is unavoidably a dreadful time of suffering and despair.

---

[13] I am happy to have received a positive answer to this question. In personal correspondence, Professor Singer replied, 'I've certainly enjoyed the years from 50 to 74 . . . So maybe 50 was premature. 75, perhaps?'

18 The Desirability and Morality of Life Extension

John K. Davis

Introduction

Life extension consists in slowing, halting, or even reversing human ageing. Merely keeping an elderly person alive longer is not life extension; life extension involves manipulating the biological processes of ageing so that we age more slowly as well as live longer. This has already been achieved in some animal studies, and many reputable geroscientists believe we may learn to do this with humans in the foreseeable future (Olshansky et al. 2002; Martin et al. 2003; Cohen 2015, 1186; Park 2015, 74). If we do, this would be one of the great changes in the human condition, up there with the development of writing, agriculture, cities, science, and technology.

There is a lot of controversy over whether life extension would be a good thing. We will explore the arguments for and against it in this chapter. As we do, bear this in mind: life extension is like most other technologies – it's not all good or all bad. It will have its upside and its downside, its good and bad consequences. This is true of the internet, plastics, the internal combustion engine, genetic engineering, and air travel, and this will be true of life extension too. Both sides have some valid arguments. In the end, we must decide whether the considerations in favor of life extension outweigh the considerations against it, or vice versa.

The Science Behind Life Extension

Why should we believe that life extension is possible? One answer is simply that ageing is a biological phenomenon governed by the laws of nature, and when we understand the natural laws that govern something, we often find ways to manipulate that thing. This may be why, centuries ago, Roger Bacon, Descartes, Benjamin Franklin, Condorcet, and William Godwin all speculated that it might someday be possible to slow human ageing. That speculation is now supported by recent developments in *geroscience*, the scientific study of the basic biological processes of ageing, especially at the cellular and molecular level. Scientists have already slowed ageing in several animal species, and the genes manipulated in these experiments are shared by humans. The National Institutes of Health have formed the NIH Geroscience Interest Group to explore the possibility of treating age-related diseases by attacking the underlying processes of ageing, noting that "a slower rate of aging leads not only to a longer life, but also to a delay in the appearance and progression of most diseases of aging, as well as a slowing in age-related functional decline."[1] The private sector is now involved: in 2013 Google founded a company called Calico to develop life extension methods, backed by $2.5 billion, and they've since invested more and partnered with pharmaceutical giant AbbVie.

When we talk about possible methods of life extension, we are talking about two things: the basic processes of ageing, and interventions that might manipulate those processes. The basic processes involve genetic pathways. These pathways are not yet fully understood, but some of the more promising pathways include one involving insulin, one that involves the TOR gene, and one that involves sirtuins and NAD precursors. As for interventions, it is premature to identify anything specific, but they are likely to include one or more of these three things: drugs, genetic engineering, and stem cells. We know this because the basic processes of ageing happen at the cellular and molecular level, and these are the three main ways to manipulate cellular and molecular-level processes.

How long might we live? Among geroscientists who consider life extension possible, conservative estimates range from 112 to 150 years (Miller 2002; Olshansky 2002, 102; Wright and Mark 2003). Others entertain estimates from 350 years to many thousands of years (Holden 2002, 1032; Richel 2003). There is even some scientific evidence that it may be possible to "reverse" ageing (Weintraub 2016).

If you never aged you would still die, but only from causes of death that are unrelated to ageing. To estimate your life expectancy under those conditions we must take current actuarial statistics for the United States and subtract all age-related causes of death, leaving only things such as accidents, violence, and medical problems unrelated to ageing. The resulting life expectancy turns out to be approximately 1000 years.[2] Keep in mind that this is merely a statistical average; it's not as though your odds of death get higher the longer you live. Because the causes of death do not become more frequent with age, your odds of death at 1000 would be the same as your odds of death at 25. Some people would live far longer than 1000 years and some would live far less.

Thus, life extension is not immortality; an immortal cannot die. Life extension confers *extended life*, which means you age more slowly or not at all, and you can still die from things such as diseases and accidents. Moreover, the decision to use life extension is reversible. As I said, life extension will probably require some combination of drugs, stem cells, and genetic engineering. Drugs

---

[1] www.nia.nih.gov/gsig (accessed June 7, 2020).
[2] This is according to calculations by Shahin Davoudpour, a demographer with whom I've worked on these issues.

and stem cells would have to be renewed periodically, and you can always cease taking them. Genetic engineering may be permanent in a sense, but it stands to reason that what can be engineered in can be engineered back out (genes removed can be replaced, genes inserted can be removed). And there is always the option of suicide.

Moral Issues

Life extension is morally controversial. Most of the moral issues can be grouped into three major areas of concern. The first concern focuses on whether extended life is desirable; some say we are better off without it. The second concern is that widespread use of life extension will cause overpopulation.[3] The third concern is that life extension will be expensive, and not everyone will be able to get it. I will argue that the first concern is not well-founded, but the other two are legitimate concerns, and life extension is morally permissible only if we take steps to avoid overpopulation and to distribute life extension fairly.

First Concern: Is Extended Life a Good Life?

Not everyone thinks so.

The value of extended life may seem obvious. If life is good, then more life (of the same quality) is better. You would have more time to enjoy life, accomplish things, and contribute to the world around you.[4] However, the value of extended life is not obvious to everyone. Surveys by the Pew Center and various universities reveal that a slight majority of those surveyed say they would refuse life extension if it were available.[5] In the Pew Center survey, 56 percent of American adults would not want extended life, and in a survey conducted by two Australian universities, only 35.4 percent said they would want it, while 38.9 percent of them thought it would do them more harm than good.

Some ethicists, particularly bioconservatives such as Leon Kass, argue that the skeptics are right. They argue that extended life would be boring and meaningless, and that facing death helps us develop virtues, accept mortality, and use our time wisely (Callahan 1998, 132; McKibben 2003, 159; Post 2003,

---

[3] I wish to thank Shahin Davoudpour, a doctoral candidate in demography at the University of California, Irvine, for working with me on the overpopulation issue over the last several years. My work on this topic is as much his work as mine, and I am greatly indebted to him.

[4] Colin Farrelly (2019) has argued for life extension on the grounds that senescence violates our liberty and life extension increases it.

[5] "Living to 120 and Beyond," Pew Research Center, www.pewforum.org/2013/08/06/living-to-120-and-beyond (accessed June 7, 2020). See also Partridge et al. (2011); Alvarez et al. (2015); Dragojlovic (2013).

77; Kass 2004, 312). Versions or antecedents of these arguments trace back at least as far as Epicurean philosopher Lucretius; they were deployed to show that we have no reason to fear death, in part because an immortal existence is not desirable.[6] Whether or not these arguments work for immortality, we must ask whether they transfer well to extended life, which (again) is not immortality. (As we do, keep this question in mind: Do these arguments establish that extended life is worse than death? To say you would be better off without extended life amounts to saying that it's a life worse than death.) So far as extended life is concerned, these are bad arguments.

The Meaning of Life

Some critics of life extension claim that extended life would lack meaning. To say that a life is meaningful is typically a way of saying that life is worth living for the person whose life it is – that is, it contains things that have value for that person. Value can be subjective or objective. A thing has subjective value when its value depends on how we react to it; a thing has objective value if its value does not depend on our reactions to it. Thus, depending on the kind of value it contains, a life might have subjective meaning or objective meaning (or both). To say that a life lacks subjective meaning is another way of saying the person living that life is not interested in it. That is boredom, which we will discuss shortly.

So let us focus on objective meaning. Why might critics of life extension think that a life that's very, very long would lack objective value? Leon Kass gives a hint when he asks, "Could life be serious or meaningful without the limit of mortality? Is not the limit on our time the ground of our taking life seriously and living it passionately?" (Kass 2004, 313). John Pauley makes a similar point: "On the condition of an infinite amount of time in existence, nothing would matter for persons" (Pauley 2007, 43). Perhaps they mean this: Beyond a certain point, a thing becomes less valuable the more of it we have. If we have infinite time, then we have an infinite amount of everything life contains, and thus what life contains – and life itself – has less value.

This argument might work for immortality, which is infinite, but it does not transfer well to extended life, which is not. Moreover, it's not clear that everything becomes objectively less valuable the more of it we have. For example, having children is not less valuable just because billions of other people are having them and billions more have already had them in centuries past. Is having more children of your own less objectively valuable just because you've already had quite a few in the previous centuries of your own life? If there were twice as many first-rate works of art in the world, would the collection in the Louvre be objectively less valuable? (I'm not talking about

---

[6] Martha Nussbaum (1994, 227) derives these points from her discussion of "On the Nature of Things" by Lucretius.

its market value here.) In any event, you can always extend your life and continue living until you find that your life lacks sufficient value, and then go off your life-extending meds, resume ageing, and die. Declining extended life to avoid a loss of value is like refusing the gift of a new coat because it will wear out eventually.

Boredom

Many critics of life extension believe that an extended life would be intolerably boring.[7] This is a way of saying that we would not value such a life or what it contains – in effect, a way of saying that extended life is subjectively meaningless.

This issue cannot be settled from an armchair. Until we live an extended life for a long time we really can't know whether extended life would be intolerably boring. Still, let's suppose you are concerned that it might be. What should you do about it? Turning down extended life (as critics of life extension seem to suggest) is one option. However, there is a better option: You can try extended life until you find it intolerably boring and *then* terminate your life, either by going off your life-extending meds or in some more immediate way. Extending your life is a reversible decision; dying of old age is not. Boredom takes a while to set in, and refusing an extended life because you fear it will become boring is like walking out of an all-day music concert at noon because you think you'll be bored with it by nightfall.

And there may be yet another option for avoiding boredom. We have drugs for depression, ADHD, anxiety, and shopping addiction. Perhaps we will find drugs for boredom. Still, some may object that such a drug doesn't prevent your life from *being* boring, it merely prevents you from *seeing* that it's boring. Bernard Williams once commented that taking a drug for boredom does not make your circumstances less boring; it would be an "impoverishment in [one's] consciousness of them" (Williams 1993, 87). This suggests that circumstances can be *objectively* boring, boring even if they are not *subjectively* boring – that is, even if you don't *find* them boring. However, if the subjective reaction of finding something boring is not what makes a life objectively boring, what does? Perhaps a life is objectively boring when it's not worth your time and attention – that is, when it lacks objective value of some kind. The solution, then, would be to spend your extended life doing things that are objectively worthwhile, such as working to preserve the environment, creating works of art, and so on. In that event, your life would be objectively interesting, and if you found that life subjectively boring, then a boredom pill might correct your perception of life in much the same way that an antidepressant helps you to see that your life is better than you thought it was.

---

[7] This is a common concern in public surveys (Partridge et al. 2009, 71). The best discussion of this is Bernard Williams, "The Makropulos Case: Reflections on the Tedium of Immortality" (1993). See also Kass (2004, 312) and Callahan (1998, 132).

Personal Identity: Will You Outlive Yourself?

Bernard Williams argues that, if you live a very, very long time, you can avoid boredom only by changing into someone else, and thereby ceasing to exist (Williams 1993, 81–83). He believes that if you live long enough, you will have to develop new interests to avoid intolerable boredom. Over time, the interests will have to be more and more different from what you found interesting early in your life. For example, you might start out life as an extroverted athlete and (centuries later) find new interests that require introversion, solitude, and intellect. Either as a result of acquiring such interests or for other reasons, you slowly change, becoming more introverted and intellectual. Later still you might explore religious ecstasy and mysticism, and change some more. Over time, you will change so much that you might as well be a different person. Your later self will be so different from the self you were in your first century that your earlier and later selves will seem like two entirely different people. This means that you will lose your earlier identity and gradually transform into someone different. In effect, your earlier self will cease to exist and a new self will come into existence.[8] (Williams does not say that you *will* change, only that if you don't, you won't be able to acquire these new interests.)

However, the fact that you will eventually fade away and gradually be replaced by a different self does not imply that it's not in your interest to extend your life. First, at any given time, you do have a lot in common with the next stage. At age 425 you have a lot in common with the self you were at 400 and the self you will be at 450. There is never a point when you are trembling on the brink of ceasing to exist, for the transition to a new self is gradual. In that event, the question is not whether to live for several centuries longer; the question is whether to live for another few decades, and the fact that you're looking at decades rather than centuries is not a good reason to turn down another few decades.

Death Benefits

Kass and other bioconservatives argue that living with a normal life expectancy, and facing death within a few decades, has several benefits (Jonas 1985, 19; Nussbaum 1994, 227; McKibben 2003, 159; Post 2003, 78; The President's Council on Bioethics 2003; Kass 2004, 311). They argue that living with the expectation of a normal life expectancy teaches us to value our time and appreciate the precious gift of life, as well as driving us to accomplish something instead of frittering our lives away. Facing death, they say, teaches us to accept mortality and acquire courage and other virtues that come from facing

---

[8] There is room for debate over whether you would truly be a different person, or merely be such a different version of yourself that you have little reason to care about that future version of you. I will pass over this issue; both accounts have the same implications for the value of extended life.

danger. Accepting our mortality forces us to invest our hopes in the next generation, thereby learning selflessness, rather than obsessing narcissistically on personal survival.

They are right to an extent. Facing death has a silver lining. However, whether these benefits are great enough to make extended life a life worse than death is another matter. Moreover, these benefits are not absent in an extended life. Extended life is biologically just like normal life, except that you age more slowly or not at all. You can still die at any time, and you must still deal with mortality even if you don't know when death may arrive. You'll still have motivation to use your time well and acquire whatever virtues facing death helps us develop. In fact, you'll have a lot more time to do these things. At worst, the death benefits may be somewhat muted in an extended life (perhaps you'll fritter away more time than you would in a normal life), but they will still be present.

Now flip the arguments around. If death teaches us to appreciate life, life must be precious. Why, then, should we turn down more of it? If we want to avoid wasting time, then turning down extra years of life is a waste of *that* time. Accepting death may be easier, not harder, when you've lived long enough to accomplish what you wanted to. Turning down life extension in order to learn to accept death amounts to dying early in order to learn to accept dying early.

The Optional Afterlife Argument

So far we have considered arguments that extended life is bad for you. Now consider an argument that extended life is good for you. Imagine that you are dying, and God appears to you. You ask whether there is an afterlife. He answers:

That's up to you. I've found that many people worry that the afterlife will be intolerably boring, or lack the finitude and challenges that make us appreciate life, so I give people a choice at the moment of death. You can have an afterlife, or you can cease to exist once you die. Moreover, just to reduce anxiety about what the afterlife will be like, I've made it resemble this life, with all its hazards and challenges, except for one thing – you will stop ageing in your twenties.

You ask if this would be permanent. He answers:

That too is up to you. You can end your afterlife by dying (again) any time you like, but once you do, that's it. Annihilation is forever.

The afterlife described above is essentially the same as extended life, for it's just like this life except without ageing. If you truly think extended life would be a bad life, then you should (to be consistent) decline God's offer and opt for annihilation. If you would opt for the afterlife God offers, then you should (to be consistent) opt for life extension and extended life.

If a Longer Life Expectancy Is Bad, Would a Shorter Life Expectancy Be Better?

If extended life (or an afterlife just like it) is worse than a normal lifespan, would a shorter lifespan be better? We can put the same point another way by asking what life expectancy is best for us. If living much longer than the eighty or so years we can now expect is not good, would a shorter life expectancy be better? Is there something about eighty years that is both better than forty and worse than 120? According to the archaeological record, tens of thousands of years ago, before agriculture and other developments, humans once routinely died in their forties or sooner. Was that better for us? Would the human race be better off if a mutant virus rewrote our DNA so that we aged twice and fast and died in our late thirties? If God offered you that choice on an individual basis, would you take it? Anyone who argues that living much longer than eighty years is bad for us must also explain why living much less than eighty years is not good for us.

Second Concern: The Overpopulation Problem

The first area of concern about life extension was that extended life might be a bad life. The second concern is that widespread use of life extension will cause severe overpopulation, partly because people use their extra time to have more babies, and partly because everyone is living longer, hanging around like guests who have stayed too long at a party. This is a common concern among both the general public (Partridge et al. 2009, 74; Alvarez et al. 2015, 90) and academic ethicists (Singer 1991; Harris 2000; Glannon 2002a; Ackerman 2007, 334).

It is a mistake to try to predict life extension's effect on population trends. We don't know how much longer people will live, or what percentage of the human race will have life extension, or how many children they will have. However, we can *project* what population trends would be under various hypothetical circumstances. I worked with a demographer, Shahin Davoudpour, to do just that. Mr. Davoudpour developed a formula that can be used to project population trends once we plug in an assumed life expectancy, an assumed number of people who have life extension, an assumed number of children per woman, and an assumed age at which women give birth. (I speak of "children per woman" rather than "children per couple" only because that's how demographers talk about this; men are not off the hook here.) We plugged in a wide variety of variables to see what would happen in various scenarios.[9]

---

[9] The projections cited in this chapter have not yet been published; two articles to present them are in preparation. Readers who would like to see these projections in greater detail are welcome to write to the author. Christopher Wareham (2015b), working from different assumptions, generated different projections.

Moderate life extension (e.g., a life expectancy of 120 years) does not increase the population by much more than it would increase when people have a normal life expectancy, but radical life extension can make a dramatic difference to population growth. For example, the fertility rate in the United States is currently close to 1.8 children per woman. When people have a normal life expectancy this rate is fairly close to replacement level; the population will not increase. If, however, women in a population with a 1000-year life expectancy have 1.8 children per woman when they are, on average, twenty years old, the population increases to *10 times* its original size by forty-nine generations, then declines over the next twenty-four generations. Even though this population eventually declines, it increases for the first 1000 years.

There are two ways to avoid this. The obvious way is to lower the fertility rate. If we want to avoid any increase at all in a population with a 1000-year life expectancy, the total number of births must be no higher than the number of deaths from non-ageing-related causes. Under current American conditions, a population of 1 billion who never age would lose 252,500 people to non-ageing-related causes every year. Thus, to avoid any increase to a population of 1 billion people with a life expectancy of 1000 years, only 252,500 women can give birth each year – roughly one woman out of every 1,980.

That's a pretty severe limit. We can relax that a bit if we are willing to tolerate an increase of around one-third. For example, we found that if a population of 1 billion with a life expectancy of 1000 years has a fertility rate of 0.5 children per woman at an average birth age 20, the population rises by one-third in five generations, to 1.333 billion. The population stays at that level for another 44 generations, and then begins a rapid decline, dwindling away to almost nothing in another century. Perhaps a one-third increase is tolerable; after all, the United Nations Population Division says we may see a population increase as high as 45 percent during the twenty-first century (United Nations 2015). If we could keep life extension from making that increase any worse, at least the environment would be no worse off as a result of life extension.

The fertility rate can be raised to 1 child per woman if the women in this population are divided into four groups and each group has one child at age 20 for the first quarter, age 40 for the second, age 800 for the third and age 900 for the fourth. The population will then rise by nearly 30 percent, to 1.285 billion, by generation 4, and stay at that level until generation 40, when it rises to 1.571 billion over the next 9 generations. It then drops to .571 billion by generation 50 and declines sharply from then on. Perhaps this is tolerable if, 40 generations from now, we find a way to sustain a 57 percent increase in population for a few generations.

The other way to avoid overpopulation is to delay the age at which women give birth. Thus, this is also a way to tolerate a higher fertility level. For example, if the women in our hypothetical population are divided into four groups and each group has one child at age 20 for the first quarter, 40 for the second, 800 for the third, and 900 for the fourth, then the population will rise by nearly 30 percent, to 1.285 billion, by generation 4, and stay at that level until generation 40, when it rises to 1.571 billion over the next 9 generations. It then drops to .571 billion by generation 50 and declines sharply from then on. Perhaps this is tolerable because, 40 generations from now, we may find a way to sustain that increase in population for a few generations. The fertility rate can be raised to two children per woman if births are delayed even more, and the women are divided into two groups. The first group has their first child at age 500 and their second at age 800, while the second group has their first child at age 540 and their second child at age 900. The population increases by approximately 50 percent by 27 generations, and doubles (from its original size) by 46 generations, remaining at that level for 5 generations and then declining back to its original size. That might be tolerable, depending on other factors. (Notice, though, that waiting 500 years to have a child is probably no easier to take than simply giving up on having children at all.)

The bottom line is that, if we develop radical life extension and make it widely available, severe overpopulation is almost inevitable unless the government severely limits how many children you can have (and when you have them) *if* you use life extension. I call this a policy of *Forced Choice* – you're forced to choose between extending your lifespan and having as many children as you wish.

There are obvious enforcement issues, but let's set those aside and ask: Is a policy like Forced Choice morally permissible? China's one-child policy comes to mind. Many people believe such a policy is an unjust intrusion into very personal matters – an unacceptable violation of personal liberty. John Stuart Mill argued that people have something like a right to liberty, and that it's wrong for anyone (including the government) to force them to act against their own choices, even when it's done for their own good. However, Mill also said that there's a limit to respecting liberty. It's called the *harm principle*, and it says that your liberty can be limited in order to prevent you from harming other people. Moreover, Forced Choice limits reproduction only for those who get life extension – it doesn't apply to everyone. It is, in a sense, consensual.

Third Concern: Unequal Access to Life Extension

The third major moral concern about life extension is that not everyone will be able to afford it, at least at first (Harris 2000, 59; Juengst et al. 2003, 1323). This seems obviously unjust for two reasons. First, those who live far longer have greater opportunities. If everyone has a right to equal opportunity, then this situation may violate that right. Second, if the current distribution of social goods is too unequal to be just, then increasing that unequal distribution increases that injustice.[10]

---

[10] Colin Farrelly (2017) has argued that such inequality is unjust for reasons related to beneficence and equality of opportunity.

There is no question that this would be a morally disturbing state of affairs. The interesting questions concern what to do about it. I will focus on the two most important ones:

A. There are two ways to prevent this inequality: Either make sure everyone gets life extension, or make sure no one gets it. Is this way of achieving equality consistent with justice?
B. Should we prohibit life extension until other, more pressing social needs have been met?

Is Justice Served by Making Sure No One Gets Life Extension?

The first of these questions concerns achieving equality. Those who argue that life extension should not be developed because it will not be available to everyone are effectively arguing that we should achieve equality by making sure no one gets it. This is a form of what philosophers call *levelling-down*.[11] There are two contexts where we might practice levelling-down in connection with life extension. First, it may arise when it's impossible to provide life extension to everyone who wants it, perhaps because there simply isn't enough money in the world to do so, or perhaps because some people are unable to benefit from life extension for biological reasons that medical science cannot alter. Second, it may be possible to provide it to everyone who wants it, but society fails to do so.

Let's start with the first scenario, where universal access is not possible. If it's simply not possible to provide life extension to everyone, then unequal access to life extension is like unequal access to human organs for transplant. There are not enough hearts available for everyone who needs a heart transplant, but we don't ban heart transplants just because not everyone can get them. In general, we do not think equality requires levelling-down in any context, so intellectual consistency tells us not to require it for life extension. Moreover, prohibiting life extension until it becomes cheap enough to provide it to everyone (and requiring that society provide it to everyone before anyone else gets it) delays the day when that technology becomes cheap enough to provide to everyone, thereby harming those who would live longer if the technology were developed in time for them.

Now consider the second scenario, where it *is* possible to subsidize access to life extension for everyone who wants it but cannot afford it, yet society fails to do this. Is *that* a reason to prohibit life extension? The very question implies that some people have an obligation to help fund the subsidy. If *everyone* who is rich enough to have that obligation refuses to pay it, then perhaps justice requires prohibiting life extension until they step up to the plate and do their duty to the rest of society. However, things will be more complicated in the real

---

[11] Walter Glannon argues for this approach (2002b, 292–293).

world. There will be some rich people who are willing to be taxed for this, and some who even donate to charities to provide it. The problem is that prohibiting life extension altogether punishes the generous ones along with the selfish ones.

Moreover, we do not outlaw medicine just because not all the poor receive publicly subsidized healthcare, nor do we think we should. To be consistent, we should therefore not prohibit life extension in those circumstances either. There is also a question about *why* we cannot get society to fund life extension for everyone but can manage to prohibit life extension altogether. If we have the social discipline to prohibit it, we probably have the social discipline to subsidize it. If so, then prohibiting it when we could be subsidizing it for everyone amounts to a kind of preventive levelling-down.

Should We Prohibit Life Extension Until We Address Other Needs?

The second question is whether society should prohibit life extension until other, more pressing social needs have been met. This objection takes the point of view of what I call a *total planner*, someone who has the power to decide the distribution of all goods, and who, therefore, can effectively refuse to distribute life extension to anyone until other needs, such as basic healthcare, have been met.

However, the parties who will be in a position to decide how to distribute life extension will not be total planners. They will be *partial planners* – people or agencies with the power to determine the distribution of only certain goods. Even if it is true that other needs are more pressing and should be met first, the problem is that refusing to let anyone have access to life extension until those needs are met does not make it more likely that those needs will be met. If withholding life extension would make it more likely that other needs would be met, perhaps the objection would have significant weight. However, withholding life extension when doing so makes no difference merely denies a great benefit to some people without conferring a benefit on anyone else.

Conclusion

Life extension, like many things, is not altogether good or altogether bad. When we ask whether it is *desirable*, we must ask whether the considerations and arguments in favor of life extension outweigh those against it. I have argued that the arguments against the desirability of extended life are mostly bad arguments. To the extent that those arguments have merit, they apply to immortality, where we cannot die, not to extended life, where we can. Moreover, the decision to extend your life will be a reversible decision; if you get it wrong by living too long, you can terminate that life.

When we ask whether life extension is *morally permissible* we must think about whether it will be made available to everyone who wants it even if they cannot afford it, and whether it will cause severe overpopulation. I have argued that justice requires society to subsidize life extension to make it as widely available as reasonably possible. I have also argued (based on demographic projections) that a genuine Malthusian catastrophe is likely if a large portion of the human race use life extension and they have more than one child per woman. My support for developing life extension and making it available is therefore conditioned upon society subsidizing life extension for those who cannot afford it, and upon society imposing strict limits on reproduction for those who extend their lives (these limits would not apply to those who do not use life extension).

If we fail to prevent life extension from causing intolerable overpopulation, or fail to make it as widely available as we reasonably can, then, in my judgment, the considerations against life extension will outweigh those in favor of it. I am optimistic that we *can* do these things. Whether we *will* is a question we will answer with our actions over time.

References

AARP Public Policy Institute. 2007. *Women and Long-Term Care.* Washington, DC: AARP Fact Sheet number 77 R. https://assets.aarp.org/rgcenter/il/fs77r_ltc .pdf

Abraham, William E. 1962. *The Mind of Africa.* Chicago, IL: The University of Chicago Press.

Ackerman, Felicia Nimue. 2007. 'Death is a Punch in the Jaw'. In *The Oxford Handbook of Bioethics*, ed. Bonnie Steinbock, 324–48. Oxford: Oxford University Press.

Adams, Robert Merrihew. 1999. *Finite and Infinite Goods: A Framework for Ethics.* Oxford: Oxford University Press.

2006. *A Theory of Virtue.* New York: Oxford University Press.

Aiyar, Shekhar, Christian H. Ebeke, and Xiaobo Shao. 2016. 'The Impact of Workforce Aging on European Productivity'. *IMF Working Papers* WP/16/238. Washington, DC: International Monetary Fund.

Alber, Erdmute, Tabea Häberlein, and Jeannett Martin. 2010. 'Changing Webs of Kinship: Spotlights on West Africa'. *Africa Spectrum* 45(3): 43–67.

Alexandrova, Anna. 2017. *A Philosophy for the Science of Well-being.* Oxford: Oxford University Press.

Alighieri, Dante. 1321. *La Divina Commedia.* http://dantelab.dartmouth.edu/read er?reader%5Bpanel_count%5D=4

Alvarez, Allen, Lumberto Mendoza, and Peter Danielson. 2015. 'Mixed Views about Radical Life Extension'. *Etikki i praksis Nordic Journal of Applied Ethics* 9(1): 87–110.

Alzheimer's Society. 2014. *Dementia UK: Update*, 2nd ed. London: Alzheimer's Society.

American Association of Suicidology. 2017. '"Suicide" is not the same as "Physician Aid in Dying"'. *Statement of The American Association of Suicidology* (October 30). https://bit.ly/3CjngQq

American Psychiatric Association. 2013. *Diagnostic and Statistical Manual of Mental Disorders: DSM-5.* Washington, DC: American Psychiatric Association.

Améry, Jean. 1994. *On Aging: Revolt and Resignation.* Bloomington/Indianapolis: Indiana University Press.

Ames, Roger. 2010. "Achieving Personal Identity in Confucian Role Ethics." *Oriens Extremus* 49: 143–166.

Anderson, Elizabeth. 1993. *Value in Ethics and Economics.* Cambridge, MA: Harvard University Press.

Anedo, Onukwube. 2012. 'A Cultural Analysis of Harmony and Conflict'. *Unizik Journal of Arts and Humanities* 13: 16–52.

Angell, Marcia. 2004. 'The Quality of Mercy'. In *Physician-Assisted Dying: The Case for Palliative Care and Patient Choice*, ed. Timothy E. Quill and Margaret Pabst Battin, 15–23. Baltimore and London: Johns Hopkins University Press.

Anton, Audrey L. 2016. 'How Long Should People Work? The Debate over the Retiring Age'. In *The Palgrave Handbook of the Philosophy of Aging*, ed. Geoffrey Scarre, 495–516. Basingstoke: Palgrave Macmillan.

Appel, Lora, Eva Appel, Orly Bogler, Micaela Wiseman, Leedan Cohen, Natalie Ein, Howard B. Abrams, et al. 2019. 'Older Adults With Cognitive and/or Physical Impairments Can Benefit from Immersive Virtual Reality Experiences: A Feasibility Study'. *Frontiers in Medicine* 6(329): 1–13.

Appiah, Anthony. 1998. 'Ethical Systems, African'. In *Routledge Encyclopedia of Philosophy*, ed. Edward Craig. London: Routledge. https://bit.ly/3yUpHbu

Applewhite, Ashton. 2017. 'A Stigma Rooted in Denial: On Ageism and "Aging Thoughtfully"'. *Los Angeles Review of Books* (November 2). https://bit.ly/2XQ3tJA

2019. *This Chair Rocks: A Manifesto Against Ageism*. New York: Celadon Books.

Aristotle. 1954. *The Nicomachean Ethics*, trans. David W. Ross. London: Oxford University Press.

2005. *Nicomachean Ethics*, 2nd ed., trans. Terence Irwin. Indianapolis, IN: Hackett.

Arneson, Richard. 1998. Commentary for BEARS (Brown Electronic Article Review Service) Symposium on John Kekes's 'A Question for Egalitarians' (26 February). www.brown.edu/Departments/Philosophy/bears/9803arne.html

2002. 'Egalitarianism'. In *The Stanford Encyclopedia of Philosophy*, ed. Edward N. Zalta. https://plato.stanford.edu/entries/egalitarianism/

Arnquist, Sarah. 2009. 'How Old Do You Feel? It Depends on Your Age'. *The New York Times* (30 June). www.nytimes.com/2009/06/30/health/30aging.html

Arnsperger, Christian and Philippe Van Parijs. 2004. *Economic and Social Ethics*. Sao Paulo: Loyola.

Arpaly, Nomy. 2005. 'How it is Not Just Like Diabetes: Mental Disorders and the Moral Psychologist'. *Philosophical Issues* 15: 282–98.

Ash, Elliott and William Bentley MacLeod. 2020. 'Mandatory Retirement for Judges Improved Performance on U.S. State Supreme Court'. *National Bureau of Economic Research (NBER) Working Paper Series 28025*. Cambridge, MA: NBER Inc. www.nber.org/papers/w28025

Auden, W. H. 2019 [2002]. *Lectures on Shakespeare*, ed. Arthur C. Kirsch. Princeton, NJ: Princeton University Press.

Awad, Edmond, Sohan Dsouza, Richard Kim, et al. 2018. 'The Moral Machine Experiment'. *Nature* 563: 59–65.

Baars, Jan. 2012. *Aging and the Art of Living*. Baltimore, MD: Johns Hopkins University Press.

2020. 'Living in a Temporal Perspective. Aging between Metric and Narrative Time'. In *Aging and Human Nature*, eds. Mark Schweda, Michael Coors, and Claudia Bozzaro, 113–27. Cham: Springer.

Baezner-Sailer, Elke M. 2008. Physician-Assisted Suicide in Switzerland: A Personal Report. In *Giving Death a Helping Hand. International Library of Ethics, Law, and the New Medicine*, eds. D. Birnbacher and E. Dahl, 141–8. Dordrecht: Springer.

Bai, Tongdong. 2019. *Against Political Equality: The Confucian Case*. Princeton, NJ: Princeton University Press.

Balasubramaniam, Meera. 2018. 'Rational Suicide in Elderly Adults: A Clinician's Perspective'. *Journal of the American Geriatrics Society* 66(5): 998–1001.

Barnes, Julian. 1989. *A History of the World in 10½ Chapters*. New York: Vintage Books.

2008. *Nothing to Be Frightened Of*. London: Random House Canada.

Bartky, Sandra Lee. 1999. 'Unplanned Obsolescence: Some Reflections on Aging'. In *Mother Time: Women, Aging, and Ethics*, ed. Margaret Urban Walker, 61–74. Maryland, MD: Rowman and Littlefield.

Bash, Anthony. 2007. *Forgiveness and Christian Ethics*. Cambridge: Cambridge University Press.

Bates, Winton. 2009. 'Gross National Happiness'. *Asian-Pacific Economic Literature* 23(2): 1–16.

Battin, Margaret Pabst. 1999. 'Can Suicide Be Rational? Yes, Sometimes'. In *Contemporary Perspectives on Rational Suicide*, ed. James L. Werth, Jr., 13–21. Philadelphia, PA: Brunner/Mazel.

Bearon, Lucille B. 1996. 'Successful Aging: What Does the "Good life" Look Like'. *The Forum* 1(3).

Beauvoir, Simone de. 1989. *The Second Sex*. New York: Vintage.

1996. *The Coming of Age*. New York: WW Norton and Company.

Bell, Daniel A. and Chenyang Li, eds. 2013. *The East Asian Challenge for Democracy*. New York: Cambridge University Press.

Bell, Daniel A. and Thaddeus Metz. 2011. 'Confucianismand Ubuntu: Reflections on a Dialogue between Chinese and African Traditions'. *Journal of Chinese Philosophy* 38(S1): 78–95.

Bell, Daniel A. and Yingchuan Mo. 2014. 'Harmony in the World 2013: The Ideal and the Reality'. *Social Indicators Research* 118: 797–818.

Bell, Nora K. 1989. 'What Setting Limits May Mean: A Feminist Critique of Daniel Callahan's Setting Limits'. *Hypatia* 4(2): 169–78.

Benatar, David. 2006. *Better Never to Have Been: The Harm of Coming into Existence*. New York: Oxford University Press.

2012. *The Second Sexism: Discrimination Against Men and Boys*. Chichester, UK: Wiley-Blackwell.

Bennett, Catherine. 2018. 'We Applaud the Active Old but If They Carry On for Ever, the Young May Lose Out'. *The Guardian* (2 December). https://bit.ly /3GoR5Sc

Bennett, Gilllian. 2014. 'Goodbye and Good Luck!' *DeadAtNoon*. http://deadatnoon
.com

Bidadanure, Juliana Uhuru. 2017. 'Discrimination and Age'. In *The Routledge Handbook of the Ethics of Discrimination*, ed. Kasper Lippert-Rasmussen, 243–53. New York: Routledge.

2021. *Justice Across Age: Treating Young and Old as Equals.* New York: Oxford University Press.

Forthcoming. 'Justice between Coexisting Generations'. In *The Oxford Handbook of Intergenerational Ethics*, ed. Stephen M. Gardiner. New York: Oxford University Press. https://bit.ly/3qeVcZT

Blackham, Alycia. 2016. *Extending Working Life for Older Workers: Age Discrimination Law, Policy, and Practice.* Oxford: Hart Press.

Blanchflower, David G. 2021. 'Is Happiness U-Shaped Everywhere? Age and Subjective Well-Being in 145 Countries'. *Journal of Population Economics* 34(2): 575–624.

Blanchflower, David G. and Andrew J. Oswald. 2008. 'Is Well-Being U-Shaped Over the Life Cycle?' *Social Science and Medicine* 66: 1733–49.

2009. 'The U-Shape Without Controls: A Response to Glenn." *Social Science and Medicine* 69(4): 486–8.

Boorse, Christopher. 1976. 'What a Theory of Mental Health Should Be'. *Journal for the Theory of Social Behavior* 6: 61–84.

Bradford, Gwen. 2015. *Achievement.* Oxford: Oxford University Press.

Bradley, Ben. 2004. 'When is Death Bad for the One Who Dies?' *Nous* 1–28.

2015. 'Is Death Bad for A Cow?' In *The Ethics of Killing Animals*, eds. Tatjana Visak and Robert Garner, 51–64. Oxford: Oxford University Press.

Bråkenhielm, Carl Reinhold. 1993. *Forgiveness*, trans. Thor Hall. Minneapolis, MN: Fortress Press.

Brennan, Samantha. 2014. 'The Goods of Childhood and Children's Rights'. In *Family-Making: Contemporary Ethical Challenges*, eds. Françoise Baylis and Carolyn McLeod, 29–48. Oxford: Oxford University Press.

Brighouse, Harry and Adam Swift. 2014. *Family Values: The Ethics of Parent-Child Relationships.* Princeton, NJ: Princeton University Press.

Brodkey, Harold. 1996. *This Wild Darkness.* New York: Henry Holt.

Browning, Christopher R. 1998. *Ordinary Men: Reserve Police Battalion 101 and the Final Solution in Poland*, 2nd ed. New York: HarperCollins.

Bujo, Bénézet. 1997. *The Ethical Dimension of Community*, Cecilia Namulondo Nganda, trans. Nairobi: Paulines Publications.

Bujo, Bénézet. 2005. 'Differentiations in African Ethics'. In *The Blackwell Companion to Religious Ethics*, ed. William Schweiker. Malden, MA: Blackwell, 423–37.

Burroughs, Augusten. 2002. *Running with Scissors: A Memoir.* New York: Picador.

Burrow, John Anthony. 1986. *The Ages of Man: A Study in Medieval Writing and Thought.* Oxford: Clarendon Press.

Burton, Diana Helen. 1997. *The Search for Immortality in Archaic Greek Myth*. Doctoral dissertation. London: University College London.

Busby, Eleanor. 2019. 'Oxford Professor Forced to Quit before 70th Birthday Wins Ageism Battle'. *The Independent* (December 31). https://bit.ly/33zcn0v

Butler, Joseph. 1970 [1727]. *Fifteen Sermons Preached at the Rolls Chapel and a Dissertation on Virtue*, ed. Tom Aerwyn Roberts. London: SPCK Publishing.

Buttonwood. 2012. 'Keep on Trucking: Why the Old Should Not Make Way for the Young'. *The Economist* (February 11). https://econ.st/3s9Yi40

Calhoun, Chester. 1992. 'Changing One's Heart'. *Ethics* 103(1): 76–96.

Callahan, Daniel. 1987. *Setting Limits: Medical Goals in an Aging Society*. Washington, DC: Georgetown University Press.

    1998. *False Hopes: Why America's Quest for Perfect Health is a Recipe for Failure*. New York: Simon and Schuster.

Campbell, Stephen M. 2015. 'When the Shape of a Life Matters'. *Ethical Theory and Moral Practice* 18(3): 565–75.

Carr, David. 2016. 'The Story of Our Lives: Aging and Narrative'. In *The Palgrave Handbook of the Philosophy of Aging*, ed. Geoffrey Scarre, 171–85. London: Palgrave Macmillan.

Carstensen, Laura L., Bulent Turan, Susanne Scheibe, Nilam Ram, Hal Ersner-Hershfield, Gregory R. Samanez-Larkin, et al. 2011. Emotional Experience Improves with Age: Evidence Based on Over 10 Years of Experience Sampling'. *Psychology and Aging* 26(1): 21–33.

Casal, Paula. 2007. 'Why Sufficiency is not Enough'. *Ethics* 117(2): 296–326.

    2015. 'Distributive Justice and Female Longevity'. *Law, Ethics and Philosophy* 3: 90–106.

Chabal, Patrick. 2005. *Africa: The Politics of Suffering and Smiling*. London: Zed Books.

Chachine, Isaias. 2008. *Community, Justice, and Freedom: Liberalism, Communitarianism, and African Contributions to Political Ethics*. Uppsala: Uppsala University Library.

Chan, Joseph. 2014. *Confucian Perfectionism: A Political Philosophy for Modern Times*. Princeton, NJ: Princeton University Press.

Chandler, J. 1996. 'Mandatory Retirement and Justice'. *Social Theory and Practice* 22(1): 35–46.

Cheever, John. 1990a. 'The Swimmer'. In *The Stories of John Cheever*, 776–88. London: Vintage.

    1990b. 'The World of Applies'. In *The Stories of John Cheever*, 789–802. London: Vintage.

    2010. *The Journals of John Cheever*. London: Vintage.

Christianson, Eric S. 2006. *Ecclesiastes through the Centuries*. Hoboken, NJ: Wiley-Blackwell.

Cohen, Jon. 2015. 'Death-Defying Experiments: Pushing the Limits of Life Span in Animals Could Someday Help Lengthen Our Own'. *Science* 350(6265): 1186–7.

Cole, Thomas R. 1992. *The Journey of Life: A Cultural History of Aging in America*. Cambridge: Cambridge University Press.

Comer, Amber Rose, Margaret Gaffney, Cynthia L. Stone, and Alexia Torke. 2017. 'Physician Understanding and Application of Surrogate Decision-Making Laws in Clinical Practice'. *AJOB Empirical Bioethics* 8(3): 198–204.

Confucius. ca. 500 BC. *The Analects*. http://classics.mit.edu//Confucius/analects .html

Conrad, Joseph. 2007 [1900]. *Lord Jim*, eds. Allan H. Simmons and John H. Stape. Harmondsworth: Penguin Classics.

Conselice, Christopher J., Aaron Wilkinson, Kenneth Duncan, and Alice Mortlock. 2016. 'The Evolution of Galaxy Number Density at Z < 8 and its Implication'. *The Astrophysical Journal* 830(83): 1–17.

Conwell, Yeates, Paul R. Duberstein, and Eric D. Caine. 2002. 'Risk Factors for Suicide in Later Life'. *Biological Psychiatry* 52(3): 193–204.

Conwell, Yeates, Kimberly Van Orden, and Eric D. Caine. 2011. 'Suicide in Older Adults'. *Psychiatric Clinics of North America* 34(2): 451–68.

Cormier, Andree-Anne and Mauro Rossi. 2019. 'Is Children's Wellbeing Different from Adults' Wellbeing?' *Canadian Journal of Philosophy* 49(8): 1146–68.

Corna, Laurie M., John Cairney, David L. Streiner. 2010. 'Suicide Ideation in Older Adults: Relationship to Mental Health Problems and Service Use'. *Gerontologist* 50(6): 785–97.

Cowley, Christopher. 2016. 'Coming to Terms with Old Age – And Death'. In *The Palgrave Handbook of the Philosophy of Aging*, ed. Geoffrey Scarre, 187–206. London: Palgrave Macmillan.

Crisp, Roger. 1997. *Routledge Philosophy Guidebook to Mill on Utilitarianism*. London: Routledge.

2004. *Aristotle: Nicomachean Ethics*. Cambridge: Cambridge University Press.

Croll, Elisabeth. 2006. 'The Intergenerational Contract in the Changing Asian Family'. *Oxford Development Studies* 34: 473–91.

Csikszentmihalyi, Mihaly. 1990. *Flow: The Psychology of Optimal Experience*. New York: Harper and Row.

Damasio, Antonio R. 1994. *Descartes' Error: Emotion, Reason, and the Human Brain*. New York: Random House.

Daniels, Norman. 1996. *Justice and Justification: Reflective Equilibrium in Theory and Practice*. Cambridge: Cambridge University Press.

2003. 'Reflective Equilibrium'. *The Stanford Encyclopedia of Philosophy*, ed. Edward N. Zalta. https://stanford.io/3dZa8pf

2007. *Just Health: Meeting Health Needs Fairly*. Cambridge: Cambridge University Press.

Davis, Dena S. 2014. 'Alzheimer Disease and Pre-emptive Suicide'. *Journal of Medical Ethics* 40(8): 543–9.

Davis, John K. 2004. 'Precedent Autonomy and Subsequent Consent'. *Ethical Theory and Moral Practice* 7(3): 267–91.

Deaton, Angus. 2008. 'Worldwide, Residents of Richer Nations More Satisfied'. *Gallup.*

de Bellaigue, Christopher. 2019. 'Death on Demand: Has Euthanasia Gone Too Far?' *The Guardian* (January 18). https://bit.ly/31ZBhpD

DeGrazia, David. 2005. *Human Identity and Bioethics.* Washington, DC: Cambridge University Press.

2010. 'Is it Wrong to Impose the Harms of Human Life? A Reply to Benatar'. *Theoretical Medicine and Bioethics* 31(4): 317–31.

2012. *Creation Ethics: Reproduction, Genetics, and Quality of Life.* New York: Oxford University Press.

De Grey, Aubrey and Michael Rae. 2007. *Ending Aging: The Rejuvenation Breakthroughs That Could Reverse Human Aging in Our Lifetime.* New York: St. Martin's Griffin Press.

De Lazari-Radek, Katarzyna and Peter Singer, eds. 2014. *The Point of View of the Universe.* Oxford: Oxford University Press.

Demakakos, Panayotes, Elizabeth Hacker, and Edlira Gjonça. 2006. 'Perceptions of Ageing'. In *Retirement, Health, and Relationships of the Older Population in England: The 2004 English Longitudinal Study of Ageing (Wave 2)*, eds. James Banks, Elizabeth Breeze, Carli Lessuf, and James Nazroo, 339–66. London: The Institute for Fiscal Studies.

De Medeiros, Kate. 2018. 'What Can Thinking Like a Gerontologist Bring to Bioethics?' *The Hastings Center Report: What Makes a Good Life in Late Life? Citizenship and Justice in Aging Societies* 48(5): S10-S14.

Derrida, Jacques. 2001. *On Cosmopolitanism and Forgiveness.* London: Routledge.

Deutscher, Penelope. 2003. 'Beauvoir's Old Age'. In *The Cambridge Companion to Simone de Beauvoir*, ed. Claudia Card, 286–304. Cambridge: Cambridge University Press.

Diener, Ed, Richard E. Lucas, and Shigehiro Oishi. 2002. 'Subjective Well-Being: The Science of Happiness and Life Satisfaction'. In *Handbook of Positive Psychology*, eds. Charles Richard Snyder and Shane J. Lopez, 63–73. New York: Oxford University Press.

Dillon, Robin. 2001. 'Self-Forgiveness and Self-Respect'. *Ethics* 112(1): 53–83.

Dixon, Nicholas. 1995. 'The Friendship Model of Filial Obligations'. *Journal of Applied Philosophy* 12(1): 77–87.

Docquier, Frédéric and Hillel Rapoport. 2012. 'Globalization, Brain Drain, and Development'. *Journal of Economic Literature* 50(3): 681–730.

Dolan, P. 2014. *Happiness by Design: Finding Pleasure and Purpose in Everyday Life.* London: Penguin Books.

Dorsey, Dale. 2015. 'The Significance of a Life's Shape'. *Ethics* 125(2): 303–30.

Dove, Mary. 1986. *The Perfect Age of Man's Life.* Cambridge: Cambridge University Press.

Dowbiggin, Ian. 2011. *The Quest for Mental Health.* Cambridge: Cambridge University Press.

Downie, Jocelyn. 2018. 'An Alternative to Medical Assistance in Dying? The Legal Status of Voluntary Stopping Eating and Drinking (VSED)'. *Canadian Journal of Bioethics* 1(2): 48–58.

Dragojlovic, Nick. 2013. 'Canadians' Support for Radical Life Extension Resulting from Advances in Regenerative Medicine'. *Journal of Aging Studies* 27(2): 151–8.

Dresser, Rebecca. 1995. 'Dworkin On Dementia: Elegant Theory, Questionable Policy'. *Hastings Center Report* 25(6): 32–8.

Du Plessix Gray, Francine. 1996. 'The Third Age'. *The New Yorker* (February 26): 186. www.newyorker.com/magazine/1996/02/26/the-third-age

—— 1994. *Life's Dominion: An Argument about Abortion, Euthanasia, and Individual Freedom.* New York: Vintage.

Dyke, Heather, ed. 2003. *Time and Ethics: Essays at the Intersection.* Dordrecht: Springer.

Eberl, Jason T. 2020. *The Nature of Human Persons: Metaphysics and Bioethics.* Notre Dame: University of Notre Dame Press.

Ebert, Roger. 1968. 'The Swimmer'. *Reviews.* www.rogerebert.com/reviews/the-swimmer-1968

Ehrenreich, Barbara. 2018. *Natural Causes: An Epidemic of Wellness, the Certainty of Dying, and Killing Ourselves to Live Longer.* New York: Hachette Book Group.

Eidinow, Esther. 2011. *Luck, Fate and Fortune: Antiquity and its Legacy.* London: Tauris.

Eliot, T. S. 1970 [1943]. *Four Quartets.* London: Faber and Faber.

—— 1986 [1963] '"East Coker", V, Four Quartets'. In *Collected Poems 1909-1962*, 201–2. London; Boston, MA: Faber and Faber.

Emanuel, Ezekiel J. 2014. 'Why I Hope to Die at 75'. *The Atlantic* (October). https://bit.ly/3E0sFvX

Engelhardt, H. Tristram Jr. 1986. *The Foundations of Bioethics*, 2nd ed. New York: Oxford University Press.

English, Jane. 1992. 'What Do Grown Children Owe Their Parents?' In *Aging and Ethics*, ed. Nancy Jecker. New York: Springer, 147–54.

Enkvist, Åsa, Henrik Edström, and Sölve Elmståhl. 2012. 'What Factors Affect Life Satisfaction Among the Oldest Old?' *Archives of Gerontology and Geriatrics* 54 (1): 140–5.

Epictetus. 2008 [1768]. *Discourses and Selected Writing*, trans. Robert F. Dobbin. New York: Penguin.

Erikson, Erik H. and Joan M. Erikson. 1998. *The Life Cycle Completed (Extended Version).* New York: WW Norton and Company.

Estabrooks, Carole A. and Janice Keefe. 2020. 'COVID-19 Crisis in Nursing Homes is a Gender Crisis'. *Policy Options Politiques* (May 19). https://bit.ly/3DYSTis

Fan, Ruiping. 2007. 'Which Care? Whose Responsibility? And Why Family? A Confucian Account of Long-Term Care for the Elderly'. *Journal of Medicine and Philosophy* 32: 495–517.

2010. *Reconstructionist Confucianism: Rethinking Morality after the West.* Dordrecht: Springer.

Farrelly, Colin. 2017. 'Justice and Life Extension'. In *Ethics at the End of Life: New Issues and Arguments*, ed. John K. Davis, 235–47. New York: Routledge.

2019. 'Aging, Geroscience, and Freedom'. *Rejuvenation Research* 22(2): 163–70.

Farwell, Paul. 1995. 'Aristotle and the Complete Life'. *History of Philosophy Quarterly* 12(3): 247–63.

Fass, Paula S. 2016. 'The End of Adolescence'. *Aeon* (October 26). https://bit.ly /3yujMJK

Feldman, Fred. 2004. *Pleasure and the Good Life: Concerning the Nature, Varieties, and Plausibility of Hedonism.* Cambridge, MA: Harvard University Press.

Finnis, John. 1995. 'A Philosophical Case Against Euthanasia'. In *Euthanasia Examined: Ethical, Clinical, and Legal Perspectives*, ed. John Keown, 23–35. Cambridge: Cambridge University Press.

Firlik, Andrew D. 1991. 'Margo's Logo'. *Journal of the American Medical Association* 265(2): 201.

Fletcher, Guy. 2016. 'Objective List Theories'. In *The Routledge Handbook of Philosophy of Well-Being*, ed. Guy Fletcher, 148–60. Abingdon: Routledge.

Fletcher, Joseph. 1954. *Morals and Medicine.* Princeton, NJ: Princeton University Press.

1972. 'Indicators of Humanhood: A Tentative Profile of Man'. *Hastings Center Report* 2(5): 1–4.

Fleurbaey, Marc, Marie-Louise Leroux, and Grégory Ponthière. 2014. 'Compensating the Dead'. *Journal of Mathematical Economics* 51: 28–41.

Ford, Ford Madox. 2008 [1915]. *The Good Soldier*, ed. Thomas C. Moser. Oxford: Oxford University Press.

Franklin-Hall, Andrew. 2013. 'On Becoming an Adult: Autonomy and the Moral Relevance of Life's Stages'. *The Philosophical Quarterly* 63(251): 223-47.

Frijters, Paul and Tony Beatton. 2012. The Mystery of the U-Shaped Relationship between Happiness and Age. *Journal of Economic Behavior and Organization* 82(2–3): 525–42.

Ganzini, Linda, Elizabeth R. Goy, and Steven K. Dobscha. 2009. 'Why Oregon Patients Request Assisted Death: Family Members' Views'. *Journal of General Internal Medicine* 23(2): 154–7.

Garrard, Eve. 2003. 'Forgiveness and the Holocaust'. In *Moral Philosophy and the Holocaust*, eds. Eve Garrard and Geoffrey Scarre, 231–45. Aldershot: Ashgate.

Garrard, Eve and David McNaughton. 2010. *Forgiveness.* Durham: Acumen.

Garson, Justin. 2019. *What Biological Functions Are and Why They Matter.* Cambridge: Cambridge University Press.

Gaster, Barak, Eric B. Larson, and J. Randall Curtis. 2017. 'Advance Directives for Dementia: Meeting a Unique Challenge'. *Journal of the American Medical Association* 318(22): 2175–6.

Gawande, Atul. 2014. *Being Mortal: Medicine and What Matters in the End.* Toronto: Doubleday Canada.

Gheaus, Anca. 2015a. 'Unfinished Adults and Defective Children: On the Nature of Value of Childhood'. *Journal of Ethics and Social Philosophy* 9(1): 1–21.

2015b. 'The "Intrinsic Goods of Childhood" and the Just Society'. In *The Nature of Children's Wellbeing: Theory and Practice*, eds. Alexander Bagattini and Colin Macleod, 35–52. Dordrecht: Springer.

Gibson, Diane. 1996. 'Broken Down by Age and Gender: "The Problem of Old Women" Redefined'. *Gender and Society* 10(4): 433–48.

Glannon, Walter. 2002a. 'Extending the Human Life Span'. *Journal of Medicine and Philosophy* 27(30) 339–54.

2002b. 'Reply to Harris'. *Bioethics* 16(3): 292–7.

Glover, Jonathan. 1977. *Causing Death and Saving Lives: The Moral Problems of Abortion, Infanticide, Suicide, Euthanasia, Capital Punishment, War and Other Life-Or-Death Choices.* London: Pelican Books.

Gosseries, Axel. 2008. 'Theories of Intergenerational Justice: A Synopsis'. *SAPIENS* 1(1): 61–71.

2009. 'Three Models of Intergenerational Reciprocity'. In *Intergenerational Justice*, eds. Axel Gosseries and Lukas H. Meyer, 119–46. Oxford: Oxford University Press.

2011. 'Qu'est-Ce Que Le Suffisantisme?' *Philosophiques* 38(2): 465–92.

2014. 'What Makes Age Discrimination Special? A Philosophical Look at the ECJ Case Law'. *Netherlands Journal of Legal Philosophy* 43(1): 59–80.

Forthcoming. 'Generational Metaphors'. In *Oxford Handbook of Intergenerational Ethics*, ed. Stephen M. Gardiner. Oxford: Oxford University Press.

Gosseries, Axel and Danielle Zwarthoed. 2016. 'Generations and Global Justice'. In *Global Political Theory*, eds. David Held and Pietro Maffetone, 281–304. Cambridge: Polity Press.

Govier, Trudy Rose. 1999. 'Forgiveness and the Unforgivable'. *American Philosophical Quarterly* 36(1): 59–75.

2002. *Forgiveness and Revenge.* New York: Routledge.

Graham, Carol, and Julia Ruiz Pozuelo. 2017. 'Happiness, Stress, and Age: How the U Curve Varies Across People and Places'. *Journal of Population Economics* 30 (1): 225–64.

Graham, George. 2013. *The Disordered Mind.* Abingdon: Routledge.

Griffiths, John, Heleen Weyers, and Maurice Adams. 2008. *Euthanasia and Law in Europe.* Oxford: Hart Publishing.

Griffiths, Paul E. and John Matthewson. 2018. 'Evolution, Dysfunction, and Disease: A Reappraisal'. *British Journal for the Philosophy of Science* 69: 301–27.

Griswold, Charles L. 2007. *Forgiveness: A Philosophical Exploration.* New York: Cambridge University Press.

Gullette, Margaret Morganroth. 2004. *Aged by Culture.* Chicago, IL: University of Chicago Press.

2018. 'Ageism Ignores and Insults the Competence of Adults'. *Cognoscenti* (July 12). https://wbur.fm/3ytJBd7

2019. 'Unwanted at Midlife: Not Old but "Too Old"'. Los Angeles Review of Books. February 20. https://bit.ly/3s7dlLG

Gwozdz, Wencke and Alfonso Sousa-Poza. 2010. 'Ageing, Health, and Life Satisfaction of the Oldest Old: An Analysis for Germany'. *Social Indicators Research* 97(3): 397–417.

Gyekye, Kwame. 1992. 'Traditional Political Ideas: Their Relevance to Development in Contemporary Africa'. In *Person and Community; Ghanaian Philosophical Studies, I.* eds. Kwasi Wiredu and Kwame Gyekye. Washington, DC: Council for Research in Values and Philosophy, 243–55.

1997. *Tradition and Modernity: Philosophical Reflections on the African Experience.* New York: Oxford University Press.

2010. 'African Ethics'. In *The Stanford Encyclopedia of Philosophy*, ed. Edward Zalta. https://stanford.io/3yEBGJV

Hannan, Sarah. 2018. 'Why Childhood is Bad for Children'. *Journal of Applied Philosophy* 35: 11–28.

Harlow, John Martyn. 1868. 'Recovery from the Passage of an Iron Bar through the Head'. *Publications of the Massachusetts Medical Society* 2: 327–47.

Harpham, Wendy S. 2019. 'View From the Other Side of the Stethoscope: Introducing "The New Normal" for Now'. *Oncology Times* 41(19): 12.

Harris, John. 1985. *The Value of Life: An Introduction to Medical Ethics.* London: Routledge and Kegan Paul.

2000. 'Intimations of Immortality'. *Science* 288 (5463): 59.

2005. 'The Age-Indifference Principle and Equality'. *Cambridge Quarterly of Healthcare Ethics* 14(1): 93–9.

Hatton, Celia. 2015. Mother or Girlfriend––Who Do You Save? BBC News 28 September, www.bbc.com/news/blogs-china-blog-34377611

Hauskeller, Michael. 2020. *The Meaning of Life and Death: Ten Classic Thinkers on the Ultimate Question.* London: Bloomsbury Academic.

Haybron, Dan. 2019. 'Happiness'. In *The Stanford Encyclopedia of Philosophy*, ed. Edward N. Zalta. https://plato.stanford.edu/entries/happiness/

Heathwood, Chris. 2005. 'The Problem of Defective Desires'. *Australasian Journal of Philosophy* 83(4): 487–504.

Heidegger, Martin. 2008. *Being and Time.* New York: Harper and Row.

Heilbrun, Carolyn G. 1998. *The Last Gift of Time: Life Beyond Sixty.* New York: Ballantine Books.

Henig, Robin Marantz. 2015. 'The Last Day of Her Life'. *The New York Times Magazine* (May 14). https://nyti.ms/3yj0IhK

Henrich, Joseph, Steven Heine, and Ara Norenzayan. 2010. 'The Weirdest People in the World?' *Behavioral and Brain Sciences* 33: 61–135.

Hieronymi, Pamela. 2001. 'Articulating an Uncompromising Forgiveness'. *Philosophy and Phenomenological Research* 62(3): 529–55.

Hilton, Tim. 2000. *John Ruskin: The Later Years.* London: Yale University Press.

Holden, Constance. 2002. 'The Quest to Reverse Time's Toll'. *Science* 295(5557): 1032–3.

Holm, Soren. 1996. 'The Moral Status of the Pre-personal Human Being: The Argument From Potential Reconsidered'. In *Conceiving the Embryo*, eds. Donald Evans and Neil Pickering, 193–220. Dordrecht: Klüwer.

2013. 'The Implicit Anthropology of Bioethics and the Problem of the Aging Person'. In *Ethics, Health Policy and (Anti-) Aging: Mixed Blessings*, eds. Maartje Schermer and Wim Pinxten, 59–71. Dordrecht: Springer.

2016. 'What Do the Old Owe the Young?' In *The Palgrave Handbook of the Philosophy of Aging*, ed. Geoffrey Scarre, 385–400. London: Palgrave Macmillan.

2020. 'Wise Old Men (and Women): Recovering a Positive Anthropology of Aging'. In *Aging and Human Nature*, eds. Mark Schweda, Michael Coors, and Claudie Bozzaro, 233–40. Cham: Springer.

Holmgren, Margaret R. 2012. *Forgiveness and Retribution: Responding to Wrongdoing*. New York: Cambridge University Press.

Holowchak, Mark Andrew. 2008. *The Stoics: A Guide for the Perplexed*. London/ New York: A&C Black.

Horsdal, Marianne. 2011. *Telling Lives: Exploring Dimensions of Narratives*. Abingdon: Routledge.

Howell, Elizabeth. 2018. 'How Many Stars Are in the Milky Way?' www.space.com /25959-how-many-stars-are-in-the-milky-way.html

Hubbard, Thomas K. 1985. *The Pindaric Mind: A Study of Logical Structure in Early Greek Poetry*. Leiden: Brill Archive.

Hudson, Frederic M. 1999. *The Adult Years. Mastering the Art of Self-Renewal*. San Francisco, CA: Jossey-Bass Publishers.

Hume, David. 1985. 'My Own Life'. In *Essays: Moral, Political, and Literary*, ed. Eugene F. Miller, xxi–xli. Indianapolis, IN: Liberty Classics.

Humphry, Derek. 1991. *Final Exit: The Practicalities of Self-Deliverance and Assisted Suicide for the Dying*. Eugene, OR: Hemlock Society.

Huppert, Felicia A. and Timothy T. C. So. 2013. "Flourishing Across Europe: Application of a New Conceptual Framework for Defining Well-Being." *Social Indicators Research* 110(3): 837–861.

Hurka, Thomas. 2001. *Virtue, Vice, and Value*. New York: Oxford University Press.

Hursthouse, Rosalind. 1999. *On Virtue Ethics*. Oxford: Oxford University Press.

Huxtable, Richard and Maaike Möller. 2007. "'Setting a Principled Boundary"? Euthanasia as a Response to "Life Fatigue"'. *Bioethics* 21(3): 117–26.

Ikuenobe, Polycarp. 2006. *Philosophical Perspectives on Communalism and Morality in African Traditions*. Lanham, MD: Lexington.

Irwin, Terence H. 1985. 'Permanent happiness: Aristotle and Solon'. In *Oxford Studies in Ancient Philosophy*, Volume III, ed. Julia Annas, 89–124. Oxford: Oxford University Press.

1999. *Aristotle: Nicomachean Ethics*. Indianapolis, IN: Hackett.

Jacoby, Susan. 2011. *Never Say Die: The Myth and Marketing of the New Old Age*. New York: Pantheon.

Jecker, Nancy S. 1990. 'The Role of Intimate Others in Medical Decision Making'. *The Gerontologist* 30: 65–71.

    2013. 'Justice between Age Groups: An Objection to the Prudential Lifespan Approach'. *The American Journal of Bioethics* 13(8): 3–15.

    2020a. *Ending Midlife Bias: New Values for Old Age.* Oxford: Oxford University Press.

    2020b. 'African Conceptions of Age-Based Moral Standing'. *Hastings Center Report* 50: 35–43.

Jecker, Nancy, Joseph Carrese, and Robert Pearlman. 1995. 'Caring for Patients in Cross-Cultural Settings'. *Hastings Center Report* 25: 6–14.

Jeske, Diane. 2008. *Rationality and Moral Theory: How Intimacy Generates Reasons.* New York: Routledge.

    2017. 'Aging, Getting Older, and the Good Life'. In *The Palgrave Handbook of the Philosophy of Aging*, ed. Geoffrey Scarre, 327–45. London: Palgrave Macmillan.

    2019. *Friendship and Social Media: A Philosophical Exploration.* New York: Routledge.

Jeske, Diane, and Richard Fumerton. 1997. 'Relatives and Relativism'. *Philosophical Studies* 87(2): 143–57.

Jeste, Dilip V., Gauri N. Savla, Wesley K. Thompson, et al. 2013. 'Association Between Older Age and More Successful Aging'. *American Journal of Psychiatry* 170(2): 188–96.

Jianxiong, Ge. 2018. 'The "Passing Down" and "Inheritance" of the Traditional Culture'. In *The Collected Works at the Symposium on China Studies 2017*, ed. Chinese Academy of Social Sciences. Beijing: China Social Sciences Press, 93–105.

Joerißen, Peter and Cornelia Will. 1983. *Die Lebenstreppe. Bilder der menschlichen Lebensalter. Städtisches Museum Haus Koekkoek, Kleve.* Köln: Rheinland-Verlag /Habelt.

Johnson, Carl. 2009. 'Freedom and Confucianism'. *International Journal of the Asian Philosophical Association* 1: 52–61.

Jonas, Hans. 1985. *The Imperative of Responsibility: In Search of an Ethics for the Technological Age.* Chicago, IL: University of Chicago Press.

Juengst, Eric T., Robert H. Binstock, Maxwell J. Mehlman, and Stephen G. Post. 2003. 'Aging: Antiaging Research and the Need for Public Dialogue'. *Science* 299(5611): 1323.

Kagan, Shelly. 1998. *Normative Ethics.* Boulder, CO: Westview Press.

Kahneman, Daniel. 2011. *Thinking, Fast and Slow.* London: Penguin.

Kant, Immanuel. 1963 [1930]. *Lectures on Ethics*, trans. Louis Infield. New York: Harper and Row.

    2005 [1785]. *Groundwork of the Metaphysics of Morals*, trans. Jonathan Bennett. Cambridge: Cambridge University Press.

Kass, Leon R. 2004. 'L'Chaim and Its Limits: Why Not Immortality?' In *The Fountain of Youth: Cultural, Scientific, and Ethical Perspectives on a Biomedical Goal*, eds. Stephan G. Post and Robert H. Binstock, 304–20. Oxford: Oxford University Press.

Kaufman, Sharon R. 2015. *Ordinary Medicine: Extraordinary Treatments, Longer Lives, and Where to Draw the Line*. Durham and London: Duke University Press.

Kauppinen, Antti. 2012. 'Meaningfulness and Time'. *Philosophy and Phenomenological Research* 84(2): 345–77.

Kekes, John. 1997. 'A Question for Egalitarians'. *Ethics* 107(4): 658–69.

Kellaway, Lucky. 2012. 'The Best I Can Do for Today's Youth is Quit'. *Financial Times* (January 29). https://on.ft.com/3yDzZwn

Keller, Simon. 2009. 'Welfare as Success'. *Nous* 43(4): 656–83.

2013. *Partiality*. Princeton, NJ: Princeton University Press.

2020. 'What Does Mental Health Have to Do with Well-Being?' *Bioethics* 34(3): 228–34.

Kennedy, David. 2006. *Changing Conceptions of the Child from the Renaissance to Post-modernity: A Philosophy of Childhood*. New York: Edwin Mellen Press.

Kenyon, Gary, Ernst Bohlmeijer, and William L. Randall, eds. 2010. *Storying Later Life: Issues, Investigations, and Interventions in Narrative Gerontology*. Oxford: Oxford University Press.

Keyes. Corey L. M. 2009. 'Toward a Science of Mental Health'. In *Oxford Handbook of Positive Psychology*, eds. C. R. Snyder and S. J. Lopez, 89–95. Oxford: Oxford University Press.

Kohlberg, Lawrence. 1984. *The Psychology of Moral Development*. San Francisco, CA: Harper & Row.

Kohli, Martin, and John W. Meyer. 1986. 'Social Structure and Social Construction of Life Stages'. *Human Development* 29(3): 145–9.

Kolnai, Aurel. 1973. 'Forgiveness'. *Proceedings of the Aristotelian Society* 74: 91–106.

Kotre, John N. 1996. *Outliving the Self: How We Live On in Future Generations*. London/New York: Norton and Co.

Kraut, Richard. 1994. 'Desire and the Human Good'. *Proceedings and Addresses of the American Philosophical Association* 68(2): 39–54.

2007. *What is Good and Why: The Ethics of Well-Being*. Cambridge, MA: Harvard University Press.

2018. *The Quality of Life: Aristotle Revised*. Oxford: Oxford University Press.

Kruse, Andreas. 2016. 'Benefactors or Burdens? The Social Role of the Old'. In *The Palgrave Handbook of the Philosophy of Aging*, ed. Geoffrey Scarre, 401–24. London: Palgrave Macmillan.

Krznaric, Roman. 2017. *Carpe Diem Regained: The Vanishing Art of Seizing the Day*. London: Unbound Publishing.

Kuhse, Hoyt and Peter Singer. 1985. *Should the Baby Live? The Problem of Handicapped Infants*. Oxford: Oxford University Press.

Lacey, Heather P., Dylan M. Smith, and Peter A. Ubel. 2006. 'Hope I Die Before I Get Old: Mispredicting Happiness Across The Adult Lifespan'. *Journal of Happiness Studies* 7(2): 167–82.

Langerak, Edward A. 1979. 'Abortion: Listening to the Middle'. *Hastings Center Report* 9(5): 24–8.

Larkin, Philip. 1990. 'Aubade'. In *Collected Poems*, ed. Anthony Thwaite. London; Boston, MA: Marvell Press; Faber and Faber.

Laslett, Peter. 1991. *A Fresh Map of Life. The Emergence of the Third Age.* Cambridge, MA: Harvard University Press.

Lazear, Edward P. 1979. 'Why Is There Mandatory Retirement?' *Journal of Political Economy* 87(6): 1261–84.

Lee, Timothy B. 2016. 'New Research Suggests an Aging Workforce is Holding Back Economic Growth'. *Vox.* www.vox.com/a/new-economy-future/aging-population-slow-growth

Levi, Becca R., Martin D. Slade, Robert H. Pietrzak, and Luigi Ferrucci. 2018. 'Positive Age Beliefs Protect against Dementia Even among Elders with High-Risk Gene'. *PLoS ONE* 13(2): e0191004.

Lewis, Penney. 2007. *Assisted Dying and Legal Change.* Oxford: Oxford University Press.

Li, Chenyang. 2006. 'The Confucian Ideal of Harmony'. *Philosophy East and West* 56: 583–603.

2014a. *The Confucian Philosophy of Harmony.* London: Routledge.

2014b. 'The Confucian Conception of Freedom'. *Philosophy East and West* 64: 902–19.

Lin, Eden. 2017. 'Against Welfare Subjectivism'. *Nous* 51(2): 354–77.

2020. 'Objective Theories of Well-Being'. In *The International Encyclopedia of Ethics*, ed. Hugh LaFollette. Hoboken, NJ: Wiley-Blackwell.

Lindemann, Hilde. 2014. *Holding and Letting Go: The Social Practice of Personal Identities.* New York: Oxford University Press.

Lippert-Rasmussen, Kasper. 2018. 'The EU and Age Discrimination: Abolish Mandatory Retirement!' *Twelve Stars* (January 26). www.twelvestars.eu/post/kasper-lippert-rasmussen

Liu, Qingping. 2003. 'Filiality versus Sociality and Individuality: On Confucianism as "Consanguinitism"'. *Philosophy East and West* 53: 234–50.

Loch, Christopher, Fabian J. Sting, Nikolaus Bauer, and Helmut Mauermann. 2010. 'How BMW is Defusing the Demographic Time Bomb'. *Harvard Business Review* 88(3): 99–102.

Locke, John. 1975. *An Essay Concerning Human Understanding*, ed. Peter H. Nidditch. Oxford: Oxford University Press.

Luper, Steven. 2009. *The Philosophy of Death.* New York: Cambridge University Press.

Lynn, Joanne. 2005. 'Living Long in Fragile Health'. *Hastings Center Report* 35(6). S14–S18.

Macleod, Colin. 2010. 'Primary Goods, Capabilities, and Children'. In *Measuring Justice: Primary Goods and Capabilities*, eds. Harry Brighouse and Ingrid Robeyns, 174–92. Cambridge: Cambridge: University Press.

2015. 'Agency, Authority and the Vulnerability of Children'. In *The Nature of Children's Wellbeing: Theory and Practice*, eds. Alexander Bagattini and Colin Macleod, 53–64. Dordrecht: Springer.

Magesa, Laurenti. 1997. *African Religion: The Moral Traditions of Abundant Life.* Maryknoll, NY: Orbis Books.

Maier, Karl. 1992. 'Free-Market Africa's Age of Disrespect: Traditional Care of the Elderly Is Declining as Western Ways Take Their Toll'. Independent, 12 July. https://bit.ly/30zDbMS

Mann, J. John. 2002. 'A Current Perspective of Suicide and Attempted Suicide'. *Annals of Internal Medicine* 136(4): 302–11.

Marquis, Don. 1989. 'Why Abortion is Immoral'. *The Journal of Philosophy* 86(4): 183–202.

Martin, George M., Kelly LaMarco, Evelyn Strauss, and Katarina L. Kelner. 2003. 'Research on Aging: The End of the Beginning'. *Science* 299(5611): 1339–41.

Martin, Mike W. 2012. *Happiness and the Good Life.* Oxford: Oxford University Press.

Martin, Sandra. 2014. 'Kim's Choice: Inside One Woman's Decision to Starve Herself to Death'. *The Globe and Mail* (July 17). https://tgam.ca/322yiNc

2016. *A Good Death: Making the Most of Our Final Choices.* Toronto: HarperCollins.

Masolo, Dismas. 2010. *Self and Community in a Changing World.* Bloomington: Indiana University Press.

Mathison, Eric, and Jeremy Davis. 2018. 'The Case for an Autonomy-Centred View of Physician-Assisted Death'. *Journal of Bioethical Inquiry* 17(8): 345–56.

Mauron, Alexandre. 1996. 'The Human Embryo and the Relativity of Biological Individuality'. In *Conceiving the Embryo,* eds. Donald Evans and Neil Pickering, 55–74. Dordrecht: Klüwer.

Mbiti, John. 1990. *African Religions and Philosophy,* 2nd ed. Oxford: Heinemann.

McClay, Wilfred M. 2018. 'Being There'. *The Hedgehog Review* 20 (3). https://bit.ly/3H18gsn

McDaniel, Kris, Jason R. Raibley, Richard Feldman, and Michael J. Zimmerman, eds. 2006. *The Good, the Right, Life and Death: Essays in Honor of Fred Feldman.* Aldershot: Ashgate.

McKerlie, Dennis. 2012. *Justice between the Old and the New.* Oxford: Oxford University Press.

McKibben, Bill. 2003. *Enough: Staying Human in an Engineered Age.* New York: Henry Holt and Company.

McMahan, Jeff. 1988. 'Death and the Value of Life'. *Ethics* 99(1): 32–61.

2002. *The Ethics of Killing: Problems at the Margins of Life.* Oxford: Oxford University Press.

2020. 'Review of Richard Kraut, *The Quality of Life: Aristotle Revised*'. *Notre Dame Philosophical Reviews,* https://bit.ly/3q0kQ4q

2021. 'Suffering and Moral Status'. In *Rethinking Moral Status,* eds. Stephen Clarke, Hazem Zohny, and Julian Savulescu, 23–39. Oxford: Oxford University Press.

Mengxi, Liu. 2018. 'The Reasoning regarding Values of the Six Classics and the Ethos of the Chinese Culture'. In *The Collected Works at the Symposium on China Studies 2017,* ed. Chinese Academy of Social Sciences. Beijing: China Social Sciences Press, 24–38.

Menkiti, Ifeanyi. 1984. 'Person and Community in African Traditional Thought'. In *African Philosophy: An Introduction*, 3rd ed, ed. Richard Wright, 171–81. Lanham: University Press of America.

——— 2004. 'On the Normative Conception of a Person'. In *A Companion to African Philosophy*, ed. Kwasi Wiredu. Oxford: Blackwell, 324–31.

Metz, Thaddeus. 2013. 'The Western Ethic of Care or an Afro-Communitarian Ethic? Finding the Right Relational Morality'. *Journal of Global Ethics* 9: 77–92.

——— 2014. 'Dignity in the Ubuntu Tradition'. In *Cambridge Handbook on Human Dignity*, eds. Marcus Düwell, 310–18. Cambridge: Cambridge University Press.

——— 2015a. 'How the West Was One: The Western as Individualist, the African as Communitarian'. *Educational Philosophy and Theory* 47(11): 1175–84.

——— 2015b. 'Values in China as Compared to Africa: Two Conceptions of Harmony'. In *The Rise and Decline and Rise of China: Searching for an Organising Philosophy*, ed. Hester du Plessis, 75–116. Johannesburg: Real African Publishers.

——— 2017a. 'Toward an African Moral Theory, Revised Edition'. In *Themes, Issues and Problems in African Philosophy*, ed. Isaac Ukpokolo, 97–119. London: Palgrave Macmillan.

——— 2017b. 'Confucianism and African Philosophy'. In *The Palgrave Handbook of African Philosophy*, eds. Toyin Falola and Adeshina Afolayan, 207–22. New York: Palgrave Macmillan.

Miller, Richard. 2002. 'Extending Life: Scientific Prospects and Political Obstacles'. *Milbank Quarterly* 80(1): 155–74.

Mitchell, Susan L., Betty S. Black, Mary Ersek, et al. 2012. 'Advanced Dementia: State of the Art and Priorities for the Next Decade'. *Annals of Internal Medicine* 156 (1 Pt 1): 45–51.

Mkhize, Nhlanhla. 2008. 'Ubuntu and Harmony'. In *Persons in Community: African Ethics in a Global Culture*, ed. Ronald Nicolson, 35-44. Pietermaritzburg: University of KwaZulu-Natal Press.

Mnyaka, Mluleki, and Mokgethi Motlhabi. 2005. 'The African Concept of Ubuntu/ Botho and Its Socio-moral Significance'. *Black Theology* 3: 215–37.

Mokgoro, Yvonne. 1998. 'Ubuntu and the Law in South Africa'. *Potchefstroom Electronic Law Journal* 1: 15–26.

Mothersill, Mary. 1999. 'Old Age'. *Proceedings and Addresses of the American Philosophical Association* 73(2): 7–23.

Mroczek, Daniel K. and Avron Spiro III. 2005. 'Change in Life Satisfaction during Adulthood: Findings from the Veterans Affairs Normative Aging Study'. *Journal of Personality and Social Psychology* 88(1): 189–202.

Munnell, Alicia Haydock and April Yanyuan Wu. 2013. 'Do Older Workers Squeeze Out Younger Workers?' *SIEPR Discussion Paper 13-011*. Stanford, CA: Stanford Institute for Economic Policy Research.

Murove, Munyaradzi Felix. 2007. 'The Shona Ethic of Ukama with Reference to the Immortality of Values'. *The Mankind Quarterly* 48: 179–89.

2016. *African Moral Consciousness*. London: Austin Macauley Publishers Ltd.

Murphy, Jeffrie G. 1976. 'Rationality and the Fear of Death'. *The Monist* 59(2): 187–203.

2003. *Getting Even: Forgiveness and Its Limits*. New York: Oxford University Press.

Mutwa, Credo. 1998 [1964]. *Indaba, My Children*. Repr. Edinburgh: Payback Press.

My Death My Decision (MDMD). 2016. *When Is a Life Complete?* (June) https://bit .ly/3yuh9YB

Nabudere, Dani. 2006. '*Towards an Afrokology of Knowledge Production and African Regeneration*'. *International Journal of African Renaissance Studies* 1: 7–32.

Nagel, Thomas. 1970. 'Death'. *Nous* 4(1): 73–80.

1979. *Mortal Questions*. Cambridge: Cambridge University Press.

Narecki, Krzysztof. 2012. 'The Image of the River in the Fragments of Heraclitus'. *Philotheos* 12: 66–77.

National Institute on Aging. 2019. 'What Is Dementia? Symptoms, Types, and Diagnosis'. *Basics of Alzheimer's Disease and Dementia*. https://bit.ly /3dWYF9O

National Population Projections. 2018. 'Older People Projected to Outnumber Children for First Time in U.S. History'. *United States census Bureau* (September 6). https://bit.ly/30vEs7F

Nelson, James Lindemann. 1999. 'Death's Gender'. In *Mother Time: Women, Aging, and Ethics*, ed. Margaret Urban Walker, 113–29. Maryland: Rowman and Littlefield.

Nelson, Lawrence and Erick Ramirez. 2017. 'Can Suicide in the Elderly Be Rational?' In *Rational Suicide in the Elderly: Clinical, Ethical, and Sociocultural Aspects*, eds. Robert E. McCue and Meera Balasubramaniam, 1–21. New York: Springer.

Nesse, Randolph M. 2019. *Good Reasons for Bad Feelings*. New York: Dutton.

Nicholson, Caroline, Julienne Meyer, Mary Flatley, Cheryl Holman, and Karen Lowton. 2012. 'Living on the Margin: Understanding the Experience of Living and Dying with Frailty in Old Age'. *Social Science and Medicine* 75 (8): 1426–32.

Nkulu-N'Sengha, Mutombo. 2009. 'Bumuntu'. In *Encyclopedia of African Religion*, eds. Molefi Keti Asante and Ama Mazama, 142–7. Los Angeles: Sage.

Normann, Hans K., Kenneth Asplund, Stig Karlsson, Per-Olof Sandman, and Astrid Norberg. 2006. 'People with Severe Dementia Exhibit Episodes of Lucidity. A Population-Based Study'. *Journal of Clinical Nursing* 15(11): 1413–17.

Nothelle, Stephanie and Thomas Finucane. 2017. 'States Worse Than Death'. *The Journal of the American Medical Association Internal Medicine* 177(4): 593.

Novitz, David. 1998. 'Forgiveness and Self-Respect'. *Philosophy and Phenomenological Research* 58(2): 299–315.

Nozick, Robert. 1974. *Anarchy, State, and Utopia*. Oxford: Basic Book.

Nussbaum, Martha C. 1994. *The Therapy of Desire: Theory and Practice in Hellenistic Ethics*. Princeton, NJ: Princeton University Press.

2001. *The Fragility of Goodness: Luck and Ethics in Greek Tragedy and Philosophy*. Cambridge: Cambridge University Press.

Nussbaum, Martha C. and Saul Levmore. 2017. *Aging Thoughtfully: Conversations about Retirement, Romance, Wrinkles, and Regret*. New York: Oxford University Press.

NVVE. 2016. *The Final Stages of Life: Guidelines to Help You Consider, Discuss and Decide*. Amsterdam: NVVE.

Oates, Whitney J. 1957. *The Stoic and Epicurean Philosophers*. New York: Random House.

Oeppen, Jim and James W. Vaupel. 2002. 'Broken Limits to Life Expectancy'. *Science* 296(5570): 1029–31.

Office for National Statistics. 2016. *Measuring National Well-Being: At What Age is Personal Well-Being the Highest?* (February 2). https://bit.ly/3GSL6EJ

2021. *Statistical Bulletin: Personal Well-being in the UK: April 2020 to March 2021*. https://bit.ly/32tc9aQ

Olshansky, Stuart Jay. 2002. 'Replacement Parts: A Survey of Recent Articles'. *The Wilson Quarterly Magazine* 26:102.

Olshansky, Stuart Jay, Bruce A. Carnes, and Christine Cassel. 1990. 'In Search of Methuselah: Estimating the Upper Limits to Human Longevity'. *Science* 250 (4981): 634–40.

Olshansky, Stuart Jay, Leonard Hayflick, and Bruce A. Carnes. 2002. 'Position Statement on Human Aging'. *The Journals of Gerontology Series A: Biological Sciences and Medical Sciences* 57(8): 292–7.

Oregon Health Authority, Public Health Division. 2017. *The Oregon Death with Dignity Act: 2017 Data Summary*. (February 9). https://bit.ly/3q3BhNb

Overall, Christine. 2000. 'Return to Gender, Address Unknown: Reflections on the Past, Present and Future of the Concept of Gender in Feminist Theory and Practice'. In *Marginal Groups and Mainstream American Culture*, eds. Yolanda Estes, Arnold Lorenzo Farr, Patricia Smith, and Clelia Smyth, 24–50. Lawrence, KS: University Press of Kansas.

2003. *Aging, Death, and Human Longevity: A Philosophical Inquiry*. Berkeley, CA: University of California Press.

2016. 'How Old is Old? Changing Conceptions of Old Age'. In *The Palgrave Handbook of the Philosophy of Aging*, ed. Geoffrey Scarre, 13–30. London: Palgrave Macmillan.

Owen, Adrian M. 2019. The Search for Consciousness. *Neuron* 102(3): 526–8.

Oxford Dictionary. 2020. 'Integrity, n'. *OED Online*. Oxford University Press.

Parfit, Derek. 1984. *Reasons and Persons*. Oxford: Oxford University Press.

1987 (reprint). *Reasons and Persons*. Oxford: Oxford University Press.

2000. 'Equality or Priority?' In *The Ideal of Equality*, eds. Matthew Clayton and Andrew Williams, 81–125. Basingstoke: Macmillan.

Paris, Peter. 1995. *The Spirituality of African Peoples*. Minneapolis, MN: Fortress Press.

Paris, Wendy. 2018. 'Not Raging against the Dying of the Light'. *Los Angeles Review of Books* (June 7). https://bit.ly/3dVZsYe

Park, Alice. 2015. 'A Cure for Aging'. *Time* (February 23). https://time.com/3706701/cure-for-aging/

Partridge, Brad, Jayne Lucke, Helen Bartlett, and Wayne Hall. 2011. 'Public Attitudes towards Human Life Extension by Intervening in Ageing'. *Journal of Aging Studies* 25(2): 73–83.

Partridge, Brad, Mair Underwood, Jayne Lucke, Helen Bartlett, and Wayne Hall. 2009. 'Ethical Concerns in the Community about Technologies to Extend Human Life Span'. *The American Journal of Bioethics* 9(12): 68–76.

Pasman, H. Roeline W. , Pam J. Kaspers, Dorley J. H. Deeg, and Bregie D. Onwuteaka-Philipsen. 2013. 'Preferences and Actual Treatment of Older Adults at the End of Life: A Mortality Follow-Back Study'. *Journal of the American Geriatrics Society* 61(10): 1722–9.

Paul, Laurie A. 2014. 'Experience and the Arrow'. In *Chance and Temporal Asymmetry*, ed. Alastair Wilson, 175–93. Oxford: Oxford University Press.

Pauley, John. 2007. 'Agency, Identity, and Technology: The Concealment of the Contingent in American Culture'. *Janus Head* 10(1): 43.

Pearson, Hesketh. 1977. *The Smith of Smiths*. London: The Folio Society.

Pence, Gregory E. 2019. 'Should I Want to Live to 100?' *Bioethics* 33(7): 820–6.

Pettigrove, Glen. 2009. 'The Standing to Forgive'. *The Monist* 92(4): 583–603.

    2012. *Forgiveness and Love*. Oxford: Oxford University Press.

Pew Research Center. 2013. 'Living to 120 and Beyond'. (August 6). www.pewforum.org/2013/08/06/living-to-120-and-beyond/

Pfaller, Larissa and Mark Schweda. 2019. 'Excluded from the Good Life? An Ethical Approach to Conceptions of Active Ageing'. *Social Inclusion* 7(3): 44–53.

Picard, André. 2021. *Neglected No More: The Urgent Need to Improve the Lives of Canada's Elders in the Wake of a Pandemic*. Toronto: Penguin Random House Canada.

Pipher, Mary. 2019a. 'The Joy of Being a Woman in Her 70s'. *The New York Times* (January 12). https://nyti.ms/3q1Hhq0

    2019b. *Women Rowing North: Navigating Life's Currents and Flourishing as We Age*. New York: Bloomsbury Publishing.

Ponthière, Grégory. 2017. *Économie Du Vieillissement*. Paris: La Découverte.

Posner, Richard. 1995. *Aging and Old Age*. Chicago, IL: University of Chicago Press.

Post, Stephen G. 2003. 'Decelerated Aging: Should I Drink From a Fountain of Youth?' In *The Fountain of Youth Cultural, Scientific, and Ethical Perspectives on a Biomedical Goal*, ed. Stephen G. Post and Robert H. Binstock, 72–93. New York: Oxford University Press.

Pruchno, Rachel. 2012. 'Not Your Mother's Old Age: Baby Boomers at Age 65'. *The Gerontologist* 52(2): 149–52.

Quill, Timothy E. 1991. 'Death and Dignity – A Case of Individualized Decision Making'. *The New England Journal of Medicine* 324:691–4.

Rabbas, Øyvind, Eyjólfur K. Emilsson, Hallvard Fossheim, and Miira Tuominen. 2015. 'Introduction'. In *The Quest for the Good Life: Ancient Philosophers on Happiness*, eds. Øyvind Rabbas, Eyjólfur K. Emilsson, Hallvard Fossheim, and Miira Tuominen. Oxford: Oxford University Press.

Radding, Charles M. 1992. 'Fortune and Her Wheel: The Meaning of a Medieval Symbol'. *Mediaevistik* 5: 127–38.

Raijmakers, Natasja J. H., Agnes van der Heide, Pauline S. C. Kouwenhoven, Ghislaine van Thiel, Johannes J. M. van Delden, and Judith Rietjens. 2015. 'Assistance in Dying for Older People without a Serious Medical Condition Who Have a Wish to Die: A National Cross-Sectional Survey'. *Journal of Medical Ethics* 41(2): 145–50.

Railton, Peter. 1984. 'Alienation, Consequentialism, and the Demands of Morality'. *Philosophy and Public Affairs* 13(2): 134–71.

Rauch, Jonathan. 2014. 'The Real Roots of Midlife Crisis'. *The Atlantic* (December). https://bit.ly/3p3wkoz

  2018. *The Happiness Curve: Why Life Gets Better After Midlife.* New York: Bloomsbury Publishing.

Rawls, John. 1971. *A Theory of Justice.* Cambridge, MA: Harvard University Press.

Rentsch, Thomas. 2016. 'Aging as Becoming Oneself: A Philosophical Ethics of Late Life'. In *The Palgrave Handbook of the Philosophy of Aging*, ed. Geoffrey Scarre, 347–64. London: Palgrave Macmillan.

Richards, Naomi. 2017. 'Old Age Rational Suicide'. *Sociology Compass* 11(3): e12456.

Richel, Theo. 2003. 'Will Human Life Expectancy Quadruple in the Next Hundred Years? Sixty Gerontologists Say Public Debate of Life Extension is Necessary'. *Journal of Anti-Aging Medicine* 6(4): 309–14.

Richey, Jeff. n.d. 'Confucius'. In *The Internet Encyclopedia of Philosophy*, ed. James Fieser. www.iep.utm.edu/confuciu/

Riley, Matilda White, Robert Louis Kahn, Anne E. Foner, and Karin A. Mack. 1994. *Age and Structural Lag: Society's Failure to Provide Meaningful Opportunities in Work, Family, and Leisure.* Oxford: John Wiley and Sons.

Roberts, Robert. 1995. 'Forgivingness'. *American Philosophical Quarterly* 32(4): 289–306.

Robson, John M. and Jack Stillinger, eds. 1981. *Collected Works of John Stuart Mill I: Autobiography and Literary Essays.* Toronto: University of Toronto Press.

Rodger, Daniel, Bruce P. Blackshaw, and Calum Miller. 2018. 'Beyond Infanticide: How Psychological Accounts of Persons Can Justify Harming Infants'. *The New Bioethics* 24(2): 106–21.

Rosenmayr, Leopold. 1987. 'On Freedom and Aging: An Interpretation'. *Journal of Aging Studies* 1(4): 299–316.

Royal College of Psychiatrists. 2018. 'Suffering in Silence: Age Inequality in Older People's Mental Health Care CR221'. *Campaigning-For-Better-Mental-Health -Policy* (November). https://bit.ly/3F64AVQ

Rubin, Emily B. 2017. 'States Worse Than Death – Reply'. *JAMA Internal Medicine* 177(4): 593–4.

Rubin, Emily B., Anna E. Buehler, and Scott D. Halpern. 2016. 'States Worse Than Death among Hospitalized Patients with Serious Illnesses'. *Journal of the American Medical Association Internal Medicine* 176(10): 1557–9.

Russell, Bertrand. 1930. *The Conquest of Happiness*. London: George Allen and Unwin.

Sanderson, Warren and Sergei Scherbov. 2008. 'A Publication of the Population Reference Bureau: Rethinking Age and Aging'. *Population Bulletin* 63(4). https://assets.prb.org/pdf08/63.4aging.pdf

Scanlon, Thomas M. 1998. *What We Owe to Each Other*. Cambridge, MA: Harvard University Press.

Scarre, Geoffrey. 2004. *After Evil: Responding to Wrongdoing*. Hampshire: Ashgate.

    2016. 'The Ageing of People and of Things'. In *The Palgrave Handbook of the Philosophy of Aging*, ed. Geoffrey Scarre, 87–99. London: Palgrave Macmillan.

Schapiro, Tamar. 1999. 'What is a Child?' *Ethics* 109(4): 715–38.

Schechtman, Marya. 2010. *Staying Alive. Personal Identity, Practical Concerns, and the Unity of a Life*. Oxford: Oxford University Press.

Schloss, David F. 1891. 'Why Working-Men Dislike Piece-Work'. *The Economic Review* 1(3): 311–26.

Schneewind, Jerome B. 1998. *The Invention of Autonomy: A History of Modern Moral Philosophy*. Cambridge: Cambridge University Press.

Schneller, Johanna. 2018. 'Old is the New Cool: Why the Silver Screen Is Finally Living Up to Its Name'. *The Globe and Mail* (December 8): R1, R15. https://tg am.ca/3GOiVqo

Schwandt, Hannes. 2016. 'Unmet Aspirations as an Explanation for the Age U-Shape in Wellbeing'. *Journal of Economic Behavior and Organization* 122: 75–87.

Schweda, Mark. 2020. 'The Autumn of My Years. Aging and the Temporal Structure of Human Life'. In *Aging and Human Nature*, eds. Mark Schweda, Michael Coors, and Claudia Bozzaro, 143–59. Cham: Springer.

Scott, Dominic. 2000. 'Aristotle on Posthumous Fortune'. *Oxford Studies in Ancient Philosophy* 18: 211–29.

Sears, Elizabeth. 1986. *The Ages of Man: Medieval Interpretations of the Life Cycle*. Princeton, NJ: Princeton University Press.

Sedaris, David. 2004. *Dress Your Family in Corduroy and Denim*. New York: Little, Brown, and Company.

Segal, Lynne. 2014. *Out of Time: The Pleasures and Perils of Ageing*. London: Verso.

Sen, Amartya. 1979. 'Utilitarianism and Welfarism'. *Journal of Philosophy*. 76(9): 463–88.

Shakespeare, William. 1623. *Comedies, Histories, and Tragedies*. London: Iaggard and Blount.

Shapiro, Susan O. 1996. 'Herodotus and Solon'. *Classical Antiquity* 15(2): 348–64.

Shutte, Augustine. 2001. *Ubuntu: An Ethic for the New South Africa*. Cape Town: Cluster Publications.

Sidgwick, Henry. 1981 [1907]. *The Methods of Ethics*, seventh edition. Indianapolis, IN: Hackett.

Singer, Abraham A. 2019. *The Form of the Firm: A Normative Political Theory of the Corporation*. New York: Oxford University Press.

Singer, Peter. 1975. *Animal Liberation: A New Ethics for Our Treatment of Animals*. New York: Harper Collins.

    1991. 'Research into Aging: Should it Be Guided by the Interests of Present Individuals, Future Individuals, or the Species?' In *Life Span Extension: Consequences and Open Questions*, ed. Fréderic C. Ludwig, 138–9. New York: Springer.

Skelton, Anthony. 2015. 'Utilitarianism, Welfare, Children'. In *The Nature of Children's Well-Being: Theory and Practice*, eds. Alexander Bagattini and Colin Macleod, 85–104. Dordrecht: Springer.

    2016. 'Children's Well-Being: A Philosophical Analysis'. In *The Routledge Handbook of Philosophy of Well-Being*, ed. Guy Fletcher, 366–77. Abingdon: Routledge.

    2018. 'Children and Well-Being'. In *The Routledge Handbook of the Philosophy of Childhood and Children*, eds. Anca Gheaus, Gideon Calder, and Jurgen De Wispelaere, 90–100. Abingdon: Routledge.

Skelton, Anthony, Lisa Forsberg, and Isra Black. 2021. 'Overriding Adolescent Refusals of Treatment'. *Journal of Ethics and Social Philosophy* 20(3): 221–47.

Skoog, Ingmar. 2011. 'Psychiatric Disorders in the Elderly'. *Canadian Journal of Psychiatry* 56(7): 387–97.

Slote, Michael. 1982. 'Goods and Lives'. *Pacific Philosophical Quarterly* 63(4): 311–26.

    1983. 'Goods and Lives'. In *Goods and Virtues*, ed. Michael Slote, 9–37. Oxford: Clarendon Press.

    2001. *Morals from Motives*. Oxford: Oxford University Press.

Small, Helen. 2007. *The Long Life*. Oxford: Oxford University Press.

Smith, John E. 1969. 'Time, Times, and the "Right Time": Chronos and Kairos'. *The Monist* 53(1): 1–13.

Smoliga, Jamed M., Joseph A. Baur, and Heather A. Hausenblas. 2011. 'Resveratrol and Health – A Comprehensive Review of Human Clinical Trials'. *Molecular Nutrition and Food Research* 55(8): 1129–41.

Snijdewind, Marianne C., Dick L. Willems, Luc Deliens, Bregje D. Onwuteaka-Philipsen, and Kenneth Chambaere. 2015. 'A Study of the First Year of the End-of-Life Clinic for Physician-Assisted Dying in the Netherlands'. *The Journal of the American Medical Association Internal Medicine* 175(10): 1633–40.

Snow, Nancy. 1994. 'Self-Forgiveness'. *Journal of Value Inquiry* 28: 75–80.

Statistics Canada. 2011. 'Centenarians in Canada: Age and Sex, 2011 Census'. *Census in Brief.* https://bit.ly/3yNZLON

2017. 'Age and Sex, and Type of Dwelling Data: Key Results from the 2016 Census'. *The Daily* (May 3). https://bit.ly/3FhbXtN

2018. 'Life Satisfaction Among Canadian Seniors'. *Insights on Canadian Society* (August 2). https://bit.ly/3penxzX

Steptoe, Andrew, Angus Deaton, and Arthur A. Stone. 2015. 'Subjective Wellbeing, Health, and Ageing'. *The Lancet* 385(9968): 640–8.

Stocker, Michael. 1976. 'The Schizophrenia of Modern Moral Theories'. *Journal of Philosophy* 73(14): 453–66.

Stokes, Patrick. 2010. 'Fearful Asymmetry: Kierkegaard's Search for the Direction of Time'. *Continental Philosophy Review* 43(4): 485–507.

Stone, Arthur A., Joseph E. Schwartz, Joan E. Broderick, and Angus Deaton. 2010. 'A Snapshot of the Age Distribution of Psychological Well-Being in the United States'. *Proceedings of the National Academy of Sciences* 107(22): 9985–90.

Strawson, Galen. 2009. *Selves: An Essay in Revisionary Metaphysics.* Oxford: Clarendon Press.

Sumner, L. W. 1992. "Welfare, Happiness and Pleasure." *Utilitas* 4(2): 199–223.

1996. *Welfare, Happiness, and Ethics.* Oxford: Clarendon Press.

2011. *Assisted Death: A Study in Ethics and Law.* Oxford: Oxford University Press.

Sung, Kyu-taik. 2000. 'Respect for Elders: Myths and Realities in East Asia'. *Journal of Aging and Identity* 5: 197–205.

Supreme Court of Canada. 2015. *Carter v. Canada (Attorney General).* 1 S.C.R. 331 (3559).

Swiss National Advisory Commission for Biomedical Ethics. 2005. *Models of Euthanasia.* https://bit.ly/3q4ZaUH

Tengland, Per-Anders. 2001. *Mental Health: A Philosophical Analysis.* Dordrecht: Springer.

Thackeray, William Makepeace. 1937. *Vanity Fair.* New Jersey: Garden City Publishing.

The President's Council on Bioethics. 2003. 'Chapter 4: Ageless Bodies'. In *Beyond Therapy: Biotechnology and the Pursuit of Happiness.* Washington: PCB. https://bit.ly/3yAB6wS

The Standing Committee on Health, Aged Care and Sport. 2018. *Report on the Inquiry into the Quality of Care in Residential Aged Care Facilities in Australia.* https://bit.ly/3mdgbL8

Tong, Rosemarie. 2014. 'Vulnerability and Aging in the Context of Care'. In *Vulnerability: New Essays in Ethics and Feminist Philosophy*, eds. Catriona Mackenzie, Wendy Rogers, and Susan Dodds, 288–307. Oxford: Oxford University Press.

Tooley, Michael. 1983. *Abortion and Infanticide.* Oxford: Clarendon Press.

Tornstam, Lars. 2005. *Gerotranscendence: A Developmental Theory of Positive Aging.* New York: Springer.

Tremain, Shelley. 2020. 'COVID-19 and the Naturalization of Vulnerability'. *Biopolitical Philosophy* (April 1). https://bit.ly/3scV4MY

Tu, Wei-Ming. 2010. 'Confucian Encounter with the Enlightenment Mentality of the Modern West'. *Oriens Extremus* 49: 249–308.

Tutu, Desmond. 1999. *No Future without Forgiveness.* London: Rider.

Ulloa, Beatriz F. L., Valerie Møller, and Alfonso Sousa-Poza. 2013. How Does Subjective Well-Being Evolve with Age? A Literature Review. *Journal of Population Ageing* 6(3): 227–46.

Unger, Peter. 1992. *Identity, Consciousness, and Value.* Oxford University Press.

United Nations. 2015. *World Population Prospects: The 2015 Revision.* https://bit .ly/3DZLCyF

Vandenberghe, Vincent and Axel Gosseries. 2016. 'Augmenter L'âge De La Retraite: La Seule Réponse Possible Au Vieillissement?' *Le Soir.* Bruxelles: Rossel & Cie.

Vandeschrick, Christophe. 2001. 'The Lexis Diagram, a Misnomer'. *Demographic Research* 4(3): 97–124.

Van Parijs, Philippe. 2015. 'Four Puzzles on Gender Equality'. *Law, Ethics, and Philosophy* 3: 79–89.

Van Parijs, Philippe and Pascale Vielle. 2001. 'La prime De Virilité'. *Le Soir.* Bruxelles: Rossel & Cie.

Van Wijngaarden, Els, Carlos Leget, and Anne Goossensen. 2014. 'Experiences and Motivations Underlying Wishes to Die in Older People Who Are Tired of Living: A Research Area in its Infancy'. *Omega – Journal of Death and Dying* 69(2): 191–216.

    2015. 'Ready to Give Up on Life: The Lived Experience of Elderly People Who Feel Life is Completed and No Longer Worth Living'. *Social Science and Medicine* 138: 257–64.

    2016. 'Caught between Intending and Doing: Older People Ideating on a Self-Chosen Death'. *BMJ Open* 6(1): e009895.

Velleman, James David. 1991. 'Well-Being and Time'. *Pacific Philosophical Quarterly* 72(1): 48–77.

    2000. 'Well-Being and Time'. In *The Possibility of Practical Reason*, ed. David Velleman, 56–84. Oxford: Oxford University Press.

Verdelho, Anna, and Manuel Gonçalves-Pereira, eds. 2017. *Neuropsychiatric Symptoms of Cognitive Impairment and Dementia.* Cham: Springer.

Wakefield, Jerome C. 2007. 'The Concept of Mental Disorder: Diagnostic Implications of the Harmful Dysfunction Analysis'. *World Psychiatry* 7: 149–56.

Walasek, Lukasz, Gordon D. A. Brown, and Gordon D. Ovens. 2019. 'Subjective Well-Being and Valuation of Future Health States: Discrepancies between Anticipated and Experienced Life Satisfaction'. *Journal of Applied Social Psychology* 49(12): 746–54.

Walker, Margaret Urban. 1999. *Mother Time: Women, Aging, and Ethics*. New York: Rowman and Littlefield Publishers.

2013. 'Third Parties and the Social Scaffolding of Forgiveness'. *Journal of Religious Ethics* 41(3): 495–512.

Walker, Mark. 2007. 'Superlongevity and Utilitarianism'. *Australasian Journal of Philosophy* 85(4): 581–95.

Walker, Tom. 2007. 'Why Economists Dislike a Lump of Labor'. *Review of Social Economy* 65(3): 279–91.

Walls, Jeannette. 2006. *Glass Castle*. New York: Scribner.

Wareham, Christopher Simon. 2015a. 'Youngest First? Why It's Wrong to Discriminate against the Elderly in Healthcare'. *South African Journal of Bioethics and Law* 8(1): 37–9.

2015b. 'Slowed Ageing, Welfare, and Population Problems'. *Theoretical Medicine and Bioethics* 36(5): 321–40.

2016. 'The Transhumanist Prospect: Developing Technology to Extend the Human Lifespan'. In *The Palgrave Handbook of the Philosophy of Aging*, ed. Geoffrey Scarre, 517–38. London: Palgrave Macmillan.

2018. 'What is the Ethics of Ageing?' *Journal of Medical Ethics* 44: 128–32.

2021. 'Between Hoping to Die and Longing to Live Longer'. *History and Philosophy of the Life Sciences* 43(2): 40.

Warren, Mary Anne. 1997. *Moral Status: Obligations to Persons and Other Living Things*. Oxford: Clarendon Press.

Wax, John W. ,Amy W. An, Nicole Kosier, and Timothy E. Quill. 2018. 'Voluntary Stopping Eating and Drinking'. *Journal of the American Geriatrics Society* 66 (3): 441–5.

Wedeking, Gary A. 1990. 'Is Mandatory Retirement Unfair Age Discrimination?' *Canadian Journal of Philosophy* 20(3): 321–44.

Wei, Xiaohong and Qingyuan Li. 2013. 'The Confucian Value of Harmony and Its Influence on Chinese Social Interaction'. *Cross-Cultural Communication* 9: 60–6.

Weintraub, Karen. 2016. 'Aging Is Reversible—at Least in Human Cells and Live Mice'. *Scientific American* (December 15). https://bit.ly/3sbqOSz

Weiss, Alexander, James E. King, Miho Inoue-Murayama, Tetsuro Matsuzawa, and Andrew J. Oswald. 2012. 'Evidence for a Midlife Crisis in Great Apes Consistent With the U-Shape in Human Well-Being'. *Proceedings of the National Academy of Sciences* 109(49): 19949–52.

Weiss, Gail. 2014. 'The Myth of Woman Meets the Myth of Old Age: An Alienating Encounter with the Aging Female Body'. In *Simone de Beauvoir's Philosophy of Age: Gender, Ethics, and Time*, ed. Silvia Stoller, 47–67. Berlin: Walter De Gruyter.

Weiss, Robert S. and Scott A. Bass. 2002. *Challenges of the Third Age: Meaning and Purpose in Later Life*. Oxford: Oxford University Press.

Werth, James L., Jr. 1999. 'Introduction to the Issue of Rational Suicide'. In *Contemporary Perspectives on Rational Suicide*, ed. James L. Werth, Jr., 1–12. Philadelphia: Brunner/Mazel.

Wester, Gry and Jonathan Wolff. 2010. 'The Social Gradient in Health: How Fair Retirement Could Make a Difference'. *Public Health Ethics* 3(3): 272–81.

Westover, Tara. 2018. *Educated.* New York: Random House.

White, Carol J. 2017. *Time and Death: Heidegger's Analysis of Finitude.* London: Routledge.

Widdows, Heather. 2018. *Perfect Me: Beauty as an Ethical Ideal.* Princeton, NJ: Princeton University Press.

Wikler, D. 2009. 'Paternalism in the Age of Cognitive Enhancement: Do Civil Liberties Presuppose Roughly Equal Mental Ability? In *Human Enhancement*, eds. Julian Savulescu and Nick Bostrom, 341–56. Oxford: Oxford University Press.

Williams, Alan. 1997. 'Intergenerational Equity: An Exploration of the "Fair Innings" Argument'. *Health Economics* 6(2): 117–32.

Williams, Bernard. 1973. 'The Makropulos Case: Reflections on the Tedium of Immortality'. In *Problems of the Self: Philosophical Papers 1956–1972.* Cambridge: Cambridge University Press.

    1981. *Moral Luck: Philosophical Papers 1973–1980.* Cambridge: Cambridge University Press.

    1993. 'The Makropulos Case: Reflections on the Tedium of Immortality'. In *The Metaphysics of Death*, ed. John Martin Fischer, 73–92. Stanford: Stanford University Press.

Williamson, Oliver E. 1985. *The Economic Institutions of Capitalism.* New York: Free Press.

Wiredu, Kwasi. 1996. *Cultural Universals and Particulars: An African Perspective.* Bloomington: Indiana University Press.

Wong, Odalia and Beatrice Chau. 2006. 'The Evolving Role of Filial Piety in Eldercare in Hong Kong'. *Asian Journal of Social Science* 34: 600–17.

Woodard, Christopher. 2016. 'Hybrid Theories'. In *The Routledge Handbook of Philosophy of Well-Being*, ed. Guy Fletcher, 161–74. Abingdon: Routledge.

World Bank. 2019. 'Life Expectancy at Birth, Total (Years)'. https://data .worldbank.org/indicator/sp.dyn.le00.in

World Health Organization (WHO). 2009. 'Women and Health: Today's Evidence Tomorrow's Agenda (Executive Summary)'. https://bit.ly/3qiZAqR

    2001. *Strengthening Mental Health Promotion.* Geneva: World Health Organization.

Wren-Lewis, Sam and Anna Alexandrova. 2021. 'Mental Health without Wellbeing'. *Journal of Medicine and Philosophy* 46(6): 684–703.

Wright, Karen and Mary Ellen Mark. 2003. 'Staying Alive'. *Discover* (November 6), http://discovermagazine.com/2003/nov/cover

Yao, Xinzhong. 2000. *An Introduction to Confucianism.* Cambridge: Cambridge University Press.

Yu-wei, Hsieh. 1959. 'Filial Piety and Chinese Society'. *Philosophy East and West* 9: 56–7.

Zhang, Hong. 2006. 'Family Care or Residential Care? The Moral and Practical Dilemmas Facing the Elderly in Urban China'. *Asian Anthropology* 5: 57–83.

Index